INTERNATIONAL SURVEY OF FAMILY LAW

Published on behalf of the International Society of Family Law

INTERNATIONAL
SOCIETY OF FAMILY
LAW

INTERNATIONAL SURVEY OF FAMILY LAW

2024 Edition

Edited by
Robin Fretwell Wilson
June Carbone

In collaboration with
Emma Kruger

Abstracts translated by
Christine Bidaud

INTERSENTIA

Intersentia
Lefebvre Sarrut Belgium SA
Rue Haute, 139/6
1000 Bruxelles
Belgium
Email: contact@larcier-intersentia.com

Distribution for the UK and
Rest of the World (incl. Eastern Europe)
Ingram Publisher Services UK
1 Deltic Avenue, Rooksley
Milton Keynes MK13 8LD
United Kingdom
Tel: +44 1752 202 301 | Fax: +44 1752 202 331
Email: orders@nbninternational.com

Distribution for France and Other Countries
Interforum Editis
92 avenue de France
75013 Paris
France

Distribution for the USA and Canada
Independent Publishers Group
Order Department
814 North Franklin Street
Chicago, IL 60610
USA
Tel: +1 800 888 4741 (toll free) | Fax: +1 312 337 5985
Email: orders@ipgbook.com

International Survey of Family Law. 2024 Edition

ISBN 978-1-83970-434-5
D/2024/06040/0333
NUR 828

British Library Cataloguing in Publication Data. A catalogue record for this book is available from the British Library.

PREFACE

The 2024 edition of the International Survey of Family Law continues the celebration of the International Society of Family Law's (ISFL) fiftieth anniversary. This second of two Jubilee editions begins with memorials to Professor Sanford Katz, a giant in the field of family law and an important figure in the Society's creation. It then adds reflections on the Society's history, its contributions to the global development of family in the context of controversial issues such as the same-sex marriage debate, its continuing relevance to newly emerging family discussions, and the Golden Jubilee Conference of 2023 in Antwerp Belgium.

The Second Jubilee edition, in the manner of the first, presents substantive retrospectives on fifty-years of family law transformations. Olga A. Khazova-Gurvich describes one of ISFL's most consequential contributions to the global family law order: the reshaping of the status of children that produced the International Convention on the Rights of the Child, which has been ratified by every member country in the United Nations other than the United States. Individual chapters focused on specific countries then review the changes in doctrine, concepts, and procedure that have remade family law in one country after another. The chapters on Brazil and China describe the evolution of family from patriarchal traditions (colonial Catholic in Brazil and feudal in China) to a modern enterprise that enshrines legal equality between men and women. In Brazil, Juliana Maggi Lima explains how Brazilian family law now views the family not as an end in itself but as a means of human fulfilment that serves the needs and development of all of its members. In a parallel way, Ran Qiyu recounts the transformation of Chinese family law to promote 'good family traditions' and the 'construction of family civilisation', rethinking both the doctrines and the aspirations underlying Chinese family law. Family law in France and Italy, by contrast, has changed as part of a dialogue between the national courts and the European Court of Human Rights, requiring reconsideration of judicial methodology as well as the substance of family law decisions. In both countries, family law evolution combines distinctive national developments (Christine Bidaud and her co-authors discuss, for example, the adoption of the French Civil Solidarity Pact Act in 1999, recognising nonmarital cohabitation, and Federica Giardini describes Italy's restrictive assisted reproduction laws) with reforms prompted by European Court rulings. Similarly, in Portugal, Rosa Cândido Martins describes how that country's efforts to ensure children's participation in family law decision-making started with the Constitution of the Portuguese

Republic, adopted in 1974 as part of a revolution replacing a dictatorial regime with a democratic one based on the dignity of the human person. She then shows how children's participatory rights developed further with ratification of the UN Convention on the Rights on the Child, EU membership subject to the Charter of Fundamental Rights of the European Union, and Portuguese courts' construction of children's rights in the context of these principles. Chao-Ju Chen reviews fifty years of change in Taiwanese family law through a feminist lens, emphasising the country's growing embrace of gender equality even as it maintains a system of marital supremacy. Finally, June Carbone, in a chapter on fifty years of family law change in the United States, focuses on federalism. In the US, family law is state law and the country, through a variety of procedures, has produced periods of growing convergence in marital property, child custody, and child support regimes followed by periods of greater dissension, particularly over matters such as abortion, parental rights, and the recognition of functional parenthood without marriage, biological ties or adoption.

The Second Jubilee edition also includes chapters that address a wide range of more recent developments. Leading with an assessment of global developments is Ursula Basset's chapter 'Rethinking the Links between the Changing Family, Law, and Gender'. The fifty-year perspectives emphasise the changing role of women as a major factor in family law transformation; Basset questions whether the move toward equality has run its course – or worse, triggered a backlash. The chapter focuses on the tensions between 'protective, empowering and neutralising' approaches and asks whether a new framework, perhaps one focused on vulnerability and empathy rather than gender may provide an answer.

The chapters addressing individual countries then discuss a host of new family issues, including Małgorzata Balwicka-Szczyrba and Anna Sylwestrzak's analysis of the challenges posed by the large influx of Ukrainian refugees, many of them minors, into Poland and Damali Nicholls and Kinda Jacob's discussion of the difficulties in implementing a right to education for migrant children who come to Trinidad and Tobago from other countries. Melanija Jančić Mihić's chapter on Serbia assesses the impact of the European Court of Human Rights and the contrasting developments based on Serbian law in protecting LGBT rights. Two parallel chapters by Katlego Mashiane and Seroné Stal examine fathers' rights in the abortion context in South Africa. And the final two chapters address family law developments in the United States. Catherine Smith, Robin Walker Sterling and Tanya Washington consider the Supreme Court's failure to develop a comprehensive jurisprudence addressing children rights and Robin Fretwell Wilson documents the difficulty of evaluating the current state of abortion regulations in light of the Supreme Court's reversal of the constitutional right to abortion in *Roe v. Wade* and the return of the issue to the fifty states. She critiques the limitations of existing abortion trackers and develops an alternative approach.

We are especially grateful for the French translation of abstracts. The translation continues to be done by the Family Law Centre of the University Jean Moulin Lyon 3 under Christine Bidaud's direction. This year's volume was produced in collaboration with Emma Kruger. We are also grateful to Pamela Melton for her assistance with the preparation of the Survey.

June Carbone, Minnesota
Robin Fretwell Wilson, Illinois

CONTENTS

LIST OF CONTRIBUTORS

Massilia Amzal
PhD Student, Family Law Center, Université Jean Moulin Lyon 3, France

Nicholas Bala
W.R. Lederman Distinguished University Professor, Faculty of Law, Queen's University, Canada

Małgorzata Balwicka-Szczyrba
Professor of Law, Faculty of Law and Administration, Department of Commercial Law, University of Gdańsk, Poland

Ursula Basset
Professor of Law, Faculty of Law, Director of the Center of Research in Family Law, Pontifical Catholic University of Buenos Aires, Argentina

Bastien Baret
Associate Professor, Research Team Confluence, Sciences and Humanities – EA 1598, Lyon Catholic University, France

Christine Bidaud
Professor and Director of the Family Law Center, Co-Director of the Research Team Louis Josserand, Université Jean Moulin Lyon 3, France

Hugo Bordin-Escharavil
PhD Student, Family Law Center, Research Team Louis Josserand, Université Jean Moulin Lyon 3, France

Giselle Câmara Groeninga
Psychologist, Psychoanalyst Member of FEBRAPSI – Federação Brasileira de Psicanálise; Consultant for Family Law Offices, Psychological Expert and Mediator in Family Disputes; Master and PhD in Civil Law by the University of São Paulo; President of Interdisciplinary Relations of IBDFAM – Instituto Brasileiro de Direito de Família, Ex-Vice-President and Member of the Executive Council of ISFL – International Society of Family Law; Convenor of the XIV ISFL World Conference, Recife, Brazil

Aurore Camuzat
PhD Student, Family Law Center, Research Team Louis Josserand, Université Jean Moulin Lyon 3, France

Rosa Cândido Martins
Assistant Professor, Faculty of Law, Researcher at the Family Law Centre and at the University of Coimbra Institute for Legal Research, University of Coimbra, Portugal

June Carbone
Robina Chair of Law, Science and Technology, University of Minnesota, United States of America

Chao-ju Chen
Distinguished Professor of Law, National Taiwan University College of Law, Taiwan

Ruth Deech, Baroness Deech of Cumnor, DBE, KC (Hon)
Member of the House of Lords, United Kingdom

Clara Delmas
PhD in Law, Researcher, Family Law Center, Research Team Louis Josserand, Université Jean Moulin Lyon 3; Temporary Research and Teaching Assistant, Université Paris Descartes – Paris V, France

John Eekelaar
Emeritus Fellow, Pembroke College, University of Oxford, United Kingdom

Éric Fongaro
Professor, College of Law, Political Science, Economics & Management and Deputy Director of the Research Institute of Business and Heritage Law, Université de Bordeaux, France

Hugues Fulchiron
Professor, Co-Director of the Family Law Center, Research Team Louis Josserand, Université Jean Moulin Lyon 3, France; Judge at the Cour de cassation

Federica Giardini
Professor of Private Comparative Law and of Private Law of the European Union, School of Law, University of Padua, Italy; Lawyer, Giardini Law Firm, Padua, Italy

Kinda Jacob
Attorney at Law, Former Legal Officer, Caribbean Centre for Human Rights

Melanija Jančić Mihic
Associate Professor, Faculty of Business Studies and Law, University 'Union-Nikola Tesla', Belgrade, Serbia

Hugo Jolly
PhD Student, Family Law Center, Research Team Louis Josserand, Université Jean Moulin Lyon 3, France

Guillaume Kessler
Associate Professor, Research Law Center Antoine Favre, Université de Savoie Mont Blanc, France

Olga A. Khazova-Gurvich
Professor, Visiting Research Fellow, Minerva Center for Human Rights, Hebrew University of Jerusalem, Israel; Leading Legal Scholar, Family and Inheritance Law Department, The Private Law Research Centre named after S.S. Alekseev, Moscow, Russia

Juliana Maggi Lima
Master of Civil Law from the University of São Paulo, Co-Coordinator of the Study Group on Family Law, Succession Law, and Asset Management at FGV, Lawyer

Katlego Mashiane
LLD Candidate, University of Limpopo, Attorney at Mashiane (KF) Attorneys, Lecturer, North-West University, South Africa

Guillaume Millerioux
PhD Student, Temporary Research and Teaching Assistant, Family Law Center, Research Team Louis Josserand, Université Jean Moulin Lyon 3, France

Margot Musson
PhD Student, Family Law Center, Research Team Louis Josserand, Université Jean Moulin Lyon 3, France

Damali Nicholls
Attorney at Law, Senior Legal Officer, with the Government of Trinidad and Tobago

Amélie Panet
Senior Lecturer, Family Law Center, Research Team Louis Josserand, Université Jean Moulin Lyon 3, France

Marie Pincet
PhD Student, Family Law Center, Research Team Louis Josserand, Université Jean Moulin Lyon 3, France

Ran Qiyu
Associate professor, Civil and Commercial Law School, Southwest University of Political Science and Law, Chongqing 401120, China

Catherine Smith
Vincent L. Bradford Professor of Law, Washington and Lee University School of Law, United States of America

Seroné Stal
LLB and LLM Graduate from North-West University and PhD Candidate at the same institution. Former Lecturer at North-West University (2020–2022). Lecturer and Researcher in the Public and Constitutional Law Department at Fort Hare University, East London, South Africa. Golden Key Honor Society Member and Holder of the Vice Chancellor's Emerging Researcher Award

Anna Sylwestrzak
Associate Professor of Law, Faculty of Law and Administration, Department of Civil Law, University of Gdańsk, Poland

Hazel Thompson-Ahye
Independent Senator, Republic of Trinidad and Tobago Parliament; Former Family Law Course Director, Council of Legal Education, Hugh Wooding Law School, Republic of Trinidad and Tobago

Richard Vessaud
PhD Student, Family Law Center, Research Team Louis Josserand, Université Jean Moulin Lyon 3, France; Consultant at Lyon Notarial Research, Information and Documentation Centre (CRIDON), France

Robin Walker Sterling
Associate Dean for Clinical Education, Director of the Bluhm Legal Clinic, and Mayer Brown/Robert A. Helman Professor of Law at the Northwestern Pritzker School of Law, United States of America

Tanya M. Washington
Marjorie F. Knowles Chair in Law Professor of Children's Constitutional Rights Georgia State University College of Law Atlanta, Georgia, United States of America

Robin Fretwell Wilson
Mildred Van Voorhis Chair in Law, University of Illinois College of Law, University of Illinois System, United States of America

PART I

MEMORIALS

SANFORD N. KATZ

John EEKELAAR*

23 December 1933 – 10 February 2024.

Sanford Katz was born in Holyoke, Massachusetts on 23 December 1933, the son of Jacob and Rebecca Katz, and one of seven children. He graduated from Boston University and the University of Chicago Law School, then joined the Air Force Judge Advocate General Division and served at the Pentagon. After a fellowship at Yale Law School, he began his illustrious teaching career at Catholic University Law School, and then moved to the University of Florida, before Dean Robert Drinan, SJ, brought him to Boston College Law School, where he taught family law and contract law for 47 years. He leaves behind several generations of devoted students – who will fondly remember his absolute commitment to their success in the legal profession – as well as countless colleagues, scholars and practitioners who he inspired.

His contribution to family law scholarship in the United States was immense. From 1968 to 1979, he was director of law and child development, funded by the Field Foundation, the Grant Foundation and the US Department of Health, Education, and Welfare, conducting research on child abuse and neglect, child custody in divorce and model legislation. He was chief drafter of the Model State Subsidized Adoption Act and Regulation 1975, and of the Model Act to Free Children for Permanent Placement. This was followed by chairmanship of the Family Law Section of the American Bar Association (1980–81), appointment to membership of the Special Massachusetts Commission on Probate and Family Court Procedures, in 1980, and receipt of the Distinguished Service Award of the Family Law Section of the American Bar Association, in 1982. During this period, he was also editor-in-chief of the Family Law Quarterly from 1970 to 1983, later serving as editor of the Millennium Issue of the Family Law Quarterly, in 2000, and of the Special Fiftieth Anniversary Issue of the Family Law Quarterly, in 2008. This list is not exhaustive.

There is also a large quantity of books, journal articles and monographs, many centred on child protection, adoption and other issues concerning children.

* Emeritus Fellow, Pembroke College, Oxford, England.

When Parents Fail: The Law's Response to Family Breakdown,[1] of 1971, was a groundbreaking book that drew attention to the problems of legal intervention in the parent–child relationship and demonstrated what was to be a life-long concern with child law issues. *Child Neglect Laws in America* (with Melba McGrath and Ruth-Arlene W. Howe)[2] and *Adoptions Without Agencies: A Study of Independent Adoptions* (with William Meezan and Eva Manoff Russo)[3] were further examples. His 1994 *Cases and Materials on Family Law: Legal Concepts and Changing Human Relationships* (with Walter O. Weyrauch and Frances Olsen)[4] stood the test of time, producing supplements in 2000, 2001, 2002, 2003, 2004, 2005, 2006, 2007 and 2008. To the outsider, the multi-jurisdictional nature of US family law is very confusing, and in 2003 Sanford took on the challenge of producing a succinct account of *Family Law in America*, which proved so successful that Oxford University Press brought out a second edition in 2014 and a paperback edition in 2015. He retired from his full-time teaching position at Boston College Law School in 2015, becoming the Darald and Juliet Libby Millennium Professor of Law Emeritus there.

But in addition to that, it was his inspiration to bring together lawyers and other experts in family matters working in the two traditions of the common law, in England and the United States. The result was *Cross Currents: Family Law and Policy in the United States and England*, published by Oxford University Press in 2000. His long association with England began in 1973, when he was an associate at Clare Hall in the University of Cambridge. From then on, he was a regular visitor to that country, holding visiting fellowships at the Hampstead Child Therapy Clinic in London, in 1973, at All Souls College, Oxford, in 1997, and at Pembroke College, Oxford, in 1999–2000 and 2006. It was, therefore, quite natural that Sanford was one of only two scholars working outside the English legal system who were invited to contribute to a tributary volume to Stephen Cretney, one of England's most eminent family lawyers, in 2012.[5]

But Sanford did not only establish relationships with family lawyers in England. He was present at a meeting in Birmingham, England, in 1973, where, on the initiative of Zeev Falk of the Hebrew University of Jerusalem and John Neville Turner of Birmingham University, the International Society of Family Law was founded. Sanford was its president from 1982 to 1985, and we collaborated in the publication of papers given at three world conferences.[6]

---

1 Beacon Press, 1971.

2 American Bar Association Press, 1976.

3 Child Welfare League of America, 1978.

4 West Publishing Company, 1994.

5 'Fifty Years of Transformation of American Family Law 1960–2011' in R. Probert and C. Barton (eds.), *Fifty Years in Family Law: Essays for Stephen Cretney*, Intersentia, 2012.

6 *Family Violence: An International and Interdisciplinary Study*, Butterworths, 1978; *Marriage and Cohabitation in Contemporary Societies: An International and Interdisciplinary Study,*

Sanford remained active in the Society, both as a member of the Executive Council and presenting and publishing papers in subsequent meetings. In 2000, he received a Distinguished Service Award from the Society.

Sanford occupied a special place in the community of family law scholars on both sides of the Atlantic, which he crossed so many times with his wife, Joan, herself experienced in, and a knowledgeable observer of, social work practice, and this was reflected in the tributary volume, *Family Law in Britain and America in the New Century: Essays in Honor of Sanford Katz*,[7] published in 2016, many of whose contributors had contributed to *Cross Currents* 16 years earlier.

Butterworths, 1980; *The Resolution of Family Conflict: Comparative Legal Perspectives*, Butterworths, 1984.

7 Brill Nijhoff, 2016.

REMEMBERING SANFORD KATZ

Ruth Deech

The loss of Sanford Katz is a shock for the international family law community. He embodied the spirit of the International Society. Sanford was larger than life and aware of his eminent stature in academia, yet totally without the pomposity that sometimes accompanies academic stars. He was gentle – even humble – in his approach to everyone and their theories. He was grateful for the good things life had given him. He was a bon viveur, although almost puritanical in his relationship with drink, and many an outing with him was devoted to finding the right restaurant and perusal of the menu. He was a founding member of the ISFL and later its president; but, more than that, he was a presence who kept all the very different attitudes of the members, their countries, their conferences and their publications together, disputing but harmonious. He had the knack of identifying trends well ahead of the time that others took, of preparing conferences on those trends, and bringing together disparate views on the topic, not only from all over the US but from all over the world, and synthesising them into a guide to family law and its direction. He did all this in a genial way and with an aptitude for smoothing over the differences.

Sanford's scholarly work was not only broad-ranging but always in step with the vogues of the family law world. His own private opinions were rather more traditional, seen not least in his life-long devotion to Joan, his sons and his grandchildren, and his love of his Newton home. He kept to himself his disapproval of some of the positions now de rigueur in family law. In his writing, he displayed that same ability to bridge various jurisdictions and viewpoints and bring them to one whole authoritative account. In his generous-spirited way he had not a bad word to say about anyone, but there was plenty of gossip to be had about the family law personalities.

He was immensely proud of his grandchildren. Lucia, a student at Northwestern, is making a name for herself as a singer and actor. Salvador is a student at Duke. Their father is Andy Katz, renowned sportswriter. Sanford's other son Daniel is a lawyer but also an actor, and his wife Meg a publicist. He was immensely protective of Joan in periods of ill health. Together they headed to Oxford every summer for many years, staying in a flat owned by All Souls College. Sanford had been a visiting fellow there, and this connection was much prized by both of them, and was an endless source of disquisition about the differences between American universities and this unique college. Joan enjoyed the annual St Hilda's College Crime Fiction Weekend during their stay. We would go to the Bangkok House for Thai dinners, sometimes joined by Nigel Lowe, John Eekelaar and other family lawyers in the vicinity, and they would enjoy outings to the theatre in London. In turn, when I visited Boston and stayed with them, Joan and Sanford would do everything they could to entertain me, including depositing me for many enjoyable hours at Chestnut Hill shopping mall!

And every year without fail he organised a Christmas gift of Fortnum & Mason biscuits for his British friends.

Sanford was especially dedicated to, and took great pride in, his students' careers. This aspect of the academic life is a joy to most teachers, but he was exceptional in the trouble he took to establish them and watch them prosper, and this was reciprocated in the affection in which they held him. He brought BC Law School to the forefront of law schools as his own work took him to the very top of family law scholarship. He was an enthusiastic participant in, and valued member of, all the important institutions in the field, including the American Bar Association and the Family Law Quarterly.

A man of warmth with a gift for friendship and broad influential intellect, whose mark on family law is permanent. I miss him already.

PART II

REFLECTIONS ON 50 YEARS OF THE INTERNATIONAL SOCIETY OF FAMILY LAW

THE SAME-SEX MARRIAGE DEBATES

Past, Present and Future

Nicholas BALA*

I was very pleased to attend the ISFL Conference in Antwerp in July 2023, my first trip to Europe since the pandemic. It gave me a good opportunity to see old friends and to reflect on the important role that the ISFL has played in my 40-plus-year career as a family law professor in Canada, and on some of the controversial issues that have been debated in the conferences and publications of the organisation, in particular regarding same-sex marriage.

Some aspects of family law are themselves international law, in particular related to the Hague Conventions, and scholarship by ISFL members in different countries is often directly cited and applied by domestic courts in Canada and elsewhere in dealing with these cases. These international aspects to family law have made the ISFL and conferences organised by prominent members like Prof. Marilyn Freeman especially valuable, providing fora for learning, discussion and debate. In some cases, a scholarly consensus developed at these meetings, such as on the need to better address issues of domestic violence in the implementation of Article 13 of the Hague Convention on Child Abduction. That ultimately resulted in Lady Brenda Hale, myself and some government representatives and Permanent Bureau staff undertaking a project to prepare a *Guide to Good Practice*[1] on the implementation of that provision of the Hague Convention.

Most of family law is domestic, and in a federal country like Canada, often based on subnational laws, making international perspectives less immediately central, and controversies in other jurisdictions sometimes seem a little less pressing. At the Antwerp Conference, I much appreciated a spirited debate at one session between English colleagues about the minutiae of proper interpretation of the Gender Recognition Act 2004 of the United Kingdom. The issue of the legal status of trans parents is certainly a live issue in my jurisdiction, but we have our own legislative and constitutional context, so the details of the discussion were

---

* bala@queensu.ca.

1 Hague Conference on Private International Law – Permanent Bureau, *Guide to Good Practice Under the Convention on the Civil Aspectsc of Child Abduction*, 2020.

less interesting to me than witnessing the level of passion and hearing about the social context of the debate.

While most members of the ISFL and conference attendees are lawyers, judges and law professors, the social scientists and mental health professionals involved also have a very important role. An understanding of the social and psychological effects of legal regimes, especially on children, is critical, so presentations in Antwerp, such as those by sociologist Bruce Smyth, from Australia, and social work professor Rachel Birnbaum, from Canada, were especially valuable. These two scholars participated in one of the vigorous debates that occurred in a session at the 2023 Conference about the legal significance (and even the existence) of parental alienation. Although this is clearly an issue of domestic law in each country, the international psychological research and legal scholarship are critical to the issues under debate, and developments in one jurisdiction clearly affect other jurisdictions as well.

The controversies about same-sex marriage and related issues of the nature of marriage and significance of conjugality have been prominent at ISFL meetings for more than two decades. In Canada, where by the late 1980s there was already significant legal recognition of unmarried cohabitation for different-sex partners, in 1999 the Supreme Court held that it was unconstitutional discrimination based on sexual orientation to deny same-sex unmarried cohabiting partners the same rights and obligations as cohabiting heterosexual partners.[2] This led to further litigation and debate in Canada about recognition of same-sex marriage.

In 2001, the ISFL North American Conference was held at Queen's University in Kingston, Ontario, and well over 100 scholars from many countries attended. I was the convenor for that meeting, and remember dealing with such 'innovations' as allowing registration online using a credit card rather than expecting a cheque to be sent by post.

The Law Commission of Canada, at that time at independent federal government-funded agency, agreed to provide some financial support for the 2001 Conference, since same-sex marriage was very much on the Conference agenda, and the Commission was doing work on the issue. A keynote speaker at the Conference was the president of the Commission, Nathalie Des Rosiers. She spoke about the Commission's Report, *Beyond Conjugality: Recognizing and Supporting Close Personal Adult Relationships*, which represented an effort to see the debate about same-sex marriage as part of the larger discussion that should be undertaken about what rights and obligations should arise out of which types of 'close personal adult relationships'.[3] The Commission advocated rethinking the ways in which conjugality is used by governments as a proxy for

2 *M v. H*, [1999] 2 SCR 3 (Can.).

3 Law Commission of Canada, *Beyond Conjugality: Recognizing and Supporting Close Personal Adult Relationships*, 2002.

the recognition of adult personal relationships, and argued that marriage and cohabitation are poor proxies for the relational attributes relevant to legislative objectives. The report proposed an elegant but very ambitious effort to rewrite a long list of Canadian legislation, considering each instance in which such terms as 'marriage' and 'spouse' were used, to determine whether these were appropriate, or whether other terms and concepts should be more carefully tailored to meet the underlying objectives of state regulation for such matters as taxation, immigration, health care and pensions.

The report argued, for example, that there were situations and purposes for which two adult siblings who lived together should be entitled to certain rights, for example if one of them were sick or died. This hypothetical continued to be a topic of discussion at the 2023 Conference, as attendees wrestled with the question of when and whether rights and obligations should arise between those in dyadic intimate relationships or polyamorous relationships, or more broadly.

Some academics,[4] including some members of the ISFL in attendance at the 2001 Conference, were very enthusiastic about the intellectual sophistication of the *Beyond Conjugality* report of Canada's Law Commission, recognising it as 'a radical challenge to the presumed naturalness and ensuing privilege of the heteronormative married family'. The position of the Commission was reported in the Canadian media as a proposal to 'get the government out of marriage business', and was viewed by many politicians as an attack on the institution of marriage. In the end, the Liberal government in power at the time did not seriously consider the report, but a combination of constitutional litigation and an increase in public support in Canada led to Parliament enacting legislation in 2005 to allow same-sex partners to marry.[5]

While intellectually provocative, the proposal of the *Beyond Conjugality* report was far too ambitious and out of touch with public support for marriage and conjugality as social institutions to be seriously considered. *Beyond Conjugality* did not mark an end of marriage or the centrality of conjugality as social and legal concepts in Canada, but the controversy over it played a very significant role in the political decision of the newly elected Conservative government to end funding for the Commission in 2006.

In 2005, the ISFL held its international conference in Salt Lake City, Utah, convened by its President Lynn Wardle, and the issue of same-sex marriage was a topic of many sessions. Prof. Wardle was a strong proponent of 'traditional marriage', but a genial host and always prepared to engage in civil debate. The following year, he organised a conference at Brigham Young University in Utah focusing solely on same-sex marriage, inviting some of speakers from the ISFL Conference, wisely recognising that opponents of same-sex marriage in

---

4 B. Cossman and B. Ryder, 'Beyond Beyond Conjugality' (2017) 30(2) *Canadian Journal of Family Law* 227.

5 *Civil Marriage Act*, S.C. 2005, c. 33 (Can.).

the US needed to be very familiar with the arguments being put forward by its proponents, both domestic and international. I was invited to present a paper, later published,[6] arguing that the recognition of same-sex marriage in Canada was a positive social development, whose benefits included promoting the welfare of children, and that its adoption in the US seemed inevitable as well as desirable. Canadian decisions were cited by the Massachusetts Supreme Court[7] in its 2003 decision recognising same-sex marriage in that state.

The 2013 US Supreme Court decision in *United States v. Windsor*[8] allowed for legal recognition of a marriage ceremony that two American lesbians had celebrated in Toronto, which for a period had a thriving business catering to foreign same-sex partners seeking to marry. This set the stage for the 2015 US Supreme Court decision in *Obergefell v. Hodges*,[9] which ruled the prohibition on same-sex marriage unconstitutional in that country.

With the enactment of the legislation recognising same-sex marriage in Canada, the issue has largely disappeared from the legal and political landscape in my country, although issues around whether 'gay pride' flags should be flown at municipal buildings spark occasional controversy, and concerns about social prejudice and violence against members of the LGBTQ+ communities remain. In Canada, public support for same-sex marriage has increased over the years since it was legalised in 2005. Unlike in the US, there has not been litigation about issues like limitations on rights of same-sex partners to adopt[10] or allowing for discrimination in the provision of commercial services, like designing a website for a same-sex partner wedding.[11]

At the Antwerp Conference, Prof. Robin Fretwell Wilson gave an important plenary presentation on some of the latest developments in the US about the laws governing same-sex marriage.[12] She reassured the audience that the *obiter dicta* comments of Justice Clarence Thomas in *Dobbs v. Jackson Women's Health*[13] about revisiting *Obergefell* are not to be taken seriously. The social, political, Congressional and now legal support for same-sex marriage in the US will undoubtedly protect it.

Prof. Wilson is surely correct, for in most liberal democracies, including the US, apex appeal courts are reluctant to stray too far from dominant public

---

6 N. Bala, 'The Debates About Same-sex Marriage in Canada & the United States: Controversy Over the Evolution of a Fundamental Social Institution' (2006) 20 *Brigham Young University Journal of Public Law* 195.

7 *Goodridge v. Deaprtment of Health*, 798 N.E. 2d 941 (Mass. 2003).

8 *United States v. Windsor*, 570 U.S. 744 (2013).

9 *Obergefell v. Hodges*, 576 U.S. 644 (2015).

10 *Fulton v. City of Philadelphia*, 593 U.S. 522 (2021).

11 *303 Creative LLC v. Elenis*, 600 U.S. 570 (2023).

12 See D. Laycock, T.C. Berg, C.H. Esbeck and R. Fretwell Wilson, 'The Respect for Marriage Act: Living Together Despite our Deepest Differences' (2024) *U. Ill. L. Rev.* 511.

13 *Dobbs v. Jackson Women's Health*, 597 U.S. 215 (2022).

opinion. *Dobbs* was highly controversial in holding that women do not have a constitutional right to abortion. In my view, it was very unwise for the majority of the Court to have so cavalierly dismissed its own precedents, let alone to have violated the fundamental rights of women in the US. The reality, however, is that a significant portion of the American public, and a majority of Republicans, remain in favour of some restrictions on access to abortion. In many states, the controversy is not about whether to have a total ban on abortion or complete freedom for women to decide, but rather on how to restrict access to abortion. On the other hand, a clear majority of Americans believe that same-sex marriage is socially desirable, so judicial reversal of the core precedent in *Obergefell v. Hodges*,[14] even by a politically activist and conservative Court, seems inconceivable at present.

A growing number of countries allow same-sex marriage or are at least giving some legal recognition to same-sex relationships, and the controversy within the ISFL over same-sex marriage seems to be over. However, those who are its members and attend its conferences may not fully reflect their societies, as the issue of same-sex marriage remains highly contentious in many countries,[15] especially outside of Western liberal democracies. It is notable that, at the Antwerp Conference, there did not seem to be any representatives of jurisdictions where shari'a laws are in force and same-sex marriage presently seems inconceivable, or from the many countries where homosexual acts are criminalised. It was, however, very important that there were Muslim colleagues from non-sharia law countries, like Nazia Yaqub of Leeds University, who were attending, giving presentations and actively participating. There need to be continuing efforts to expand the diversity of membership in the ISFL and participation in its events.

14 *Obergefell v. Hodges*, 576 U.S. 644 (2015).

15 S. Gubbala, J. Poushter and C. Huang, 'How people around the world view same-sex marriage', *Pew Research Center*, 27 November 2023.

A TRIBUTE TO ISFL

Giselle Câmara Groeninga

When Prof. Robin Fretwell Wilson, Vice President of ISFL, and editor of the *International Survey of Family Law* together with Prof. June Carbone, invited me in Antwerp, at the 18th ISFL World Conference, to write a few pages about my experience with ISFL, I was surprised at how many years had passed by. Nevertheless, at each World Conference I find myself in the same excited mood as at the first one that I attended in 1999.

As I am writing this short testimony, I feel a deep gratitude to all my colleagues that I am sure would not fit into a few lines, and some of these colleagues continue to be among us as indelible memories. I kindly ask all my colleagues to feel represented by those few I nominate here.

As a reflex of the subject that brought us together – families – I can say that we do form a big family: old and new generations of scholars exchanging experiences that are a product not only of academic education, teaching and professional expertise, but also of personal emotional experiences. And that includes the affective bonds we create as a family law institution. Unlike an objective text, this reflection uses many adjectives to express emotions.

From my perspective, the ISFL makes the magic of strengthening the attachments of different people and cultures by uniting them with a common aim: protecting what I call 'the right of being human'.

The beginning: a book, *Liber Amicorum Marie-Thérèse Meulders-Klein: Droit Comparé des Personnes et de la Famille*, 1998.[1] To my surprise, my name was in the subscription list. I took this as a kind of invitation for me, as a psychoanalyst, to study international family law. And I must confess that today I still have the same feeling of warm acceptance of our different perspectives – family law and psychoanalysis – in every ISFL encounter. Our family law institution is inclusive not only regarding different cultures, but also in respect of diverse points of views.

Prof. Marie-Thérèse Meulders-Klein was one of the grande dame of the ISFL. She was as elegant in manners as she was in addressing key and controversial family law issues – a woman ahead of her time.

---

1 J. Pousson-Petit (ed.), *Liber Amicorum Marie-Thérèse Meulders-Klein – Droit Comparé des Personnes et de la Famille*, Bruylant, 1998.

Another grande dame that I have the privilege to know is the Baroness Prof. Ruth Deech, who is relentless in bringing to light the necessity of social consciousness in sensitive and controversial issues in family law.

As a clinical psychoanalyst working with individuals and families, I was dissatisfied and began to be interested in other ways of approaching family conflicts and human sufferings, which, surprisingly enough, increased in the face of legal demands.

The horizon was broader than my consulting room, and the aim was to travel through different family law landscapes around the world. At that time, mediation appeared, as a path to approach other areas of knowledge and practices. This was my bridge to interdisciplinarity and family law.

The year: 2000. The place: Brisbane, Australia. The event: 10th ISFL World Conference. The theme: 'Family Law: processes, practices and procedures'. the conveners: Prof. John Dewar and Prof. Stephen Parker. Looking back, I know that it took a lot of boldness to make my debut, as well as the encouragement of older members of ISFL, whom I deeply acknowledge. We sent an abstract by three mediators: two psychoanalysts and a family lawyer. To our surprise, it was accepted. At our panel, there was only the name of the lawyer at the table: 'Excuse me Sir but we're all going to present …'. Prof. Andrew Bainham, editor of the *Survey* at the time, was presiding over the session. He was a bit astonished but, elegantly, did not say anything other than a phlegmatic 'so it is'. Afterwards, he thanked us for the competent presentation; he acted as the true gentleman that he is.

Subsequently, I was requested to be the director of interdisciplinary relationships of IBDFAM, the Brazilian Institute of Family Law, and we invited Prof. Andrew Bainham to come to Brazil for a series of lectures. The cooperation between IBDFAM and ISFL was flourishing.

Enchanted with the new horizon, I wanted to speak the 'language of family law', and in the following years I took Master's and PhD degrees at the São Paulo Faculty of Law.

In 2001, at the 3rd IBDFAM National Conference, in Ouro Preto, Minas Gerais, Prof. Lynn Wardle was invited to represent ISFL as a keynote speaker. No words would be enough to describe Prof. Lynn's serenity, intelligence and capability to conciliate different perspectives and interests, and to transform them into action. His contributions to our Executive Council and the enthusiasm he showed regarding interdisciplinary approaches, and in expanding ISFL to other continents, were priceless.

Then came the 11th ISFL World Conference, held in Copenhagen, Denmark, and Oslo, Norway, with the theme 'Family Life and Human Rights'. The President of IBDFAM, Prof. Rodrigo da Cunha Pereira, and myself were invited to be keynote speakers – an extreme honour and incentive. Our convenors were Prof. Peter Lødrup and Prof. Eva Modvar.

In 2005, we had the 12th World Conference, in Salt Lake City, Utah, United States, with the theme 'Family Law: Balancing Interests and Pursuing Priorities'. The convenor was Prof. Lynn Wardle, who organised a magnificent experience at Brigham Young University. At that time, thanks to the incentive of Prof. Paul Vlaardingerbroek, another enthusiast of the interdisciplinary approach, I ran for vice presidency and was elected one of the six vice presidents.

In 2008, we had the 13th World Conference, with a provocative theme: 'Family Finances'. The romantic Vienna, Austria, was the perfect setting to discuss existential and material aspects of family law. The convenor was Prof. Bea Verschraegen. Her sensible and keen objectivity was embodied in the atmosphere of this conference.

In 2011, it was the time for Lyons, France, to be the venue for the 14th World Conference. The theme was 'Generation Solidarities'. Our convenor was Prof. Hugues Fulchiron, and his elegant and outstanding competence, and his capacity for identifying and making visible what had been cloaked but key issues in family law, were distinctive marks of this World Conference. The programme brought into the spotlight issues such as the responsibility of newer generations to past ones, and reflections about the existential role played by gratitude.

To be elected as vice president brought me even more responsibility. And, in another impulse of courage, I offered to hold a World Conference in Brazil. Only my gratitude to ISFL could make me undertake such a challenge.

As a convenor, I can testify to the great amount of work that is required to organise an international conference; nevertheless, it is a most rewarding experience. I express my recognition to all past conveners and my encouragement to the many to come.

To organise a World Conference in Brazil, in my case with no university financing, was quite an experience. It was only possible with the collaboration of IBDFAM, and the support of the ISFL president at the time, Prof. Patrick Parkinson, and the extra- competent general secretary, Prof. Marsha Garrison. Their backing, and an extra 'little big' help from some friends, was decisive to managing it. 'Family Law: Singularities and Universalities' was a successful event, resulting in an increase in the number of ISFL members from Brazil, with a significant attendance at our World Conferences ever since – mission accomplished!

A few words about Prof Patrick Parkinson: from my standpoint, he has a privileged vision of what is needed to have more effectiveness in family law: taking knowledge gained from the courts into other spheres, for example compiling statistics and expanding the participation of the State in solving problems that, despite occurring in family relations, in fact belong to the whole society. Amidst many other challenges, he focuses on the importance of mediation in disputes, and in using the internet to foster communication and agreements in several conflicting situations.

And I need a few more words now to praise Prof. Marsha Garrison. Her most evident qualities – a bright intelligence, objectivity, impressive efficiency and an energetic presence – could not disguise the warmth of her soul, and happiness when meeting each one of us. She played, and plays, a major role in our Society, always ready to collaborate.

The 15th World Conference, in 2017, was in Amsterdam, the Netherlands, with the theme 'Family Law and Family Realities'. Our convenor, Prof. Masha Antokolskaia, received all the attendants in the progressive and charming atmosphere of Amsterdam.

And, oddly enough, during Prof. Antokolskaia's mandate, family realities were overrun by the coronavirus pandemic. With serenity, she guided the Society, together with Prof. Ursula C. Basset, our bright, very active and irreplaceable General Secretary, through those misty times.

Our dear Prof. Hazel Thompson Ahyé – has, in recent times, been sharing with us her keen sense of humour and sensibility in making poetic summaries of the key issues presented at the closing of the conferences. She was organising a World Conference in Barbados, but the pandemic impeded the ability of all her efforts to come to the desired end. Her amazing work was recognised, like that of other convenors, with a permanent place in the Executive Council. And that is another key mark of our society – recognition.

Our very active representative of Latin America, Prof. Ursula Basset, brought even more enthusiasm to our society, with an impressive gentle willpower, organising the 17th World Conference online. The theme was 'Family Law and Crisis: Going Through Pandemics'. It is needless to say how crucial it was to gather together in those shadowy times. Despite the melancholic times, our Society was active.

And the pandemic made even more clear the importance of celebrating: our society's 25th birthday deserved a Golden Jubilee Conference. The 18th World Conference was held in Antwerp, Belgium, in 2023. The theme was 'Rethinking Law's Families & Family Law?'. The convenors were Prof. Frederik Swennen and Prof. Elise Goossens.

Trying to keep up with new forms of communication, the society began to rethink the use of social media and the internet to democratise access to knowledge and family law. In the Antwerp Conference we had a glance of that, with the immediate access to all the richness of the papers during the presentations. We have much to be thankful to our current President, Prof. Federick Swennen, for.

A metaphor that I brought from the experience of Antwerp and its diamond district is the ever-glowing multifaceted shine of our ISFL, as many are the countries and cultures comprised in our Society.

Over the years, I have accompanied the growing of an interdisciplinary perspective in a world of rapid changes. What we see is a deeper understanding of how our human nature and subjectivity contribute, for good and bad, to family relations and the conduct of judicial disputes. Consequently, there is a growing need to integrate the existential and material aspects of family law, and to adopt practices that address both perspectives.

In parallel, we have been facing a change from a binary paradigm of opposition between reason and emotions, and between objectivity and subjectivity, to a more integrative paradigm, and accordingly we can observe an increase in the value given to the affective bonds in the family. The very concept of the family has been evolving, and there is a clear need to carefully address, and to acknowledge those aspects, including the subjectivity of legal practitioners.

Along that path, mediation, counselling and therapies are increasingly used together – prior to, in parallel with, or after a judicial claim. On the other hand, with this broader view of family relations, we are facing a certain overlap between a judicial and a 'therapeutic' approach. Of course, this overlap is neither desirable nor effective. There is a need to clarify the realm of family law and how to deal with those vectors, material and existential, and the use of tools other than judicial tools.

One of the effects of an interdisciplinary approach is to question the limits and possibilities of each discipline, to find the areas of possible cooperation, so as to strength the identity of each discipline. And I believe this is the direction in which we are heading.

In a rapidly changing world, some key issues are drawing our attention: polygamous relationships, reproductive techniques and so-called reproductive tourism, the contractualisation of family relationships, migration, and so on; and, in a broader sense, the role of family law, and of the judiciary, in our contemporary world. These issues have been competently discussed in recent World and Regional Conferences. And there is much more to come.

The venue for the next World Conference has not yet been chosen. Nevertheless, what one can be sure of is the growing contribution of ISFL, not only to family law, but as an example that respect for our differences can be achieved through curiosity, knowledge, respect and dialogue. From my point of view, that is what most characterises our ISFL and its members' personal initiatives.

An example of the compromise with diversity, inclusiveness and the need for effective communication is the work of Robin Fretwell Wilson – 'Tolerance means Dialogue' – in seminars held in several universities, discussing approaches for living together in a diverse society. And certainly, there are many other similar initiatives, and many more to come, among our valuable members.

Long live ISFL in addressing the three basic existential questions of humankind: where do we came from? Who are we? And, most importantly, where we are heading to? In ISFL we are heading to the 'right of being human', with the consciousness that we live in a shared world in which we should share our human resources.

THOUGHTS ABOUT THE BENEFITS OF GETTING INVOLVED WITH THE ISFL

Thomas OLDHAM

An ISFL conference affords one the opportunity to meet interesting people from different cultures. I have greatly enjoyed interacting with attendees at various conferences. In addition, you learn about recent legal initiatives in other countries. For example, at the 2023 conference, I learned that the English Law Commission has started an investigation into whether premarital agreements should be formally recognised and whether a system of equitable distribution of property at divorce should be adopted.

Similarly, meeting people from other countries expands your professional network and gives you colleagues you can contact in the future if you have questions about legal developments in their countries. Conversations at conferences can catalyse interesting ideas about scholarly collaborations. This has happened to me more than once.

Other professional opportunities can result from ISFL participation. For example, over the years, I have been invited by ISFL colleagues to be a visiting scholar at various universities. I have travelled to Australia a number of times for various projects. This eventually resulted in a Fulbright appointment in Sydney and Canberra, which was great fun.

Finally, by attending ISFL conferences, you will encounter interesting and challenging new ideas. I still remember a statement made at a plenary presentation at the Copenhagen conference almost thirty years ago. The speaker predicted that same-sex marriage would be accepted throughout Western Europe in ten years. I thought, 'Is he out of his mind?' (At the time, I don't think any jurisdiction accepted same-sex marriage.) Well, guess what? He was essentially correct. Ten years later, many European countries had accepted same-sex marriage.

REMEMBERING AND CELEBRATING ISFL AT OUR GOLDEN JUBILEE

Hazel THOMPSON-AHYE*

In 1973, in Birmingham, the International Society of Family Law was born.
Professor Falk was the one in whose brain this brilliant idea took form.
The objective of the Society was the study and discussion of Family Law.
Furtherance of international research, dissemination of ideas and much more.
The **first ISFL World Conference** was held in West Berlin, in 1975.
Its theme, 'The Child and the Law', is still so very much alive.
The **second World Conference** in Montreal, Canada, in 1977,
was on 'Violence in the Family', an ever-present painful cry to heaven.
'Family Living in a Changing Society' was theme of **World Conference three**.
In 1979, in Sweden, new knowledge gained, we didn't leave ignorantly.
Come 1982 at Harvard Law School, the **fourth World Conference** was held.
The first in the USA, but the theme, I do not know, and no one could tell.
Belgium in 1985 was the **fifth**, on 'The Family, the State and Individual Security'.
Still so relevant and concerning to all, whether you live in country or the city.
The **sixth World Conference** in 1988, in Tokyo, Japan, was the first in Asia.
'Issues of the Ageing in Modern Society' was the theme chosen for us to hear.
The **seventh World Conference** in 1991, in Croatia, had longest title you'd see:
'Parenthood, The Legal Significance of Motherhood and Fatherhood in a Changing Society'.
The **eighth World Conference**, in 1994, in Cardiff, Wales, was my first.
'Families Across Frontiers', an intellectual fare, birthed in me an insatiable thirst.
For the **ninth World Conference** in 1997, I went to Durban, South Africa, to dine.
One of the conference presentations later published in the *Survey* was mine.
'Changing Family Forms: World Themes and African Issues' was the topic.

* Senator Hazel Thompson-Ahye, HBM, Vice President ISFL.

'The Relationship Between Social Change and the Law – The Concept of
"Family" and the Child Born Out of Wedlock' was my pick.
The **tenth World Conference** was held in 2000, in Queensland, Australia.
The theme, 'Family Law Processes, Practices and Pressures' was good to hear.
The **eleventh World Conference** was held in Copenhagen and Oslo,
on the theme, 'Family Law and Human Rights', one that we all know.
The **twelfth World Conference** in Utah, organised in 2005 by Lynn Wardle,
on 'Family Law, Balancing Interests and Pursuing Priorities' was a good model.
My paper on 'The Law and the Cohabitant', and the law we had recently passed,
was published in the conference book and West Indian Law Journal superfast.
The **thirteenth World Conference** was held in Vienna, Austria in 2008.
'Family Finances' was the theme and the planned social events were great.
The **fourteenth** was in Lyons, France, on 'Solidarities between Generations'.
I presented on our problems of the aged that were similar to all nations.
In the midst of my research, I discovered the UN classified me as old.
An idea on which, despite my children's concurrence, I was not sold.
The **fifteenth World Conference** in Recife, Brazil, in 2011, was a joy.
To interact with the students, who were so enthusiastic, both girls and boys.
The topic was 'Family Law: Universalities and Singularities'.
And we learnt that each country has its own peculiarities.
I presented on 'Corporal Punishment: A Painful Blow to Children's Rights'.
A solution to which, despite commitment to child rights, no end is in sight.
The **sixteenth World Conference** 2017, on 'Family Law and Family Realities',
in Amsterdam, the Netherlands, revealed many situations of families.
The **seventeenth**, 'Family Law and Crisis Going through Pandemics',
conducted online, showed Secretary Ursula's resourcefulness and work ethic.
For our **eighteenth**, we explored 'Rethinking Law's Families and Family Law?'
It was our **Golden Jubilee**, a grand reunion in Belgium and so much more.

ISFL GOLDEN JUBILEE CONFERENCE 2023

Hazel THOMPSON-AHYE

ISFL Golden Jubilee Conference 2023
will always remain a treasured memory.
The theme, 'Rethinking Law's Families and Family Law'
brought many family law researchers to this conference door.
From every continent of the world to Antwerp they came
to share family law problems that really were all the same.
What is a parent and what is a partner?
What is the legal position of a minor?
Care and protection of the elderly is an important duty.
Soon someone will have to take care of you, and even me.
Lest you think I seek volunteers for this important function,
let me quickly turn my attention to assisted reproduction.
Attribution of parenthood and the right to know one's original family
involve complicated issues of surrogacy, identity and technology.
Abortion and reproductive rights are hot topics creating strife,
for which some Christians are prepared to lay down their life.
Money, property, gender and the law, digital law,
are issues which can have the family engaged as though fighting a war.
International child abduction and parental alienation,
with the issue of domestic violence, there may be a connection.
Research, policy formation and the law.
That was a topic I do not recall our discussing before.
After years of women power, Bea, Marsha and Masha, hard acts to follow
We passed the baton to Frederik, seems a decent enough fellow.

I wish him a successful presidential term without too much strife.
You know the first thing this man do, was buy a new wardrobe to look nice.
We look forward to the expansion of our ISFL membership.
Who will continue to build great scholarship and form lasting friendships.

PART III

50-YEAR RETROSPECTIVES ON FAMILY LAW

GLOBAL PERSPECTIVES

FIFTY YEARS OF FAMILY LAW

Child's Rights and the Family

Olga A. Khazova-Gurvich

Résumé

Le présent chapitre vise à explorer l'évolution du statut juridique de l'enfant au sein de la famille au cours des cinquante dernières années, en commençant par

1973, année de la signature de la Convention internationale sur la protection des droits de tous les travailleurs migrants et des membres de leur famille. À l'époque, la Convention des Nations unies sur les droits de l'enfant n'existait pas et l'intérêt supérieur de l'enfant n'était pas l'un des principes fondamentaux gouvernant les droits de l'enfant. La garde des enfants après un divorce était traditionnellement confiée à la mère et les pères qui n'étaient pas satisfaits de leur droit de visite avaient tendance à résoudre le problème, du moins dans les cas transfrontaliers, en enlevant leurs enfants. Les enfants n'étaient pas encore considérés comme titulaires de droits à part entière et les parents les traitaient plutôt comme leur « propriété ». L'année 1989 a été marquée par l'adoption de la Convention des Nations unies relative aux droits de l'enfant dont, aujourd'hui encore, nous n'avons pas pleinement saisi l'importance. Elle a institué le droit de l'enfant d'être entendu et de participer aux procédures le concernant et ce droit demeure l'une des questions les plus délicates, en particulier en matière familiale. Les progrès de la science et de la procréation médicalement assistée ont donné une nouvelle dimension aux relations parents-enfants et il n'est pas toujours évident de savoir qui sont les parents légaux de l'enfant et où tout cela mènera le droit de la famille : enfants conçus par donneur, enfants nés d'une mère porteuse, filiation multiple et, quel que soit le scénario, le droit de l'enfant à l'identité. À cela s'ajoute une augmentation du nombre de divorces et de remariages, ce qui signifie une augmentation du nombre de familles où au moins l'une des personnes qui s'occupe de l'enfant n'a pas de lien biologique avec lui : la notion de parenté sociale est de plus en plus à l'ordre du jour. Enfin, le fait que les enfants se connectent à Internet ajoute une nouvelle dimension aux relations parents-enfants. Où va donc le droit de la famille et comment l'adapter aux réalités sociales d'aujourd'hui et à l'évolution de la place de l'enfant au sein de la famille ? Quel avenir pour le droit de la famille ?

1. 1973 – THE ISFL LAUNCHED: THE BEGINNING

Although '[c]hildren are the most valuable members of the family life', they 'have not always been treated well by family law'.[1] In the early 1970s, 'a significant number of manifestos' appeared, 'proclaiming the urgent need for children to be liberated'.[2] Despite this, among legal scholars there were hardly any discussions on children's rights – not to mention on children's rights within the family – comparable to those that we witness today. Children's rights were hardly taken

1 M. Henaghan, '50 Years of Contributions to Family Law by Leading ISFL Members' in R. Fretwell Wilson and J. Carbone (eds.), *The International Survey of Family Law 2023*, Intersentia, 2023, p. 90.

2 D. Archard, *Children: Rights and Childhood*, 3rd ed., Routledge, 2015, p. 64.

seriously at that time,[3] and the concept of children's rights was, at best, just beginning to take shape. There was not yet a UN Convention on the Rights of the Child[4] ('UNCRC' or 'UN Convention'), *The Rights and Wrongs of Children* had yet to be written by Michael Freeman,[5] and the best interests of the child had yet to become one of the fundamental principles in children's rights theory and practice.

To briefly describe a picture of the time when the ISFL was launched, the following matters should first of all be highlighted. Parental custody after divorce was traditionally assigned to the mother; fathers not satisfied with their access rights tended to respond, at least in cross-border cases, by abducting their children, and this raised concerns about increased numbers of international child abductions. The 'illegitimacy' of children born outside legal marriage was still a prevailing legal rule in most jurisdictions globally. Non-married fathers had yet to prevail in their claims for recognition as part of the right to respect for family life under Article 8 of the European Convention on Human Rights and Fundamental Freedoms[6] (ECHR, or European Convention). Children were not yet considered fully fledged holders of rights, and parents treated their children as their 'property'. The parental rights of same-sex couples were not discussed either, as the issue of same-sex marriage itself was not yet part of the agenda. The same is true regarding many other issues, such as, for instance, those that follow from advancements in assisted reproduction, which nowadays constitute an integral part of contemporary family law.

At the same time, it was obvious that family law would go through tremendous changes, but probably only a few could have foreseen the true scale of those changes. In this regard, it is remarkable that the ISFL was an organisation that had 'anticipated issues that only became highly topical later',[7] particularly having chosen 'The Child and the Law' as the theme of its very first conference in 1975 – 'a subject that had just begun to be of concern to scholars and legislators'.[8] To quote Baroness Ruth Deech, '[t]hose were exciting times for family law'.[9]

---

3 See M. Freeman, *The Moral Status of Children: Essays on the Rights of the Child*, Martinus Nijhoff Publishers, 1997, pp. 19, 29–30.

4 A/RES/44/25: Convention on the Rights of the Child, available at <https://documents.un.org/doc/resolution/gen/nr0/547/84/img/nr054784.pdf>, last accessed 12.09.2024.

5 M. Freeman, *The Rights and Wrongs of Children*, Francis Pinter, 1983.

6 Council of Europe, 'Convention for the Protection of Human Rights and Fundamental Freedoms', Council of Europe Treaty Series 005, 1950, available at <https://rm.coe.int/1680a2353d>, last accessed 12.09.2024.

7 J. Eekelaar, 'The Origins and Development of the Society' in R. Fretwell Wilson and J. Carbone (eds.), above n. 1, p. 23.

8 S.N. Katz, 'Remembrance of Things Past' in R. Fretwell Wilson and J. Carbone (eds.), above n. 1, p. 34.

9 R. Deech, Baroness Deech of Cumnor, 'Memories of the International Society of Family Law' in R. Fretwell Wilson and J. Carbone (eds.), above n. 1, p. 16.

A single chapter can hardly claim to fully cover all aspects of child rights in the context of the family, not to mention that the term 'family' itself is not clearly defined, and its definition keeps expanding as the social realities change. Therefore, this chapter will focus on identifying key issues or milestones that have characterised the evolution of the legal status of the child in the family over the period under review.

2. BEFORE THE UN CONVENTION ON THE RIGHTS OF THE CHILD

2.1. THE 1924 DECLARATION OF THE RIGHTS OF THE CHILD

The work on the draft UNCRC would not begin until 1979, but the idea of children's rights did not come out of nowhere. From a legal point of view, the origins of children's rights go back to the Geneva Declaration of the Rights of the Child, adopted by the League of Nations in 1924.[10] The main concern at that time was a great number of children that had become orphans or had been displaced as a result of World War I, who needed assistance and protection.[11] The 1924 Declaration contained five principles to be used by those who worked in international child welfare.[12] It is based on a paternalistic approach to children, and there are no signs of the idea of child participation being important to children's rights. In fact, the word 'right' is not used in the text of the Declaration; it appears only in the title. Nevertheless, the 1924 Declaration, despite its legal nature as a non-binding instrument, was a milestone in children's rights evolution,[13] as it was, technically, the first international document that explicitly acknowledged the idea of children's rights.[14]

---

10 Geneva Declaration of the Rights of the Child, 26 September 1924, League of Nations, O.J. Spec. Supp. 21 at 43 (1924), available at <http://www.un-documents.net/gdrc1924.htm>, last accessed 12.09.2024.

11 For more detail see, e.g. Office of the UN High Commissioner for Human Rights, *Legislative History of the Convention on the Rights of the Child ('Travaux preparatoires')*, vol. I, United Nations, 2007, p. 3, available at <https://www.ohchr.org/sites/default/files/Documents/Publications/LegislativeHistorycrc1en.pdf>, last accessed 12.01.204; S. Detrick, *A Commentary on the United Nations Convention on the Rights of the Child*, Martinus Nijhoff Publishers, 1999, pp. 13 ff; T. Buck, *International Child Law*, Routledge, 3rd ed., 2014, pp. 21–22, 89 ff.

12 See *Travaux preparatoires*, vol. I, above n. 11, p. 22.

13 See Child Rights Connect, 'Milestones in Children's Rights', <https://www.childrightsconnect.org/wp-content/uploads/2019/09/milestoneschildrights_27_07_2019_sm.pdf>, last accessed 12.01.2024.

14 See *Travaux preparatoires*, vol. I, above n. 11, p. 3.

2.2. THE 1959 DECLARATION OF THE RIGHTS OF THE CHILD

After World War II, which also brought a lot of misery and suffering to children, the General Assembly of the newly established United Nations decided to revise the 1924 Declaration. However, a significantly revised text, which became a new Declaration of the Rights of the Child, was adopted only in 1959.[15]

The 1959 Declaration of the Rights of the Child is considered of 'far greater importance'[16] than the 1924 Declaration, and not only because it has ten Principles compared with the five of the earlier Declaration. Both Declarations have the same titles but their wording is different. Importantly, the 1959 Declaration reflected the evolution of views on the rights of the child since 1924, and many of its principles 'are formulated in terms of rights of children',[17] thereby reflecting 'the conception of a child as more than merely a passive recipient of international humanitarian aid, but rather as an active participant in the enjoyment of human rights and freedoms'.[18] Moreover – and this is of particular significance – the 1959 Declaration was the first international human rights document that referred 'specifically to the "best interests of the child"'[19] (in Principles 2 and 7).

The 1959 Declaration is considered to be 'the conceptual parent' of the UNCRC,[20] and remains a very important instrument in the field of children's rights. Nevertheless, it should be borne in mind that it was adopted 65 years ago, and some of its provisions may not be fully up to date. This is particularly true of the provisions of Principle 6 that specifically address issues related to the child's family life, namely the one that states that 'a child of tender years shall not, save in exceptional circumstances, be separated from his mother'.[21] The provision reflects 'outmoded stereotyped ideas about the roles to be played by mothers and fathers in the lives of their children',[22] a subject which will be returned to later in this chapter.

---

15 Declaration of the Rights of the Child, G.A. res. 1386 (XIV), 14 U.N. GAOR Supp. (No. 16) at 19, U.N. Doc. A/4354 (1959), available at <https://digitallibrary.un.org/record/195831?ln=en&v=pdf>, last accessed 12.09.2024.

16 J. Fortin, *Children's Rights and the Developing Law*, CUP, 2005, pp. 37–38.

17 See S. Detrick, above n. 11, p. 14.

18 See T. Buck, above n.11, at p. 89.

19 See S. Detrick, above n. 11, p. 15.

20 G. van Bueren, *The International Law on the Rights of the Child*, Brill/Nijhoff, 1998, p. 14.

21 The full text of Principle 6 reads as follows: 'The child, for the full and harmonious development of his personality, needs love and understanding. He shall, wherever possible, grow up in the care and under the responsibility of his parents, and, in any case, in an atmosphere of affection and of moral and material security; a child of tender years shall not, save in exceptional circumstances, be separated from his mother. Society and the public authorities shall have the duty to extend particular care to children without a family and to those without adequate means of support. Payment of State and other assistance towards the maintenance of children of large families is desirable.'

22 See J. Fortin, above n. 16, p. 38.

2.3. DRAFTING THE UN CONVENTION ON THE RIGHTS OF THE CHILD

The work on the draft UNCRC, as has been noted, began in 1979, and it took ten years to finalise the instrument.

During the thirty-fourth session of the UN Commission on Human Rights, in 1978, Poland submitted a proposal to draft an international convention on the rights of the child.[23] Poland proposed that the draft convention be based on the ten principles contained in the 1959 UN Declaration of the Rights of the Child. Therefore, the draft could have been considered as basically complete, and the expectation was that the convention could be adopted by the next year, 1979, which the UN General Assembly had proclaimed as the International Year of the Child. The governments' response, however, was highly ambivalent. Although there was general support for the idea of the convention as such, and, to a certain extent, that it be based on the 1959 Declaration, strong concerns were expressed that the proposed content and style of the convention, among other things, were unsuitable for an internationally binding instrument. In addition, several Member States noted that the draft, being based on the 1959 Declaration, 'did not reflect the social, economic and cultural developments and changes that had taken place since then'.[24] Particularly, as noted by a representative of Sweden:

> Since the adoption of the Declaration, views on the situation of the child have developed in many parts of the world. It is clear, for instance, that in many countries, views on the family, on marriage, on the relations between children and parents and on the child as an individual having its own needs and rights have undergone important changes. Nor are the material conditions and the social structures in which children live always the same today as they were 20 years ago. This development should, in the view of the Swedish Government, affect the contents of the convention which is to be drafted at the present time.[25]

In 1979, after extensive and prolonged discussions of the Polish proposal that involved not only the UN Member States but also competent specialised agencies, and regional intergovernmental and non-governmental organisations, the UN

---

23 For more details on the drafting history of the UNCRC, see, e.g. S. Detrick, above n. 11, pp. 14–18; *Travaux preparatoires*, vol. I, above n. 9, pp. 29 ff; S. Detrick, J.E. Doek and N. Cantwell, *The United Nations Convention on the Rights of the Child: A Guide to the 'Travaux Préparatoires'*, Martinus Nijhoff Publishers, 1992; T. Buck, above n. 11, pp. 89–91; N. Cantwell, 'Words that Speak Volumes. A short history of the drafting of the UNCRC' in Institut international des droits de l'enfant, *18 Candles. The Convention on the Rights of the Child Reaches Majority*, IDE, 2007, pp. 22–29, available at: https://www.ohchr.org/sites/default/files/Documents/Publications/crc18.pdf, last accessed 12.01.2024.

24 See S. Detrick, above n. 11, p. 16.

25 See *Travaux preparatoires*, vol. I, above n. 11, p. 62 (para. 4).

Commission on Human Rights established a working group on the question of a convention on the rights of the child. The ten years that it took to develop the final text of the convention 'proved to be years extremely well-spent'.[26]

Of those issues that were identified as the most controversial during the drafting process, three areas related, directly or indirectly, to family law: the definition of the minimum age of the child (the question was at what point childhood begins: at conception or at birth), freedom of religion, and adoption.[27] However, there were also other issues on child–parent relations which were perhaps less controversial, but nevertheless provoked debates that resulted in the adoption of several important provisions.

The first of these that should be noted in this regard relates to the provision of Principle 6 of the 1959 Declaration that was mentioned earlier – that a child of tender years shall not, save in exceptional circumstances, be separated from his mother. This provision was directly linked to the issues of fathers' rights and parental equality, and received a clear and strong response at the drafting stage. It was particularly noted that the role of the father for the normal development of children had, so far, been 'underestimated and should be stressed in the future'.[28] Several State representatives expressed concerns that, if the wording of Principle 6 was kept unchanged in the convention, the ties of a child with their father would 'be weakened or broken' and 'jeopardized or severed'.[29] As we know, Article 18(1) of the UNCRC is based on the idea of parental equality, and fixes parents' 'common responsibilities for the upbringing and development of the child'.

The second child–parent-related issue that raised an interesting discussion during the drafting process, but which did not become part of the convention, concerned the duties of children, particularly towards their parents. A corresponding proposal, submitted by the representative of Senegal, included the following provision: 'the child has the duty to respect his parents and to give them assistance, in case of need'.[30] Although some participants shared the concerns of the author's proposal, even they hesitated to support it, and argued that the duty to respect parents was 'a moral obligation [rather] than a legal one'.[31] Besides, as was also pointed out, it would hardly be possible for the States Parties to report on their compliance with such a provision of the convention.[32]

---

26 See N. Cantwell, above n. 23, at p. 22.

27 The fourth one was the age at which children should be permitted to participate in armed conflict. See discussion in S. Detrick, J.E. Doek and N. Cantwell, above n. 23, p. 26.

28 See Office of the UN High Commissioner for Human Rights, *Legislative History of the Convention on the Rights of the Child ('Travaux preparatoires')*, vol. II, United Nations, 2007, p. 499.

29 See *Travaux preparatoires*, vol. I, above n. 11, p. 392; vol. II, above n. 28, p. 498.

30 See *Travaux preparatoires*, vol. II, above n. 28, pp. 893–94.

31 See ibid., p. 894 (para. 706).

32 Ibid.

At the same time, as some of the participants voiced the opinion that the idea about respect for the parents should at least be included in the convention, the proposal of the observer for Canada to incorporate this idea within the Article that dealt with the objectives of education of the child was accepted.[33] This was a creative solution to a delicate problem, and, as the final text of UNCRC Article 29(1) demonstrated,[34] its wording was 'sufficient to satisfy the morality of the issue'.[35]

Conversely, a corresponding provision on the responsibility of the child was included in the African Charter on the Rights and Welfare of the Child, adopted in 1990.[36] Article 31 of the African Charter stated that, as far as it concerns the family and parents, 'every child shall have responsibilities towards his family', and 'subject to his age and ability, and such limitations as may be contained in the present Charter, shall have the duty … to work for the cohesion of the family, to respect his parents, superiors and elders at all times and to assist them in case of need'. Although this Article has a predominantly moral significance, and was partly influenced by the 1948 Universal Declaration of Human Rights[37] and the Preambles of two 1966 UN Covenants[38] that refer to the duties of the individual, it also reflects the distinctive character of the African human rights system.[39] Article 31 aims 'to underscore the point that responsibilities are complementary to rights, rather than being undermining of them', and 'reveals that children should be required to play a role at family, community, national and continental

33 Ibid., pp. 893–94 (paras. 706–07; 709–10).

34 The final wording of UNCRC Art. 29, in a part dealing with the aims of education, states that the education of the child shall be directed, among other things, to '[t]he development of respect for the child's parent'.

35 N. Vuskovic Sahovic, J.E. Doek and J. Zermatten, *The Right of the Child in International Law*, Stämpfli Publishers, 2012, p. 162.

36 African Charter on the Rights and Welfare of the Child, adopted by by the 26th Ordinary Session of the Assembly of Heads of State and Government of the OAU Addis Ababa, Ethiopia, July 1990, entered into force on 29 November 1999, available at <https://au.int/en/treaties/african-charter-rights-and-welfare-child>, last accessed 15.09.2024. See J. Sloth-Nielsen and B.D. Mezmur, 'A Dutiful Child: The Implications of Article 31 of the African Children's Charter' (2008) 52(2) *Journal of African Law* 169 ff.

37 United Nation General Assembly, 'The Universal Declaration of Human Rights (UDHR)', New York, adopted and proclaimed by General Assembly resolution 217 A (III) of 10 December 1948, available at <https://www.un.org/en/about-us/universal-declaration-of-human-rights>, last accessed 15.09.2024.

38 'The International Covenant on Civil and Political Rights', adopted and opened for signature, ratification and accession by General Assembly resolution 2200A (XXI) of 16 December 1966, entry into force 23 March 1976, available at https://www.ohchr.org/en/instruments-mechanisms/instruments/international-covenant-civil-and-political-rights, last accessed 15.09.2024; the International Covenant on Economic, Social and Cultural Rights, adopted and opened for signature, ratification and accession by General Assembly resolution 2200A (XXI) of 16 December 1966, entry into force 3 January 1976, available at <https://www.ohchr.org/en/instruments-mechanisms/instruments/international-covenant-economic-social-and-cultural-rights>, last accessed 15.09.2024.

39 See J. Sloth-Nielsen and B.D. Mezmur, above n. 36, 160, 164 ff.

levels, in accordance with their age and maturity as they grow up'. Therefore, together with 'the ideals that it envisages', Article 31 'must be situated within a positive developmental context' that, among other things, 'aims to nurture child participation'.[40]

There was also a set of provisions that were proposed but not even discussed during the drafting process.[41] Among these, two in particular deserve attention in the context of this chapter.

The first concerns definition or interpretation of the term 'parent(s)',[42] a matter which is absent from the final text of the UN Convention; not only was this issue not discussed during the drafting process, but it was not even posed. According to the only proposal, the term 'parents' should 'be interpreted to include, where appropriate, other family members or guardians who have de facto responsibility for the care and upbringing of the child'. It is submitted here that refusal to discuss this proposal can be explained by the fact that the problem of interpretation of this term was solved in a different way, avoiding the need to give a definition of the term 'parents'.[43] However, remarkably, this proposal was not even used as a basis for raising the questions of 'who is a parent?' and 'what is a parent?', which nowadays belong to one of the most topical family law issues.[44] Probably, drafters of the UN Convention did not see any serious problems in this regard, although it would be interesting to figure out what such a discussion might have looked like at that time.

Other proposals that were not discussed but seem prescient in retrospect relate to genetic engineering. Thus, the representative of Colombia suggested that '[t]he item concerning the convention should include as a topic of discussion the development of new scientific methods for the fertilization and preservation of human reproductive cells and experiments concerning their genetic structure'.[45] The World Association of Children's Friends submitted a more expanded proposal based on the Council of Europe Recommendation No. 1046 (1986).[46] This proposal, amongst other important issues, contained provisions aiming to ensure 'protection of a child, conceived but not yet born, against genetic

40 Ibid., 188.

41 See *Travaux preparatoires*, vol. II, above n. 28, pp. 897 ff.

42 Ibid.

43 Art. 5 of the UNCRC lists the persons whose responsibilities, rights and duties towards the child the States Parties shall respect: these are 'parents, or, where applicable, the members of the extended family or community as provided for by the local custom, legal guardians or other persons legally responsible for the child'.

44 It is enough to refer to one of the first books on this topic: A. Bainham, S.D. Sclater and M. Richards, *What is a Parent? A Socio-Legal Analysis*, Hart Publishing, 1999.

45 See *Travaux preparatoires*, vol. II, above n. 28, p. 898.

46 Council of Europe, Parliamentary Assembly, Recommendation 1046 (1986), adopted on 24 September 1986 (18th Sitting), available at <https://assembly.coe.int/nw/xml/XRef/Xref-XML2HTML-en.asp?fileid=15080&lang=en>, last accessed 15.09.2024.

experiments or engineering contrary to his physical, moral or mental integrity, or his health', and also to oblige the States Parties to take all measures to forbid 'the creation of embryos from the sperm of different individuals' and 'the creation of children from people of the same sex'.[47]

It would obviously have been premature to include provisions of that kind in an internationally binding instrument at that time, although the discussion itself might have been important, and might have shed some light on understanding the child's rights in the context of advances in biomedicine. It is particularly worth mentioning in this regard that the first child with DNA from three people (two mothers and one father), through the use of mitochondrial replacement therapy, was born in UK in 2015.[48] Taking into account that, technically, the child had two genetic mothers, was it the creation of a child 'from people of the same sex' that it had been suggested to prohibit? I will take the risk of giving a positive answer to this question.

2.4. EUROPEAN COURT OF HUMAN RIGHTS: THE END OF THE CONCEPT OF ILLEGITIMACY OF CHILDREN BORN OUT OF WEDLOCK IN EUROPE

By pure coincidence, in 1979, the same year that work on the draft UNCRC began, the European Court of Human Rights (ECtHR) ruled in the *Marckx v. Belgium* case. This is known as a 'landmark case'[49] because it put an end to the illegitimacy of children born out of wedlock, at least in Europe.[50] In *Marckx v. Belgium*, the Court found a violation of ECHR Article 8 (on the right to respect for private and family life) together with Article 14 (on prohibition of discrimination)

---

47 See *Travaux preparatoires*, vol. II, above n. 28, pp. 898–900.

48 I. Sample, 'First UK baby with DNA from three people could be born next year', *The Gardian*, 15 December 2016, available at <https://www.theguardian.com/science/2016/dec/15/three-parent-embryos-regulator-gives-green-light-to-uk-clinics?CMP=Share_iOSApp_Other>, last accessed 12.01.2024; J. Gallagher, 'Baby born from three people's DNA in UK first', *BBC*, 9 May 2023, available at <https://www.bbc.com/news/science-environment-65538866>, last accessed 12.01.2024.

49 See, e.g. D. Coester-Waltjen, 'The Impact of the European Convention on Human Rights and the European Court of Human Rights on European Family Law' in J. Scherpe (ed.), *European Family Law*, vol. I, Edward Elgar, 2016, p. 57; J. Scherpe, *The Present and Future of European Family Law*, vol. IV, Edward Elgar, 2016, p. 7.

50 To be fair, it should be noted that, much earlier, in Russia after the 1917 revolution, the notion of an illegitimate child was abolished by the first Russian Family Code – the Code of Laws on Acts of Civil Status, Marriage, Family and Guardianship Law of 22.10.1918 (S. 133), where it was stated that true filiation was the basis of the family, and that there was no difference between children born within and outside marriage. Later, it became one of the main principles of the Soviet law on parentage (see O. Khazova, 'The New Codification of Russian Family Law' in J. Eekelaar and T. Nhlapo (eds.) *The Changing Family: International Perspectives on the Family and Family Law*, Hart Publishing, 1998, pp. 74–76, 81).

because, due to the complicated and restrictive rules on establishing maternal affiliation with regard to a child born outside wedlock, such a child '[was] likely to remain motherless in the eyes of Belgian law' (para. 39). As was stated by the ECtHR, Article 8 applies to the 'family life' of the 'illegitimate' family as it does to that of the 'legitimate' family (para. 31), and 'in acting in a manner calculated to allow the family life of an unmarried mother and her child to develop normally … the State must avoid any discrimination grounded on birth: this is dictated by Article 14 taken in conjunction with Article 8' (para. 34).

Later, protection under Article 8 ECHR was extended to unmarried couples who live together with their children and, depending on the facts, also to relations between a child and their natural 'unmarried father', provided, however, that there are close family ties between them. As the ECtHR stated in *Keegan v. Ireland*,[51] with reference to the Court's jurisprudence and specifically its judgment in *Marckx v. Belgium*, 'where the existence of a family tie with a child has been established, the State must act in a manner calculated to enable that tie to be developed and legal safeguards must be created that render possible as from the moment of birth the child's integration in his family'.[52]

3. FAMILY LAW ISSUES AND THE UN CONVENTION ON THE RIGHTS OF THE CHILD

The year 1989 was marked by the adoption of the UNCRC, a 'Magna Carta for Children',[53] the significance of which we have yet to grasp.

As stated in the Preamble to the UNCRC, the family is the natural environment for children's growth and well-being, and for the full and harmonious development of their personalities; they 'should grow up in a family environment, in an atmosphere of happiness, love and understanding'. The family is where children usually live, develop and start to exercise their rights. Therefore, it is not surprising that the UNCRC pays considerable attention to the rights of the child in the context of the family. There are several Articles in the UNCRC that specifically deal with family issues: Articles 5, 7, 8, 9, 10, 11, 18, 20, 21 and 27 (para. 4). These Articles concern different aspects of a child's family life and selected Articles will be discussed in more detail in the context of the respective questions raised in each section below.

But what is the family?

---

51 *Keegan v. Ireland*, no. 16969/90, 26 May 1994.

52 Ibid., para 50. For detailed discussion see, e.g. ECtHR, *Guide on Article 8 of the European Convention on Human Rights – Right to Respect for Private and Family Life, Home and Correspondence*, Council of Europe, 2022, pp. 85–86; see D. Coester-Waltjen, above n. 49, pp. 49–94.

53 M. Freeman, *A Magna Carta for Children?: Rethinking Children's Rights*, CUP, 2020.

3.1. WHAT IS THE FAMILY?

There is limited or no consensus on what family is and how it should be defined. Although there are 'three dovetailing concepts'[54] of family in international law – 'family', 'family environment' and 'family life'[55] – there is no formally established legal definition of the family that is internationally accepted. The Preamble to the UNCRC defines family as 'the fundamental group of society'. This definition, based on those used in the 1948 Universal Declaration of Human Rights (Article 16) and the 1966 International Covenant on Economic, Social and Cultural Rights (Article 10),[56] does not, however, answer the question of what exactly a family is, and who exactly family members are.

In accordance with the interpretation of the UN Committee on the Rights of the Child ('UNCRC Committee' or 'Committee'), the term 'family' shall be understood broadly to include biological and adoptive parents or, where applicable, members of the extended family or community as provided for by local custom (Article 5).[57] Moreover, when discussing the issues related to prevention of family separation and preservation of family unity, particularly in the context of Article 9, the UNCRC Committee added to that list 'persons with whom the child has a strong personal relationship'.[58]

It seems obvious that the answer to this question is fact-specific and depends on the particular situation regarding the existing family relationships between particular persons – or, more specifically, that between a child and a particular person. The jurisprudence of the ECtHR in this regard is illustrative, as the existence of family relations with a child protected by Article 8 ECHR is recognised as 'essentially a question of fact'.[59] It is defined on a case-by-case basis and depends on the existence of family ties between a child and the person concerned.

Therefore, it is not a surprise that none of the numerous attempts to define the concept of family can offer a definition that would be exhaustive and cover all possible situations. Family is a changing construction; it may take different forms, which depend on different factors, among them historical, cultural, social and legal ones.[60] As was noted in 1994, proclaimed by the UN General Assembly as the International Year of the Family, 'families assume diverse forms

---

54 G. van Bueren, *Child Rights in Europe*, Council of Europe Publishing, 2007, p. 118.

55 In the UN 1966 Covenant on Economic, Social and Cultural Rights (ICESCR), the UNCRC and the ECHR (Art. 8), respectively.

56 International Covenant on Economic, Social and Cultural Rights (ICESCR), 1966, Art. 23.

57 UNCRC Committee, 'General comment No. 14 on the right of the child to have his or her best interests taken as a primary consideration' (2013), CRC/C/GC/14, para. 59.

58 Ibid., para. 60.

59 B. Rainey, E. Wicks and C. Ovey, *Jacobs, White and Ovey: The European Convention on Human Rights*, 6th ed., OUP, 2014, p. 335.

60 See N. Vuskovic Sahovic, J.E. Doek and J. Zermatten, above n. 35, p. 57.

and functions from one country to another, and within each national society. These express the diversity of individual preferences and societal conditions.'[61] At present, this statement seems, at least in Western countries, where the range of family structures 'is characterized by the coexistence of traditional, newer and unfamiliar forms of family life',[62] to be as true as it ever was.

The UNCRC Committee confirms such a fact-specific approach in its jurisprudence. For instance, as the Committee notes in its General comment No. 7 on implementing child rights in early childhood, 'family', as mentioned in the Preamble to the UNCRC, is understood as 'a variety of arrangements that can provide for young children's care, nurturance and development, including the nuclear family, the extended family, and other traditional and modern community-based arrangements, provided these are consistent with children's rights and best interests'.[63] This interpretation, although it formally concerns early childhood development, has an obviously broader meaning and relates to all children irrespective of their age. Thus, in 2016, the UNCRC Committee expressed concerns that the definition of a stable family contained in Slovak legislation, as consisting of the child's father and mother as the most suitable environment for the complex and harmonious development of the child, did not take into account the different kinds of families that exist, and was not in conformity with the definition of the family environment as set out in the UNCRC. Therefore, the UNCRC Committee recommended that the State Party amend its legislation 'to bring it into full compliance with the Convention, focusing on the well-being of the child rather than the composition of the family'.[64]

3.2. CHILD'S RIGHT TO A FAMILY ENVIRONMENT

When speaking about the child's rights and the family, amongst the key issues is the child's right to a family environment,[65] as this impacts on all other issues

61 United Nations Division for Social Policy and Development, 'International Year of the Family (IYF)', available at https://www.un.org/development/desa/family/international-year-of-the-family.html, last accessed 12.01.2024.

62 H. Keller, 'Article 8 in the System of the Convention' in A. Büchler and H. Keller (eds.), *Family Forms and Parenthood: Theory and Practice of Article 8 ECHR in Europe*, Intersentia, 2016, pp. 3–28.

63 UNCRC Committee, 'General comment No. 7 on implementing child rights in early childhood' (2005), CRC/C/GC/7/Rev.1, para.15.

64 UNCRC Committee, 'Concluding observations: Slovakia' (2016), (CRC/C/SVK/CO/3–5), paras. 32–33.

65 It is well recognised that children, as well as adults, 'do not have a right to family per se under international law'; any question on whether the child has the right to family can only arise in respect to marriage, fostering and adoption. See G. van Bueren, *The International Law on the Rights of the Child*, above n. 20, at p. 93.

that may arise in the family context. The child's right to a family environment logically derives from a number of provisions of the UNCRC. Thus, to repeat, the Preamble to the UNCRC states that children, for the full and harmonious development of their personalities, 'should grow up in a family environment, in an atmosphere of happiness, love and understanding'. The child has the right to know and be cared for by his or her parents (Article 7(1)). States Parties shall respect the right of the child to preserve his or her family relations as recognised by law without unlawful interference (Article 8(1)). States Parties shall ensure that a child shall not be separated from their parents against their will, except when such separation is necessary for the best interests of the child (Article 9(1)). If, for one reason or another, a child is separated from one or both parents, the State Parties shall ensure that the child is able to maintain regular personal relations and direct contact with both parents, except if this is contrary to the child's best interests (Article 9(3)). Moreover, even if the child's parents reside in different states, the child has the right, save in exceptional circumstances, to maintain regular personal relations and direct contact with both parents (Article 10(2)).

In addition, importantly, the UNCRC requires that the best interests of the child be a primary consideration in all decisions concerning the child, whether in the public or private sphere (Article 3(1)). This right of the child is one of the key provisions of the UNCRC, and one of its four general principles that govern the interpretation and realisation of all child rights.[66]

However, to apply this principle in practice, in order to determine which solution is in the best interests of a particular child, requires a holistic approach – an understanding of what criteria should underpin such a decision and what other factors should be taken into account in making the decision. The child's right to a family environment has a special place in this regard. The UNCRC Committee has compiled a non-exhaustive list of elements that are important to consider when making an assessment of a child's best interests in a particular situation.[67] These elements necessarily include preserving the family environment and maintaining relationships,[68] an element that essentially constitutes the child's right to a family environment. The very name of this element – preserving the family environment and maintaining relationships – reflects the primary goal in addressing virtually all issues related to children in the family context. Such issues may concern disputes between parents about the child's place of

66 UNCRC Committee, 'General comment No. 5 on general measures of implementation of the Convention on the Rights of the Child' (2003), CRC/GC/2003/5 (para. 12); 'General comment No. 12 on the right of the child to be heard' (2009), CRC/C/GC/12, para. 2.

67 See General comment No. 14, above n. 57, paras. 52–84.

68 Ibid., paras. 58–70. Such elements also include the child's views; the child's identity; care, protection and safety of the child; situation of vulnerability; the child's right to health; and the child's right to education.

residence or parental custody, the relocation of a parent with the child, access or visitation rights of a non-resident parent, disputes related to child maintenance, or the removal of a child from the family, and it does not matter whether these disputes are domestic or cross-border in nature. In all such cases, the aim is to ensure, provided that it is not harmful to the child, that the child is not deprived of the care of their parents and, if the child is separated from one of them, of meaningful contact with the non-resident parent.

3.3. CHILD–PARENT RELATIONS

Recognition of a child as an independent rights-holder, separate from their parents,[69] has seriously impacted on how parent–child – or, rather, child–parent – relations should be conceptualised and operationalised, and has contributed significantly to the child's more active role within the family. To repeat, the child was traditionally considered as the 'property' of their parents, and was deprived of the right to have a voice in the family. The child was seen 'as a dependent, invisible and passive family member'.[70] The UNCRC, while acknowledging a child as a subject of rights, also extends to children who are capable of forming their own views the right to express those views freely in all matters affecting them, with the views of the child being given due weight in accordance with their age and maturity (Article 12(1)). It should be acknowledged that the child's right to have a say, stipulated in UNCRC Article 12 – or, in a broader sense, child participation – turns out to be one of the most challenging issues for parents, as it requires that they reconsider how relationships with their children should be built.

3.3.1. Evolving Capacities

The concept of evolving capacities stipulated in UNCRC Articles 5 and 14(2)[71] was designed to balance the rights of the child and the rights of the parents, and to solve the problem that, under the UNCRC, all children, including newborns and the very youngest children, are recognised as the holders of all the rights

---

69 UNCRC Committee, 'Statement on article 5 of the Convention on the Rights of the Child', 11 October 2023, para. 4, <https://www.ohchr.org/sites/default/files/documents/hrbodies/crc/statements/CRC-Article-5-statement.pdf>, last accessed 12.01.2024.

70 UNCRC Committee, 'Report on the seventh session', 1994, CRC/C/34, para. 192.

71 As stated in UNCRC, Art. 5, 'States Parties shall respect the responsibilities, rights and duties of parents or, where applicable, the members of the extended family or community as provided for by local custom, legal guardians or other persons legally responsible for the child, to provide, in a manner consistent with the evolving capacities of the child, appropriate direction and guidance in the exercise by the child of the rights recognised in the present Convention.'

enshrined in the Convention,[72] and are to 'be respected as persons in their own right'.[73] This concept also allows States to avoid the need 'to set arbitrary age limits or definitions of maturity tied to particular issues'.[74]

From UNCRC Article 5, it follows that 'the child has a right to direction and guidance, which have to compensate for the lack of knowledge, experience and understanding of the child and are restricted by his or her evolving capacities'.[75] Accordingly, parental responsibilities change as the child matures, and the more the child knows and understands – the more experienced the child is – 'the more the parent, legal guardian or other persons legally responsible for the child have to transform direction and guidance into reminders and advice and later to an exchange on an equal footing'.[76] As the UNCRC Committee explains, the evolving capacities concept should be seen as a positive and enabling process, not an excuse for authoritarian practices that restrict children's autonomy and self-expression, and which are often inaccurately justified by pointing to children's relative immaturity.[77] Children, thus, have acquired the 'most dangerous but most precious of rights: the right to make their own mistakes'.[78]

Parental rights over their children, as well as their direction and guidance in their children's development, are not absolute. They are limited, firstly, by the concept of the evolving capacities of the child and, secondly, by the UNCRC Article 5 requirement that direction and guidance be 'appropriate'. Thirdly, and importantly, when parents are exercising their parental responsibilities, they are limited by the requirement that they act in the best interests of the child, which, under Article 18(1), 'will be their basic concern'. In this regard, the child's interest is that the parent 'should make the best decision' for the child, and the parent is 'no more than the agent for fulfilling' the child's interests.[79] The requirement to respect the principle of the best interests of the child is an important restrictive factor and 'creates balance between parental responsibilities and children's rights, particularly in cases of conflicting interests between those parties'.[80]

---

72 UNCRC Art. 1: 'a child means every human being below the age of eighteen years unless under the law applicable to the child, majority is attained earlier'.

73 See General comment No. 7, above n. 63, para. 5.

74 R. Hodgkin and P. Newell, *Implementation handbook for the Convention on the Rights of the Child*, 3rd ed., UNICEF, 2007, p. 77.

75 See General comment No. 12, above n. 66, para. 84.

76 Ibid.

77 See UNCRC Committee, 'Statement on article 5', above n. 69, para. 10; General comment No. 7, above n. 63, para. 17.

78 J. Eekelaar, 'The Emergence of Children's Rights' (1986) 6(2) *Oxford Journal of Legal Studies*, p. 182.

79 Ibid p. 169.

80 See N. Vuskovic Sahovic, J.E. Doek and J. Zermatten, above n. 35, p. 160.

3.3.2. 'Digital Parenting'

The concept of the child's evolving capacities has acquired particular significance in the context of the digital environment, which is increasingly becoming part of children's normal lives.[81] For parents, maintaining the balance between their children's evolving capacities and their desire to be independent and autonomous is not an easy task; with today's children living online, the challenge for child–parent relations has become that much greater.[82] In the digital environment, the process of a child's gradual development and acquisition of understanding of themselves is accompanied – or, rather, complicated – by the fact that 'children can engage more independently from supervision by parents and caregivers'.[83] The digital environment thus poses new opportunities and new risks. All the risks are obvious, and the fact that children often reach a much more advanced stage with regard to digital environments, and may start experimenting 'with digital opportunities and encountering risks at a younger age than their parents ... may anticipate',[84] only exacerbates the task. To address this problem, the UNCRC Committee developed the General comment on children's rights in relation to the digital environment,[85] in which it particularly recommended that States 'support parents and caregivers in acquiring digital literacy and awareness of the risks to children in order to help them assist children in the realisation of their rights, including to protection, in relation to the digital environment'.[86]

3.3.3. Prohibition of Corporal Punishment

To reiterate, the change in the child's status within the family inevitably necessitates changes in parenting techniques. This change, first of all, requires

---

81 At the global level, it has been estimated that one child in three is an internet user, and that one in three internet users is a child under 18 years of age. See UNICEF, *Growing up in a connected world: Understanding Children's Risks and Opportunities in a Digital Age*, UNICEF, 2019, p. 10, available at <https://www.unicef-irc.org/growing-up-connected#:~:text=At%20the%20global%20level%2C%20it,shift%20over%20the%20past%20decade>, last accessed 12.01.2024.

82 See, for instance, S. Livingstone and J. Byrne, 'Parenting in the Digital Age. The Challenges of Parental Responsibility in Comparative Perspective' in G. Mascheroni, C. Ponte and A. Jorge (eds.), *Digital Parenting: The Challenges for Families in the Digital Age*, Nordicom, Univerity of Gothenburg, 2018, pp. 19–29, available at <https://www.nordicom.gu.se/en/publications/digital-parenting>, last accessed 15.09.2024.

83 UNCRC Committee, 'General comment No. 25 (2021) on children's rights in relation to the digital environment', CRC/C/GC/25, para. 19.

84 Ibid., para. 85.

85 Ibid. Although the UNCRC was created in the predigital age, it turns out that its provisions are completely applicable to children's lives online, and hardly any of its Articles have no relation to the digital environment.

86 Ibid., p. 21.

prohibition of the use of corporal punishment as a disciplinary method.[87] In exercising parental rights, parents may not harm the physical and mental health or moral development of their children. Corporal punishment, even in its lightest form, is, in any case, neglectful, insulting, degrading and humiliating treatment. Although UNCRC Articles 19 and 28(2) do not explicitly refer to corporal punishment, it is obvious that corporal punishment is violent and causes harm to children;[88] in the view of the UNCRC Committee, 'corporal punishment is invariably degrading'.[89] The UNCRC Committee defines 'corporal' punishment as 'any punishment in which physical force is used and intended to cause some degree of pain or discomfort, however light. Most such punishment involves hitting ("smacking", "slapping", "spanking") children, with the hand or with an implement – a whip, stick, belt, shoe, wooden spoon, etc.'[90] It can also involve other forms of physical or non-physical punishment specifically named in the UNCRC Committee's General comment No. 8 on the right of the child to protection from corporal punishment and other cruel or degrading forms of punishment (Arts. 19; 28, para. 2; and 37, inter alia).[91]

Corporal punishment is one of the most common forms of violence against children, and it begins in the family, often starting with slapping and spanking. The negative consequences of violence, in general, and the use of corporal punishment by parents, in particular, even in mild forms, are well known and described in the literature;[92] the results from research demonstrate a direct link between the use of corporal punishment against children and children's subsequent behavioural problems.[93] And, conversely, according to the research,

87 Some, however, would justify a certain level of 'reasonable' or 'moderate' corporal punishment as necessary for a child's upbringing. For discussion, see, e.g. B. Shmueli, 'The Influence of the UN Convention on the Rights of the Child on Corporal Punishment – A Comparative Look' (2008) 10 *Oregon Review of International Law* 189, available at <https://papers.ssrn.com/sol3/papers.cfm?abstract_id=1514367>, last accessed 12.01.2024.

88 There are no records of any discussion of corporal punishment during the drafting sessions either. However, as the UNCRC Committee notes, the prevalence of corporal punishment of children in their homes, schools and other institutions has become more visible through the reporting process under the UNCRC, and through research and advocacy. The Committee further explains that the UNCRC, like all human rights instruments, must be regarded as a living instrument whose interpretation develops over time. See UNCRC Committee, General comment No. 8 (2006) on the right of the child to protection from corporal punishment and other cruel or degrading forms of punishment (Arts. 19; 28, para. 2; and 37, inter alia), paras 11, 20, CRC/C/GC/8.

89 See ibid., para. 11; see also General comment No. 13 (2011) on the right of the child to freedom from all forms of violence, CRC/C/GC/13.

90 See General comment No. 8, above n. 88, para. 11.

91 For further examples, see ibid.

92 See, e.g. End Violence Against Children/End Corporal Punishment, 'Corporal punishment of children: review of research on its impact and associations. Full working paper, September 2021', available at <https://endcorporalpunishment.org/wp-content/uploads/2021/09/Research-effects-full-working-paper-2021.pdf>, last accessed 12.01.2024.

93 E.T. Gershoff and S.H. Bitensky, 'The Case against Corporal Punishment of Children: Converging Evidence from Social Science Research and International Human Rights Law

children who have not experienced violence, and who develop in a healthy manner, are less likely to act violently, both in childhood and when they become adults.[94] As the UNCRC Committee notes, '[p]reventing violence in one generation reduces its likelihood in the next'.[95]

3.3.4. *Parental Responsibility versus Parental Custody*

In line with the understanding of children as rights-holders, the UNCRC moved away from the notions of 'parental custody', 'parental authority' or similar expressions, which were not child's rights-focused, but rather parents' rights-focused, replacing them with the term 'parental responsibilities'.[96] The Convention sought to emphasise the parental responsibility component in the child–parent relationship. Words matter, and changes in terminology represent changes in 'thinking about parent-child relationships'.[97] Indeed, it is now very clear that many parental rights, in reality, are not rights at all, but parental responsibilities, and 'can only be interpreted in a way that upholds the dignity of children in the family'.[98]

Following the UNCRC, legislatures in many European countries have shifted to the 'parental responsibility' terminology, and a similar shift may be observed in the documents of the European Commission and the Council of Europe.[99] Illustrative in this respect is the change in terminology in the Hague Children's Conventions adopted before and after the UNCRC: from 'custody' in the 1980 Convention on Civil Aspects of International Child Abduction to 'parental responsibility' in the 1993 Convention on Protection of Children and Co-operation in Respect of Intercountry Adoption and the 1996 Convention on Jurisdiction, Applicable Law, Recognition, Enforcement, and Co-operation in Respect of Parental Responsibility and Measures for the Protection of Children. As noted in the explanatory report to the 1996 Convention, the expression 'parental responsibility' drew 'its inspiration from the Convention on the Rights of the Child (Article 18)'.[100]

---

and Implications for U.S. Public Policy' (2007) 13(4) *Psychology, Public Policy, and Law* 231 ff, 236.

94 See General comment No. 13, above n. 89, para. 14.

95 Ibid. Currently, there are 67 states that prohibit all corporal punishment of children, including in the home; 26 more states have also announced plans to fully ban corporal punishment. See End Corporal Punishment, 'Countdown', <https://endcorporalpunishment.org/countdown/>, last accessed 15.09.2024.

96 See J. Scherpe, *The Present and Future of European Family Law*, above n. 49, p. 102.

97 Ibid., p. 101.

98 G. van Bueren, KC, 'Children's Rights in the Family' in B. Stark and J. Heaton (eds.), *Routledge Handbook of International Family Law*, Taylor & Francis, 2019, p. 208.

99 For discussion, see, e.g. J. Ferrer-Riba, 'Parental responsibility in a European perspective' in J. Scherpe (ed.), *European Family Law*, vol. II, Edward Elgar, 2016, pp. 284–310.

100 P. Lagarde, *Explanatory report on the 1996 Hague Child Protection Convention*, HCCH Publications, 1998, para. 14, available at <https://assets.hcch.net/upload/expl34.pdf>, last accessed 12.01.2024.

4. NEW SOCIAL REALITIES: NEW CHALLENGES FOR LAWYERS, AND NOT ONLY FOR LAWYERS

Life is not static; things are constantly developing, and new social realities bring new challenges and require legislatures and judiciaries to respond accordingly. Amongst major family law challenges, there seem, firstly, to be those encountered in relation to social parenting and assisted reproduction, and in whichever scenario the issue arises of the child's right to identity. A rise in divorce rates and remarriages, an increase in same-sex parenting, and the widespread use of assisted reproductive technologies have led to an increase in the number of families where at least one of the caregivers is not genetically related to the child, and to recognition of social parentage becoming an increasingly important issue. Nevertheless, there are still no answers on who a child's parents are, or who they should be,[101] or on what social parenting is and how it is different from 'natural' parenting, as well as on many others questions related to new family realities.

4.1. CHILD AND SOCIAL PARENTING

Until recently, social, genetic and legal parentage almost always coincided. The legal parent was traditionally a genetic parent. The only exception to this was adoption, where adoptive parents, as a rule, replaced natural parents both legally and socially. However, due to transformations in family relations, being a legal parent does not, nowadays, necessarily mean being simultaneously a genetic parent and a social parent. And social parentage may create family ties as well. As has been noted above, social parenthood is on the rise, and increasing attention is now being paid to this phenomenon. Despite this obvious trend, the legal status of a social parent is far from clear, and is hotly debated.[102] At the same time, for a child, in most cases 'a social parent *is* a parent',[103] and to deprive a child of all contact with the social parent may seriously traumatise the child.

The ECtHR jurisprudence is illustrative in this respect. As the Court has noted in a number of judgments, the notion of 'family life' under ECHR Article 8 is not confined to marriage-based relationships and includes other de facto family ties.[104] And the Court has held that the existence or non-existence of family life

101 See A. Bainham, 'Parentage, parenthood and parental responsibility: subtle, elusive yet important distinctions' in A. Bainham, S.D. Sclater and M. Richards (eds.), above n. 44, p. 1.

102 See, e.g. C. Huntington, C.G. Joslin and C. von Bary (eds.), *Social Parenthood in Comparative Perspective*, New York University Press, 2023, p. 1.

103 Ibid.

104 See *Anayo v. Germany*, no. 20578/07, 21 December 2010, para. 55; *Nazarenko v. Russia*, no. 39438/13, 16 July 2015, para. 56.

for the purposes of Article 8 is 'essentially a question of fact depending on the real existence in practice of close personal ties'.[105] Thus, for instance, the Court has found that 'the relationship between a foster family and a fostered child who had lived together for many months amounted to family life within the meaning of Article 8 §1, despite the lack of a biological relationship between them'.[106]

In this case, important for the Court was a close emotional bond that 'had developed between the foster family and the child, similar to the one between parents and children, and that the foster family had behaved in every respect like the child's parents'.[107]

An interesting and educative case is *Nazarenko v. Russia*, considered by the ECtHR in 2015.[108] In the *Nazarenko* case, the child was born during the applicant's marriage to the child's mother and was registered as his daughter. The applicant did not initially have any doubts about his paternity and raised and provided care for the child for more than five years. As established by the childcare authority and expert psychologists, a close emotional bond existed between the applicant and the child. However, the applicant eventually discovered that he was not the child's biological father. Because the applicant's parental status had been terminated and his name deleted from the child's birth certificate after it had been established that he was not her biological father, he did not have any entitlement under domestic law to maintain contact with her.[109] The point is that Russian law set out an exhaustive list of persons who were entitled to maintain contact with a child, without providing for any exceptions taking into account the variety of family situations and the best interests of the child. In the opinion of the ECtHR, 'the complete and automatic exclusion' of the applicant from the child's life after his parental status was terminated, 'as a result of the inflexibility of the domestic legal provisions – in particular the denial of contact rights without giving proper consideration' to the child's best interests, amounted to a failure to respect the applicant's family life.[110]

---

105 *K. and T. v. Finland* [GC], no. 25702/94, para. 150, ECtHR 2001-VII.

106 In *Nazarenko v. Russia*, above n. 104, para. 57, the ECtHR referred to *Moretti and Benedetti v. Italy*, no. 16318/07, 27 April 2010, paras. 49–50, and *Kopf and Liberda v. Austria*, no. 1598/06, 17 January 2012, para. 37. See also *V.D. and Others v. Russia*, no 72931/10, 9 April 2019, which concerned the right of the former foster mother and other children in the foster family to keep in contact with a disabled child who had been returned to his biological parents after he had been with that foster family for nine years.

107 *Nazarenko v. Russia*, above n. 104, para. 57.

108 *Nazarenko v. Russia*, above n. 104. See also *Fatkhutdinov v. Russia*, no. 36335/18, 29 September 2020, where the facts were literally identical to those in the *Nazarenko* case. For more detailed discussion of *Nazarenko* case see O. Khazova, 'Some Reflections on a European Court Case *Nazarenko v. Russia*' in J.M. Scherpe (ed.), *Family Matters – Essays in Honour of John Eekelaar*, Intersentia, 2022, pp. 611–621.

109 *Nazarenko v. Russia*, above n. 104, paras. 51, 58, 64.

110 Ibid., para. 68.

Although the *Nazarenko* case was about very specific circumstances, its importance goes far beyond its specific facts. The decision underscored the conclusion that, even if legal relations between a child and their social parent are formally terminated, the child still has a continuing right to contact with individuals with whom they had developed a de facto family relationship. The case recognised that 'life has a timeless quality and is to be held to have value in and of itself', and that 'that value does not disappear even if intervention is justified'.[111]

4.2. CHILD AND ASSISTED REPRODUCTION

Among numerous other legal and ethical challenges, developments in biomedical science and assisted reproductive technologies (ART) have brought a new dimension to the regulation of parental rights and created unprecedented difficulties in determining who a child's parents are. So far, there has been no consensus on whether the legal parent may be a genetic parent, including one who has had no contact with the child, or an intended parent who may not be genetically related to the child born through ART. The Roman law concept 'the mother is always certain' is not currently working with the same precision as in the past, particularly when it concerns a child born through use of a surrogate. Thus, should a gestational mother who is genetically unrelated to the child to whom she gave birth be recognised, by default rule, as a legal mother? If the answer is positive, the next question is whether such a rule is in line with the best interests of the child born to the surrogate, especially because, in most cases, the gestational carrier did not intend to act as that child's mother or to care for him or her. What is the status of a gamete donor, and should such a donor, particularly in the context of UNCRC Article 7(1), be considered a child's legal parent at all? Finally, under what circumstances should post-mortem conception be permitted, and how could the practice affect the potential offspring, both legally and psychologically?

Responses to these challenges differ considerably between national jurisdictions, and there is no clear solution offered at the international level either.[112] For instance, in some countries, the law strictly stipulates that the mother of a child is the woman who gave birth to the child; in other words, surrogates are legal mothers. In some countries, the law may permit the

---

[111] J. Eekelaar, 'Respect' in L.D. Wardle and C.S. Williams (eds.), *Family Law: Balancing Interests and Pursuing Priorities*, William S. Hein and Co., 2007, p. 51.

[112] See the Hague Conference on Private International Law, 'Parentage/Surrogacy Project', <https://www.hcch.net/en/projects/legislative-projects/parentage-surrogacy>, accessed 12.01.2024.

reassignment of legal parenthood to the intended parents at a later stage, through a post-birth legal process. In other countries, the law permits, under certain circumstances, an intended mother to be registered on a birth certificate as the child's legal mother.[113]

In countries where the law strictly prohibits surrogate motherhood arrangements, and the intended parents travel abroad to more surrogacy-friendly jurisdictions, problems with the child's parentage or legal status can arise on their return to their home country. To illustrate, it is enough to refer to one of the most well-known case considered by the ECtHR, *Mennesson v. France*.[114] Because the French authorities in that case refused to recognise the American birth certificates that identified the intended parents as the legal parents of two children born to a surrogate in the US, the children could not acquire French nationality with all the consequences arising therefrom. In the opinion of the ECtHR, such a refusal to recognise the children's French citizenship put the children in a position of legal uncertainty, restricted their ability to establish their identity in law, and constituted a violation of Article 8 ECHR. In this case, adoption was used to finalise the legal relationships between the two children and their – not genetically related – intended mother, which is the routine practice in many countries for resolving parentage in surrogacy cases. This raises the additional question of whether adoption is an appropriate mechanism for such purposes, or whether legislatures should invent a special legal framework.

As developments in biomedical science and assisted reproduction evolve, new challenges are emerging. Thus, for instance, what should be the legal response to the possibility, mentioned earlier, of a child having three genetic parents?[115] Should this mean legal acceptance of the 'multiple parentage' phenomenon, and if so, what should the legal consequences entail? In 2017, for the first time, the possibility of multiple parentage was clearly fixed in legislation: California law stated that 'a court may find that more than two persons with claim to parentage … are parents if the court finds that recognising only two parents would be detrimental to the child'.[116]

The connections between being a biological or genetic parent, being a social parent, and being a parent in a legal sense are complex and currently unclear in the complicated situations that arise, especially in the context of assisted

113 See K. Trimmings and P. Beaumont (eds.), *International Surrogacy Arrangements: Legal Regulation at the International Level*, Hart Publishing, 2013. See also the relevant chapters in K. Trimmings, S. Sharkagy and C. Achmad (eds.), *Research Handbook on Surrogacy and the Law*, Edward Elgar, 2024.

114 *Mennesson v. France*, no. 65192/11, 26 June 2014; see also *Labassée v France*, no. 65941/11, 26 June 2014.

115 See J. Scherpe, *The Present and Future of European Family Law*, above n. 49, p. 100.

116 West's Ann. Cal. Fam. Code §7612.

reproduction. Can the concept of 'parental responsibilities' be adapted to cases of multiple parenting, as well as to broader situations of social parenthood, by allocating different amounts of responsibility to different 'parents'?[117] Such a proportional approach would allow a differentiated approach to determining the scope of parental rights and duties, depending on the circumstances of a particular situation, and taking into consideration the best interests of the child.

4.3. CHILD'S RIGHT TO IDENTITY

It is widely recognised that knowledge of one's own origin is an important part of the right to identity, and is a vital part of children's interests.[118] This interest is not limited to the need to know one's medical history for health purposes; the importance of knowing one's origin has a much broader significance. According to recent findings in developmental psychology, 'knowledge of one's genetic origins plays a crucial role in identity formation as it enables the individual to locate him- or herself in a world of interpersonal relations'.[119]

As a legal concept, the child's right to identity is relatively new: the UNCRC was the first international human rights treaty that expressly recognised it. However, discussion of the problems relating to children's identities began quite some time ago, particularly in the context of adoption secrecy, which, until recently, was an almost universal legal rule. Psychologists were the first to raise concerns about 'severe psychological distress of adopted persons', which was 'not experienced – according to their findings – by children raised by their real parents'.[120] They poetically called it 'genealogical bewilderment' and argued that '[k]nowledge of and definite relationship to his genealogy is … necessary for a child to build up his complete body image and world picture.'[121]

Although the child's right to identity has increasingly received formal recognition, we find ourselves in a situation of even greater 'bewilderment' due

117 See discussion in J. Scherpe, *The Present and Future of European Family Law*, above n. 49, pp. 109 ff, 118; A. Bainham, 'Parentage, parenthood and parental responsibility: subtle, elusive yet important distinctions' in A. Bainham, S.D. Sclater and M. Richards (eds.), above n. 44, pp. 25–46.

118 For discussion, see, e.g. S. Schmahl, *United Nations Convention on the Rights of the Child: Article-by-Article Commentary*, Nomos/Beck and Hart, 2021, pp. 150 ff.

119 P.M. Reuss, 'Surrogacy' in B. Stark and J. Heaton (eds.), above n. 98, pp. 231–32.

120 E. Wellisch, 'Children Without Genealogy – A Problem of Adoption' (1952) 13 *Mental Health* 41–42; H.J. Sants, 'Genealogical Bewilderment in Children with Substitute Parents' (1964) 37 *British Journal of Medical Psychology* 133–41.

121 E. Wellisch, above no. 120, p. 41.

to the confusion that has been brought by advances in biomedical science and the increased popularity of surrogacy, especially with use of donor gametes. In Article 8(1),[122] the UNCRC lists 'family relations' as one of the elements of a child's identity, but, as discussed above, the Article does not clearly explain what the notion of 'family relations' includes, although the concept 'reflects a growing recognition of the importance of children's relationships not only with their immediate family but also with the wider family'.[123] But what is a wider family, and can donors and a surrogate be classified as a part of it? And what about siblings? The UNCRC is silent about siblings and access to information about them.[124] However, a donor's children are half-brothers and half-sisters of children conceived with that donor's gametes.

Finally, and importantly, can a child access information about their origins in the context of ART? The current trend is obvious: the child should have access to such information. In this respect, one needs to be reminded that the increasing availability of genetic testing has made it more likely that the child will be able to discover such information. But many questions remain: what specific information should children be able to access, at what age, and under what conditions? And how should the child's right to identity be balanced with the rights of other persons involved?

5. QUESTIONS INSTEAD OF CONCLUSION

Looking back at the evolution of family law during the last 50 years, one cannot help but wonder what our family law will look like 50 years from now. Where is the development of family law heading?

Of course, it is too risky to predict this. Nevertheless, it seems obvious that family law is again on the threshold of tremendous changes. These changes, insofar as they relate to the legal status of the child in the family, would obviously appear to lie in the area of social parenthood. But what is social parenting, and how is it different from 'natural' parenting? What rights and duties might social parents have, particularly when some may also be genetic or biological parents at the same time? What criteria, apart from the principle of the best interests of the child, should additionally be used when making a decision on the scope of their responsibilities? What about those who were not directly involved in a child's coming into being, such as gamete donors' other children, who are,

---

122 In Art. 8(1), it is stated that 'States Parties undertake to respect the right of the child to preserve his or her identity, including nationality, name and family relations as recognized by law without unlawful interference'.

123 R.C. Akhtar and C. Nyamutata, *International Child Law*, 4th ed., Routledge, 2020, p. 162.

124 See G. van Bueren, *The International Law on the Rights of the Child*, above n. 20, p. 83.

as already noted, half-siblings of a donor-conceived child? The half-siblings should probably be considered as that child's family members, but should such recognition lead to any legal consequences?

These are just some of the most obvious questions that the law has yet to answer.

Perhaps we are now on the eve of another era of 'exciting times' for family law?!

BRAZIL

BRAZILIAN FAMILY LAW IN THE LAST FIVE DECADES

A 180-Degree Change

Juliana MAGGI LIMA

Résumé

Il y a cinquante ans, le Brésil ne reconnaissait légalement qu'une seule forme de famille : la famille fondée sur le mariage. Elle était hétérosexuelle, indissoluble, avait pour but d'avoir des enfants et dirigée par l'homme. Mais la société brésilienne a beaucoup changé depuis 1973, et par conséquent le droit de la famille aussi.

Lors du dernier congrès de l'ISFL, des juristes brésiliens ont présenté l'évolution du droit de la famille au cours des dernières décennies, intégrant des concepts juridiques et des liens familiaux inimaginables dans d'autres pays. Le droit brésilien ne fait pas de discrimination entre les différents types de filiation, biologique ou par adoption, et possède un lien juridique familial très spécifique : l'affectivité, qui peut même constituer un lien parental.

Il y a cinquante ans, le Brésil était soumis à une dictature militaire et, en 1988, après la fin de ce gouvernement, une avancée juridique a eu lieu : la Constitution actuelle. Cette nouvelle constitution a modifié les fondements juridiques de la famille, en reconnaissant les unions stables[1], les familles monoparentales et en plaçant définitivement les hommes et les femmes sur un pied d'égalité dans la famille.

Au cours des décennies qui ont suivi l'adoption de la Constitution, la jurisprudence a joué un rôle de premier plan dans l'élargissement de la définition de la famille. Par exemple, elle a reconnu les familles homoparentales et l'existence de la socio-affectivité, une relation parentale qui n'est pas fondée sur la biologie. Ces transformations ont suscité des critiques dans un pays déjà profondément divisé sur le plan idéologique et politique. Cependant, malgré les nombreux changements survenus au cours des cinq dernières décennies, la famille reste un concept fondamental de la société brésilienne. C'est un sujet majeur du débat politique, et les politiciens utilisent souvent les valeurs familiales pour justifier leurs décisions et leurs votes. La famille reste un concept sujet à discussion dans un pays fortement polarisé.

1. INTRODUCTION

In 2023, the ISFL celebrated its fiftieth anniversary. In this context, this chapter aims, within its limitations, to present an overview of the changes in Brazilian family law over these five decades. The concept of family evolved very slowly from Brazil's independence in 1822 until the early 1970s, the initial period of interest in this chapter. However, in the 50 years that coincide with the existence of ISFL, the reality has been different: Brazilian family law has undergone a true revolution.

At the beginning of the 1960s, Brazil took its first steps towards revising the family model established during Portugal's colonisation, maintained after independence, and followed even after the effective inclusion of Brazilian norms into the family law system. The origin of the Brazilian legal family (according to legislation imposed by Portuguese colonisers) was Catholic (during the nineteenth century, marriage was exclusively celebrated by the Catholic Church, and initially only marriage between Catholics was allowed), and it was patriarchal (in 1916, the first Brazilian Civil Code was promulgated, containing a series of provisions that legally oppressed and financially restrained women who wished to marry, as, upon marriage, they became legally submissive to their husbands).

The 1916 Civil Code imposed a series of restrictions on married women, including: relative legal incapacitation upon marriage; mandatory change of surname to that of the husband; submission to the domicile chosen by the husband; exclusive administration of the couple's assets by the husband; and need for husband's authorisation to work (outside the home) or travel. Such

1 Concept dérivé de la constitution, art. 226, §3°, Code civil, art. 1,723, *caput*, avec l'interprétation constitutionnelle basée sur le jugement *erga omnes* ADPF 132/ADI 4277.

impositions limited women's personal and financial autonomy and potentially distanced them from their families of origin.

Furthermore, the Code did not offer children legal protection against parental abuse and discriminated against children according to their origin (marital, extramarital, or through adoption). At the time, Brazil was one of the last Western countries not to allow divorce;[2] the inability to dissolve marriage gave women locked into abusive relationships little ability to leave. The marriage could not be dissolved during life but only by death. Certainly, the impossibility of dissolution of marriage brought serious individual and social problems. There was an intermediate remedy for the dissolution of the marital partnership: 'desquite', a procedure similar to a legal separation that did not allow people to marry again, was permitted in exceptional situations, and brought great social stigma to those who adopted this solution.[3]

Over the course of the last 50 years, Brazilian family law has evolved significantly. Brazilian family law now recognises legal equality between men and women, and between children of different origins, and provides full protection for children and adolescents, including protection from violence and abuse. In addition, divorce is freely available at the initiation of either spouse, without preconditions or the consent of the other spouse.

The family has ceased to be an end in itself and has become a means of human fulfilment; the special protection that the family must receive is solely to the extent that it is an instrument for the development of children (especially infants, adolescents and young people) and the promotion of the dignity of the people who compose it.[4]

Institutions similar to those developed in other countries were introduced into the Brazilian legal system, such as stable unions (initially permitted only between heterosexual couples,[5] but later extended by the Supremo Tribunal Federal (STF), the Brazilian Constitutional Court, to homosexual couples).[6]

---

2 A. Palladino and V. Palladino, *Il divorzio: comento teorico-pratico ala legge sulla disciplina dei casi di sciglimento del matrimonio*, Giuffrè, Milan 1975, p. 44.

3 Art. 317, Civil Code of 1916 defined the exceptional circumstances as adultery, attempted murder, cruelty, serious injury, voluntary abandonment of the home for more than two years or mutual agreement.

4 G. Tepedino, 'The Civil-Constitutional Discipline of Family Relations' in V. Barreto (org.), *The New Family: Problems and Perspectives*, Renovar, Rio de Janeiro 1997, pp. 47–70, p. 50.

5 Indeed, a milestone of the 1988 Constitution, which honoured the long-awaited rupture in the monopoly of matrimonial family, was the recognition of unofficial families. The demand for such recognition had existed for many years, due to the absence of divorce in the legal system before 1977 or the difficulties in obtaining it even after its insertion into Brazilian law, among various other reasons. These circumstances led to extensive discussion of the justifications for such recognition in theory and jurisprudence, mainly before the 1988 Constitution (A. Azevedo, *Estatuto da Família de fato*, Editora Jurídica Brasileira, São Paulo 2001, pp. 221 and 296).

6 See the joint judgment of Direct Action of Unconstitutionality 4,277 and Direct Action of Constitutional Precept 132, in which the existence of stable union between same-gender

However, Brazilian family law (or families law, a term that is increasingly being adopted by more and more jurists) has developed new institutions specific to Brazil. Affection (or the principle of affectivity) is recognised as a legal value capable of giving rise to a new type of filiation called socio-affective filiation, which our Supreme Court has already recognised as legally possible (although the Civil Code does not expressly provide for this type of filiation), entitled to equal recognition with biological filiation.[7] In this ruling, the STF also held that multiparentality (that is, more than the binary solution of two parents) is possible.

In addition to the emerging legal themes surrounding children, there has been a recent discussion about the treatment of domestic animals as members of the family, but this has still not been consolidated in jurisprudence and the Civil Code continues to treat animals as property.

Despite all these ruptures, it is interesting that the STF, in 2021, decided against the legal possibility of simultaneous[8] parallel families. Thus, monogamy continues to be a fundamental principle of the Brazilian family, according to the Constitutional Court.

2. FAMILY LAW TREATMENT PRIOR TO 1988 CONSTITUTION AND SOME SOCIOCULTURAL TRANSFORMATIONS

During the initial period under discussion in this chapter, Brazil was under a military regime. In 1964, Brazil underwent a military coup that initiated a regime that lasted until 1985. This was a period of significant consequences for the country.

At the beginning of the military coup, Brazil was under the Constitution of 1946. The Constitution was soon amended, in 1967, with successive amendments aimed at reducing political rights and allowing the top of the military regime to control Congress and society. Regarding the family, the changes between the Constitutions of 1946 and 1967 were of little relevance; Brazilian law continued to maintain the monopoly of the matrimonial family and the indissolubility of

individuals was unanimously recognised, and it was, by majority vote, understood that this recognition was with the same rights as heterosexual stable unions, and therefore included the right to have children, and to marriage – in short, to all inherent rights of a family in Brazil. This decision was made in May 2011.

7 STF, RE 898,060/SC, Reporter Minister Luiz Fux, judgment on 21 September 2016, https://redir.stf.jus.br/paginadorpub/paginador.jsp?docTP=TP&docID=14300644.

8 Leading Case: RE 104,527, https://portal.stf.jus.br/jurisprudenciaRepercussao/verAndamentoProcesso.asp?incidente=5181220&numeroProcesso=1045273&classeProcesso=RE&numeroTema=529.

marriage until 1977, when a constitutional amendment was approved, allowing divorce in Brazil.[9]

Aside from the constitutional provisions, the family was essentially regulated by the Civil Code of 1916, then in force, which made it clear that there was a head of the family – the man – that marriage and family were synonymous, and that what mattered was the institution and not the people who constituted it.

In conjunction with the legal theme, it is necessary to highlight that Brazil is a country of continental extension, and over these past 50 years, Brazilian society has undergone profound transformations, directly impacting the family structure. It is impossible to talk about family – the foundation of society – without recognising how this society has changed in these 50 years, and what it went through during this period (and even before then, which still impacts on families today). The profound social, demographic and cultural changes allowed the institution of the family, so important to Brazilian society, to detach somewhat from its origins – origins that initially merged with the concept of family from the Catholic religion.[10]

Brazilian families are becoming smaller and longer-lived. The Brazilian fertility rate decreased from 6.2 children per woman in 1960, to 1.73 in 2020.[11]

---

9 Six-decade-long disputes between proponents and opponents of divorce were waged among jurists and in Congress. The approval of the Constitutional Amendment that legalised divorce in Brazil was made possible at that time thanks to a legislative strategy by proponents of divorce: 'In 1977, against the backdrop of the defeat of the Judicial Reform, but also slowing down the transition to democracy, with the imminent election of 1978, Geisel decreed the recess of the National Congress (Complementary Act 102/1977), which lasted fourteen days, taking the opportunity to approve modifications to the Constitution, based on Institutional Act 5, of 1968, which gave the President of the Republic the power to both close Congress and legislate on all matters. The set of measures approved by Geisel during the parliamentary recess decreed by him became known as the April Package. To ensure the approval of constitutional amendments favorable to the government, after the reopening of Congress, the quorum for approval of constitutional amendments was reduced from two-thirds to one-third (EC 8, of 1977, which amended art. 48 of the Constitution of 1967, as amended by EC 1, of 1969). Faced with this change, which would allow the approval of divorce in Brazil after many years of legislative dispute, in August of the same year, Proposal for a Constitutional Amendment 14, of 1977, was presented, which was approved and converted into Constitutional Amendment 9/1977. EC 9/1977 modified the text of art. 175, whose original wording was: "Art. 175. The family is constituted by marriage and shall be entitled to protection by the Public Authorities. §1 The marriage is indissoluble." Article 175, §1, was amended to read as follows: "Marriage may only be dissolved, in cases provided for by law, provided there has been prior judicial separation for more than three years."' (J.M. Lima, *The Homoaffective Family in the Jurisprudence of the Superior Court of Justice and the Federal Supreme Court*, Foco Publishing House, Indaiatuba 2022, p. 34).

10 G.M.F.N. Hironaka, 'The concept of family and its legal organization' in R. da Cunha Pereira, (coord.), *Treaty on Family Law*. IBDFAM, Belo Horizonte 2016, p. 31. During the Brazilian Empire, only the Catholic Church could celebrate marriages, as per the Decree of 3 November 1827.

11 IBGE, 'In 2022, women spent 9.6 hours more per week than men on household chores or caring for people', 11 August 2023, https://agenciadenoticias.ibge.gov.br/agencia-noticias/

Among the main consequences of this decrease is the rapid inversion and flattening of the base of the demographic pyramid, something that has already impacted on generations that have to care for their elders (sometimes with more than one living generation) and descendants, necessitating the consideration of public policies so that the younger generations are not excessively burdened with caring for the elderly.

Another positive but noteworthy data point in the same vein as the previous one is that there has been a significant increase in life expectancy, from 62.5 years in 1960 to 76.6 years in 2020.[12] Brazil is a country experiencing rapid aging, which means that families have more elderly members, posing new intergenerational challenges. The State is not able to take care of all vulnerable people (children, young people and the elderly); thus, the importance of families is growing. On the one hand, conservatives continue to advocate for the exclusive creation of families in a single type of social unit, through marriage. On the other hand, it is the State's economic interests for responsibility for the vulnerable to be shared among more families, regardless of their different formats.

Another major change has been the increased concentration of the Brazilian population in urban areas, with the percentage increasing from 45 per cent in 1960 to 87 per cent in 2023. This change certainly influenced family relationships, for example allowing greater State interference in family relations. In rural areas, families lived further away from State facilities, such as schools and police stations, and vulnerable people were seen less by the State.

In the 1960s, women essentially worked in domestic services (in their own homes or in the homes of others, with very low wages, a remnant of slavery that officially persisted in Brazil until 1888).[13] It is worth noting that an important law, the Married Woman Statute, which amended the country's civil legislation, was passed in 1962.It was only with the Married Woman Statute that women were allowed to work without their husband's authorisation. As a result of the legal change, the increase in female participation in the labour market increased from 22 per cent in 1970 to 52 per cent in 2020.[14] Despite this, the data indicate that Brazil is far from achieving material equality for women, which is reflected in the allocation of family responsibilities. In 2022, women still took on

---

2012-agencia-de-noticias/noticias/37621-em-2022-mulheres-dedicaram-9-6-horas-por-semana-a-mais-do-que-os-homens-aos-afazeres-domesticos-ou-ao-cuidado-de-pessoas#:~:text=A%20divis%C3%A3o%20das%20taref.

12 Ibid.

13 T. Querino, Episode 05, 2023, transcription available at https://projetoquerino.com.br/wp-content/uploads/2022/07/Ep-05_Os-piores-patroes_Querino-1.pdf.

14 IBGE, 2023, above n. 10.

9.6 hours a week more of household or caregiving tasks than men,[15] and in 2019, men earned 30 per cent more than women.[16]

It should be noted that Brazil still faces a serious problem of children registered only in their mother's name. According to official data from 2012, there were at least 5.5 million children without their father's registration on their birth certificates at that time.[17]

The inequality between women and men is still evident with respect to violence in family relationships. Brazil now has a comprehensive law combating domestic violence[18] (although its application has flaws). Despite the legal reforms, Brazil continues to be a country of extreme violence against women in family relationships. The numbers from the Anuário Brasileiro de Segurança Pública of 2023 indicated increases in domestic violence, with records of 245,713 assaults and 1,437 femicides, 70 per cent of the cases of feminicides occurred within the woman's own home.[19]

The social and cultural changes meant that the legal family no longer covered all of the social formations that recognised themselves as families and wanted the special social protection that the State confers on families. This refers not only to homoaffective[20] families but, long before this agenda gained ground, heterosexual couples who could not marry – particularly during the period when divorce did not exist in Brazil – or who had not formalised their relationships, for various reasons.[21]

---

15 Here, a racial perspective demonstrates that black women are even more vulnerable. According to the IBGE, 'women who identified as black had the highest rate of performing household chores (92.7%)' (ibid.).

16 IBGE, 2020, 'Men earned nearly 30% more than women in 2019', 6 May 2020, https://agenciadenoticias.ibge.gov.br/agencia-noticias/2012-agencia-de-noticias/noticias/27598-homens-ganharam-quase-30-a-mais-que-as-mulheres-em-2019.

17 Conselho Nacional de Justiça, 'Pai Presente program completes five years and consolidates in the country', 6 August 2015, https://www.cnj.jus.br/programa-pai-presente-completa-cinco-anos-e-se-consolida-no-pais/.

18 Law 11.340/2006, nicknamed the Maria da Penha Law, was enacted after a conviction of Brazil by the Inter-American Commission on Human Rights of the Organization of American States. It was nicknamed as such precisely because of the case that led to said conviction, regarding the Brazilian State's negligence in processing the crimes committed by the then-husband of pharmacist Maria da Penha, which ended up having serious physical consequences. The story of Mrs Maria da Penha Maia Fernandes, the law, and even the law translated to English, can be found on the website of the Maria da Penha Institute, available at https://www.institutomariadapenha.org.br/.

19 Anuário Brasileiro de Segurança Pública 128 (2023), https://assets-dossies-ipg-v2.nyc3.digitaloceanspaces.com/sites/3/2023/07/17-Anurio-Brasileiro-de-Seguranca-Publica_FBSP_2023.pdf.

20 A term specific to Brazilian family law.

21 Brazil is a country of continental size and poor, for example.

3. THE NEW LEGAL MODEL OF FAMILY: IMPACTS OF THE 1988 CONSTITUTION

In the evolution of Brazilian family law over the last 50 years, the 1988 Constitution marks a significant milestone. The 1988 Constitution is such a relevant landmark that it allowed some authors, such as Maria Berenice Dias, to start referring to the subject matter as 'families law' rather than 'law of the family', alluding to the overcoming of what this author has previously called the monopoly of matrimonial families.[22]

The 1988 Constitution established a new legal regime. Breaking with decades of military dictatorship, the new Constitution ensured recognition of fundamental rights and guarantees, among which should be highlighted, for its importance to families, the legal equality of all, with an emphasis on equality between men and women in families and the inviolability of intimacy and private life.[23] The Constitution also recognised, among the objectives of the Federative Republic of Brazil, the construction of a free, just and fraternal society and the promotion of the well-being of all, without prejudice to origin, race, sex, colour, age and any other form of discrimination.[24]

The 1988 Constitution also dedicated a specific chapter to the family, addressing the themes of children, adolescents, youths and the elderly; that is, people presumed to be vulnerable, who deserve protection both from the State and from families, and maintaining the provision that the family deserves special protection from the State but also affirming for the first time that the family is the foundation of society.[25]

It was through the 1988 Constitution that the monopoly of matrimonial families was definitively broken, as it expressly recognised the existence of families formed through stable non-marital unions or single parenthood. Furthermore, the 1988 constitutional text finally eliminated differential treatment between children from different origins, determining that, 'children, whether born of the marriage relationship or not, or by adoption, shall have the same rights and qualifications, forbidden any discriminatory designations regarding parentage.'[26]

The contours of what constitutes a family have changed; families have ceased to be places of oppression for women and children, and have instead become places of human development. Nonetheless, the constant regarding the constitutional legal treatment of the family is that the family deserves special treatment from the State.

---

22 J.M. Lima, above n. 8, p. 25.

23 Arts. 5, *caput*, I, and 226, 1988 Constitution.

24 Ibid., Art. 3º, I and IV.

25 Ibid., Art. 226.

26 Ibid., Art. 227, §6º.

4. THE PRINCIPLE OF AFFECTIVITY AND ITS IMPACTS: SOCIO-AFFECTIVITY AND MULTIPARENTALITY

The principle of affectivity had its initial seed planted by João Baptista Vilella in 1979, when he wrote about his proposal to value the act of nurturing, which he called the 'debiologization of paternity'.[27] Since then, affection has become a legal value or a legal principle of affectivity. Despite scholars having delved into the topic since at least Ricardo Calderón's 2011 Master's thesis, and his subsequent work making him a leading figure in the field, there have been criticisms of the lack of clarity in defining the difference between the legal value of affection and the principle of affectivity, as already mentioned by this author in other texts.[28]

This imprecision is reflected in the judgments of even the highest courts in the country, which sometimes use affection and affectivity synonymously, and do not clarify what affectivity is. The term is not defined and is non-existent in legislation, only recent in doctrine, and still not an entirely settled concept.

This lack of clarity is not a criticism of the principle of affectivity but a point that offers encouragement for the continued development of the concept, especially due to affectivity's importance to the development of socio-affective filiation, which has solved legal problems in family law – or, rather, social problems of Brazilian families. Regardless of the lack of a definitive definition, Flávio Tartuce emphasises that the principle of affectivity derives from constitutional precepts, such as human dignity, social solidarity, and equality between children.[29]

Socio-affective paternity and maternity have developed as legal concepts based on the notion of breaking the absolute relevance of biological ties in favour of the legal value of affection. Socio-affective paternity first reached the Superior Court of Justice (STJ) at the end of the 2000s. Unless there is a constitutional matter at issue, the STJ is the Brazilian court that, as a matter of last resort, interprets infra-constitutional legislation and unifies national jurisprudence.

One of the first cases to reach the STJ, in 2009, shows that the creation of the principle of affectivity is a solution to a problem that is very Brazilian – the so-called 'Brazilian-style adoption' – a pejorative way of referring to adults registering a child as if it were their biological offspring, knowing that it is not. This case reached the STJ when, after the child's recorded father died, a daughter

---

27 J.B. Villela, 'Desbiologização da Paternidade' *Journal of the Faculty of Law of the Federal University of Minas Gerais*,. Year XXVII, n. 21 (new phase); Belo Horizonte, 1979.

28 J.M. Lima, above n. 8, p. 128.

29 F. Tartuce, *Civil Law: Family Law*, v.5. GEN Group, 2023, e-book, p. 25.

of the deceased father requested the annulment of her brother's paternity, as she was aware that he had been 'Brazilian-style adopted'. The STJ ruled that the father knowingly registered the child despite the absence of biological ties and, therefore, dismissed the sister's claims, reaffirming paternity based on socio-affectivity due to the possession of the status of a child.[30]

In addition to filiation, the STJ, in a 2020 case, has also recognised the 'socio-affective bond between siblings, using the term "socio-affective siblinghood"', but the case was only reported through the Court's newsletter, as the case data were kept confidential.[31]

The STF has also delved into the issue, analysing whether there is a hierarchy between socio-affective and biological filiation, and deciding that there is not.[32] Regarding this decision, Flávio Tartuce draws three conclusions from the votes: (1) that some STF ministers recognise the existence of the principle of affectivity as a legal principle;[33] (2) that there is the legal possibility of filiation and, therefore, of kinship, through socio-affectivity on equal terms with biological filiation; and (3) that the insertion into Brazilian family law of a new concept – multiparentality – breaks with the historical paradigm of only two people as parents (father and mother; mother and mother; father and father – the latter two admitted by the STF in 2011).[34]

5. RECOGNITION OF THE POSSIBILITY OF SAME-GENDER COUPLES FORMING A FAMILY

In May 2011, the STF recognised the legal existence of homoaffective families (a term coined in Brazil, and even adopted by the STF, to avoid using a term

30 The determination of a child's status, which is at the origin of affective filiation, is characterised by three elements: treatment *(tractus)*, as a parent and child act towards each other as if they were parent and child; reputation *(reputatio)* – recognition by society of that parental bond; and name *(nomen)*, when the child informally uses the surname of the affective parent – this is considered non-essential but complementary (ibid., p. 457).

31 Ibid., p. 461.

32 STF, RE 898,060/SC, Justice Luiz Fux, judgment on 21 September 2016.

33 At this point, it is worth noting that, in 2011, in the ruling where the same Court recognised the existence of same-sex families, Justice Ayres Britto highlighted the 'preponderance of affectivity over biologicality' (J.M. Lima, above n. 8, p. 154), with other justices, such as Luis Fux and Celso de Mello, mentioning affection as a basis for the decision.

34 F. Tartuce, above n. 27, p. 462. Regarding multiparentality, José Fernando Simão recently wrote that he regretted having in the past defended affection as a legal value, precisely because this was one of the justifications that led to what he considers to be the excessive and ill-considered recognition of cases of multiparentality (J.F. Simão, 'Affection: from legal value to perversion. I was wrong. A lot', Parts 1 and 2, *Conjur*, 17 December 2023, https://www.conjur.com.br/2023-dez-17/afeto-de-valor-juridico-a-perversao-eu-errei-e-muito/ and https://www.conjur.com.br/2023-dez-24/afeto-de-valor-juridico-a-perversao-eu-errei-e-muito-parte-2/).

associated with something sexualised) and also ruled that such families were guaranteed the same legal framework as heterosexual unions.

This judgment resulted from two actions of concentrated constitutional control, ADI 4.277/DF (proposed by the Attorney General's Office) and ADPF 132 (proposed by the then governor of Rio de Janeiro). The requests were similar and were, therefore, judged together.

Based essentially on the principles and fundamental rights enshrined in the 1988 Constitution, the STF recognised the fundamental right of same-gender couples to form families (considered the basis of our society), and that the wording of the Constitution and the Civil Code 2002 required the terms 'man' and 'woman' to be interpreted in light of the specific need to value men and women equally, and not to exclude homosexuals.

The Attorney General and the governor of Rio de Janeiro argued that the grounds in favour of their requests were essentially of a constitutional nature, in accordance with the principles of human dignity, intimacy, private life and equal treatment (all people are equal before the law). The grounds for recognising a family formed by a same-gender couple were also of a constitutional nature, and affection and the principle of affectivity were also widely used in the ministers' votes.[35]

6. OTHER TOPICS IN BRAZILIAN FAMILY LAW TODAY

Brazilian family law continues to evolve in significant ways. Until 2010, there were still requirements for divorce, but Constitutional Amendment 66/2010 removed any waiting period or prior judicial separation requirement. Since this change, divorce has become a potestative right of either party, with no possibility of discussing blame for legal purposes regarding the end of the marriage, and divorce is even possible without the other party being heard, as there would be no argument capable of maintaining the marriage, as has been the case in the judicial decisions of state courts.[36]

Another issue on the horizon of Brazilian family law is the legal treatment of domestic animals. With the decline in fertility rates and many couples not having children at all, the importance of pets has increased for many families.

---

35 J.M. Lima, above n. 8, pp. 127–32.

36 E.g. São Paulo Court of Justice, Case No. 2086675-97.2021.8.26.0000, presiding judge Rômolo Russo, 7th Private Law Chamber, date of judgment 3 March 2022; Paraná Court of Justice, Case No. 0041434-50.2020.8.16.000, presiding judge Rosana Amara Girardi Fachin, 12th Civil Chamber, date of judgment 24 September 2020.

Couples who have dissolved their bonds have started to dispute rights over pets. There are current proposals that animals be treated as chattels or property, as animals are already treated under the 2002 Civil Code, while others propose that pets be treated as family members, effectively creating a multi-species family, and thus becoming a matter of family law. There is even a bill pending in the Federal Congress that aims to recognise the multi-species family as one formed by humans and their pets.[37]

These are just some of the topics that reveal the tendency of Brazilian family law to continue evolving and expanding the framework of the concept of family, which has increasingly moved away from the traditional concept of family (and here it is not only about the marital concept, but also about a concept which was originally exclusionary, essentially aimed at white, Catholic individuals, with the purpose of controlling sexuality, attributing paternity and being a means of transmitting wealth and a source of labour).[38]

7. FINAL CONSIDERATIONS

Juscelino Kubitschek served as Brazil's president from 1956 to 1961 and had a plan (or motto) to make Brazil grow '50 years in 5'. In a loose adaptation of this motto, the last 50 years of Brazilian family law have overcome centuries of established paradigms. Legal traditions stemming from Roman law and Portuguese law, which formed the basis of Brazilian family law, had changed little until the early 1970s. However, since then, the changes have been considerable, to the point where we now speak of 'families law' rather than 'family law', recognising unions previously considered non-existent as families (homosexual unions). The country has developed the concept of socio-affectivity, which is highly particular to Brazil – like the jabuticaba, a fruit unique to Brazil. This concept denotes a filial relationship without biological ties and legal formalities – a relationship that develops from the Brazilian principle of affectivity.

Despite being a country of civil law, the force of constitutional provisions regarding the family and fundamental rights, such as the family being the foundation of society, have grown immensely since 1988, and have made the recognition of socio-affective filiation and homosexual families possible. We are in a civil-constitutional regime regarding family law.

---

37 The progress of the bill 179/2023 can be followed at the link https://www.camara.leg.br/proposicoesWeb/fichadetramitacao?idProposicao=2346910.

38 J.M. Lima, above n. 8, p. 14.

As in the rest of the world, the family continues to be a central topic of public and political debate in Brazil, and is now once again the subject of legislative changes, with the creation of a commission by the Federal Senate, in 2023, to update the Civil Code, including its family law section.[39]

---

[39] At the time of drafting this chapter, the commission had provided the bill draft the Congress (available at https://legis.senado.leg.br/sdleg-getter/documento/download/68cc5c01 1f3e 491a-836a-7f376cfb95da).There is no guarantee that this bill will even advance through the legislative process, let alone be approved. In any case, considering that the commission was created by Congress itself, it is interesting to highlight some points of the draft delivered by the commission: socio-affectivity is recognised as a legal means of establishing filiation and kinship and regulated; the word affection is only used once, when dealing with the parameters for assigning guardianship of children and adolescents who are not under family power – their parents 'power' – and are not in a family placement programme); and affectivity only when dealing with the recognition that animals make up the socio-familial environment (Art. 19). Monogamy is, once again, reinforced as the foundation of family law, preventing the recognition of parallel unions, even for exclusively patrimonial purposes. The bill recognises three types of family: those formed by marriage, stable unions and parental families. The latter can be formed in two ways: by at least one ascendant and their descendant, or by collateral relatives living under the same roof, sharing personal and patrimonial family responsibilities (Art. 1.511-B). This second type of parental family brings an interesting possibility in which collateral relatives who live together can spontaneously assume – more than they would just by law – the reciprocal rights and responsibilities inherent to families, and even register this in their civil records. Whether or not it is approved by Congress, the mere inclusion in a draft law of the possibility for individuals to recognise themselves as a family is highly modern. It aligns with the principle of autonomy in private life and marks a departure from the traditional dogmas that originally shaped the concept of the legal family in Brazil.

CHINA

HOW THE LAW PROTECTS CHINESE MARRIAGES AND FAMILIES

Evolution, New Developments and Challenges of China's Family Law

Ran QIYU*

* Ran Qiyu (female), associate professor, Civil and Commercial Law School, Southwest University of Political Science and Law, Chongqing 401120, China, email: ranqiyu@swupl.edu.cn.

Résumé

À l'image d'un microcosme des changements sociaux, le développement et l'évolution du droit de la famille dans la Chine contemporaine, après la fondation de la République populaire de Chine, sont étroitement liés à cette époque particulière et à un certain environnement social. S'appuyant sur les excellentes traditions juridiques et culturelles chinoises, le droit de la famille dans le Code civil de 2020 a été élaboré en incorporant le droit initial du mariage et ses interprétations jurisprudentielles, avec les caractéristiques nationales et les particularités de l'époque. Le Code civil inclut le droit de la famille, accorde une grande importance à la construction de la « civilisation » familiale, fait de la liberté, de l'égalité et de la justice les valeurs fondamentales en la matière, met l'accent sur la protection des mariages et des familles par l'État, respecte l'intérêt supérieur des enfants et renforce les mesures d'aide pour les groupes défavorisés ou le conjoint innocent, ce qui constitue une étape capitale dans l'histoire législative de la nouvelle Chine. Parallèlement, le droit de la famille inscrit dans le Code civil de 2020 est également confronté à de nouveaux défis. Il est nécessaire d'élaborer de nouvelles orientations sur la validité et l'application des accords de fidélité entre époux sur la base d'études de cas. La clause relative aux « bonnes traditions familiales » doit être étudiée afin de déterminer si elle peut être appliquée en tant que disposition normative dans la construction de la « civilisation » familiale. Il est important d'observer et d'étudier l'effet de la mise en œuvre de la disposition relative au délai d'attente dans le cadre du divorce et de prendre des mesures pour améliorer son fonctionnement. Des règles distinctes du Code civil sont nécessaires pour réglementer les relations de cohabitation et traiter les litiges découlant de la cohabitation. Les règles de protection du droit à l'identité sont trop vagues et fondées sur de grands principes. Il est également possible d'améliorer le système du droit des relations parents-enfants.

1. INTRODUCTION

The historical evolution of China's Marriage Law is, to a certain extent, a microcosm of the social changes in contemporary China.[1] The development and evolution of family law are both a requirement and a reflection of social changes in families. The legislation on marriage and family law reflects the unique circumstances of the period, and is of profound significance. Over the course of 70 years, China's family law developed from the Marriage Law 1950 of the People's Republic of China (PRC), to the Marriage Law 1980 of the PRC, to the current Marriage and Family volume of the Civil Code 2020 of the PRC. This evolution process shows the continuous development and improvement of China's family law through inheritance, innovation and leaps forward. During the development and evolution of family law since the founding of the PRC, general rules on kinship, and provisions on marriage, property relations between husband and wife, divorce, parentage, etc. have gradually been improved. The systemic, logical and scientific nature of family law has been increasingly enhanced. The Marriage Law 1950 was enacted to oppose the feudal marriage and family system, while the Marriage Law 1980 was enacted at the beginning of adopting the 'reform and opening-up'[2] policy that began in 1978, and the 1980 Law was further revised in 2001, at the turn of the twenty-first century. The Civil Code 2020 of the PRC is a code modelled on the French, German and Japanese civil codes, etc. The compilation and implementation of the Civil Code is a milestone in the legislative history of China, marking a new era in Chinese legislation and the gradual establishment of a socialist legal system with Chinese characteristics. The Marriage and Family volume repealed the former Marriage Law and changes the previous legislative mode of family law as a separate Act. Family law returning to the Civil Code indicates the beginning of China's

[1] L. Weifang, 'A Trial Discussion on the Historical Evolution of the Marriage Law of the PRC' 21 *Contemporary China History Studies* 59 (2014).

[2] On 18–22 December 1978, the Third Plenary Session of the Eleventh Central Committee of the CPC (the Communist Party of China) was held in Beijing. The conference decided to shift the focus of the CPC and the attention of the whole nation to socialist modernisation construction. The task of domestic reform and opening up to the outside world was put forward, and a new process of rural reform was initiated. The Third Plenary Session of the Eleventh Central Committee achieved a great turning point in the history of the Party following the founding of the PRC, which opened a new era of China's legislation and judiciary.

codification era of family law. However, the Civil Code has not been in effect for a long time, and some new problems in the process of its application are likely to gradually emerge. This chapter reviews the development and evolution of family law in China, and analyses the achievements of the Civil Code in protecting marriage and family in the twenty-first century, and the challenges facing the Code, in the hope of understanding family law in the Civil Code and exploring future research directions.

2. EVOLUTION OF CHINA'S FAMILY LAW

After the founding of the PRC, family law was enacted, reformed or abolished at different distinct social stages and each legislative activity undertook specific legislative missions. The Marriage Law 1950 ended the feudal marriage and family regime. The Marriage Law 1980 terminated the politicised era of family law. As a code to comprehensively construct new family relations in the twenty-first century, the compilation of the Civil Code 2020 has realised the systematisation and codification of family law.

2.1. THE MARRIAGE LAW 1950: ABOLISHING THE FEUDAL MARRIAGE AND FAMILY REGIMES

The first law promulgated after the founding of the PRC was the Marriage Law 1950, which is called the 'first child' of the legislation of New China. The Marriage Law 1950 gradually abolished the old family law system in China and transplanted in its place the marriage and family law legislation of the former Soviet Union. Soviet family law vastly influenced the Marriage Law 1950, both in form – as the new legislation was adopted independently of the **civil law** – and in substance, as Chinese family law absorbed the basic principles and theories of Soviet family law.[3] The Marriage Law 1950 completed the historical task of 'abolishing the feudalistic marriage and family system and implementing a new democratic marriage and family system', which was regarded as a revolution in the history of family legislation in New China.[4] Some family systems in the old society, such as arranged and forced marriages, male superiority over females, and ignoring the interests of children were repealed. New and democratic marriage principles like marriage freedom, monogamy, equal rights between

---

3 L. Xiuqing, 'The Growth of Marriage Law in New China and the Influence of the Soviet Model' 119 *Legal Science* 76–82 (2002).

4 Y. Dawen, 'Three Milestones of Two Marriage Laws', *Work of Shandong People's Congress* 64 (2017).

men and women, and protection of the legitimate rights and interests of women and children were introduced. Some acts in the old society, like bigamy, taking concubines, child brides, interference with the freedom of marriage of widows, and the exaction of money or gifts in connection with marriage etc. were completely prohibited in the Marriage Law 1950. After the promulgation of the Marriage Law 1950, a public propaganda campaign was carried out throughout China. March 1950 was designated the Marriage Law propaganda campaign month, to promote the support of the new rules on families.

2.2. THE MARRIAGE LAW 1980: FAMILY PROTECTION IN THE ERA OF REFORM AND OPENING UP

During the ten years of the Cultural Revolution from May 1966 to October 1976, marriage and family relations in China were seriously damaged. China began to adopt reforms and opening-up policy in 1978. The Marriage Law 1980 was enacted in time to put an end to the politicisation of family law and address the new problems faced by families during the reform and opening-up. Amidst the controversy over 'just reasons' and the 'breakdown of feelings', the Marriage Law 1980 finally established the principle that divorce should be granted on the basis of 'breakdown of feelings' rather than 'just reasons'. This means that divorce can be permitted when the People's Court confirms the breakdown of feelings between spouses because of separation, severe diseases or the fault of one party, with divorce not necessarily being based on the fault of either spouse. In addition, the Marriage Law 1980 established the rules that incomes acquired during marriage by either spouse are joint marital property of husband and wife, and stipulated that husband and wife can reach an agreement on the ownership of incomes gained by either spouse during the marriage.

In 1992, Comrade Deng Xiaoping's southern tour speech marked the beginning of China's comprehensive transformation into a socialist market economy.[5] China's social transformation concerned transition in economy, social governance, ideology, rural society, family structure and cultures.[6] In the twenty-first century, China's social transformation has been further intensified, which has brought about tremendous changes to family structures, interpersonal relationships and functions. With the acceleration of social modernisation, Chinese families faced new phenomena and problems, 20 years after the implementation of the the Marriage Law 1980. However, the provisions of the

---

5 Y. Shanhua, 'Family Changes in Rural China in the Past 30 Years', *Decision & Information* 37 (2009).

6 W. Jun and L. Yuting, 'A Review and Prospects of China's Social Transformation Research in the Past 40 Years: Taking Papers Collected by CNKI and CSSCI as Examples', *Jianghuai Forum* 137–38 (2019).

Marriage Law 1980 in fields such as kinship, marriage, marital relationships and divorce lagged behind social development, shifting between tradition and modernisation.[7] In 2001, the Standing Committee of the National People's Congress amended the Marriage Law 1980 to modernise the rules of family law, and to regulate family relations during the period of social transition. In this 2001 amendment, provisions on invalid or revocable marriages were incorporated into the marriage system. As regards marital property relations, the family law distinguished the scope of personal and joint property of husband and wife, and more rules on the marital property agreement were added. With the development of society, attitudes of the public towards marriage had gradually changed, and high divorce rates required a further legislative response to the consequences of family breakdown. More divorce remedies, like divorce damage compensation and divorce financial compensation, were added to the divorce law to relieve the impact of social transformation on family members.

2.3. FAMILY LAW IN THE CIVIL CODE 2020: FAMILY RELATIONSHIPS IN THE TWENTY-FIRST CENTURY

In the legislative history of New China, the codification of civil law has been initiated four times: in the years 1954, 1962, 1979 and 2001. In 1979 and 2002, a two-step legislative plan was confirmed. The first step was to enact separate Acts as the components of civil law, and the second step was to compile a unified civil code. After decades of efforts, the constituent parts of China's civil law, such as the General Principles of the Civil Law of the PRC, the Property Law of the PRC, the Contract Law of the PRC, the Marriage Law of the PRC, the Inheritance Law of the PRC, the Tort Liability Law of the PRC, and so on, have been enacted and continuously revised and improved. The Civil Code – the first code of the PRC – was adopted on 28 May 2020, and indicates a new phase of protection for marriages and families. During the compiling of the Civil Code, the Legal Affairs Commission of the National People's Congress conducted in-depth research, listened extensively to the opinions of experts, scholars and social groups, and responded to the concerns of the public. The Civil Code summarised past legislative experiences, drawing on China's excellent 5,000-year cultural heritage and long-term judicial experience. The Marriage and Family volume of the Civil Code was compiled based on the original Marriage Law and its judicial interpretations. Some inappropriate old provisions were deleted or modified, while some new regulations were added to meet the need for social development.

---

7 M. Yinan, 'The Tradition and Modernization of Chinese Marriage and Family Law – on the Occasion of the Amendment of Marriage Law' 38 *Journal of Peking University* 62–65 (2001).

2.3.1. *The National Characteristics*

China's legislation has distinctive native features, especially in family law. Based on the national circumstances and current situation of Chinese families, the Civil Code respects good traditions, summarises historical experiences in the construction of family cultures, and realises the integration of law and emotion, and the rule of law and morality. The goal of the national character of the Civil Code is to interpret Chinese spirit and culture by establishing a legal system that reflects the Chinese spirit and unifies the Chinese culture.[8] The Marriage and Family volume absorbs the rich family culture in Chinese history, stipulates that marriages and families are protected by the State, and writes good family traditions into the Code. The Civil Code pays great attention to the construction of family civilisation in the new era, and this is the new basic value orientation of the Marriage and Family volume of the Civil Code. It reflects the philosophical standpoint of the Civil Code on how to regard 'family' and 'coordinate relations between persons',[9] as well as demonstrating the State's protection of 'marriages and families'. The Civil Code promotes socialist core values and places special emphasis on protecting the legitimate rights and interests of women, minors, the elderly and the disabled; equality between men and women; the autonomy of will; and care for and protection of the weak, which reflects the fact that 'the fundamental value orientation and legislative purpose of China's family legislation are to build harmonious family relations all along'.[10] Bigamy,cohabitation of a spouse with another person, domestic violence and abuse and desertion of family members are prohibited in the Code (Article 1042). The Civil Code advocates mutual fidelity, respect and love within families, and emphasises harmonious family relationships in which fathers are kind and sons are filial, the elderly are respected and loved, and family members support and assist each other.

2.3.2. *Features of the Times*

Inheritance and innovation have accompanied the development of family law. The Marriage and Family volume of the Civil Code adapts to the development of society and the times, and the suggestions of experts and scholars have been heard with an inclusive and open attitude. The Civil Code abolished the provision on diseases that prohibited marriage, to keep up with social developments.

---

8 X. Zhongyuan, 'Political, Ethnic, Systematic Characteristics of China's Civil Code', *The Jurist* 36 (2018).

9 W. Lei, 'The Construction of Family Civilization in the Civil Code', *Journal of Shandong University (Philosophy and Social Science Edition)* 91 (2021).

10 C. Wei and R. Qiyu, 'The Construction of Harmonious Marriage and Family – Six Decades of Chinese Marriage and Family Law', *Hebei Law Science* 43–44 (2009).

In cases where a man or a woman is suffering from a serious illness, the validity of the marriage is decided according to the spouses' own wishes. Given the importance of the family, the Civil Code provides for a principle that marriage and family are protected by the State, to enhance the status of marriages and families, and to promote the functions of families in modern society. With the development of the society and economy, external transactions of families and debts incurred by families have increased. The Civil Code stipulates the rules for the identification and discharge of joint debts of spouses based on experiences in judicial practice and the achievements of judicial interpretation, to protect transaction safety. With China's population ageing, the one-child family policy that began in the late 1970s has been adjusted in recent years to allow a couple to have three children, and the issue of family planning does not fall into the field of private law,[11] so the family planning principle established in the Marriage Law 1980 has not been retained in the Code. In the face of the increasing numbers of both registered divorces and rash divorces, the Civil Code adopted a one-month waiting period for registered divorces, in order to prevent frivolous actions. In addition, in an era when family laws in different jurisdictions have focused on protecting the interests of the weak, the Civil Code increases special protection for the old, the disabled and minors.

3. NEW DEVELOPMENTS OF THE FAMILY LAW IN THE CIVIL CODE

3.1. FAMILY LAW AS A COMPONENT OF THE CIVIL CODE

The relationship between family law and civil law has been controversial in the compilation of the Civil Code. Influenced by the legislative model of the former Soviet Union, China's family law, since the founding of New China, has adopted an independent legislative model under which family law is independent from civil law. In terms of whether family law should return to civil law, the 'return' opinions[12] and 'independent' arguments[13] have expressed their different views.

---

11 Chief Editor of the Leading Group for the Implementation of the Civil Code of the Supreme People's Court, *Understanding and Application of the Marriage, Family and Inheritance Volume of the Civil Code of the PRC*, People's Court Press, 2020, p. 36.

12 L. Chunhong, 'The Orientation of Marriage and Family Law: "Independence" or "Return": Discussion with Dr. Wu Ruozhi', *Academic Forum* (2010); Y. Dawen, 'The Legislative Model and System Structure of the New Marriage and Family Law' 16 *Legal and Commercial Studies* (1999).

13 L. Huixing, 'The Proposed Draft of China's Civil Code and Reasons', Law Press, 2004; C. Shiquan, 'The Fundamental Reconstruction of China's Marriage Law' 18 *Legal Studies* 104 (1996); Y. Zongren, 'Marriage and Family Law Should Be Incorporated into the Civil

The Civil Code finally ended the debate, with family law returning to the Civil Code. The Civil Code is composed of seven volumes, comprising General Rules, Real Rights, Contract, Personality Rights, Marriage and Family, Inheritance, and Tort Liability. The Marriage and Family volume consists of five chapters – general provisions, marriage, family relations, divorce and adoption – with a total of 79 articles. On 25 December 2020, Judicial Interpretation I of the Supreme People's Court on the Application of the Marriage and Family Volume of the Civil Code of the PRC was issued, to guide the proper application of the Marriage and Family volume. The Marriage and Family volume of the Civil Code and Judicial Interpretation (I) of the Marriage and Family Volume constitute the basic norms regulating marriage and family relations. On the date the Marriage and Family volume came into effect, the former Marriage Law 1980, as revised in 2001, and its corresponding judicial interpretations were all repealed.

3.2. CONSTRUCTION OF FAMILY CIVILISATION

The construction of family civilisation and the inheritance of good family traditions are emphasised in the Civil Code. Article 1043 of the Code stipulates that 'families shall establish good family traditions, promote family virtues, and attach importance to the construction of family civilization', and that '[h]usband and wife shall be loyal to each other, respect each other, and care for each other. Family members shall respect the elderly, love the children, help each other, and maintain a marital and familial relationship of equality, harmony, and civility.'

The good family traditions clause enriches the value of the provisions on spiritual civilisation construction, and expands the provisions on spiritual civilisation construction and moral regulations in the Constitution Law, which integrates and reflects core socialist values.[14] The provision on good family traditions is a symbol that China's Civil Code attaches great importance to the construction of families, and civilised family education and family morals, which will be helpful for constructing new family relations of gender equality, kindness and love, and civilisation and harmony, in the new era of China.

The Civil Code advocates respecting the elderly and caring for the young, which is conducive to preventing the expansion of individualism in families, and responds to traditional family ethics and morals.[15] For example, the Civil Code stipulates that parents are obliged to raise and educate their minor children,

---

Law System', *Academic Exchange* (1992); W. Ruozhi, 'Examination of the "Return of Chinese Marriage Law to Civil Law" in the Past 30 Years', *Legal System and Social Development* (2009).

14 N. Kaihui, 'The Constitutional Value of China's Civil Code', *Journal of Jianghan University (Social Science Edition)* 10 (2020).

15 Z. Jianyuan, 'Distinguishing between Traditional Family Ethics and Moral Circumstances' *Journal of Chongqing University Social Sciences* 53 (2015).

and that children should support their parents when they are unable to work or have no means of self-support (Article 1068). Family members should care for the young, and respect and care for the elderly (Articles 1067 and 1069), and grandchildren and grandparents are legally obligated to support each other under certain circumstances (Article 1074).

3.3. PROTECTION OF MARRIAGES AND FAMILIES BY THE STATE

3.3.1. *Protection of Marriages and Families by the State*

Family is a 'community of shared future' constructed face-to-face between individuals.[16] The Universal Declaration of Human Rights adopted by the United Nations,[17] the International Covenant on Economic, Social and Cultural Rights,[18] and the International Covenant on Civil and Political Rights[19] all require special protection for families. The Constitution of the PRC also states that marriages, families, motherhood and children are all protected by the State. The provision that marriages and families shall be protected by the State is recognised in the Civil Code, to meet the requirement of the Constitution Law and reflect an emphasis on the protection of the marriage and family[20] In addition, Article 112 of the Civil Code provides that the identity rights[21] of natural persons arising from marriages and families are protected by law. Reference shall be made to the provisions in the Personality Rights volume of the Code, where there are no special provisions (Article 1001).

---

16 P. Yunfu and C. Guangyun, 'Traditional Chinese Ethical Culture and Modern Construction of Family as the Basic Unit', *Journal of Jianghai Studies* 230 (2019).

17 Art. 16: 'The family is the natural and fundamental group unit of society and is entitled to protection by society and the State.'

18 Art. 10: 'The States Parties to the present Covenant recognize that the family, as the natural and fundamental group unit of society, shall be accorded the widest possible protection and assistance, particularly with regard to its establishment and when it is responsible for the care and education of children who are not independent.'

19 Art. 23: 'The family is the natural and fundamental group unit of society and is entitled to protection by society and the State. The right of men and women of marriageable age to enter into marriage and to found a family shall be recognized.'

20 H. Wei, *Interpretation of the Marriage and Family Volume of the Civil Code of the People's Republic of China*, China Legal Publishing House, 2020, p. 11.

21 Identity rights in Chinese law involve a person's right to recognition as a family member, whether through marriage, birth, adoption or other relationship. Art. 112 of the Civil Code stipulates that the personal rights of a natural person arising from marriage or family relations shall be protected by law, which is deemed to have recognised identity rights in the Civil Code. However, it is difficult to apply Art. 112, as it is too simple and abstract. Meanwhile, given the growing role of non-marital cohabitation, provisions on identity rights have become too rigid and vague, and there is space to clarify the application of provisions on identity rights.

3.3.2. *The Waiting Period in Divorce Registration*

Article 16 of the deleted Regulations on the Administration of Marriage Registration 1994, issued by the Ministry of Civil Affairs, provided for a one-month review period for registered divorces. The regulation stipulated that the marriage registration authority should examine the divorce application within one month from the date of accepting the application. A divorce was to be registered, and a divorce certificate issued, if the conditions for divorce were met. In 2003, the new Marriage Registration Regulations promulgated by the Ministry of Civil Affairs replaced the Regulations on the Administration of Marriage Registration 1994, and the provision for a one-month review period for registered divorces was also repealed. Article 13 of the Marriage Registration Regulations stipulates that the marriage registration authority shall examine the documents and proofs submitted to the divorce registration and inquire about the relevant matters. Where the divorce is indeed voluntary, and husband and wife have reached an agreement on child support, property division, debt payment and other issues, divorce shall be registered on the spot, and a divorce certificate shall be issued. The Marriage Law 1980, which was revised in 2001, also stipulated that divorce should be granted if a man and a woman divorced voluntarily. When the marriage registry found that they are indeed voluntarily agreeing to divorce, and that the issues of child support and property division had been properly solved, a divorce certificate could be issued.

However, since the implementation of the revised Marriage Law in 2001 and the Marriage Registration Regulations, the divorce rate in China has been on a continuous rise, with the number of registered divorces increasing substantially. According to statistics, the total number of divorces in China rose from 1.177 million to 4.374 million between 2002 and 2017, and the crude divorce rate rose from 0.9 per cent to 3.2 per cent.[22] In addition to the high divorce rate, an increase in the remarriage rate can somewhat explain the number of impulsive divorces. Some NPC (National People's Congress) deputies and CPPCC (the Chinese People's Political Consultative Conference)members proposed to address the problem of rash divorce in the compilation of the Civil Code.[23] Based on thorough research and discussion, the legislature adopted the opinions of experts and scholars, and a one-month waiting period for divorce registration was stipulated in the Code.[24]

---

22 M. Yinan, 'The Consideration Period at Divorce is a Restriction on Frivolous Divorce' 160 *Journal of Chinese Women's Studies* 104 (2020).

23 H. Wei, above n. 20, at 175–77.

24 Art. 1077: 'Where either party is unwilling to divorce, he may withdraw the divorce registration application within thirty days after such an application is received by the marriage registration authority. Within thirty days after expiration of the period provided in the preceding paragraph, both parties shall personally visit the marriage registration

The divorce waiting period in the Civil Code is the confirmation and reflection of practical experiences in dealing with impulsive divorces; the waiting period is valuable in maintaining the stability of marriages and families and building equal, harmonious and civilised family relations.

3.4. RESPECT FOR AUTONOMY OF WILL

The Civil Code inherits the principle of autonomy of will from the former Marriage Law and stipulates that a man and a woman shall enter into marriage freely and voluntarily (Article 1046). The opinions of adopted children shall be heard if they are eight years old or older, concerning the establishment or dissolution of an adoption (Article 1104, 1114). The Civil Code respects agreements on the property of the spouses. A man and woman may agree that property acquired during their marriage and premarital property shall be owned separately, jointly, or partially owned separately and partially jointly. The agreement should be in writing. Where no agreement has been reached or agreement is unclear, the provisions of Article 1062 and Article 1063 of the Civil Code apply. The couple's agreement on property acquired during the marriage and premarital property is legally binding on both parties (Article 1065).

The most significant change in the Civil Code with regard to autonomy of will is the change in attitude towards marriages in which either party suffers from a serious disease. The original Marriage Law 1950 stipulated that a marriage was prohibited if either party suffered from venereal disease or mental disorder, or from leprosy or any other disease that was considered medically inadvisable for marriage. The Marriage Law 1980 no longer enumerated the diseases that prohibited marriage; instead, it stipulated that 'either party [who] suffers from diseases that are considered medically inadvisable for marriage is prohibited to marry', and provided that marriages were null and void if either party to the marriage was suffering from a disease that prohibited marriage.

What diseases should give rise to prohibition from marriage is a complicated issue, and one that should be determined by professionals. Besides, with medical developments, some diseases can now be cured or controlled. When a man or woman suffers from a severe disease, but the other party knows about the disease and is willing to marry him or her, it will conflict with the principle of marriage freedom if marriage is prohibited.[25] Considering the factors above, the Civil Code changed the provision addressing disease. Under the Civil Code, if one of the parties suffers from a serious disease, marriages are voidable but not void. The Civil Code respects the autonomy of will of

authority to apply for granting a divorce certificate, and failing to do so will cause the divorce registration application to be deemed as withdrawn.'

25 H. Wei, above n. 20, pp. 59–61.

both man and woman, and stipulates that if one of the parties suffers from a severe disease, they shall truthfully inform the other party of such disease before marriage registration; where they fail to do so, the other party may apply to the People's Court to annul the marriage. This legislative shift constiutes a respect for marriage freedom and a guarantee of marriage freedom for persons suffering from diseases.

3.5. RELIEF MEASURES FOR DISADVANTAGED GROUPS OR THE INNOCENT SPOUSE

Compared with the original Marriage Law, the Civil Code strengthens relief measures for disadvantaged groups and the innocent parties in families, including improving provisions for financial compensation in divorce (Article 1088) and divorce damage compensation (Article 1091), increasing the damage compensation claim right of the no-fault party in invalid and revocable marriages, and stipulating the right to divide marital property in marriages under specific circumstances.

3.5.1. Remedy for No-Fault Parties in Invalid and Revocable Marriages

According to the Marriage and Family Law volume, when a marriage is void or revoked, the common property should be divided in favour of the innocent party. But this provision cannot make up for the damage caused to the innocent party by a void or revocable marriage. Some experts and the public proposed to grant the no-fault party a right to claim damages, which is conducive to protecting the legitimate rights and interests of the no-fault party.[26] The Civil Code adopted this opinion. In addition to the consequences of invalid and revocable marriages stipulated in the original Marriage Law, a new provision is stipulated that if the marriage is invalid or revoked, the innocent party is entitled to claim damages.[27] Meanwhile, the Code extends the period to claim the revocation of a marriage. The provision in the original Marriage Law that '[t]he period for revoking the marriage shall be within one year from the date of marriage registration' has

26 Ibid., p. 69.

27 Art. 1054: 'A void or revoked marriage has no legal effect from the beginning, and neither party to such a marriage shall have any rights or duties arising from the marital relationship. Property acquired during the cohabitation period shall be disposed of by mutual agreement. Where the parties fail to reach such an agreement, the People's Court shall adjudicate the case in compliance with the principle of favoring the no-fault party. When disposing of the property acquired during a marriage which has been voided due to bigamy, the property rights and interests of the parties to the lawful marriage shall not be infringed upon. The provisions of this Code on parents and children shall apply to the children born by the parties to a void or revoked marriage.'

been modified to 'within one year from the date on which the coercion ceased' or 'within one year from the date when the personal freedom is restored'. Where either husband or wife suffers from a serious disease without informing the other party of such disease prior to marriage registration, the other party may apply to the People's Court to revoke the marriage 'within one year from the date when he or she knows or should have known the cause for revocation'.

3.5.2. *Divorce Damage Compensation*

The amended Marriage Law in 2001 stipulates a divorce damage compensation system, but the legal reasons for the innocent party to claim divorce damage compensation under the law are strictly limited to four situations, namely bigamy, cohabitation with another person of the opposite sex, domestic violence, or maltreatment or desertion of family members. However, in some other cases where the acts by either spouse do not fall into these enumerated circumstances, damage caused to the no-fault party cannot be ignored. Furthermore, in divorce practice, it is difficult to obtain the proof necessary to prove the fault. As a result, in judicial practice the proportion of cases claiming for divorce damage compensation is low, and claims in fewer cases are supported, such that this system is not properly performing its function. Hence, the Civil Code expands the circumstances for obtaining divorce damages by adding a 'pocket provision' that other grave faults establish grounds for the no-fault spouse to claim divorce compensation.[28]

3.5.3. *Divorce Financial Compensation*

'As a special form of human labour, domestic work is a kind of labour that requires costs, generates benefits and social values.'[29] The provision on financial compensation in divorce was first stipulated in the amended Marriage Law in 2001, which reflected respect for the value of domestic work, and offered relief and balance for the rights of the party burdened with more domestic work.[30] However, the precondition for claiming financial compensation in divorce was the spouses having agreed in writing that the property acquired during the marriage would be owned separately. This premise greatly limited the claim for divorce financial compensation, which was unfair on divorced women.

28 Art. 1091: 'Under any of the following circumstances resulting in divorce, the no-fault spouse shall be entitled to claim for compensation: (1) bigamy; (2) cohabitation with other persons of an opposite sex; (3) committing domestic violence; (4) maltreatment or desertion of any family member; (5) any other grave faults.'

29 R. Qiyu, 'Cost and Benefit: a Law and Economics Analysis of the Value of Husband and Wife's Housework' 217 *The Northern Forum* 145 (2009).

30 Chief Editor of the Leading Group for the Implementation of the Civil Code, above n. 11, p. 317.

According to the Fourth National Survey on the Status of Women, women shouldered the primary responsibility for family care. Women were mainly responsible for daily care (76.1 per cent), helping children with their homework (67.5 per cent) and transporting children aged 17 or under (63.6 per cent); women spent an average of 136 minutes per day caring for children, helping children with their homework, transporting children or caring for the old or sick and other family members. Married women spent an average of 120 minutes per day on household chores.[31] Considering these factors, the existence of an agreement to keep property separate, as a prerequisite for claiming financial compensation in divorce, was cancelled in the Civil Code.[32]

3.5.4. *Division of Marital Property in Marriage*

In China, the legal property system for spouses is the joint system of marital incomes. During the period of the marital relationship, no request shall be filed for the division of common property, unless otherwise stipulated by law or agreed by the parties. But when one spouse infringes upon the rights and interests of common property, too strict restrictions on the division of common property may damage the rights and interests of the other spouse. Hence, the relevant rules in the judicial interpretations of the Supreme People's Court were incorporated into Article 1066[33] of the Civil Code to establish a system of dividing joint property during marriage, providing a new remedy for the fair protection of the property rights and interests of both spouses.[34] Considering that the legal property system in China is a joint system of marital proceeds, Article 38 of the Judicial Interpretation (I) of the Marriage and Family volume strictly limits the situations in which a request for division of joint property within marriage can be heard. The People's Court will not support the request of one spouse to divide joint property during the marriage

---

31 'Main Data Report of the Fourth Survey on the Social Status of Chinese Women' (2022) Women's Studies Series.

32 Art. 1088: 'Where one spouse burdens more duties for raising children, looking after the old, or assisting the other spouse in his work, the aforementioned spouse is entitled to request compensation upon divorce against the other party. Specific compensation shall be agreed upon by both parties; where such an agreement fails, the People's Court shall make a decision.'

33 Art. 1066: 'During the period of marital relationship, one party may request the division of the joint property in one of the following situations: (1) where one of the parties has conducted acts that seriously damage the interests of common property, such as hiding, transferring, selling, destroying or squandering the joint property of the husband and wife or forging joint debts, and other acts seriously damaging the property interests of the husband and wife; (2) a person, whom one of the spouses is statutorily obligated to support, is suffering from a severe disease and needs medical treatment, but the other spouse does not agree to pay the relevant medical expenses.'

34 J. Yue, 'On the Division of Marital Joint Property and its Improvement' 53 *Journal of Yunnan Normal University* (Philosophy and Social Science) 114 (2021).

relationship, except for in the circumstances stipulated in Article 1066 of the Civil Code.

3.6. EQUAL RELATIONSHIP BETWEEN HUSBAND AND WIFE

The primary family relationship is that between husband and wife. The value orientation of equality and harmony from the original Marriage Law is upheld in the Civil Code. The Code stipulates that husband and wife are equal in marriages and families (Articles 1041 and 1055). It also prescribes the right of the husband and wife to use their surnames and given names (Article 1056) and respects their personal freedom (Article 1057), their rights to decide on marital domiciles (Article 1050), and the duty of mutual support and right of inheritance. As regards the property relationship between husband and wife, the legal property system and conjugal agreed property system coexist in the Code, under which what constitutes common property or private property is clear, and both the husband and wife have equal rights to dispose of the common property (Article 1062).

The amended Marriage Law 2001 and its three subsequent judicial interpretations focused mainly on the property relationship between husband and wife, while little attention was paid to their personal relationship; this was criticised as 'seeing only property but no persons'.[35] One of the critiques was that the judicial interpretation of the former Marriage Law had regressed to become an integral part of the Property Law or the Partnership Enterprise Law, and that the Marriage Law had shifted from personal relationship law to investment promotion law.[36] In order to build a more equal and harmonious relationship between husband and wife and enhance the protection of marriages and families, the Civil Code confirms that the personal rights of a natural person arising from marriage or family relations are protected by law, which is conducive to promoting harmony and equality between husband and wife. At the same time, in order to adapt to modern developments, meet the needs of daily life and maintain transaction safety, on the basis of the former judicial interpretation, the agent right for daily affairs of families between husband and wife is supplemented in the Civil Code.[37]

35 D. Hui, 'The Tendency of the Philosophy of Chinese Family Law – Discussion with Professor Xu Guodong' 7 *Law Science Magazine* 69 (2012).

36 Z. Xiaoli, 'The Horn of Chinese Family Capitalism' 1 *Cultural Landscape* 32 (2011).

37 Art. 1060: 'A civil juristic act performed by either spouse to meet the daily needs of the family is binding on both parties thereto unless otherwise agreed between the third person and the spouse performing the act. Restrictions on the scope of the civil juristic acts that may be performed by either spouse shall not constitute a defence against a third person in good faith.'

3.7. JOINT DEBTS OF HUSBAND AND WIFE

In the history of Chinese family law, the identification and liquidation rules of the joint debts of husband and wife have experienced several changes. With the advancement of reform and opening-up, assets in ordinary families have increased, and so have the debts incurred by either spouse in daily life, agricultural production and enterprise business. In judicial practice, the number of disputes on the joint debts of husband and wife handled by the courts has been increasing in recent years. In such cases, usually the debts have been incurred by one of the spouses, but the debtors have requested both husband and wife to pay off the debts jointly, especially where the husband and wife have divorced. How to recognise the joint debts concerns not only the interests of the parties but also transaction safety.

The Marriage Law, amended in 2001, adopted the term 'used for the joint life' to identify the joint debts between husband and wife; that is, Article 41 stipulates that:

> 'At the time of divorce, the debts incurred by the husband and wife for their common life shall be paid off jointly. If the joint property or the private property is insufficient to pay off the debts, both husband and wife shall reach an agreement on the payment; if agreement fails, the People's Court shall make a judgment.'

However, family life is a private field; it is difficult for debtors to prove whether or not debts were incurred by the husband and wife for their joint life. In some cases, husband and wife have even colluded to infringe upon the rights of creditors. Hence, the Supreme Court issued Judicial Interpretation (II) on the Application of the Marriage Law 2003, Article 24 of which shifts from the 'used for the joint life' to the 'time presumption'[38] method to recognise joint debts.

Some new problems arose in the application of Article 24 of Judicial Interpretation (II). Due to the wide scope of joint debts, debts incurred by either spouse not for common life, agricultural production or enterprise operation were, in judicial practice, also recognised as joint debts. As a result, the proportion of cases in which appeals and retrials were applied for increased greatly. Hence, the Supreme People's Court made supplementary

---

38 Art. 24: 'Where a creditor claims a debt incurred by either spouse in his or her own name during marriage, it shall be treated as a joint debt between the spouses, except that one of the spouses can prove that the creditor and the debtor clearly agreed on the debt as a private debt, or can prove that it falls under the circumstances stipulated in paragraph 3 of Article 19 of the Marriage Law.' Para. 3, Art. 19 of Marriage Law: 'Where the husband and wife agree to own the property separately obtained during the duration of the marriage relationship, if the third party knows the agreement, the debts incurred by either husband or wife shall be paid off by husband or wife from his or her own property.'

provisions to Article 24 of Judicial Interpretation (II), by means of new judicial interpretations in 2017 and 2018, which excluded debts arising from illegal activities such as gambling and drug addiction, and forged debts, from the joint debts of husband and wife. In 2018, the judicial interpretation of the Supreme Court further reduced the scope of joint debts between husband and wife. Joint debts between husband and wife were limited strictly to co-signed debts, debts incurred for daily needs of the family, and debts arising from joint production and business operation. These provisions have been incorporated into the Civil Code.[39]

As for liquidation of joint debts, it is stipulated that the common debts of the spouses shall be jointly paid off upon divorce. If the common property is insufficient to pay off the debt or the property is owned by husband and wife separately, the debt shall be paid off on the basis of an agreement; if agreement cannot be reached, the People's Court shall decide the matter (Article 1089). Creditors are entitled to request that both the man and woman pay off the joint debts regardless of the divorce agreement of the parties or the verdict, ruling or mediation made by the People's Court on the division of the joint property at divorce. Where one party has assumed the responsibility of paying off the common debt, the People's Court will support his or her claim requiring the other party to bear the corresponding debt in accordance with the divorce agreement or the legal documents made by the People's Court (Article 35 of Judicial Interpretation (I) of the Marriage and Family volume).

3.8. THE BEST INTERESTS OF CHILDREN PRINCIPLE

'The best interests of children' principle is a basic principle to deal with child-related matters in modern countries.[40] Based on the principle in the original Marriage Law of protecting the legitimate rights and interests of minor children, the principle of 'the best interests of children' has been further embodied in the Civil Code. It stipulates that adoption shall adhere to the principle of the best interest of the adoptee (Article 1044), and that the rights and interests of children born out of wedlock are protected by law (Article 1071).

---

39 Art. 1064: 'A debt jointly signed by both spouses and a debt signed by either spouse and subsequently ratified by the other spouse, and debts incurred by either spouse in his or her name during the marriage to meet the daily needs of the family, shall be joint debts of the husband and wife. A debt incurred by either spouse in his or her name during the marriage that exceeds the daily needs of the family is not the joint debt of husband and wife, except that the creditor can prove that such a debt is incurred for the joint life, production and operation of the couple or is incurred based on the common intention of both husband and wife.'

40 R. Qiyu, 'From Idea to System: The Principle of "the Best Interests of Children" in Parent-Child Divorce Law', *Hubei Social Sciences* 170 (2012).

In addition, opinions of minor children are respected by law. The 'Several Specific Opinions on the Handling of Child Support Issues in Divorce Cases by People's Courts' in 1993 by the Supreme People's Court(which was abolished in 2001) stipulated that, where disputes over the upbringing of their children arise between husband and wife at the time of divorce, the wishes of the children who have reached the age of ten shall be heard. The precondition, in the original judicial interpretation, of disputes over child custody between parents is repealed in the Code, so that it directly stipulates that,

> 'after divorce, children under the age of two shall be in the direct custody of the mother. If the parents cannot reach an agreement on the custody of the child who has reached the age of two, the People's Court shall make a judgment under the specific circumstances of the parents and the principle of what is most favourable to the minor child. If a child has reached the age of eight, his true wishes shall be respected.'

Furthermore, on the establishment or dissolution of the adoption relationship of minor children, the children's opinions shall be listened to, provided that they have reached the age of eight.

Meanwhile, the Civil Code establishes a new lawsuit for the recognition or denial of parenthood' so that the regime of parent–child relationship law is more systematic. Article 1073 states that, where a parent challenges the parent–child relationship for legitimate reasons, he or she may file a lawsuit to the People's Court to request confirmation or denial of the parent–child relationship. Where an adult child challenges the parent–child relationship with legitimate reasons, he or she can bring a lawsuit to the People's Court to request confirmation of the parent–child relationship.

4. NEW FAMILY LAW CHALLENGES OF CHINA'S CIVIL CODE

The promulgation of the Civil Code is just the beginning of the Code era, but the pace of legislation and judicial interpretation will not slow because of the arrival of the codification. Due to the gap between legislation and practice, some controversies will inevitably arise in the application of the Civil Code. Thus, it will be necessary to study the understanding and application of the Civil Code correctly. On the other hand, legal rules and regulations in the Code have not solved all the problems in the family field, so some new rules will be necessary to fill in the blanks in the Code. Furthermore, as a new code, the Civil Code is not impeccable, and cannot solve all practical problems once and for all. In the era of the Civil Code, the Code will develop continuously with the times, and 'it is necessary to issue Judicial interpretations and conduct case studies to make up for the limitations of the Code itself'.[41] In addition, the effects of some new regimes need further observation. All these are new challenges the Civil Code should address.

4.1. NECESSARY GUIDANCE ON SPOUSAL FIDELITY AGREEMENTS

The validity of a loyalty agreement[42] between husband and wife is a long-debated issue in judicial practice.[43] Will an agreement on the legal consequences of acts infringing upon marital and family rights between the husband and wife be effective in the era of the Civil Code? How can the legal rules be applied to solve the disputes concerned? In judicial practice, some courts, influenced by cases decided before the Civil Code, insist that such agreements are invalid, but others support the validity of fidelity agreements. There is no consensus in the academic field on the effect of such agreements. One viewpoint is that, for the purpose of maintaining marriages and enhancing the self-healing of family relationships, the theory of civil legal behaviour should not be applied to the interpretation of such loyalty agreements.[44] The opinion of the First Division

41 L. Yongjun, 'Breakthroughs and Deficiencies of Marriage and Family Legislation in the Era of Civil Code', *Legal System and Social Development* 133 (2020).

42 A loyalty agreement specifies that, when either husband or wife violates their duty of loyalty, they will bear adverse consequences in terms of property, which do not involve issues related to child custody and divorce freedom.

43 A survey of the People's Court's decisions on the validity of spousal fidelity agreements shows that the courts' decisions are highly controversial. The proportion of agreements that were recognised as valid is 23.64%; 9.08% were deemed invalid; 9.1% were deemed conditionally valid; the proportion that distinguished the content of the agreement was 5.45%; and 52.73% of lawsuits were not accepted, or the court did not make a decision on the validity. In the highest proportion of cases, the court made no judgment or did not accept a lawsuit on this kind of agreement. As spousal fidelity agreements do not violate the legal provisions of spousal fidelity obligations, do not violate public policy and good customs, and meet the effective requirements of civil legal acts, they have been recognised as valid by some courts; the main reason for their invalidity is that a fidelity agreement concerning marriage status is not subject to contract regulation. Some courts held that a fidelity agreement between spouses was conditional on divorce, and so the agreement would not come into effect during marriage. Some courts handled fidelity agreements by distinguishing terms concerning status rights and property. Provisions on status restrictions often fail to take effect, while agreements on property are valid. See Z. Xiaohui, 'An Empirical Study on the Effect of Marital Loyalty Agreement' (2023) *Journal of Taiyuan Normal University (Social Science Edition)* 70. A spousal loyalty agreement is essentially an emotional and moral promise, and the status law (marriage law) does not acknowledge this kind of agreement, so such an agreement can be regarded as a natural debt beyond the jurisdiction of the People's Court. See X. Ninglan and C. Dan, 'Identification, Types, and Legal Application of Identity Relationship Agreements' (2022) *Legal Research* 75.

44 S. Lei, '"Good Family Traditions" in Law: Nature Analysis, Meaning and Application', *Journal of Southwest University of Political Science and Law* 60 (2021).

of the Supreme People's Court on loyalty agreements between husband and wife is that, if one party is unwilling to perform it, the agreement should not be enforced. Just like a debt where the time limitation period has expired, whether to perform the agreement depends entirely on the willingness of the debtor to honour the terms of the agreement.[45] Another viewpoint holds that a loyalty agreement can be legally effective for the reason that such an agreement is one reached in advance on how to determine the compensation standard and calculate the amount of compensation in divorce where either spouse commits marital faults.[46]

There is also controversy over the law applicable to spousal loyalty agreements. The controversial issues include whether spousal loyalty agreements are subject to the provisions of the Contract volume or the general provisions of the Civil Code on civil legal acts, as well as whether they are subject to the provisions of Article 464 or 467 of the Contract volume, etc. Article 464,[47] which addresses agreements concerning marriage, adoption and guardianship, specifies that, in the absence of other provisions specifically governing such issues, the Contracts volume of the Code shall be referred to according to the nature of the contracts. In the present author's opinion, since the contracts clauses of the Code are applicable to agreements on personal topics such as adoption and guardianship, they should also apply to property agreements. As a fidelity agreement addressing property is not an agreement on an 'identity relationship', such as marriage or parentage, its validity should be determined by reference to the rule of an innominate contract in Article 467 rather than Article 464. Meanwhile, acknowledging the validity of the fidelity agreement is consistent with the legislative spirit of Article 1045 on good family traditions and the promotion of socialist core values. Analysing this issue from the perspective of the civil legal acts, there is no obstacle to the validity of such an agreement either. In this regard, the Supreme People's Court may release judicial interpretations or guidance on the legal application and validity of loyalty agreements, to 'enhance the uniformity of legal application to a greater extent' and 'meet the urgent need for a relatively uniform legal order'.[48]

---

45 Chief Editor of the Leading Group for the Implementation of the Civil Code, above n. 11, pp. 37–39.

46 Z. Li, 'Determination of the Validity of the "Conjugal Loyalty Agreement" on the Background to the Civil Code', *Procuratorate Daily*, 29 (July 2020, 7th ed.).

47 Art. 464(2): 'Agreements concerning personal relations such as marriage, adoption, and guardianship shall be regulated by the provisions on the relevant personal relations; or absent such provisions, reference shall be made to this Part according to the nature of such agreements.'

48 J. Yan, 'Legal Doctrine in the Context of Civil Code Compilation: Orientation and Approaches', *Journal of Yantai University (Philosophy and Social Science Edition)* 41 (2018).

4.2. FURTHER STUDY OF THE CLAUSE ON GOOD FAMILY TRADITIONS

With regard to the provisions on good family traditions in Article 1043 of the Civil Code,[49] it is necessary to engage in theoretical and practical research. Firstly, is this Article just an 'advocacy' provision or can it be applied as a legal norm? The view of the Civil First Division of the Supreme Court is that Article 1043 is an advocacy or oath clause, which reflects the legal spirit of regulating families under the rules of law and morality.[50] A different view is that Article 1043 is not simply an 'advocacy' or 'oath' clause, but should play the function of a basic principle in the Marriage and Family volume of the Civil Code. On the one hand, its function is to review the effect of legal acts of husband and wife, and on the other, it is to restrict the exercise of marital rights.[51] Another position held is that the provision on good family traditions in Article 1043 has normative effect. It not only exerts its normative effect as a principle and general clause, but can also be the basis of relevant legal claims.[52] The nature of the clause on good family traditions determines its status in the Civil Code and whether it can be used as a legal norm to make a decision in judicial practice.

4.3. INTERPRETATION OF RULES ON THE IDENTITY RIGHT

The Civil Code stipulates that the identity rights of a natural person arising from marriages and family relations are protected by the State. Although the Civil Code does not explicitly stipulate that family members are obligated not to arbitrarily disrupt their families, it is clear from the provisions on good family traditions in Article 1043, divorce damage compensation in Article 1091 and the situations in which divorce can be granted in Article 1079[53] that both husband

---

49 Art. 1043: 'Families shall establish good family traditions, promote family virtues, and value the construction of family civilization. Husbands and wives should be faithful to each other, respect and care for each other; family members shall respect the elderly and take care of the young children, help each other, and maintain equal, harmonious and civilized marriage and family relationships.'

50 Chief Editor of the Leading Group for the Implementation of the Civil Code, above n. 11, p. 36.

51 Y. Chengyuan, 'The Path Choice of Marriage Law Returning to the Civil Law – Also on the Application of the Referral Norms of the Civil Code', *Social Sciences in Chinese Higher Education Institutions* 140 (2012).

52 Z. Li, 'The Normative Effect of Good Family Traditions in China's Civil Code' 278 *Jinan Journal (Philosophy and Social Sciences Edition)* 118 (2022).

53 Art. 1079: 'Where either husband or wife claims divorce, the relevant organizations may conduct a mediation or a divorce lawsuit may be directly filed to the People's Court. In dealing with a divorce case, the People's Court shall carry out mediation; a divorce shall be granted where mutual affection no longer exists and mediation fails. Where mediation

and wife shoulder the responsibility not to damage their marriages and families arbitrarily. In practice, the People's Court also supports family members having the obligation to maintain the stability of their marriages and families.[54]

Whether a third party outside marriage, other than a third party engaged in bigamy, should bear liability for improper interference with the marriages and families of others is controversial in the academic circle. Opponents argue that a third person is not obligated to protect the marriages and families of others. They believe that the right to marital status is significantly different from the right to personality, since marital status is a 'weak claim right' without external effect on others.[55] After examining French law, Professor Ye concludes that pure adultery does not constitute a tort, as the obligation of marital loyalty is considered a relative obligation that can bind only the spouses.[56] The People's Court usually holds a negative attitude, in judicial practice, towards third-party liability. In the present author's opinion, the duty of loyalty legally binds only the husband and wife but not the third person. The Civil Code does not create types of rights such as family rights and spousal rights, either. However, a systematic interpretation of the provisions that legitimate rights and interests should be protected and natural persons should have the right to privacy supports the conclusion that a third person bears a minimum obligation not to interfere with the marriages and families of others. Not to mention that Article 112 stipulates that identity rights arising from family relations are protected by the law. A third person is surely obliged not to infringe upon the marriages and families of others.

Another question is whether a third person should shoulder liability for all actions interfering with others' marriages and families. A third person may interfere with the families of others in various forms, such as bigamy,

fails, a divorce shall be granted under any of the following circumstances: (1) bigamy or cohabitation with other persons of an opposite sex; (2) committing domestic violence or maltreatment or desertion of any family member; (3) gambling, drug abuse and other vices despite repeated education; (4) separation for two years due to relationship disharmony; (5) other circumstances resulting in the breakdown of the relationship between husband and wife.

54 In the divorce case of *Hua X v. Chen X*, the court held that a legal marriage is protected by law, and that neither of the parties to the marriage might arbitrarily destroy the stability of the marriage and family without legal reasons. See Anhui Province Guzhen County People's Court (2014). In another divorce case, between Pi Chumei and Li Jinyao, the court of first instance recognised that the plaintiff had committed domestic violence, cohabited with a third person, damaged the feelings of the other spouse, and destroyed the marriage and family. Considering the fault of the plaintiff and the spiritual damage to the defendant, the court ordered the plaintiff to compensate the defendant by paying RMB 100,000, at the discretion of the court. The appeal court upheld the decision of the first-instance court. See Huai'an Intermediate People's Court of Jiangsu Province (2014).

55 R. Keping, 'On the Civil Liability of a Third Person's Tort on the Right to Matrimonial Status', *Journal of Huazhong University of Science and Technology* 75 (2020).

56 Y. Mingyi, 'Tort Liability of a Third Person for Adultery under French Law', *Journal of East China University of Political Science and Law* 91 (2013).

cohabitation, adultery, etc. The statutory circumstances to determine whether a marital relationship has broken down, and whether compensation for divorce damages are due by one spouse to the other, are limited to bigamy, cohabitation with others and other severe faults destroying marriages and families. In the present author's opinion, it should not matter whether these acts are conducted by a family member or a third person; the damage consequences and negative value evaluations of these acts are similar. As the serious faults of husband and wife during marriage are limited to such acts as bigamy or illegal cohabitation with a third person outside marriage, where a third person commits bigamy or cohabits with either husband or wife, those behaviors can be regarded as infringements of identity rights that give rise to liabilities.

In the Civil Code, the situations in which a third party is deemed to interfere with the families of others, and the corresponding responsibilities of the third party, are too abstract and vague; it would be advisable to provide guidance to reduce divergence in judicial practice and better protect the identity rights arising from marriage and family. At the same time, certain restrictions should be imposed on the behaviours and responsibilities of a third person interfering with families of others, to distinguish the boundary between law and morality.

4.4. OBSERVATION OF IMPLEMENTATION EFFECT OF THE WAITING PERIOD

The waiting period in divorce registration has played a role in relieving marital conflicts; however, some new problems occur in its application.

The first is how to link up the provision on the waiting period in divorce registration with the litigation divorce system. According to the Statistical Bulletin of the Ministry of Civil Affairs, 4.339 million couples divorced in 2020 – a decrease of 7.7 per cent from the previous year – including 3.736 million divorces registered at Civil Affairs Departments and 603,000 couples divorced through a court judgment or mediation.[57] In 2021, 2.839 million divorce cases were handled, a reduction of 34.6 per cent from the previous year. Among these divorces, 2.141 million couples divorced through registration at Civil Affairs Departments, and 698,000 were ordered or mediated by courts.[58] From the statistics it can be seen that, although the number of divorce registrations dropped significantly in 2021, after the implementation of the Civil Code, the proportion of divorces in the courts has increased.

57 Statistical Bulletin on the Development of Civil Affairs in 2020.
58 Statistical Bulletin on the Development of Civil Affairs in 2021.

In the granting of marriage dissolution, does a lax criterion or a rigorous standard comply with the legislative purpose to establish a waiting period in divorce registration? The one-month waiting period is stipulated in divorce registration, but not in litigation divorce. However, the courts do not usually support marriage dissolution when couples apply for divorce for the first time unless there are clear reasons supporting divorce. Six months after the first ruling that divorce was not granted, the courts tend to support marriage dissolution in the second divorce lawsuit. The fact that divorce is not usually granted in the first lawsuit indicates a judicial moderation attitude towards marital life.[59] The fact that courts tend to maintain the marital relationship during the first divorce lawsuit objectively plays a role in preventing hasty divorce. Hence, some scholars doubt that the 'waiting period in divorce registration' may overlap with the court's 'no divorce first time' practice, which will weaken the marriage intention of marriageable young men and women.[60] In addition, there is a concern that some couples may resort to 'false litigation, true mediation' to avoid the waiting period in divorce registration and indirectly turn the court into a 'divorce registration authority' in a disguised way, so that the waiting period performs practically no function in registered divorce.[61] How to avoid this phenomenon is worth studying. The waiting period at divorce registration should be limited to imprudent divorce.[62] What measures, then, should be adopted to realise this legislative purpose?

The second question is whether, in applying the waiting period regulation, it is necessary to distinguish different situations and adopt supporting measures to relieve marital conflicts and promote marital reconciliation. In the formulation of the Civil Code, the provision on the waiting period for divorce has attracted much attention. One view holds that the procedural delay cannot effectively prevent risks of domestic violence or abuse. After evaluating the drafts, some scholars pointed out problems with the waiting period, for example that the one-size-fits-all rule is unsuitable, and that there are no ancillary measures to assist the waiting period in playing its role.[63] The Civil Code does not distinguish between marital death and marital crisis. Whether such a provision is truly conducive to

---

59 J. Jinliang and Z. Zhenyuan, 'How Justice Protects Marriage – Based on the Analysis of the Phenomenon of Second Lawsuit in Divorce Cases' 30 *Shantou University Journal (Humanities & Social Sciences Bimonthly)*.

60 Y. Longgang, 'Judges' Behaviors under Institutional and Social Constraints: The Experience of Divorce Dispute Resolution in Basic Courts' 165 *Leg. Sys. & Soc. Dev. (Bimonthly)* 108 (2022).

61 Z. Yutai, 'The Dilemma and the Way of the Waiting period – Article 1077 of the Civil Code' 24 *Journal of Southwest Petroleum University (Social Sciences Edition)* 101 (2022).

62 M. Zhiyong, 'The Logical Justification and Examination of the "Divorce Cooling-off Period" System', *The Jurist* 27 (2022).

63 Y. Lixin and J. Xiaohua, 'Legislative Evaluation of the Divorce Cooling-off Period in the Draft of the Marriage and Family Volume of the Civil Code' 27 *Henan Social Sciences* (2019).

protecting the legitimate rights and interests of the couples involved, and how mediation or reconciliation measures are adopted during the waiting period, requires further research on the application of the provision.

4.5. LEGAL RULES TO DEAL WITH COHABITATION RELATIONSHIPS

In 1993, the Supreme People's Court released 'Opinions of the Supreme People's Court on Several Issues Concerning the Handling of Cohabitation Relationship', which provided guidance on how to deal with cohabitation relationships. However, this judicial interpretation was abolished after the implementation of the Civil Code. The only rule to deal with cohabitation can be found in Article 3 of Judicial Interpretation (I) of the Marriage and Family volume, which states that the People's Court will not accept a lawsuit filed by a party only for the dissolution of cohabitation. If such a case has been accepted, the court shall rule to dismiss the lawsuit. If a party files a petition due to a dispute over property division or child-rearing during the period of cohabitation, the People's Court shall accept it. Under the Marriage and Family volume of the Civil Code and its judicial interpretation, the personal relationship of cohabitation, such as the formation and dissolution of a cohabitation, is not subject to legal regulation, and there are no specific rules to deal with disputes over property acquired or debts incurred during the period of cohabitation.

Can cohabitants be regarded as family members and the disputes between them handled accordingly? Article 1045 of the Civil Code enumerates family members, but the parties in a cohabitation relationship are not listed there. From a comparative point of view, more and more countries have treated cohabitation as one of the family relationships.[64] For example, while recognising the inviolability and sanctity of marriage, the Philippine Constitution, in another separate clause, stipulates that the State recognises the sanctity of family life, and protects and strengthens the family as a basic autonomous social system.[65] As early as 1995, the United Nations Secretary-General's observation report on the commemoration of the International Year of the Family mentioned families of different forms and functions, acknowledging non-traditional families.[66] What attitude should be taken towards cohabitation, and how to

---

64 R. Qiyu, 'On Families in the Civil Code of China', *Journal of China Women's University* 20 (2017).

65 T.M. Naldine N.M. Elamparo, 'Discrimination in Social Legislation: Is There State Protection for the Modern Family?' 54 *Ateneo Law Journal* 1627–55 (2020).

66 U.N. Secretary-General, 'Report of the United Nations on the Observance of the International Year of the Family', U.N. Doc. A/50/370 (6 Sep. 1995), p. 3.

establish corresponding legal rules, are issues that should be studied in the era of the Civil Code.

4.6. IMPROVEMENT ON THE PARENT-CHILD RELATIONSHIP LAW

Rules on parent-child relationships have been improved in the Civil Code; however, legal regulation of parent-child relationships has not been completely established. Firstly, the Civil Code does not fully establish a system for fathers to acknowledge children born out of wedlock. Under the Civil Code, only litigation to confirm or deny a parent-child relation is permitted. No specific provisions involve the confirmation or denial of the parent-child relationship. Secondly, the parent-child relationship created through artificial reproduction technology has not been set up completely. The determination of the parent-child relationship created by artificial reproduction technology can be found in Judicial Interpretation (I) of the Family and Marriage volume, which stipulates that, during the marriage relationship, if both husband and wife agree to conduct artificial insemination, the children born should be regarded as legitimate children, and the rights and obligations between parents and children shall be governed by the relevant provisions of the Civil Code. But this regulation cannot meet the needs of judicial practice. China's Health Commission (former Ministry of Health) has issued a number of regulations; however, these are just regulations by the former Minister of Health, and not the law enacted by the National Committee or regulations formulated by the State Council, and have mainly been enacted to regulate medical institutions and researchers, which cannot solve all the new problems brought about by artificial reproduction technology in reality. If the husband dies, can the wife request to continue the transfer of the frozen embryos kept by the husband and wife in the medical institution? Due to the lag in specific legislation on artificial reproductive technology, it is difficult for medical institutions to determine their obligations during frozen embryo transfer. The People's Court usually faces dilemmas in handling cases concerning frozen embryos. In addition, although surrogacy is illegal in China, how can parent-child relationships in surrogacy be determined? To solve all these problems depends both on the correct application of the Civil Code and further improvements in parent-child relationship legislation.

5. CONCLUSION

As a code of the twenty-first century, the Civil Code completes the systematisation and logicalisation of China's civil law, as well family law. Meanwhile, it should also be noted that the family law in the Civil Code has not solved all the problems once and for all. And the Civil Code will keep up with the times by improving some regulations in an evolutionary way. How to correctly understand and apply the rules of the Civil Code on marriage and family will certainly be a topic of research for a considerable period in the future. Research is required to strengthen relevant judicial interpretations and case studies, to enhance the practicality of the Civil Code, so that it can better play its role as an 'encyclopedia of civil society'. It is necessary to provide guidance on spousal fidelity agreements to reduce divergence in judicial practice. In the application of waiting periods in divorce, some supporting measures are needed to allow the new provisions to function better, and their implementation needs further observation. Rules on the confirmation or denial of parent–child relationships and the parent–child relationship created by artificial reproduction technology need to be systematised. It is also necessary to make rules to regulate cohabitation relationships and deal with disputes among cohabitants.

FRANCE

FIFTY YEARS OF EVOLUTION IN FRENCH FAMILY LAW

Christine BIDAUD (Dir.),
Hugues FULCHIRON, Amélie PANET, Richard VESSAUD, Clara DELMAS, Massilia AMZAL, Bastien BARET, Aurore CAMUZAT, Éric FONGARO, Guillaume KESSLER, Guillaume MILLERIOUX, Margot MUSSON, Marie PINCET, Hugo JOLLY and Hugo BORDIN-ESCHARAVIL

Résumé

En 50 ans, le droit français de la famille a connu de profonds bouleversements dans tous ses aspects. C'est d'abord sur le plan des méthodes de raisonnement et d'élaboration des normes que l'évolution se constate. Ensuite, la conjugalité s'est transformée tant en consacrant de nouveaux modes de conjugalité qu'en faisant évoluer les droits des membres du couple. La parenté et la parentalité ont également connu des changements majeurs au cours des dernières décennies, tout comme le droit des personnes vulnérables. Le présent chapitre retrace ces évolutions en se focalisant sur certaines d'entre elles.

1. THE EVOLUTION OF FRENCH FAMILY LAW METHODS

1.1. THE INTRODUCTION OF THE ECHR'S PROPORTIONALITY TEST IN FRENCH FAMILY LAW[1]

The development of fundamental rights in the aftermath of World War II and the construction, on a European scale, of mechanisms guaranteeing their legal protection have, over the past 50 years, contributed to creating porosity between civil and common law legal systems. The growing influence of the European Convention on Human Rights (ECHR) has led French law to adapt to new legal rules, including in family law, via abundant and regular litigation under Article 8 ECHR, which guarantees the right to private and family life. Various decisions from the European Court of Human Rights (ECtHR), on issues ranging from assisted reproductive technologies and surrogacy to modes of partnership (from civil partnerships to same-sex marriage), and to the rights of illegitimate children and the protection of vulnerable individuals, have been major factors influencing family law reform. The ECtHR decisions, though

[1] Clara Delmas, PhD, researcher, University Jean Moulin Lyon 3, Family Law Centre, Research Team Louis Josserand, consultant in civic participation and digital democracy.

sometimes encountering resistance and always sparking significant legal debate, have gradually caused French family law to evolve.

Methodological changes complemented the substantive changes in the early twenty-first century when the highest French judicial authority expressly chose to apply the European method of proportionality control in disputes involving fundamental rights and freedoms. This method, well known to European human rights lawyers, is inspired by the common law and resides in a three-step review for judges when they examine an attempt to a fundamental right: the attempt must be prescribed by a clear and accessible law, pursue a legitimate aim, and be necessary in a democratic society.[2] Family law served as the pioneering field, with two decisive steps taken, in 2013[3] and 2016,[4] concerning incestuous marriages, making it the preferred 'laboratory'[5] for this evolution. Since then, the Court of Cassation has consistently reaffirmed this paradigm shift, which contrasts with the traditional reasoning of this jurisdiction and imposes on both lower and appellate judges the need to familiarise themselves with a new method of approaching fundamental rights in general.

1.1.1. From 1950 to 2013: Enduring Proportionality

For a long time, the proportionality test was not explicitly and expressly applied by French courts, as France's legal tradition distinguished itself from the common law. Although a form of proportionality examination was known to lower-court judges, as some legal rules required it,[6] the 'Strasbourg-style' conventionality control was neither exercised nor verified by the Court of Cassation, and was not subject to any specific formalisation, even in disputes involving fundamental rights.[7] French decisions could then be subjected to retrospective review by the

---

2 About this European method, see, for instance, J. Christoffersen, *Fair Balance: Proportionality, Subsidiarity and Primarity in the European Convention on Human Rights*, Brill, 2009; F. Sudre (dir.), *Droit européen et international des droits de l'homme*, PUF, 2023.

3 Civ. 1st, 4 December 2013, no. 12-26.066, *D.* 2014. 179, note F. Chénedé, 153, point of view H. Fulchiron, 1342, obs. J.-J. Lemouland and D. Vigneau, and 2017. 123, chron. V. Vigneau; *AJ fam.* 2014. 124, obs. S. Thouret, and 2013. 663, point of view F. Chénedé; *RTD civ.* 2014. 88, obs. J. Hauser, and 307, obs. J.-P. Marguénaud.

4 Civ. 1st, 8 December 2016, no. 15-27.201, *D.* 2016. 2568, obs. I. Gallmeister; *AJ fam.* 2017. 71, obs. J. Houssier.

5 H. Fulchiron, 'Le contrôle de proportionnalité et les évolutions contemporaines du droit de la famille' in A. Gogos-Gintrand and S. Moracchini-Zeidenberg (dir.), *2010–2020: Une décennie de mutations du droit de la famille*, Dalloz, 2021, p. 35 ff, spec. p. 36.

6 E.g. French law requires proportionality examination when it establishes prerogatives that are not absolute (in particular, Art. L. 1121-1 of the Code du travail, which compares the interests of the company with the fundamental freedoms of the employee), or when it gives the judge discretion (e.g. Art. 1231-5, para. 2, of the Civil Code, which allows the judge to moderate a penalty clause).

7 See, in particular, Cass. Civ. 1st, 29 October 1990, no. 88-19.366 (Arts. 9 and 10 ECHR) or Cass. Civ. 1st, 31 January 1989, no. 87-15.139 (Art. 10 ECHR).

ECtHR, which applied its own criteria to national decisions elaborated with their own national method, leading the ECtHR to assume control that the French Cour de cassation judge had not achieved.

Indeed, the Court of Cassation could render a decision based on the right to respect for private and family life and Article 8 ECHR without verifying whether the application of the law made by the lower courts was correct, and without detailing its reasoning according to the method required by European human rights law. Decisions based on Article 8 might have a sole motivation, such as that 'the pronouncement of divorce for the rupture of communal life is not contrary to the provisions [of the said article]',[8] or that 'succession rights are unrelated to the respect for private and family life recognized by Article 8 of the [ECHR]'.[9] This lack of explanation in French decisions prompted the ECtHR to emphasise that enriched motivation and the exercise of proportionality control by the Court of Cassation could have allowed it to better understand its own reasoning[10] and perhaps avoid European condemnation. Thus endured rather than mastered by the French high jurisdiction, proportionality control remained an attribute of European judges that did not blend well with the increasing influence of European human rights law on French law, particularly in family law. With dialogue among judges accompanying the globalisation of law, French courts have, since 2013, embarked on assimilating European methods of conventionality control (see section 1.1.2. below).

1.1.2. From 2013 to Today: Assimilating Proportionality

Since 2013, the French Court of Cassation has formalised and incorporated the use of proportionality and conventionality control into French judicial method. While the journey will be long, given that French courts were not accustomed to the exercise,[11] the paradigm shift is under way, and each decision adds a new

---

8 Civ. 2nd, 25 March 1987, no. 85-12.262.

9 Civ. 1st, 25 June 1996, no. 94-14.858 (this is the judgment that led to the first *Mazurek v. France* decision of the ECtHR: see *Mazurek v. France*, no. 34406/97, 1 February 2000).

10 See, e.g. in the area of inheritance, the judgment of the ECtHR in *Quilichini v. France*, no. 38299/15, 14 March 2019, especially §44; in the area of freedom of expression (in the case of a T-shirt worn by the applicant's three-year-old nephew at his nursery school, bearing inscriptions with terrorist connotations), see ECHR, *Z.B. v. France*, no. 46883/15, 2 September 2021, especially §66.

11 To assist the lower courts, the Court of Cassation has been producing various methodological documents since 2018, both through Memento and recommendations, as well as within its cassation decisions, detailing the various stages of its 'control of control' and specifying the criteria. The aim is to provide trial judges with sufficiently precise instructions regarding the methodology. See, e.g. Civ. 1st, 21 March 2018, No. 16-28.741. However, legal doctrine consistently raises certain risks and imperfections subject to improvement; see, in particular, F. Chénedé, 'Two lessons from classical natural law for the control of concreteness conformity: a contribution to the reflection of the Court of Cassation', *D.* 2021, 1142.

element to the progression of the French method of protecting fundamental rights and freedoms. In family law, which constitutes 'one of the privileged fields of experimentation for proportionality control',[12] and specifically under Article 8 of the ECHR, the French Court of Cassation has been led to exercise three new types of control.

Firstly, and in the majority of cases, the Court can exercise light control, *in concreto*, verifying that the lower-court judges have properly carried out the proportionality control and implemented the appropriate criteria. In this scenario, some authors refer to the 'control of control'[13] exercised by the Court of Cassation over the decisions of lower courts. It is also conceivable that this type of control may occur in disputes involving legal standards, such as the interest of the child, where the balancing requires an assessment of highly factual considerations that do not fall within the purview of the cassation judge.

However, the Court can also go further and exercise heavy control, still *in concreto*, in which, conversely, it itself carries out the proportionality control to remedy the deficiency or inadequate control exercised by the lower courts.[14] Here lies the methodological innovation, in that the high French jurisdiction must ensure not to 'descend into the facts' while applying a proportionality control necessarily based on factual elements. This type of control can also lead the Court of Cassation to set aside the application of a legal rule *in casu*, which constitutes a real innovation.

Finally, the Court of Cassation may be required to exercise heavy control, *in abstracto*, more generally addressing the conventionality of French law, which may lead it to seek a new balance to bring French rules into compliance with European requirements. This type of control has occurred in notable cases related to assisted reproductive technologies between women in same-sex partnerships[15] (before its legalisation in 2021),[16] surrogacy, and incest issued from alliances.[17] In the first two cases, proportionality control had led the French Court of Cassation to attempt to evolve national law by establishing a general principle of transcribing the civil status acts of a child born through assisted reproductive technologies or surrogacy abroad.[18] Regarding surrogacy,

---

12 H. FULCHIRON, 'Le contrôle de proportionnalité et les évolutions contemporaines du droit de la famille', above n. 5, p. 36.

13 H. FULCHIRON, 'Le contrôle de proportionnalité: questions de méthode', *D.* 2017, 656. For an example in case law, see Civ. 1st, 2 March 2022, No. 20-23.282.

14 In this case, the referring court is not required to carry out the proportionality control in turn (see Civ. 3rd, 10 June 2023, No. 19-25037).

15 See, most recently, Civ. 1st, 13 January 2021, No. 19-17.929.

16 Law No. 2021-1017 of 2 August 2021, relating to bioethics.

17 See Civ. 1st, 4 December 2013, No. 12-26.066, and Civ. 1st, 8 December 2016, No. 15-27.201, mentioned above.

18 Civ. 1st, 18 December 2019, No. 18-14751 (for PMA) and Nos. 18-11.815 and 18-14.751 (for GPA), *AJ fam.* 2020.133, note J. HOUSSIER; *RTD Civ.* 2020.81, obs. A.-M. LEROYER;

the legislature has subsequently reframed the French position by prohibiting this transcription concerning the intended parent, forcing the courts to adhere to a case-by-case assessment, depending on the speed of the procedure.[19] In the case of incest, this same control, conversely, allowed the judges not to question the French prohibition, and even to consolidate it by providing the necessary flexibility for the preservation of the fundamental rights at stake.[20]

This assimilation of substance and form concerning fundamental rights within French family law reinforces the horizontal effect of the ECHR and the rights it guarantees. By removing the Conseil Constitutionnel's and the Conseil d'État's duopoly on assessing interferences with fundamental rights, this evolution grants all French jurisdictions the tools for comprehensive protection of what must now constitute the 'alpha and omega'[21] of legal reasoning in particular, and the French legal system in general.

1.2. THE EUROPEANISATION OF PRIVATE INTERNATIONAL FAMILY LAW[22]

The need for a united Europe based on solidarity was asserted in the aftermath of World War II, against a background of destroyed countries, more than 40 million dead, and a single idea in mind: 'never again'. Two considerations governed this construction. On the one hand, it would be possible to achieve this objective first and foremost through economic union; on the other, European integration could only be a success if it was carried out step by step. Thus, in 1950, the Schuman Declaration, we can read: 'Europe will not be built all at once, or as part of an overall project. It must be built through concrete achievements, first creating de facto solidarity.'[23] This was followed by the creation of the European Coal and Steel Community (ECSC) in 1951, the European Atomic Energy

JDI 2020, No. 9, note D. Sindres. This decision was subsequently challenged by the law of 2 August 2021, and the new wording of Art. 47 of the Civil Code.

19 This was the position of the French Court of Cassation between 2019 and 2021 (Cass. Ass. Plén., 4 October 2019, No. 10-19.053, *D.* 2019.2228, note H. Fulchiron and C. Bidaud; *JCP* 2019.1184, note A. Gouttenoire and F. Sudre; *RTD Civ.* 2019.817, obs. J.-P. Marguénaud, p. 841, obs. A.-M. Leroyer; *JDI* 2020, No. 8, note J. Heymann and F. Marchadier). Since 2021, French courts have returned to this position (see, in this regard, TJ Nantes, 7 September 2023, No. 20/01421, *Dr. Fam.* No. 11, November 2023, comm. 154, V. Égéa).

20 See H. Fulchiron, 'Le contrôle de proportionnalité et les évolutions contemporaines du droit de la famille', above n. 5, p. 37.

21 In the words of H. Fulchiron (ibid., p. 40).

22 Christine Bidaud, professor at University Jean Moulin Lyon 3, director of the Family Law Centre, co-director of the Research Team Louis Josserand.

23 Robert Schuman was the French minister of foreign affairs at the time. Along with Jean Monnet, he was one of the architects of European construction.

Community and the European Economic Community in 1957, and abolition of customs duties in 1968. At the same time as strengthening its economic ties, the European Community expanded its borders. From six states in 1951 (Germany, Belgium, France, Italy, Luxembourg and the Netherlands), it grew to nine in 1973 (adding the United Kingdom, Ireland and Denmark), ten in 1981 (adding Greece), and twelve in 1986 (adding Spain and Portugal). The year 1986 also saw the adoption of the Single European Act, which completed the organisation and structuring of the single market. It was from 1992 onwards, with the adoption of the Maastricht Treaty, transforming the European Community into the European Union (EU) and creating European citizenship, that the European institutions really began to enter the sphere of private law in general, and family law in particular. Alongside the geographical enlargement of the EU to 28 Member States – before its shrinkage to 27 with the exit of the United Kingdom ('Brexit') – a twofold phenomenon gradually occurred.

First, in the name of the principle of free movement, and especially the free movement of persons, the areas of intervention of European Community law multiplied to such an extent that today it is an EU regulation that decides which court has jurisdiction in divorce cases involving a foreign element.[24] Since June 2012, it has also been a EU regulation that decides on the applicable law in this type of matter.[25] Other EU regulations have subsequently come to govern international succession,[26] matrimonial property regimes[27] and the property effects of registered partnerships[28] where there is a foreign element. A proposal for a regulation on parentage[29] is currently under discussion.

24 Council Regulation (EC) No. 2201/2003 of 27 November 2003 concerning jurisdiction and the recognition and enforcement of judgments in matrimonial matters and the matters of parental responsibility, (called 'Regulation Bruxelles 2 *bis*') [2003] OJ L338/1, replaced by Council Regulation (EU) 2019/1111 of 25 June 2019 on jurisdiction, the recognition and enforcement of decisions in matrimonial matters and the matters of parental responsibility, and on international child abduction (called 'Regulation Bruxelles 2 *ter*') [2019] OJ L178/1.

25 Council Regulation (EU) No. 1259/2010 of 20 December 2010 implementing enhanced cooperation in the area of the law applicable to divorce and legal separation (called 'Regulation Rome 3') [2010] OJ L343/10.

26 Regulation (EU) No. 650/2012 of the European Parliament and the council of 4 July 2012 on jurisdiction, applicable law, recognition and enforcement of decisions and acceptance and enforcement of authentic instruments in matters of succession and on the creation of a European Certificate of Succession [2012] OJ L2021/107.

27 Council Regulation (EU) 2016/1103 of 24 June 2016 implementing enhanced cooperation in the area of jurisdiction, applicable law and the recognition and enforcement of decisions in matters of matrimonial property regimes [2016] OJ L183/1.

28 Council Regulation (EU) 2016/1104 of 24 June 2016 implementing enhanced cooperation in the area of jurisdiction, applicable law and the recognition and enforcement of decisions in matters of the property consequences of registered partnerships [2016] OJ L183/30.

29 Proposal for a Council Regulation on jurisdiction, applicable law, recognition of decisions and acceptance of authentic instruments in matters of parenthood and on the creation of a European Certificate of Parenthood, 7 December 2022, COM(2022) 695 final, 2022/0402(CNS).

We are a long way from the economic considerations that led to the creation of this European area!

Second, the nature of what used to be known as 'Community' law has changed. From directly applicable substantive law, it gradually began to slide towards a system of conventional law. In other words, there were no longer only Community rules of pure substantive law, but also Community rules including conflict-of-law rules, conflict-of-jurisdictions rules and rules on the recognition and enforcement of judgments. Initially, these rules were the subject of conventions. The first of these was the Brussels Convention of 27 September 1968 on the jurisdiction and the effect abroad of judgments in civil and commercial matters. This convention was supplemented by another, the Brussels 2 Convention, on the jurisdiction, recognition and enforcement of judgments in matrimonial matters. But this system of conventions proved too complex when new states joined the EU. As these were conventions, the new Member States of the EU had to ratify them once they joined the Union, which multiplied the 'formalities'. In the Amsterdam Treaty of 2 October 1997, it was decided to transform this system. The judicial cooperation in civil matters put forward in this treaty made it possible to transform these conventions into real secondary Community legislation; that is, a Community regulation that we now call an EU regulation. The idea was that all Member States should apply the same European regulations, so that the rules on conflicts of jurisdictions, conflicts of laws and recognition of judgments would be the same throughout the EU, Unifying the rules of private international law compensated for the lack of unity in the substantive family laws of the Member States.

But if there is one area in which national particularities are more than predominant, it is family law. The evolution of social values is not the same from one state to another, and while some Member States have adopted laws on registered partnerships and/or same-sex marriages, double monosexual links of parenthood, medically assisted procreation for single women or lesbian couples, surrogacy, etc., other states have, on the contrary, prohibited such types of marital union or parenthood. The differences from one Member State to another have been so great on the definition of concepts such as marriage or maternity that it is no longer possible to adopt regulations that would apply in all Member States of the EU. For the first time, in 2010,[30] and on several occasions since, a special cooperation agreement procedure called 'the enhanced cooperation' has been used. This is a special procedure for creating a European regulation – a real instrument of secondary legislation rather than a convention – that is applicable only in those Member States that wish to adopt it. Those who do not initially wish to adhere to the text may do so at a later date, but are

30 With the EU Regulation called Rome 3 (see below).

not obliged to do so. Faced with the different evolution of societies and values, the pendulum's swing has reversed: the desire to speak with a single voice on behalf of all the Member States of the EU has changed to the need to respect national particularities, so as not to risk upsetting the construction of the area of freedom, security and justice that the EU is supposed to be. Just as it is almost impossible immediately to grow a tropical plant in a country with a temperate climate, it is undoubtedly through the technique of the 'acclimatisation garden' – of taming, or even legal acculturation, of the specificities of each country – that the European construction of private international family law will be solid, and will stand the test of time.

1.3. THE RISE OF AUTONOMY OF WILL IN PERSONAL STATUS[31]

Numerous principles underpin the law of persons and family, among which is the principle of the immutability of personal status. Although the notion of personal status is used regularly, it is difficult to define – so much so that there is no unanimous definition. This contribution does not aim to precisely define personal status, but rather to consider its evolution; therefore, a general definition will be retained. It might be considered that personal status is composed of the personal, family and political status of an individual. The main elements of personal status are sex, first names and surname. The main elements of family status are filiation, marriage and civil solidarity pacts. And the main element of political status is nationality.[32]

Originally, personal status was immutable. This was justified by the State's desire to ensure a certain stability by avoiding the disorders linked to the possibility of changing one's status at will. However, some components have always been modifiable, such as domicile, marital status, first names, filiation, or even nationality. For these different elements, a person's will was decisive, as it could lead to a modification of personal status. Whether it involves a change of domicile, or of marital status, the will has always had a significant place. This is also the case in matters of filiation, particularly concerning adoption and the establishment of filiation through recognition or possession of status. As for French nationality, it can be obtained through various titles which assume an expression of will by the individual concerned. Furthermore, it has always been

---

31 Aurore Camuzat, PhD student at University Jean Moulin Lyon 3, Family Law Center, Research Team Louis Josserand.

32 S. Guinchard and T. Debard (dir.), *Lexicon of Legal Terms*, see 'Personal status', Dalloz, 27th ed., 2019–20, p. 462.

possible in France to request a change of first names when they could cause prejudice[33]

However, other elements of personal status were unalterable and could not be modified by individuals' will. Yet, over the past 50 years, alteration of these elements has increasingly become available. Since 1992, it has been possible to obtain the rectification of the mention of a person's sex in civil status documents.[34] Furthermore, the law for the modernisation of justice in the twenty-first century has eased the conditions for modifying the sex listed in civil status to ensure that it conforms to social reality.[35] More recently, the law of 2 March 2022 broadened the circumstances in which an individual can change their family name. Any adult may now request a change in their family name from the civil status officer by substituting or adding the name of the parent who did not pass theirs on, in the chosen order.[36] This change strengthens the will to achieve equality between father and mother in the devolution of the family name.[37] It also illustrates the increasingly prominent place of the autonomy of will in matters of personal status.

Moreover, filiation raises new questions. The use of surrogacy agreements and medically assisted procreation poses new challenges, particularly through the establishment of filiation with regard to intended parents.[38] The notion of a parent, as well as that of a 'mother', raises many questions today. The example of the recognition, in France, of foreign documents mentioning filiation following surrogacy perfectly illustrates this issue. While such agreements are prohibited in France, intended parents, as well as children born abroad from such a process, have every interest in having their filiation established.[39] However, how can the

---

33 Art. 60, French Civil Code; P. Voirin and G. Goubeaux, *Civil Law*, vol. 1, LGDJ, 2021, p. 99, no. 138.

34 Plenary Assembly of the Court of Cassation, 11 December 1992, no. 91-11.900: *JCP* 1993. II., p. 21991, conclusions by M. Jéol, note by G. Mémeteau; *Gazette du Palais* 1993, 1, p. 180; *RTD civ.* 1993, p. 325, note by J. Hauser.

35 Law no. 2016-1547 of 18 November 2016, on the modernisation of justice in the 21st century.

36 Law no. 2022-301 of 2 March 2022, relating to the choice of name from filiation.

37 M. Lamarche, 'The name, filiation and affection', *Dr. Fam.* no. 2, February 2022, focus p. 13; M. Lamarche and J.-J. Lemouland, 'Choose your name! The use of names and the change of family name', *JCP G.* no. 14, April 2022, 466 ff.

38 See, e.g. C. Bidaud-Garon and H. Fulchiron, 'Recognition or reconstruction? Regarding the filiation of children born via surrogacy, following the *Labassée*, *Mennesson*, and *Campanelli-Paradiso* rulings of the European Court of Human Rights', *RCDIP* 2015, 1 ff; H. Fulchiron, 'Transcription of the birth certificate of a child born via surrogacy: confirmation', *Dr. Fam.* no. 2, February 2018, study 2; A.-M. Leroyer, 'Transcription of the birth certificate of children born via surrogacy', *RTD civ.* 2018, 88 ff; P. Malaurie and H. Fulchiron, *Family Law*, LGDJ, 6th ed., 2017, pp. 488 ff, 1030 ff.

39 In addition to fundamental rights, one may cite, without being exhaustive, the establishment of parental authority, the transmission of French nationality, the equivalence between social reality and being legally considered as the child's parent, etc.

principle of the permanence of personal status be ensured while reaffirming the French prohibition of surrogacy?

It must not be forgotten that the principle of permanence of personal status was forged at a time when the elements in question were almost by nature immutable. The family name was necessarily that of the father, and this could not be questioned. Biological sex could not be modified, while the law of filiation, organised around marriage, allowed for stability that was easy to record in civil status acts. Current developments seem to challenge all of these notions, which can now be modified over the course of a person's life. While some of these changes are social, such as the issue of the name, others are linked to medical progress, as shown by the current questions surrounding the notion of what constitutes a mother.

The evolution of French family law over the past 50 years illustrates a profound shift towards an increasing consideration of the autonomy of will. What was once immutable now adapts to individual will. Thus, the unavailability of personal status has increasingly given way to the individual will that shapes personal, family and political status – a significant change that may well continue to intensify in the future.

2. THE EVOLUTION OF FRENCH FAMILY LAW ON CONJUGALITY

2.1. CHANGES IN THE RIGHTS OF THE SURVIVING SPOUSE UNDER FRENCH LAW[40]

The rights of the surviving spouse under French law have evolved over a long period. In the Civil Code of 1804, the spouse inherited only if there were no relatives in the line of succession, but this situation almost never arose. Later, a law of 9 March 1891 granted the spouse a usufruct, but the proportion of this usufruct varied according to the rank of the heir with whom the spouse inherited. A law of 3 December 1930 gave the surviving spouse full ownership rights in the presence of heirs in the direct line of succession, but in 1930 the surviving spouse did not take precedence over any heir. It was only with a law of 26 March 1957 that the French legislaturellowed the spouse to take precedence over ordinary collaterals, and it was only with an ordinance of 23 December 1958 that the title of heir was granted to the surviving spouse.

[40] Eric Fongaro, professor at University of Bordeaux.

At the present time, despite some slight additions resulting from a law of 23 June 2006, it is a law of 3 December 2001 that has really improved the situation of the surviving spouse. This law granted three new rights to the surviving spouse: firstly, the surviving spouse benefited from a promotion in the devolution of the estate; then from protection of their living environment; and, finally, from the grant of minimum inheritance amounts.

Since the law of 3 December 2001, the surviving spouse is always the first heir, either because he or she excludes other heirs, or because he or she competes for the succession with other heirs. In principle, the surviving spouse excludes all other heirs when the deceased leaves no descendants, father or mother. In this case, as a matter of principle, the surviving spouse receives the entire estate. The brothers and sisters of the deceased are, in principle, excluded from the succession.

If the father and mother of the deceased are still alive, the surviving spouse will receive half of the estate in full ownership. If one of the parents is deceased, the surviving spouse will receive three-quarters in full ownership. If the deceased leaves a surviving spouse and descendants, the legislature has introduced a distinction for the determination of the spouse's rights. This distinction depends on whether or not there are descendants not descended from both spouses. According to Article 757 of the Civil Code, '[i]f the predeceased spouse leaves children or descendants, the surviving spouse receives, at his or her option, the usufruct of all existing property or ownership of a quarter of the property where all the children are descended from both spouses, and ownership of a quarter where there are one or more children who are not descended from both spouses.'

However, in 2001, the legislature also sought to protect the surviving spouse.

Protecting the living environment of the surviving spouse was one of the key measures of the law of 3 December 2001. This protection illustrates the extent to which the notion of family has become closer to the couple and their home. In 2001, the legislature gave the surviving spouse a genuine right to remain in the home, by granting them two separate rights to the home and the furniture in it. On the one hand, the legislature granted the surviving spouse, by operation of law, a temporary right of enjoyment over the principal dwelling, where that dwelling belonged to the spouses or was wholly dependent on the estate, as well as a right of enjoyment over the furniture that furnished that dwelling, where this is included in the estate. On the other hand, unless the deceased spouse's express wish is expressed in an authenticated will, the law grants the surviving spouse, for the rest of their life, a right of dwelling in the home, and a right of use over the furniture in it.

The protection of the surviving spouse's living conditions also involved the granting of minimum inheritance amounts. These minimum inheritance amounts constitute imperative rights for the surviving spouse; that is, rights that are not subject to disinheritance. The granting of a reserve to the surviving spouse is certainly one of the most symbolic measures of the 2001 law. For the surviving spouse to become a reserved heir, the deceased must leave no descendants. The surviving spouse is only entitled to reserve rights if there are no other reserved heirs; that is, if there are no descendants of the deceased. The surviving spouse's reserve covers one-quarter of the full property.

With the introduction of a reserve in favour of the spouse, it is possible to appreciate how far we have come since the introduction of the Civil Code in 1804, when the spouse inherited only in the absence of relatives to a certain degree of inheritance; that is, at the time, up to the twelfth degree. Finally, this development in the rights of the surviving spouse is most illuminating in terms of the more general development of French family law, which over the last two centuries has constantly refocused on children and spouses.

2.2. THE RECOGNITION AND CONSECRATION OF FORMS OF CONJUGALITY OTHER THAN MARRIAGE: REFLECTIONS ON THE CIVIL SOLIDARITY PACT AND COHABITATION[41]

Until the end of the twentieth century, extramarital unions had only a precarious legal status in French law.

The Civil Code of 1804, which reflected the sociological contingencies of the early nineteenth century, only recognised heterosexual marriage. However, this legal framework was quickly overtaken by the reality of human interaction, as all unions between people could not be reduced to matrimonial ties alone.

For almost 200 years, cohabitation had no strict legal or jurisprudential definition. Only a few outlines were sketched out, as and when required by practice, in scattered and limited legal provisions, which led to the emergence of certain contradictions between legal disciplines, each with a different approach to the issue. Worse still, without going into detail, against the backdrop of the Aids epidemic, same-sex couples did not enjoy the same prerogatives as heterosexual couples. The time had, therefore, come to provide formal legal recognition and give cohabitation a legal framework, especially as it was enjoying remarkable growth in French society among both heterosexual and homosexual couples. It was not until the end of the twentieth century, however, that cohabitation made a timid entry into the Civil Code, with the resounding Civil Solidarity Pact Act of 15 November 1999. Article 515-8 of the Civil Code now defines cohabitation as 'a de facto union, characterised by a stable and continuous life together,

41 Richard Vessaud, PhD, Research and Teaching Fellow, University Jean Moulin Lyon 3, Family Law Centre, Research Team Louis Josserand.

between two persons of different or the same sex who live as a couple'. However, despite this salutary definition, the enshrinement of cohabitation in the Civil Code leaves a feeling of incompleteness, as the legislature has not developed the regime for this type of union any further.

Although the Act of 15 November 1999 gave only limited recognition to cohabitation, this legislative intervention nonetheless established a new form of union unprecedented in the French legal system: the civil solidarity pact. Although this law is remarkable in terms of its contours, having put an end to the monopoly of marriage as the sole form of legal recognition of a couple, and having opened up new forms of conjugality to people of the same sex prior to the law of 17 May 2013 (which enshrines marriage for 'all'), it is not without its critics. Having enshrined the civil solidarity pact in Articles 515-1 *et seq.* of the Civil Code, the French legislature nonetheless left many grey areas regarding the nature of this form of conjugality, its opposability to third parties and its legal system (which established a presumption of joint ownership that was potentially dangerous for ill-informed litigants).

Aware of these shortcomings, the legislature intervened with the Act of 23 June 2006, providing for more effective publicity measures, in particular by including a reference to the civil solidarity pact on the partners' birth certificates, or by abandoning the presumption of joint ownership and enshrining the presumption of separation of property. More limited changes were then made by the Act of 5 March 2007, to specify the procedures for entering into a pact when one of the parties is under a legal incapacity, and again by the Act of 12 May 2009, to clarify the rules governing jurisdiction in matters of dissolution of a civil solidarity pact.

In addition to these adjustments, the legislature has also intervened twice in the last ten years to modernise the practice of this form of conjugality in line with sociological developments. Under the Act of 18 November 2016, responsibility for concluding, amending and terminating civil solidarity pacts was transferred to town hall registrars, with a view to relieving court registrars of this time-consuming task and facilitating access to this type of marriage. Lastly, under the Act of 23 March 2019, the legislature abolished the requirement for a vulnerable adult to seek a judge's agreement before entering into a civil solidarity pact, which in a way helped to modernise the French approach to the law governing protected adults.

In conclusion, it should be noted that the abandonment of the monopoly of marriage as the legal element structuring conjugal relationships is relatively recent in French law. The legal understanding of conjugal relationships has undergone major upheavals over the last 50 years, moving from a unitary approach to conjugality to recognition of a certain polymorphism in couple relationships.

2.3. FIFTY YEARS OF FRENCH DIVORCE LAW[42]

The jubilee of the *International Society of Family Law* just happens to coincide with that of France's first major divorce reform. The Law of 11 July 1975, drawn up by the famous Dean Jean Carbonnier, broke with the restrictive approach to divorce that previously required proof of fault on the part of one of the spouses. Rather than enshrining the concept of no-fault divorce, which had already become established in the United States a few years earlier, the legislature chose to address the diversity of family situations. Four models were offered to the spouses:

- Divorce by mutual consent for spouses who agree on the principle and the consequences; divorce on dual declaration.
- Divorce by double declaration for spouses who wish to divorce but are unable to agree on the consequences.
- Divorce on grounds of breakdown of cohabitation, a unilateral model that can be imposed by one spouse on the grounds that the spouses have ceased living together for six years.
- Divorce for fault.

The reform also aimed to dedramatise relations between spouses in a spirit of '*pacification*' (peacefulness). A specialised judge, the matrimonial affairs judge (*juge aux affaires matrimoniales*), was created within each *tribunal de grande instance* (ordinary court),[43] and the question of compensation after the break-up was rethought around the concept of '*prestation compensatoire*' (compensatory payment). The aim was to avoid subsequent disputes, in a clean-break approach, by replacing the maintenance obligation with a lump-sum payment.

Despite its innovative nature, the reform did not resolve all problems, and in particular not those linked to the duration and cost of the procedure, and thus a new reform was initiated almost 30 years later. The legislative debates focused on the question of creating a non-judicial divorce and abandoning divorce for fault. However, the reform ultimately abandoned that ambition and settled for a technical improvement to the law. The Law of 26 May 2004 retained most of the 1975 model while trying to improve it, although not to revolutionise it. The four models have been retained but divorce for breakdown of life together has

42 Guillaume Kessler, Senior Lecturer at Savoie Mont Blanc University, Research Law Center Antoine Favre.

43 The *juge aux affaires matrimoniales* became the *juge aux affaires familiales* (judge for family matters) in 1993, and the *tribunal de grande instance* was renamed *tribunal judiciaire* (judiciary court) in 2020.

been considerably facilitated. This model was replaced by a divorce for *altération définitive du lien conjugal* (definitive alteration of the marital bond), requiring proof of a separation of two years rather than six. The divorce on dual request has been replaced by a new *divorce accepté* (accepted divorce), whose procedure has been simplified. *Pacification* was also reinforced by facilitation of agreements between spouses and the development of family mediation. The dissociation of causes and effects has also been reinforced. The idea of a guilty spouse who would have to suffer financially the consequences of their fault, and an innocent spouse who would see their wrongs repaired has been greatly attenuated. The only traces of subjectivity that have been preserved concern the possibility for the judge to exclude the *prestation compenstatoire* if serious circumstances require this, and the possibility of requesting damages.

The next step – much more spectacular – was the introduction of a non-judicial divorce by the Law of 18 November 2016. France has, therefore, decided to jump ahead and admit the idea of a purely contractual divorce countersigned by lawyers and filed with a notary.[44] The contract must contain the complete settlement of the effects of the divorce and the liquidation of matrimonial property. In order to protect the parties from rash consent, each spouse cannot validly consent before the expiration of a 15-day period from its reception. The parties' consent, determined by the recording by the notary of the contract in his records, establishes the effective date of the termination of their relationship and the enforceability of the contract. Divorce by mutual judicial consent nevertheless persists in cases where a child requests to be heard by the judge, or if one of the spouses has been placed under a regime of protection due to an alteration of their mental faculties. It can also be useful to choose the judicial model to avoid future conflicts. Otherwise, it is possible that spouses realise they have consented a little hastily or have made mistakes, and then need to go to court to relitigate the terms of their divorce. Non-judicial divorce was, however, very quickly adopted by the French, who use it massively. A good half of divorces take place outside court, and many law firms have taken advantage of the opportunity to create low-cost divorce services with essentially online systems offering solutions costing between 150 and 300 euros.

Finally, the law of 19 March 2019 made procedural modifications that are worth mentioning. The period required for divorce due to definitive alteration of the marital bond has been reduced to one year of separation instead of two. It was also decided, in the context of accepted divorce, that acceptance could be made by legal act in a way similar to non-judicial divorce. On a more technical level, the conciliation phase has been removed, to reduce the workload of judges. The use

44 The notary, as underst ood in France, is the Latin or civil law notary, defined by the International Union of the Latin Notariat as 'a legal professional specifically designated to attest the acts and contracts that persons celebrate or perform, to draft the documents which formalize the latter, and to give legal advice to those who require the services of his office'.

of alternative dispute resolution methods, and particularly mediation, was also encouraged. This preference for voluntary settlements also appears in the decree of 29 July 2023, which promotes the amicable settlement of disputes before the ordinary court through two systems: the 'cut' or cessation of the trial *(césure du procès)* and the amicable settlement hearing *(audience de règlement amiable)*. These two systems are not specific to divorce, but can be applied in this context. Inspired by German and Dutch law, the 'cut' or cessation of the trial allows the parties to agree on certain points amicably, allowing the judge to concentrate on the most contentious points. Inspired by Quebec law, the amicable settlement hearing involves the possibility for the judge seised of the dispute to summon the parties to an amicable settlement hearing, to seek the 'amicable resolution' of the dispute between them, through the balanced presentation of their opposing points of view; the assessment of their respective needs, positions and interests; and the determination of the legal principles applicable to the dispute.

The most recent reforms, therefore, aim to speed up the process, reduce the cost for the spouses, and reduce the work of the courts. These developments show that marriage is gradually losing its specific characteristics, and that it can no longer really be considered as being at the centre of family law. The difference with civil solidarity pact (PACS), whose success is increasing, shows that it is perhaps time to rethink couple rights in a more general way.

3. THE EVOLUTION OF FRENCH FAMILY LAW ON PARENTHOOD

3.1. MAJOR CHANGES IN ACCESS TO MEDICALLY ASSISTED REPRODUCTION TECHNIQUES IN FRANCE[45]

Over the past 50 years, France, like many other countries around the world, has seen significant developments in terms of access to medically assisted reproduction techniques. First of all, it is worth pointing out that the legal framework governing these techniques dates back only to the 1990s. In France, the first bioethics law was passed in 1994.[46] The 1994 law established a legal framework for medically assisted procreation, notably authorising donor insemination for heterosexual couples. However, donor-assisted reproduction was not authorised for same-sex couples. The legal framework was later completed by the 2004 law,[47] which created the Agence de la biomédecine, a

45 Massilia Amzal, PhD student at University Jean Moulin Lyon 3, Family Law Centre, Research Team Louis Josserand.
46 Law No. 94-654, 29 July 1994.
47 Law No. 2004-800, 6 August 2004.

public agency that carries out its missions in the fields of organ, tissue and cell removal and transplantation, as well as in the fields of procreation, embryology and human genetics.

In 2013, the law opening marriage and adoption up to same-sex couples[48] did not directly modify the conditions of access to medically assisted procreation. At that time, the second spouse in a female couple could only become a statutory mother by adopting the child of their spouse. Adoption, however, required that the adoptive parent had previously married the legal parent and conceived the child abroad. In addition, for the adoption to occur, the child must not have had an established paternal lineage. Medically assisted procreation with sperm donation was, therefore, the only way to envisage such an adoption.

The French bioethics laws were revised in 2011,[49] and bioethical issues were debated in 2018 to take account of scientific advances and societal developments. These events did not necessarily broaden access to new techniques, but the new law made adjustments to existing rules. The French Bioethics Act of 7 July 2011 allows oocyte donors to store oocytes for their own use, in case of future need. By doing so, women can postpone starting a family for professional or personal reasons.

One of the most striking developments has been the extension of access to medically assisted procreation for single women and female couples, enabled by the French Bioethics Act of 2021.[50] French law now states that medically assisted procreation is intended to respond to a parental project; it is made accessible to any couple, whether made up of a man and a woman or two women, or to any unmarried woman, after individual interviews of applicants by members of a multi-disciplinary clinicobiological medical team. The law specifies that this access may not be subject to any differences in treatment, notably with regard to the marital status or sexual orientation of the applicants.[51] This law also constitutes a considerable turning point in the evolution of family law, as the legislature had to redefine parentage, in particular by creating an ad hoc method of establishing parentage for female couples.

Another major advance of this law is that donor anonymity is no longer absolute. The law indicates that any person conceived by medically assisted procreation involving a third-party donor may, if they so wish, access the identity and non-identifying data of the third-party donor at the age of majority.[52]

Advances in stem-cell research and genetics have had a significant impact on assisted reproduction techniques. These advances have opened up new perspectives and options for couples facing fertility problems. It is important to

---

48 Law No. 2013-404, 17 May 2013.

49 Law No. 2011-814, 7 July 2011 on bioethics.

50 Law No. 2021-1017, 2 August 2021 on bioethics.

51 Art. L. 2141-2 of the Public Health Code.

52 Ibid., Art. L. 2143-2.

note that access to assisted reproduction in France is governed by ethical laws, and each legislative change is often the result of in-depth debate on ethical, social and medical issues. These developments reflect French society's desire to adapt its legislation to scientific advances and social change, making this a constantly evolving topic to be monitored on a regular basis.

3.2. THE PARENTAGE OF CHILDREN BORN ABROAD BY SURROGACY: A DECADE OF UNCERTAINTY[53]

Readers of this section will be familiar with the issue of France's acceptance of surrogate pregnancies carried out abroad, as the authors have already had the opportunity to address the subject on several occasions. On this occasion, it seems appropriate to retrace the broad outlines of the issue, which has perhaps not yet reached its climax.

Surrogacy has been formally prohibited in France since 1994. This ban has remained in force to this day. However, at the beginning of the twenty-first century, French people proceeded to go abroad for surrogacy, returning with one or more children. This has led to several cases being brought before French judges, with the legislature taking its time to address the issue. The surrogacy question has been a major concern for the courts, scholars, legislators and French society in general. It is, therefore, appropriate to summarise the main stages of the evolution regarding this subject here.

Initially, when couples or single individuals returned from abroad with a child conceived as a result of surrogacy, the Court of Cassation refused to transcribe the foreign records; therefore, the court did not acknowledge the parentage created abroad.[54] Some scholars have criticised this refusal to acknowledge foreign records because of the practical problems it creates for children.[55] The issue eventually came before the ECtHR, which ruled against France on the grounds that children's right to privacy, and in particular their right to identity, had not been respected.[56] The French courts then reacted by partially accepting the transcription of foreign records. Transcription is authorised for the biological father, enabling him to be established as the child's father in France, but for the other parent, with no biological link with the child, he or she must adopt the child, according to the French adoption procedure. This position, although sometimes challenged by the French legal community, was validated

---

53 Bastien Baret, associate professor at UCLy (Lyon Catholic University), UR "Confluence, Sciences et Humanités – EA 1598".

54 Cass. Civ. 1st, 6 April 2011, no. 10-19.053, no. 09-66.486 and no. 09-17.130.

55 H. FULCHIRON and C. BIDAUD-GARON, 'Dans les limbes du droit', *D.* 2013, 2349.

56 ECHR, *Mennesson v. France*, no. 65192/11, 26 June 2014.

by an opinion of the ECtHR.[57] However, individual cases have shown that, in some specific situations, it has been impossible to proceed with the adoption of the child, and this has led to decisions advocating the transcription of foreign records for both parents.[58] This latter position pushed the legislature into acting within the Bioethics Act of 2022, by subtly amending the Article of the Civil Code relating to transcriptions of records in order to prevent transcription for the intended mother who has not given birth.[59]

This latest development could stabilise case law on this point, although it should be noted that it concerns only documents drawn up abroad and not judgments, and that it in no way prevents domestic courts from carrying out an *in concreto* proportionality review.[60]

What can we learn from these ten years of developments? First of all, that a private international law issue concerning a small number of individuals may be of interest to the entire society, as is often the case in family law. Moreover, that it is now difficult for the courts to take a clear and general position on such a legal issue, particularly given the need to take into account *in concreto* the fundamental rights of individuals. Finally, that the legislature is not quick to take up such issues, intervening only if the time and opinion are politically opportune.

To conclude, this issue will no doubt have a greater impact on relations between those involved in the law (Parliament, Court of Cassation, ECtHR), and on judicial procedures (review procedure, request for an opinion from the ECtHR),[61] than on the substance and principles of French law. However, such a development is far from negligible, and it is certain that the next 50 years will allow us to observe how France's attitude toward surrogacy (international or not) evolves.

3.3. CHANGES IN PARENTAGE LAW IN FRANCE SINCE 1972: TOWARDS GREATER EQUALITY[62]

In its most common sense, filiation represents an individual's belonging to the family of their father and mother. The essential function of filiation is to assign

57 ECHR, no. P16-2018-001, *Avis consultatif relatif à la reconnaissance en droit interne d'un lien de filiation entre un enfant né d'une gestation pour autrui pratiquée à l'étranger et la mère d'intention*, 10 April 2019.

58 B. Baret, 'The parentage of children born abroad by surrogacy: stabilisation time?' in M. Brinig (ed.), *The International Survey of Family Law 2021*, Intersentia, 2021, p. 202.

59 B. Baret, 'The parentage of children born abroad by surrogacy: the legislature's time' in R. Fretwell Wilson and J. Carbone, *The International Survey of Family Law 2022*, Intersentia, 2022, p. 162.

60 See C. Delmas, 'The Introduction of the ECHR's Proportionality Test in French Family Law' (section 1.1. above).

61 B. Baret, 'Vers un ordre public familial européen? Contribution à l'étude des rapports entre ordres juridiques' (thesis, University Jean Moulin Lyon 3, 5 March 2021).

62 Hugo Jolly, PhD student at University Jean Moulin Lyon 3, Family Law Centre, Research Team Louis Josserand.

each individual his or her personal place. In its legal meaning, filiation can be understood as the legal consecration of a specific bond between parent and child (blood relationship, social-emotional relationship). By creating this legal bond, the child becomes part of the family. In so doing, the law will form a genealogical order so as to individualise, in non-interchangeable relationships, each person within the family group. The same person cannot legally be the son and grandson of the same man or woman, for example, any more than they can be the daughter and wife of the same man, or the father and mother of the same child. This section will deal solely with the development of filiation based on a biological link (voluntary acknowledgement and recognition by operation of law) or an emotional link (possession of status).

In order to explain the development of filiation in French law over the last 50 years, it is necessary to start with the Act of 3 January 1972 reforming the system of filiation (one of the major reforms that transformed French family law), and to briefly explain how this law broke with an unequal conception of filiation, and then to explain its content.

The Act of 3 January 1972 enshrined the principle of equality between all children,[63] whether or not born of their parents' marriage. It put an end to the inequalities between legitimate and natural children,[64] and between the different categories of natural children. In this way, the law treats all filiation as legally established on an equal footing (with the exception of children born of an incestuous relationship). As regards the effects of this equality of filiation, it entails incorporation of the legal status of legitimate and natural children; that is, children born within or outside marriage. Equal status in property matters means that marital and non-marital parents have comparable levels of maintenance obligations, and non-marital children enjoy equal rights within the law of succession and gifts, and in extra patrimonial matters, in particular as regards the attribution, content and nature of parental authority.

However, while this salutary reform was hailed for the egalitarian progress it brought about with regard to methods of filiation and their effects, this equality was not entirely complete. The terms 'legitimate' and 'natural' children had not disappeared from legal texts, maintaining the distinction between children born within or outside marriage.

A fortiori, the reform was not satisfactory as regards adulterous children.[65] Equality of inheritance was tempered by the maintenance of a certain superiority of the legitimate family, insofar as the legislature had deemed it necessary to protect legitimate children's inheritance rights against natural children conceived in disregard of the duties of marriage. This is why an adulterous

63 C. Labrusse-Riou, 'Filiation – Généralités', *Rép. Civ. Dalloz*, 2023, ch. 2, 192.
64 Ibid., ch. 1, 37.
65 F. Moneger, 'Les droits successoraux des enfants adultérins', *RDSS* 2000, 607.

child's inheritance rights were reduced only in cases where he or she was in competition with legitimate children, or with the spouse of the marriage during which the adultery had been committed (former Articles 759 and 760 of the French Civil Code). The effect of this law was that a child born of adultery 'paid' for the consequences of their birth in terms of protecting legitimate children and the spouse of the adulterer.

It was not until the *Mazurek* judgment,[66] handed down by the ECHR on 1 February 2000, which condemned France for its discriminatory provisions against adulterous children, that the idea of a reform of filiation was reinforced. The legislative response came with Law no. 2001-1135 reforming inheritance law (Article 733 of the French Civil Code).

But France's condemnation was not the only reason why reform was necessary. Having lost the institutional support of marriage, the law of filiation was seeking to regain its coherence.[67] All the prevailing forces were working in favour of no longer distinguishing between legitimate filiation and natural filiation,[68] not only in terms of their effects, but also in terms of the ways in which they were established: sociological data; the gradual evolution of positive law; European case law; the examples of France's neighbours; and, finally, the need for greater neutrality within the law.

It was, finally, the regulation of 4 July 2005 and the law of 16 January 2009 that completed the establishment of equality of filiation. The adjectives 'legitimate' and 'natural' disappeared from the legal language of virtually all the codes, which meant that a great many Articles had to be adapted, both inside and outside the French Civil Code. The main development was that filiation was now legally established. Since 1972, French parentage law has been harmonised in favour of complete equality (except in the case of incestuous children).

4. THE EVOLUTION OF FRENCH FAMILY LAW ON PARENTAL RESPONSIBILITY

4.1. PARENTAL AUTHORITY UNDER FRENCH LAW: FIFTY YEARS OF CHANGE[69]

Since the 1970s, the relationship between parents and their children under French law has undergone far-reaching changes in response to the sociological

---

66 ECHR, *Mazurek v. France*, above n. 9.

67 C. Labrusse-Riou, above n. 61, 199.

68 I. Najjar, 'Libéralités: détermination et capacités des parties – Conditions relatives aux personnes physiques', *Rép. Civ. Dalloz*, 2022, 343.

69 Amélie Panet, senior lecturer at University Jean Moulin Lyon 3, Family Law Centre, Research Team Louis Josserand.

evolution of our era. Without going into the details of the various laws[70] that have succeeded one another in this area, three main principles have guided successive reforms.

First guiding principle: the pursuit of equality. First, equality between men and women led, with the law of 4 June 1970, to the disappearance of the 'paternal power' enshrined in the Code Napoleon (Civil Code), in favour of the notion of 'parental authority'. Since then, French law has been driven by the principle of co-parenthood: father and mother exercise parental authority over their child together, on an equal footing, regardless of the family context. Over the past decade, this need for equality between father and mother has evolved into equality between 'parents'. Since the law of 18 May 2013 opened up adoption to same-sex couples, and the bioethics reform adopted in the summer of 2021 opened up medically assisted procreation to female couples, parents must be 'equal' in the ownership and exercise of parental authority regardless of their sex.

Following the principle of equality between men and women is the principle of equality between children, regardless of the circumstances of their birth. The 'Malhuret law' of 1987 transposed the co-parenthood principle that had been introduced to the 'legitimate' family in 1970 to the 'natural family'. However, it was not until the law of 4 March 2002 that French law recognised a true common law of parental authority. The 2002 law eliminated the notions of 'natural child' and 'legitimate child' from the Civil Code. This very same law also specified that the separation of parents has no effect on the rules governing the devolution of parental authority (Article 373-2 of the Civil Code).

The second guiding principle is the preservation of the best interests of the child, a flexible concept that lacks any real definition yet is firmly anchored in a number of international instruments. Article 3.1 of the UN Convention on the Rights of the Child states that, 'in all actions concerning children, whether undertaken by public or private social welfare institutions, courts of law, administrative authorities or legislative bodies, the best interests of the child shall be a primary consideration'. A similar provision is to be found in the Charter of Fundamental Rights (Article 24.2) and, at domestic level, a decision by the French Constitutional Council[71] has given the principle of the best interests of the child constitutional status, placing it among the principles defended by the highest-ranking norms in French law.

These first two guiding principles are frequently combined. For example, the ever-increasing need to protect the best interests of the child has been combined

[70] Mainly the law of 4 June 1970, the 'Malhuret' law of 22 July 1987, the law of 8 January 1993, and the law of 4 March 2002.

[71] Cons. Constit, 21 March 2019, no. 2018-768. The constitutional value of the notion of the child's interest was confirmed by Cons. Constit. decision, 7 February 2020, 2019-826 QPC.

with the principle of co-parenthood to hold that it is in the child's best interests to maintain a personal relationship with both parents. A requirement of the UN Convention on the Rights of the Child (Article 10.2), of the European Charter of Fundamental Rights (Article 24.3), and of the ECHR (in terms of the right to respect for family life guaranteed by Article 8), has been enshrined in the Civil Code since the law of 4 March 2002, in Article 373-2 paragraph 2: '*Each of the father and mother must maintain personal relations with the child and respect the child's ties with the other parent.*' The best interests of the child and the maintenance of ties with their parents are the two primary guiding principles for the decisions of family court judges in cases concerning parental authority.[72]

Finally, a third guiding principle must be highlighted: the promotion of the will of individuals. Firstly, the will of the parents, which is reflected internally in France in the now well-known phenomenon of contractualisation in family law, which has been extended to the law of parental authority. Separated parents can increasingly resort to agreements, which they may submit to the family court for approval, to organise the joint exercise of parental authority.[73] Even in the absence of an express agreement, the Civil Code requires the judge, when ruling on parental authority, to take into account previous practices to which the parents agreed.[74]

Secondly, children's wishes have increasingly been taken into account in the course of the reforms. Today, the first Article concerning parental authority (Article 371-1 of the French Civil Code) has, since the law of 5 March 2007 reforming child protection, stated that parents must involve children in decisions concerning them, in accordance with their age and degree of maturity, and Article 388-1 of the Civil Code, which allows judges to hear children (and even obliges them to do so), if the child so requests.

Parental authority, now understood as a set of rights and duties belonging jointly and equally to the parents, and having the child's best interests as its ultimate goal, is now seen more as a function than a power. Its evolution, like that of family law as a whole, is simply keeping pace with the social upheavals of our times.

---

72 Art. 373-3-6 of the French Civil Code, paras. 1 and 2: 'The judge of the judicial court responsible for family matters settles the issues submitted to him/her under the present chapter, paying special attention to safeguarding the interests of minors. The judge may take measures to guarantee the continuity and effectiveness of the child's ties with each of his or her parents.'

73 Ibid., Art. 373-2-7.

74 Ibid., Art. 373-2-11.

4.2. THE PLACE OF STEP-PARENTS IN BLENDED FAMILIES UNDER FRENCH LAW: FIFTY YEARS OF DEBATE – LITTLE PROGRESS[75]

In France, as in many other countries, more and more children are sharing their lives with people – parents and, above all, step-parents – who take care of them and participate in their upbringing, without any filial ties between them. While many legal systems around the world have made room for these 'third parties', French law continues to ignore them (or almost ignore them),[76] whether in terms of the personal relationship between the children and their step-parents[77] or the transfer of property to stepchildren.[78] It is true that the issue is complex. Situations and expectations are highly diverse. Furthermore, the question of parenthood has continued to interfere with other issues which have profoundly divided French society: that of parental authority in separated families, and of homoparentality (in the past) and pluriparenthood (today).

Thus, in the 1980s, people wondered how to articulate the rights (and duties?) that would eventually be granted to 'third parties', in comparison with those of separated parents. In France, as in many other countries, contemporary law on parental authority is in fact based on the principle of coparentality, and on the idea that, in the interests of the child, the parental couple must outlive the conjugal couple. But is giving to a third party who shares a parent's life not taking from the other parent, especially from fathers, where the child's habitual residence is still mostly with the mother?

The aim was to devise a set of flexible, adaptable and evolving rules for parents and third parties, giving them the tools they needed to exercise in the child's best interests the responsibilities they were in fact assuming. More often than not, the third party is called upon to cooperate with one of the parents in raising the child: instruments based on the individual's will (educational mandates for everyday acts, delegation-sharing approved by a judge) make it possible to establish the third party's place without him or her taking over the place of one of the parents.

75 Hugues Fulchiron, professor, judge at the French Cour de Cassation, honorary director of the Family Law Centre, Research Team Louis Josserand, University Jean Moulin Lyon 3.

76 This is a long-standing debate: see I. Thery and M.T. Meulders-Klein, *Les recompositions familiales aujourd'hui*, Nathan, 1993.

77 The only specific provision concerns the right to personal relations that may be granted to step-parents after the separation of a blended family. And even then, the legislature did not dare speak of a step-parent. Instead, it used a heavy-handed periphrasis: these rights are granted to the person who 'has resided on a stable basis with him/her (the child) and one of his/her parents, has provided for his/her upbringing, maintenance, education or settlement, and has established lasting emotional ties with him/her' (Art. 371-4, al. 2 of the Civil Code).

78 In inheritance matters, children and parents-in-law are treated as foreigners for tax purposes, and are therefore taxed at 60%. The only way to pass on assets at a lower cost is through adoption. But adoption is neither always possible nor always wanted.

And in relation to cases where a third party takes charge of a child (notably in the event of the death or default of one of the parents), it was proposed that the rules laid down in the Civil Code be reviewed, in order to strengthen the powers of the third party to whom the judge entrusts the child, and to relax the rules governing the judicial delegation of parental authority, which is still too marked by the idea of abandonment.

A number of proposals were made along these lines. A commission chaired by I. Théry,[79] a working group led by F. Dekeuwer-Défossez,[80] a parliamentary information mission on the family and children's rights, chaired by P. Bloche and V. Pécresse,[81] and the 2006 Report of the Défenseure des enfants (Children's Ombudsperson)[82] all came out in favour of such a status, albeit with various nuances. But no reform was forthcoming from a legislature whose attention was focused on enhancing the father' place (or, looking at the issue from another angle, his 'empowerment') in separated families. Then came the debates surrounding same-sex marriage and, above all, homoparenting. The passions that tore French society apart are well-remembered.[83] Against this backdrop, a bill awkwardly entitled 'Preliminary bill on parental authority and the rights of third parties' was published in early 2009. No reference was made to the potential use of this law by same-sex couples, but the substitution of the neutral term 'parent' for 'father' and 'mother' in the text was not misleading: at a time when adoption was still closed to same-sex couples, the text would allow same-sex partners or cohabitants to take charge of a child raised by the couple. Once homoparentality was accepted, would homoparenthood not follow? Although very moderate in its proposals, the text provoked a veritable barrage. Jurists and 'specialists in the field of homoparenthood' were all in a frenzy, referring to the terms of the bill as unnecessary in practice, devoid of any social or legal necessity, contrary to the principle of co-parenthood on which contemporary family law is built, a symbol of the harmful 'contractualisation' of family law, dangerous for children torn between a multitude of referents, and so on. In

---

79 I. Théry, 'Couple, filiation et parenté aujourd'hui: Le droit face aux mutations de la famille et de la vie privée', Ed. Odile Jacob – La Documentation française, 1998.

80 F. Dekeuwer-Défossez, 'Rénover le droit de la famille: propositions pour un droit adapté aux réalités et aux aspirations de notre temps', La Documentation française, 1999.

81 P. Bloche and V. Pécresse (rapporteurs), 'L'enfant d'abord. 100 propositions pour placer l'intérêt de l'enfant au cœur du droit de la famille, Report on behalf of the fact-finding mission on the family and children's rights', Ass. nat., n°2832, La Documentation française, 2006.

82 D. Versini (dir.), 'L'enfant au cœur des nouvelles parentalités: pour un statut des tiers qui partagent ou ont partagé la vie d'une enfant et ont des liens affectifs forts avec lui', Report by the Children's Ombudsman, 2006.

83 For a presentation of the debates surrounding law no. 2013-404 of 17 May 2013 opening marriage to same-sex couples, see P. Malaurie and H. Fulchiron, *Droit de la famille*, 8th ed., Lextenso, 2023, pp. 159 ff. and ref. cit.

the eyes of jurists and 'child specialists', there were no words harsh enough to condemn this project. In order to calm tempers, a fact-finding mission was entrusted to a Member of Parliament accustomed to sensitive subjects, who cautiously stripped the project of its substance and placed mediation at the heart of his proposals.

The debate resumed the day after the legislature adopted the 17 May 2013 law on marriage for all. With the 'homosexual question' settled, one might have thought that spirits would have calmed down: after all, less than ten years after the vote, amid much noise and fury over the law on marriage for all, the opening-up of medically assisted procreation to female couples, and then adoption to all couples, took place in a relatively consensual climate.[84]

But when the subject came back into the spotlight, some critics denounced a new stage in the dismantling of family structures. Drawing largely on proposals made by a commission chaired by Irène Théry and Anne-Marie Leroyer,[85] a draft law on parental authority and the interests of the child suggested, instead of creating a 'status' for step-parents, offering families a 'palette' of flexible, evolving and adaptable instruments that could be put in place on a contractual basis or, if necessary, by court order.[86] These included the creation of an 'education mandate' enabling step-parents to carry out a certain number of acts, reinforcement of the powers of the third party to whom the judge has entrusted responsibility for the child (in the event, for example, of a parent's failure to act or death), and more flexible rules for delegated sharing. Passed on first reading by the French National Assembly, the bill subsequently disappeared.

Resistance remains strong. Now, a new debate is looming on the horizon, which is also likely to collide with the debate on step-parents. A new revolution in family law is underway: that of the 'plural' family. This represents a new challenge for family law: to move away from the binary system in which our law has, for centuries, conceived of and constructed the family; two spouses, or two cohabitants, parents, family lines, etc., may open up to encompass new forms of family life based on the plurality of ties.[87]

84 Law no. 2022-219 of 21 February 2022 aimed at reforming adoption.

85 I. Théry and A.-M. Leroyer, 'Filiation, origines, parentalité. Le Droit face aux nouvelles valeurs de responsabilité générationnelle', Ed. Odile Jacob, 2014.

86 Bill on parental authority and the interests of the child, no. 1856, tabled at the National Assembly on 1 April 2014.

87 The issue is only just emerging in France, whereas it is the subject of major studies in other countries, particularly in North and South America. Two distinct issues need to be distinguished: that of plurality of the link (link of the same or similar nature linking one person to several persons, e.g. spouses living in a polyamorous situation or a child in the context of a parental project involving several persons who would have filiation links with the different authors of this project), and that of plurality of links, i. e. the coexistence of links of a different nature linking one person to several persons, e.g. spouses living in a

And yet, while our legal thinking on the family has gradually freed itself, not without difficulty, from the male/female binary, this legal thinking has great difficulty in going beyond duality to consider plurality. As proof of this, the model of the conjugal couple *'à deux'* remains the reference model for all couples, whether married or unmarried, different-sex or same-sex. It continues in the model (the myth) of the conjugal couple surviving the break-up of the parental couple: two parents forever; two parents – not one less, not one more. As for filiation, here again, dual normality prevails, even in homoparental families: two parents who, because they have begotten a child, commit to each other, and to the child and society, to assume their responsibility as parents.

More and more often, however, the question arises of a parental project constructed by several people, and consequently of the child' s attachment to the different people who conceived this project together: a 'polyparenthood' that would link the child, for example, to two women and a man, or to two men and a woman, or even, in certain cases of 'crossed' parentage, to a couple of men and a couple of women.[88]

While some legal systems seem intent on building new forms of kinship, in France, reflection on the subject is only just beginning. And there is a real risk that future debates on the plural family will give rise to the same tensions between parenthood and 'pluriparenthood' (should we enshrine a plurality of filial ties or go for pluriparentality?) that arose in earlier debates; we may find the same false oppositions between parents and 'third parties', and use the child's best interests to reject the new forms of 'multiple' parenthood that are emerging here and there.

For all that, if the proposed projects pass, the need to address the role of step-parent and other third parties remains. We can only hope that, in the 50 years to come, the issue of step-parents will finally be addressed 'for its own sake'.

---

polyamorous situation or a child in the context of a parental project involving several persons who would have filiation links with the different authors of this project (i.e. the coexistence of ties of different kinds linking one person to several others (the child, its parents and the gamete donor or surrogate mother, or, for our purposes, the child, its parents and the step-parent(s))).

88 See G. Kessler, 'De la pluriparenté à la pluriparenté' in *Les métamorphoses du droit de la famille, Hommage à Jacqueline Rubellin-Devichi*, Éditions Edilaix, 2023, pp. 203 ff. In British Columbia, for example, multiple parenthood is enshrined in law (Family Law Act, SBC 2011, c 25, Art. 30–36), as it is in Ontario (Law reforming children's rights, LRO 1990, c C12, Arts. 4, 6–13). Approved by referendum, the new Family Code was adopted in September 2022 (Ley 156/2022 'Código de las Familias' (GOC-2022-919-O99)), and it is also broadly open to multiple parenthood, to the benefit of children born within the framework of a parental project constructed by several parents.

5. THE EVOLUTION OF FRENCH FAMILY LAW ON VULNERABLE PERSONS (ADULTS/MINORS OUTSIDE THE SCOPE OF PARENTHOOD)

5.1. THE EVOLUTION OF THE CHILD'S AUTONOMY IN FRENCH LAW[89]

Regarding children, the difficulty of every lawmaker is to strike a balance between children's quest for autonomy and their need for protection, resulting from their young age and consequent vulnerability. Over the last 50 years, numerous French legislative changes have increased the autonomy of children, particularly regarding new technologies and the opportunity to make their voices heard, thanks to the UN Convention on the Rights of the Child, signed in 1989, and the General Data Protection Regulation (GDPR) of 2016.

Firstly, the French legislature has incorporated into the Civil Code provisions resulting from Article 12 of the UN Convention, allowing minors to express their feelings and be heard in court. According to Article 12(1), 'States Parties shall assure to the child who is capable of forming his or her own views the right to express those views freely in all matters affecting the child, the views of the child being given due weight in accordance with the age and maturity of the child.' In the French Civil Code, Article 371-1, al. 4, states that '[p]arents shall involve their children in decisions that concern them, according to their age and degree of maturity.' The criteria are the same in the UN Convention and the French Civil Code, but the formulation of the disposition in the Civil Code is not quite as protective: it expresses, rather than a right for the child, an invitation to the parents, which seems purely symbolic without any sanctions for non-compliance.

Concerning the right to be heard, according to Article 12(2) of the UN Convention, 'the child shall in particular be provided the opportunity to be heard in any judicial and administrative proceedings affecting the child, either directly, or through a representative or an appropriate body, in a manner consistent with the procedural rules of national law'. Article 388-1 of the French Civil Code reiterates the possibility of being heard but sets the condition that the child must be discerning. Previously, French law only provided for the child to be heard concerning educational assistance, in the former Article 1183 of the Code of Civil Procedure. However, several limitations restrict the effectiveness of the minor's right to be heard, including those concerning the discerning condition – who needs to assess this condition and how? – and the fact that a

[89] Margot Musson, PhD in Law, research and teaching fellow, University Jean Moulin Lyon 3, Family Law Centre, Research Team Louis Josserand.

procedure must already have been initiated, even though the child themselves cannot go to court.

Secondly, following the GDPR, the French Information Technology, *Data* Files and Civil Liberties Act of 1978 was modified to incorporate Article 8 of the EU regulation, according to which, '[i]n relation to the offer of information society services directly to a child, the processing of the personal data of a child shall be lawful where the child is at least 16 years old.' Because the GDPR allowed for Member States to provide by law for a lower age than 16, Article 45 of the French Law now states that children over 15 years old can consent to their personal data being processed. Such disposition recognises digital autonomy for children who are judged to be mature enough to understand the consequences of data processing, although giving children autonomy is always risky, especially regarding their personal data.

This law explains why the French legislature limited this autonomy with a bill in 2023, according to which a child under 15 years old cannot register on a social network unless one of their parents agrees. It also states that providers of online social networking services must provide, to users, information on the risks associated with digital use and the means of prevention of such risks, and information about the conditions of use of their data, and their rights. The fact remains that this provision appears difficult to implement regarding the technological means to check the user's age. The French Audiovisual and Digital Communication Regulatory Authority is to establish a reference framework to guide the choice of appropriate technical solutions.

5.2. THE EVOLUTION OF FRENCH LEGAL PROTECTION OF ADULTS[90]

Over the last 50 years, French legal protection of adults has evolved, but has not been revolutionised. The law is still seeking to strike a satisfactory balance between the autonomy and protection of vulnerable persons. Since the last significant reform in 2007,[91] the legislature has pursued at least three different goals: guaranteeing greater autonomy for vulnerable adults, limiting recourse to the judge as much as possible, and encouraging protection within the family.

Vulnerable persons' autonomy, and respect for their rights, are at the heart of all concerns, mostly due to the influence of the ECHR, the recommendations of the Council of Europe's Committee of Ministers, and – more recently – the Convention on the Rights of Persons with Disabilities. Although French law

[90] Guillaume Millerioux, associate professor at Polytechnic University Hauts-de-France and Marie Pincet, PhD student at University Jean Moulin Lyon III, Family Law Centre, Research Team Louis Josserand.

[91] Law no. 2007-308 'reforming the legal protection of adults' (5 March 2007).

has considered the protected adult's autonomy primarily in terms of the adult's capacity for independent decision-making, the law is increasingly providing mechanisms enabling the individual to anticipate their own protection, and even, more broadly, their vulnerability. France has set up various mechanisms to anticipate any potential alteration in mental or physical faculties that might prevent the expression of one's wishes. These reassuring mechanisms are designed to enable people who are not under protective supervision to ensure that their decisions, choices and wishes will be heard and respected when they are no longer capable of looking after their own interests.

The best-known legal provision is undoubtedly the *'mandat de protection future'*, a fully fledged protection measure created by the 2007 reform. Inspired by foreign legislation,[92] the *'mandat de protection future'* enables a person to preventively designate one or more agents to represent them should they no longer able to look after their own interests due to an alteration to their personal faculties. The 2007 reform also introduced the possibility for adults to designate their protector in advance, before their faculties are impaired, and the judge is bound by the adult's choice, unless the appointment is not in their best interests, or the person concerned refuses to take on the role or finds it impossible to do so.[93] In the medical field, there are several ways of anticipating not just the patient's protection but also their vulnerability. Created in 2002,[94] the system of the 'person of trust', or 'trusted support person' *('personne de confiance')* enables any adult to designate a trusted support person[95] who has a dual role: he/ she is consulted if the person is unable to express their wishes,[96] and can help the patient to make decisions, if so desired.[97] Since 2015,[98] this mechanism has been extended to the social and medico-social domains. Complementing these mechanisms, it has been possible, since 2005,[99] for any adult to draw up advance directives *('directives anticipées')* – directives that have, in theory, been binding on doctors.[100] These directives, regarding the end of life, make it possible to

---

92 Quebec (1990) and Germany (1990) had already introduced mechanisms for anticipating protection: respectively, the *'mandat en cas d'inaptitude'*, which can be translated as 'mandate in case of incapacity', and the *'vorsorgevollmatch'*, which can be translated as 'mandate for foresight'.

93 Art. 448 of the French Civil Code.

94 Law no. 2002-303 'on patients' rights and the quality of the healthcare system' (4 March 2002).

95 Art. L.1111-6 of the French Public Health Code specifies that the trusted support person may be a relative, a close friend or a general practitioner.

96 Ibid., Art. L. 1111-6, para. 1.

97 Ibid., Art. L. 1111-6, para. 2.

98 Law no. 2015-1776 'on adapting society to ageing' (28 December 2015).

99 Law no. 2005-370 'on patients' rights and the end of life', also called the 'Leonetti Law' (22 April 2005).

100 There are two exceptions to Article L.1111-11 of the French Public Health Code: life-threatening emergencies and cases where 'advance directives appear to be manifestly inappropriate or inconsistent with the medical situation'.

respect the wishes expressed by patients who were capable of acting in their own interests at the time they drew up the provisions.[101]

This overview of mechanisms for anticipating vulnerability, while not exhaustive, may seem misleading. Although these mechanisms have multiplied over the last 50 years, this does not mean that French people are taking advantage of them. The lack of effectiveness of these mechanisms, observed by professionals[102] and the Défenseur des droits,[103] can be partly[104] explained by sociological factors:[105] French people are afraid to think about their future vulnerability. A wide-ranging debate on these anticipation mechanisms would, therefore, be worthwhile, since anticipation is undoubtedly the best way for protected adults to ensure that their wishes will be respected when they are no longer able to act in their own interests.

In addition to these anticipatory mechanisms, and without going into details, other changes have also improved the autonomy of vulnerable persons. It should be noted that only an impairment of personal faculties can justify limiting an adult's legal capacity, and so this excludes cases of profligacy (unless it results from a mental disorder). In other words, the grounds for reducing legal capacity have narrowed. The Civil Code now contains a general regime for personal acts for which the adult is, in principle, autonomous,[106] but where assistance or representation can be provided by way of exception, and a list of 'strictly personal acts' for which the person cannot be assisted or represented.[107] Since 2019, a judge has no longer been able to withdraw the voting rights of an adult under guardianship.[108]

One of the legislature's concerns in recent years has been to limit recourse to the courts as much as possible. For this reason, the legislature has abolished several prior judicial authorisations. These abolitions give people greater freedom (tying in with the first goal), and are intended to refocus judges on their main function: avoiding litigation. For instance, it is no longer necessary to apply to a judge to get married: the vulnerable person must only inform the

---

101 Art. L.1111-25 of the French Public Health Code refers more specifically to 'the conditions for continuing, limiting, stopping or refusing medical treatment or procedures'.

102 In its report, 'Removing the obstacles to the development of the *mandat de protection future*: proposals from the notarial profession' (2022), the Conseil supérieur du notariat sought to explain the lack of success of the '*mandat de protection future*' in France.

103 Reports by the French Défenseur des droits, 'Legal protection for vulnerable adults' (2016) and 'The fundamental rights of elderly people in residential establishments for the dependent elderly' (2021).

104 There are many other factors that may explain the ineffectiveness of vulnerability anticipation mechanisms, including a lack of publicity, ill-defined roles, inconsistencies in operation, insufficiently defined exceptions to the mechanisms, etc.

105 See 'Removing the obstacles to the development of the *mandat de protection future*', above n. 100, p. 11.

106 Art. 459 of French Civil Code.

107 Ibid., Art. 458.

108 Abolition of Art. L.5 of the French Electoral Code since Law no. 2019-222 (23 March 2019).

person responsible for their protection of their plans to marry.[109] Along the same lines, the person under guardianship no longer needs the judge's authorisation to enter a civil union pact,[110] or to divorce.[111]

Finally, the legislature wants protection to be provided by family members rather than professionals. In this respect, the creation of 'family authorisations' *('habilitations familiales')*, in 2015,[112] is significant because only some members of the person's family can be appointed by the judge to ensure their protection.[113] These new measures are more customisable than other civil measures of protection, and offer greater freedom to the person responsible for protection (because they have fewer obligations, and can carry out certain serious acts without the intervention of a judge). Accordingly, these measures have been the most widely used in France in recent years, replacing guardianships.

What will happen next? What will the law on the legal protection of adults look like in 50 years' time? The Convention on the Rights of Persons with Disabilities will certainly influence other reforms to come, and perhaps, as recommended in a report commissioned by the government in 2018,[114] guardianship will be abolished.

5.3. THE EVOLUTION OF FRENCH LAW TO TAKE ACCOUNT OF PEOPLE WITH DISABILITIES[115]

After its gradual integration into everyday language over the course of the twentieth century, the word 'disability' made its first appearance in an official French text in 1957.[116] The juxtaposition of the words 'law' and 'disability' is even more recent.[117] In the history of disability and its related law, the evolutions of vocabulary, mentalities and legislation seem inseparable. The post-war period marked the start of a long and gradual evolution in society's treatment of disabled people. The last five decades, characterised by major legislative reforms, have seen a profound change in the way people with disabilities are perceived, as well as changes in the methods of their integration into society. A gradual shift

109 Art. 460 of French Civil Code.

110 Ibid., Art. 462.

111 Ibid., Art. 249.

112 Order no. 2015-1288 'simplifying and modernising family law' (15 October 2015).

113 Arts. 494-1 ff of the French Civil Code.

114 A. Caron-Déglise, 'Changes in the legal protection of adults, Recognising, supporting and protect the most vulnerable people', Interministerial mission report, 2018.

115 Hugo Bordin-Escharavil, PhD student at University Jean Moulin Lyon 3, Family Law Centre, Research Team Louis Josserand.

116 Law no. 57-1223 of 23 November 1957 on the professional reclassification of disabled workers.

117 A. Dessertine, Colloque 'Droit et handicap', TGI de Créteil, 1981.

is taking place, from a logic of assistance, or even charity, to one of insertion and social inclusion.

The law of 30 June 1975, '*d'orientation en faveur des personnes handicapées*',[118] undoubtedly marked the beginning of a paradigm shift in 'disability law'. Although the text did not define the word 'disability', it did for the first time emphasise the need to give priority, wherever possible, to the integration of disabled people into an ordinary environment. In the absence of a definition, the task of deciding who should (or should not) be recognised as disabled was entrusted to the COTOREP and the CDES,[119] which, throughout their existence, were the subject of much criticism and discussion. A little over a decade passed before the 10 July 1987 law '*en faveur de l'emploi des personnes handicapées*'[120] adjusted a number of old measures deemed ineffective and ill-adapted to sociological and economic realities.[121] In particular, the law introduced the '*obligation d'emploi des travailleurs handicapés*' (OETH),[122] requiring all companies with more than 20 employees to hire at least 6 per cent disabled workers. This innovation led to the creation of Agefiph[123] to manage the Fonds de développement de l'insertion professionnelle des handicapés. Very recently, the legislature introduced a reform of the OETH, which came into force in 2020,[124] allowing all forms of employment (trainees, periods of work experience, etc.) to be included in the calculation of this obligation.

It was not until 2005, with the law '*pour l'égalité des droits et des chances, la participation et la citoyenneté des personnes handicapées*',[125] that the French legislature finally established a definition of 'disability' for the first time. The law of 11 February 2005 stipulates that 'a handicap is any limitation of activity or restriction of participation in society suffered in its environment by a person due to a substantial, lasting or definitive impairment of one or more physical, sensory, mental, cognitive or psychic functions, a multiple handicap or a disabling health disorder'. The contribution of this definition is considerable, since the legislature has made it possible to encompass a far greater number of disorders and pathologies within the notion of disability by no longer limiting

---

118 Law no. 75-534 of 30 June 1975 on the orientation of disabled persons.

119 Technical Commissions for Reclassification Guidance (COTOREP) and Departmental Commissions for Special Education (CDES).

120 Law no. 87-517 of 10 July 1987 on employment of disabled workers.

121 C. Hamonet, 'Chapitre VI. Droit et handicap' in C. Hamonet (ed), *Les personnes en situation de handicap*, Presses Universitaires de France, 2016, pp. 77–98.

122 Obligation to employ disabled people.

123 Association nationale de gestion du fonds pour l'insertion professionnelle des personnes handicapées (National association for the management of the fund for the professional integration of disabled people).

124 Law no. 2018-771 of 5 September 2018 'for the freedom to choose one's professional future'.

125 Law no. 2005-102 of 11 February 2005 'for equal rights and opportunities, participation and citizenship for people with disabilities'.

it to physical or mental handicaps.[126] The law's other innovation, influenced by international texts, is the beginning of a break with the strictly medical approach to disability, with the inclusion of a social and environmental approach. In most cases, the aim of the text is to enable people with disabilities to remain in an ordinary environment whenever possible (whether at school, at work, etc.). In response to the shortcomings of the 13 July 1991 law '*pour favoriser l'accessibilité aux personnes handicapées des locaux d'habitation, des lieux de travail et des installations recevant du public*',[127] the 2005 legislation introduced an accessibility obligation that applies to the various components of community life (housing, public services, etc.), but which still faces numerous obstacles.

In summary, the early 2000s marked a radical paradigm shift in disability law and policy, both internationally (EU Directive 2000/78/EC and the UN's 2006 Convention on the Rights of Persons with Disabilities) and nationally. While these major legislative changes have led to the better integration of disabled people into education and employment, progress in terms of accessibility, more appropriate compensation systems and a better understanding of the different types of disability still too often leave much to be desired. Ambitious changes – and more effective and efficient standards – are needed to bring us closer to a truly inclusive society.

---

126 F. Mananga, 'La réforme des droits des personnes handicapées: une réalité juridique entachée de quelques incertitudes dans l'application', *Journal du droit des jeunes*, vol. 257, no. 7, 2006, 33.

127 Law no. 91-663 of 13 July 1991 on various measures to promote disabled access to residential premises, workplaces and facilities open to the public.

ITALY

FIFTY YEARS OF ITALIAN FAMILY LAW

Federica GIARDINI

Résumé

Les cinquante dernières années ont été caractérisées par une importante évolution de la société italienne en général, mais aussi en tant que société insérée dans un vaste contexte européen et international. En conséquence, l'évolution du droit italien de la famille au cours des dernières années peut être définie comme une mutation d'époque. Tout en maintenant ses propres traditions juridiques, dont le système juridique italien conserve des particularités précises, le droit italien de la famille a profondément changé et certains événements marquants peuvent être identifiés dans cette évolution. Après l'introduction du divorce en 1970, la grande réforme du droit de la famille de 1975 a eu un profond effet sur les relations entre époux et sur la relation parentale envers les enfants. Entre 2012 et 2014, la réforme de la filiation a eu une incidence considérable non seulement sur la notion d'enfant, en rendant égaux tous les enfants, nés ou non en mariage, devant la loi, mais aussi sur la notion même de famille au sens juridique dans le système légal italien.

La réforme de la procédure civile dans le domaine de la famille est en cours (à l'heure où nous écrivons). La loi prévoit une délégation au gouvernement pour l'adoption de décrets d'application de grande envergure, qui traitent notamment du droit de la famille. Les profonds changements sociétaux et juridiques qui ont caractérisé le droit de la famille italien au cours des cinquante dernières années correspondent également à un profond renouvellement des sources du droit dans le domaine de la famille. Le rôle de la jurisprudence au cours des dernières décennies n'est plus ce que la tradition juridique enseigne, c'est-à-dire l'application et l'interprétation de la loi. En matière familiale, elle s'est transformée depuis longtemps en une véritable source de la règle juridique. Il s'agit d'un phénomène de grande importance d'un point de vue technique, mais aussi d'un point de vue culturel et social. La présente contribution se propose d'analyser ce phénomène, en tenant compte non seulement de la perspective italienne, mais aussi de la perspective européenne, et avec une vision comparative des institutions et des principes élaborés par la tradition juridique dite occidentale.

1. INTRODUCTION: THE TRADITION OF ITALIAN FAMILY LAW AS ESSENTIALLY MATRIMONIAL LAW

The history of Italian family law over the last 50 years has been characterised by profound changes. The importance of the family as the founding nucleus of Italian society finds its precise consecration in the Italian Constitution of 1948, which in Article 29 recognises the family as a 'natural society founded on marriage'. Under the Italian Civil Code of 1942, and even after the great family law reform of 1975 (which will be discussed below), marriage was the sole basis of the family in a legal sense, and was the institution that gave rise to all legal relationships of a family nature

During this period, Article 29 of the Constitution provided the only legal definition of family, and Italian legal doctrine opposed the recognition of family forms other than those based on the marriage of a man to a woman. This situation continued until the reform of filiation, between 2012 and 2014.

The evolution of Italian society over the last 50 years has required important interventions by the legislature to adapt the overall structure of the Italian legal system in the family context. In the following pages, this chapter analyses some of the most important stages of this profound change. In the conclusions, the chapter highlights what is perhaps the greatest critical issue that the Italian legal system faces today, not only in the family context: that of a necessary adaptation, through reform, of the process of formation of the legal rule. But let us go step by step.

2. THE GREAT REFORM OF FAMILY LAW OF 1975 (LAW NO. 151 OF 19 MAY 1975)

As stated above, the last 50 years of Italian family law have been characterised by profound changes. The first of these, chronologically, occurred in 1975. After a legislative process lasting almost nine years, the Italian Parliament approved what is now remembered as the great reform of Italian family law – the one introduced by law 19 May 1975, no. 151. This law took a decisive step towards concretely implementing Article 29 of the Italian Constitution, according to which 'marriage is based on the moral and legal equality of the spouses'. The Italian family was no longer conceived as an entity at the top of which is the husband, who until then maintained the role of head of the family, in some ways heir to the 1,000-year-old figure of the paterfamilias of Roman law. Until this reform, Article 144 of the Civil Code had provided that the husband/father was 'the head of the family', and that 'the wife follows his civil condition, she assumes his surname and is obliged to accompany him wherever he deems appropriate to establish her residence'.

The reform modified many Articles of the Civil Code of 1942. It introduced the principle that the family residence and the direction of family life were to be decided together by husband and wife. With marriage, the husband and wife each acquired the same rights and assumed the same duties (new Article 143). However, the equality of the spouses was not absolute. Some important critical issues remained. The wife acquired the ability to keep her own surname upon marriage, but was also required to add that of her husband to her own surname (Article 143-*bis*). The surname of the new family was, by law, only that of the man. Even if, after the reform, a woman who married a foreigner no longer lost her Italian citizenship, as in the past (Article 143-*ter*), the substantial inequality between men and women also remained in some aspects of the legal discipline of the reform concerning the children.

From an economic point of view, the Civil Code of 1942 provided for a family structure according to which the woman was economically dependent on her husband. Italian society at the time of the code – post-war society – was a society in which women rarely worked outside the home and instead carried out housework and childcare tasks. To better protect the position of women, the 1975 law provided that 'a woman's work is considered equivalent to that of a man', and introduced a new legal family property regime: that of the legal community of property between spouses. Until then, the separation of property between husband and wife had been in force. According to the reform, both spouses were 'required, each in relation to their assets and their ability to work professionally or at home, to contribute to the needs of the family' (new Article 143, Civil Code). The new law introduced the community property regime between spouses, subject to a different choice being made on their part, which could be made at the time of the marriage celebration, or even subsequently, during the marriage.

The 1975 reform also sought to implement greater equality between men and women by equalising the roles of the two parents with respect to their children. The new law replaced the power exercised by the father with a power 'exercised by mutual agreement by both parents' (new Article 316, Civil Code). And parents no longer only had the obligation 'to support, instruct and educate their offspring', but also had to do so, 'taking into account the abilities, natural inclinations and aspirations of their children' (new Article 147, Civil Code). Profound differences remained regarding the status of children born inside and outside marriage, who were defined as legitimate children and natural children, respectively. The reform eliminated much of the discrimination concerning the inheritance rights of natural children compared with children born in marriage (legitimate children), but other distinctions remained, and would be eliminated only with filiation reform over the years 2012 to 2014.[1] For example, based on Article 537 of the Civil Code, legitimate children could liquidate in money the inheritance share of their natural children – the so-called right of '*commutazione*' – to prevent them from entering into hereditary communion with the deceased's marital family.

3. THE INNOVATIONS REGARDING DIVORCE INTRODUCED IN THE 1970s AND 1980s: TOWARDS PROGRESSION IN CIVIL RIGHTS

The institution of divorce was introduced in Italy only in 1970, with Law 898 of 1 December 1970. Having survived a subsequent referendum, called in 1974, to attempt to repeal the divorce legislation, the introduction of divorce represents a watershed in the evolution of Italian family law, between the era before divorce and the era following its introduction.

When talking about divorce in Italy, distinctions must be made, linked to the type of marriage being referred to. In the Italian legal system, there are two forms of marriage: the civil one and the concordat one. The latter is religious marriage that also has civil effects, introduced into the Italian legal system in

[1] See *infra*, section 6.

1929 through the Lateran Pacts, an international treaty concerning the relations between the Italian State and the Catholic Church. In relation to this distinction, this chapter, according to law, will speak of both the dissolution of the marital bond and the cessation of civil effects.

Italian law talks about dissolution of marriage when the divorce occurs with respect to civil marriage, celebrated before the civil registrar, and speaks of termination of the civil effects of marriage when the divorce affects the concordat marriage (i.e. as already mentioned, the marriage celebrated church – at the beginning only a catholic one, in 1929 – and transcribed in the civil status registers, with both civil and religious effects). In the latter case, divorce only affects the civil effects of marriage, but the religious effects remain intact, since, for the Catholic Church, marriage is an indissoluble sacrament.

A peculiarity of the Italian legal system compared with other systems is that, with rare exceptions (criminal sentences, annulment or dissolution of the marriage or new marriage of a foreign spouse abroad, failure to consummate the marriage (inconsummation), sex change), even today, divorce cannot be obtained directly (through the relevant judicial proceedings), but in most cases can only be granted after a period of marital separation, which is the subject of a distinct and independent procedure with prerequisites, and consequences other than divorce. The separation can be consensual – that is, based on an agreement between the spouses – then approved by the court, or judicial – obtained through an adversarial proceeding before the court itself, which ends with a separation order.

As noted above, the Law on Divorce is considered, without a doubt, to be an important turning point in modern Italian history. The battles for civil rights, supported by popular consensus, have produced a fundamental institution in our legal system – divorce – which is the basis and foundation of the freedom of personal self-determination expressly sanctioned by the Constitution. In an overall evaluation of this historical period, the Law on Divorce was a first step towards legal reforms that undermined obsolete patriarchal privileges and propelled the Italian legal system towards recognition of new civil rights. As seen above, with the 1975 reform and the introduction of the new family law, paternal authority ceased, and was replaced by the parental authority of both parents (although the law still spoke only of parents who were spouses). In addition, the new family law recognised the equality of spouses and reduced discrimination against children born out of wedlock compared with children conceived during marriage. 1978 was also a year full of essential legislative innovations. The law on voluntary termination of pregnancy[2] allowed abortion in Italy in the cases expressly provided for by the new legislation. Also in 1978,

2 Law 22 May 1978, no. 194.

Parliament established the National Health Service,[3] which provided for prevention, treatment and rehabilitation services, constituting substantial progress towards the protection of the right to health.

Initially, Italians used the new Law on Divorce with prudence, and this attitude continued for several decades, even after reform in 1987. During the 1970s and 1980s in Italy, no more than 15,000 divorces were pronounced per year, a much lower proportion (between a fifth and a tenth) of the cases recorded in France, Germany or the United Kingdom.

The 1970 Divorce Law was modified by Laws 436/1978 and 74/1987. With these, the procedure was simplified, the time required to request a divorce after being separated was reduced (from five to three years), and the judge was given the power to issue a partial order declaring the definitive dissolution of the marital bond or the termination of the civil effects of marriage – that is, divorce – in advance of, and separately from, the discussion of further conditions, such as those on economic issues, child custody and more. In this way, the new law sought to discourage litigation tactics designed to delay the dissolution of the marital bond.

Many further reforms have reshaped divorce litigation. Article 709-*bis* of the Civil Procedure Code, for example, introduced in 2005, recognised the possibility of pronouncing a partial order on separation; that is, granting the legal separation while reserving judgement on other issues.

In 2014, the government, as part of a more general aim of 'civil justice reform', adopted the Legislative Decree of 12 September 2014, no. 1324 – later converted into Law no. 162 of 10 November 2014 – which provided for two distinct procedures, arbitration and assisted negotiation, with the declared objective of 'simplifying' the procedures for the personal separation of spouses, dissolution of marriage and termination of civil effects, as well as modification of the conditions of separation and divorce.

As part of the broader aim of dejurisdictionalisation in these topics and other interventions explicitly designed to reduce the backlog in civil proceedings and lighten the workload of the courts and tribunals, the Italian legislature offered the parties the possibility of referring pending civil proceedings on available rights (not in matters of employment, social security and social assistance) to the judgement of arbitrators. The parties can also negotiate an agreement, with the assistance of lawyers, which produces the same effects as judicial proceedings addressing legal separation, termination of the civil effects of marriage, dissolution of marriage and modification of the conditions of separation or divorce. From a theoretical point of view, these innovations have made a general principle of the Italian legal system disappear: the principle that the modification of the

[3] Law 23 December 1978, no. 833.

status of persons should find its natural place only in court proceedings. Today, in fact, thanks to these new institutions, the change of status of people, from married to separated, and from separated to divorced (ex-spouse), can also be achieved through administrative measures or streamlined judicial proceedings. Following the introduction of this new legislation on out-of-court agreements on separation and divorce, 27,040 divorces (32.8 per cent of divorces) and 17,668 separations (19.3 per cent) were, in 2015, resolved at the civil registry offices of separations, without any judicial proceedings at all.

In 2015, the duration of the separation necessary before submitting an application for dissolution of marriage was further reduced to one year from the appearance of the spouses before the president of the court, in the case of judicial separation, and six months, in the case of consensual separation (Law 6 May 2015, no. 55, the so-called law on 'short-term divorce'). This was the so-called introduction of 'short divorce'. It resulted in a significant increase in the number of divorces, which, in 2015 alone, reached 82,469 (57 per cent more than in 2014), and in 2018 reached 88,458.

In 2018, the United Sections of the Court of Cassation carried out a rereading of Article 5, paragraph 6, of the Law on Divorce, which confirmed the relevance of the post-marital solidarity and divorce allowance as an instrument that fulfils a 'balancing function', which, although not 'aimed at the reconstruction of the intra-marital standard of living', aims at 'recognition of the role and contribution provided by the economically weaker ex-spouse' to the family ménage.

After 50 years, the total number of divorces in Italy had reached 1,463,973 by 2019. According to Istat data, in 2019, 681,000 men and 990,000 women requested divorce in Italy, a notable increase compared with 2011, which saw 524,000 men and 839,000 women initiate divorce proceedings.

Since 28 February 2023, a divorce request can be submitted as part of a separation proceeding and becomes actionable as soon as the deadlines have expired and the separation decree (even if partial) has become final. If the relevant proceeding must continue in order to address the charge, financial issues or child custody, such issues will be dealt with after the non-final ruling on the separation, or could be included in the divorce case.

4. LAW NO. 40 OF 2004 REGARDING MEDICALLY ASSISTED PROCREATION (MAP)

For Italy, 2004 was a year in which Parliament legislated simultaneously in important ways in the fields of personal and family law, but with diametrically opposed approaches. On the one hand, it approved the Law of 19 February 2004, no. 40, which was the first Italian law on medically assisted fertilisation, which, as will be detailed below, was the result of an ideology full of prohibitions and restrictions; on the other hand, it introduced, in the same year, the figure of the support administrator into the legal system, with important support functions that enhanced the autonomy of the individual person.

The general approach of Law 40 of 2004 regarding MAP was extremely restrictive. It allowed the use of medically assisted procreation only 'if there are no other effective therapeutic methods to remove the causes of sterility or infertility'. Heterologous fertilisation (Article 4) – that is, fertilisation using a donor external to the couple – and human cloning were prohibited. Surrogacy in all its forms was prohibited, including the so-called uterus rental. Furthermore, any experimentation on the embryo was prohibited, as was 'any form of selection of embryos and gametes for eugenic purposes'. Article 13 banned the allocation of supernumerary embryos to research and absolutely prohibited the withdrawal of consent to MAP after the fertilisation of the egg had occurred.

It also required that the creation of the embryos must be designed to produce a single and simultaneous implantation, and, in any case, that no more than three embryos be created at a time, and that all of the embryos must be implanted. In fact, the law also prohibited, in general terms, the cryopreservation of embryos, and allowed only the cryopreservation of gametes. The only hypothesis in which cryopreservation was permitted was a case in which the mother's serious and temporary health issues prevented immediate implantation, and in such cases, the cryopreserved embryos needed to be implanted in the mother as soon as possible. Furthermore, the embryo to be implanted could not be selected and, even if not all the embryos could be implanted at the same time, no screening could be conducted to determine which embryo to implant.

Law 40 also prescribed very severe penalties for doctors and health care facilities involved in violations of the rules and prohibitions in the new law. It also established a national registry of all facilities, public and private, authorised to offer assisted procreation techniques. In three years, the registry carried out a complete mapping of such centres and produced homogeneous and reliable statistical data. Following Law 40's enactment, a substantial flow of Italian couples abroad has occurred, to overcome the law's restrictions and prohibitions. This phenomenon has been described as 'reproductive tourism'.

In the meantime, the original structure of the legislation, which has raised serious constitutional doubts since its approval, has been progressively dismantled over the years by a series of decisions from the Italian Constitutional Court.

Among the many questionable points of this law is the ban on pre-implantation genetic diagnosis. This ban affects couples who have well-founded fears of being carriers of hereditary genetic defects, for the simple reason that, regardless of the outcome of the examination, the prospective parent cannot refuse to implant the embryo. The first decision, in 2009,[4] re-established the principle that the doctor has the authority to decide how many eggs to inseminate, in agreement with the couple, taking into account the clinical situation, the age of the woman, and, above all, the need to protect the woman's health, a concern Law 40 ignored. In particular, the Constitutional Court reiterated that the doctor must try to carry out as little stimulation of the woman's ovaries as possible, and, in this way, the Court reintroduced the possibility of freezing embryos – albeit with some limitations. With the subsequent decisions of the Constitutional Court – no. 162 of 2014, no. 96 of 2015 and no. 229 of 2015 – the ban on heterologous fertilisation was repealed, in part, with respect to couples who have been diagnosed with a cause of absolute and irreversible sterility or infertility, and for fertile couples who are carriers of transmissible genetic diseases; at the same time, the Court cancelled the ban on the selection of embryos for therapeutic and diagnostic purposes.

Based on this progressive dismantling of the original structure of the law, today in Italy access to MAP techniques is also allowed for fertile couples with genetic diseases that could be transmitted to their children; further, pre-implantation genetic diagnosis is permitted, both for fertile and infertile couples, in order to discover any genetic anomalies in the embryo, and thus be able to implant only healthy embryos. There is also the possibility of resorting to heterologous fertilisation for heterosexual couples, and cryopreservation is now permitted for embryos that have accidentally been produced in excess, and which can be used by the couple if the first implantation fails, or the couple subsequently wishes to have additional children.

Surrogacy is still prohibited and only heterosexual couples are permitted access to ART techniques. These bans are at the basis of recent legal problems and judicial events involving homosexual couples. In fact, such couples often go abroad to utilise MAP techniques and then ask in Italy for the recognition of the children thus conceived as the children of both parents. This is an open topic, and remains the subject of discussions in the Italian legal system today. It is the opinion of the present writer that any legal provision which provides for bans such as those currently in force in Italy in relation to MAP techniques must necessarily take into account the fundamental rights of which every human being has been the bearer since birth, and that this principle of a general nature, which is also a principle expressed in a solemn way by Article 2 of the Italian Constitution, cannot be derogated from by legal provisions which, in the hierarchy of sources, are subordinate to the Constitution itself.

4 Corte Cost., no. 151 of 2009.

5. THE INTRODUCTION, IN 2004, OF THE SUPPORT ADMINISTRATOR FOR THE PROTECTION OF VULNERABLE PEOPLE: A SUPPORT TOWARDS THE AUTONOMY OF THE PERSON

A fundamental stage in the evolution of the Italian legal system towards the protection of the subject of law understood as a human person was reached with the law of 9 January 2004, no. 6, which introduced the figure of the support administrator (ADS) into Italian law. This introduction has implemented a real legal and cultural revolution in the protection that the Italian legal system provides to fragile people. A new instrument has been added to the more rigid traditional institutions of interdiction and disqualification; this instrument is more flexible, and therefore more adaptable to the specificity of individual situations. The law has the aim of protecting, with the least possible limitation of the ability to act, people deprived, in whole or in part, of autonomy in carrying out the functions of daily life, and carries this out through temporary or permanent support interventions.

Articles 404 *et seq.* introduced this new regulatory framework into the Civil Code. Pursuant to Article 404, support administration can be ordered to provide protection for a person 'who, as a result of an infirmity or a physical or mental impairment, finds himself unable, even partially or temporarily, to provide for his own interests'. The law requires fulfilment of two conditions for the appointment of the ADS: one of a subjective type, which consists of physical or mental impairment; the other of an objective type, which concerns the impossibility of the subject providing for their own interests. These are cumulative preconditions; that is, both must exist, and a causal relationship must exist between them. The person for whose protection the appointment of the ADS is requested must have a physical or mental impairment that does not allow them to take care of their own interests.

Over the years, particularly with respect to the progressive ageing of the population, the ADS has had a great social impact, and resort to the appointment of an ADS has become increasingly common even without a specific infirmity or pathology; that is, in all cases in which the subject lacks autonomy in carrying out the functions of daily life.

In concrete terms, the provision establishing an ADS has been extended to large categories of beneficiaries not expressly mentioned in the 2004 law, but which the subsequent jurisprudence, doctrine and case law has developed into categories that include large sectors of the civil society. Among the subjects who can be beneficiaries of an ADS are people suffering from physical infirmities, such as strokes, degenerative or terminal diseases, physical and motor handicaps, coma conditions and vegetative states or tumour pathologies; and also people affected by mental illnesses and psychological impairments, including psychiatric pathologies, mental retardation, Down syndrome, autism, Alzheimer's disease, dementia, drug abuse, alcohol dependence, prodigality, compulsive shopping, gambling addiction, and many other conditions.

The procedure to establish an ADS can be initiated by the public prosecutor, or by the beneficiary (even if minor, interdicted or disabled), a spouse, a cohabitant, a relative up to the fourth degree, a guardian of the interdicted person, a curator of the disabled person or a civil partner. In addition, a series of subjects have the obligation to start the procedure. They are the managers of health and social services directly involved in the care and assistance of the person in cases where they become aware of facts that make it appropriate to initiate the support administration procedure. They must lodge the appeal pursuant to Article 407 of the Civil Code to the tutelary judge or, alternatively, report relevant developments of which they become aware to the public prosecutor. The procedure takes place before the court (office of the guardianship judge) of the place of residence or domicile of the potential recipient of the measure. Tutelary judges have extensive investigative powers which they can use *ex officio*. At the end of the investigation, the judge then issues a reasoned and immediately enforceable decree.

The choice of the ADS is made by the tutelary judge 'with exclusive regard to the care and interests of the beneficiary'. Any designation of an ADS previously made by the beneficiary must be taken into account, as well as any preference that the beneficiary expresses during the procedure, in the event that they are still capable of doing so. In the absence of these, the judge will consider making the appointment, preferably within the categories established by law, including, among others, a spouse who is not legally separated, a permanent cohabitant, or a father, mother, child, brother, sister or other relative within the fourth degree. Furthermore, in the absence of available administrators from the designated categories, or for good cause, the judge may appoint a third party, who is usually chosen from specific lists established at the individual judicial offices. These lists contain the names of professionals in legal and economic matters who are available to carry out such assignments.

The object of the assignment is set forth in the appointment decree, which identifies the duties of the ADS. The duties are personal and financial, to be understood alternatively or cumulatively, depending on the specific situation. The ADS can, therefore, deal with the care of the person, assisting with any health care choices and relationships with medical staff; the management of the beneficiary's recreational and social activities; and the care of the beneficiary's assets. This latter activity may involve the administration of the beneficiary's assets, salary, pension and securities investments. This asset management activity must have the aim of preserving the individual's assets, so as to be able to satisfy the beneficiary's ordinary and extraordinary needs.

The ADS periodically reports on their activities to the judge, who has the discretion to determine a fair compensation and remunerate the administrator from the beneficiary's assets. If a professional from outside the family is appointed, an annual allowance is provided, taking into account the financial capacity of the beneficiary and the commitment required to carry out the office. In many courts, specific protocols and guidelines have been adopted to guide judges both on the appointment of support administrators and the determination of their compensation.

In recent years, the position of the ADS has lost some of the purposes that inspired the legislature to introduce it in 2004, and has increasingly become a real profession. However, a series of highly worthy initiatives have arisen, throughout Italy, which monitor the the relationship between the number of support administrators and the needs of the population, and carry out voluntary activities in this important sector.[5] In fact, with the progressive ageing of the Italian population, the figure of the ADS is taking on a growing value on a social level, and the related proceedings constitute one of the most important, ever-growing, burdens for the Italian courts. According to the Italian Ministry of Justice, 48,639 support administration procedures were opened between 2020 and 2021 alone. In total – and the figure corresponds to the estimates made by various experts – there are around 350,000 people in Italy who have support administrators, but the indication is that around 500,000 people need to be supported by this institution. The size of the need requires profound reforms, including greater attention to the costs of the ADS, which weigh on the beneficiaries and their families.

6. THE 2012–14 FILIATION REFORM AND ITS CONSEQUENCES ON FAMILY MATTERS AND ON LEGAL PROTECTION OF THE FAMILY IN A LEGAL SENSE

Between 2012 and 2014, the Italian legal system implemented an important reform in the field of family law. This is perhaps the most significant reform approved after the great reform of 1975, both in terms of the areas in which the legislature intervened and in terms of the innovations introduced. The legislative technique used was that of the novelisation of the Civil Code and the complementary laws already in force on the subject. There were many innovations introduced, and some of them constituted, as will be described

5 One of these is that of AIASS ODV, the Italian Association of Solidarity Support Administrators. It is a voluntary, non-profit association, which intends to provide support, assistance and training to support administrators who carry out this function not as a profession, but as a 'service' for vulnerable subjects, deprived wholly or partly of autonomy. See www.aiassonlus.it.

below, an adaptation of the Italian system to the stimuli and developments in family matters that also derive from other European systems.

These reforms were a profound positive innovation in the evolution of the Italian legal system towards the protection of rights, and the meaning of the reforms must be understood, at a general interpretative level, in a much broader and more appreciable way than the individual changes considered in isolation. Indeed, the reforms affected the very notion of family in the Italian legal system, both with respect to its definition and its fundamental structure. No longer is the family legally founded only on marriage, but by separating – as will be described below – the protection of filiation from marriage, the legislature remodelled the family institution from within through two fundamental innovations: the introduction of the uniqueness of the status of the child before the law, and the redefinition of the legal relationship between parents and children, with the replacement of parental authority with the notion of parental responsibility.

With the unification of the status of the child before the law, Italy implemented a principle that has long been adopted at a European level, and through the interventions implemented by the Court of Strasbourg since the end of the 1970s.[6] At the same time, always from a broader perspective, the equalisation of children before the law constitutes the implementation of the principles contained in the Charter of Fundamental Rights of the European Union (EU). Article 21 of the Nice Charter expressly prohibits any discrimination based, in particular, on sex, race, skin colour or ethnic or social origin, or on genetic characteristics, language, religion, personal beliefs, political or any other opinions, or on belonging to a national minority, heritage, birth, disability or sexual orientation. This provision thus outlaws distinctions tied to the circumstances of a child's birth.

The reform regarding filiation was implemented in two distinct moments: through law 10 December 2012, no. 219, and subsequently through Legislative Decree no. 154 of 2013, which came into force on 7 February 2014.

Also, following some important decisions by the Constitutional Court,[7] the reforms implemented a historic and radical change, equalising the legal

6 On the principle of equality of all children before the law, in the jurisprudence of the ECtHR, see, among others, *Markx v. Belgium*, 13 June 1979 (also in Foro it., 1979, IV, c. 342); *Johnston and Others v. Ireland*, 18 December 1986; *Inze v. Austria*, 28 October 1987; *Vermeire v. Belgium*, 29 November 1991; *Mazurek v. France*, 1 February 2000.

7 The reference is, on the one hand, to the Constitutional Court, 18 December 2009, n. 335, regarding the compatibility between the right of commutation and the Italian Constitution, but also to a series of interventions by the same Constitutional Court, dating back over time, which had configured the relationship between natural relatives as a mere factual relationship of consanguinity and not a legal bond of kinship. See, in this last area, Constitutional Court 23 November 2000, n. 532, but also, over time, Constitutional Court 4 July 1979, n. 55;

status of children before the law, whether or not their parents were married to each other at the time of their conception. There are no longer 'legitimate children' – that is, children conceived during marriage – and 'natural children', conceived outside marriage. Only 'children' exist. After the 1975 reform, the process of equalising natural and legitimate children was further continued by the legislature in 2006, which, in dictating the rules regarding parents' shared custody of children following separation and divorce, unified the substantive rules to make them the same as custody proceedings relating to children of unmarried parents (Article 4, para. 2, Law no. 54/2006).

The substantial equality between children and the change in the very notion of kinship were made possible by the fact that the new law radically modified the legal effects of the act of recognition of the child by their parent. It produced legal effects no longer only with regard to the parent by whom it is implemented, but also with regard to their relatives (Article 258, Civil Code). A consequence of this is that, today, the kinship bond exists between people who descend from the same lineage in every form of filiation, whether born inside or outside marriage (Article 74, 1st para. of Civil Code). As stated above, the law also eliminates any difference in terminology, replacing the expressions 'legitimate children' and 'natural children' with a reference solely to 'children'.[8]

From a systematic point of view, in a critical reflection on the innovative scope of the reforms, the unification of the statuses of children desired by the law marks an epochal achievement. For the first time, the full protection of filiation is clearly separated from the institution of marriage. Filiation is protected as an autonomous value, independently of the legal bond that unites the parents and, therefore, independently of the institution of marriage. Children – all children – are protected by the law in every aspect, regardless of whether there they were conceived in marriage.

From this perspective, the reforms constitute a full implementation of the principle of equality established by the Italian Constitution in Article 3, both towards the individual parent and towards the parents' relatives and family members, since they also become relatives and family members, in a broad sense, of the child who has been recognised outside marriage.

Among the other significant consequences of the new approach of the legal system to filiation and the family are matters of inheritance, because the law implements a substantial revision of the rules on necessary and legitimate

---

Constitutional Court 24 March 1988, n. 363; Constitutional Court 12 April 1990, n. 184; Constitutional Court 7 November 1994, n. 377.

8 The specification between differents categories of children remains only in some Articles in which relevance is attributed to birth in or out of marriage (see, e.g. Arts. 337, 252, 254, 262 and others of the Civil Code).

succession, as a consequence of the principle of uniqueness of the status of child, and the new legal notion of kinship. By virtue of this revision, for example, the right of commutation has been abolished; according to Article 537, 3rd paragraph, of the Civil Code, now repealed, this right allowed legitimate children – children who had been conceived during marriage – to settle in money the share of inheritance due to natural children, thus preventing them from entering into the hereditary community.

From a content perspective, the filiation reform also aims to redefine the relationships between the members of the family unit. Compared with what was previously provided, the rights of children are developed and included in a general provision that concerns all children. The right to a family, the right to relationships with relatives and the right to be heard are now regulated in general terms. The right and duty to educate children must be exercised taking into account their abilities, natural inclinations and aspirations; in cases of conflict between the parents on particularly important decisions, each of them will be able to appeal to the court – no longer to the Juvenile Court, but to the Ordinary Court – indicating the solution they deem most appropriate for the child. The decision will be up to the judge, who will also be able to indicate which of the two parents is the most suitable to decide the specific case.

The reform replaces the notion of parental authority with that of 'parental responsibility', which must be exercised by mutual agreement between both parents, whether they are married to each other or not. The previous legal provision which attributed the exclusive exercise of parental authority to the parent who first recognised the child – or with whom the minor cohabited, if the parents were neither married nor cohabiting – is therefore repealed.

The change in perspective desired by the law, in cancelling the notion of parental authority and replacing it with that of parental responsibility, in relationships between parents and children, is extremely significant. The abolition of the notion of power certainly implies, at an interpretative level, the law's desire to remove from the content of the parent–child relationship those authoritarian elements that have always characterised the parental role with respect to their children in different historical periods.

Parental responsibility obviously remains even following separation, dissolution, cessation of civil effects, annulment and nullity of marriage.

As already partially mentioned, with the filiation reform the Italian legislature is completing an important process of adapting the legal system to the needs that civil society has been expressing for years now. The legal protection of filiation, regardless of whether it takes place within a marriage, radically changes the notion of family, in the legal sense, present in the Italian legal system.

A first important step in this direction had already been taken as a result of Law No. 54 of 2006 regarding shared custody of children between parents. In fact, since 2006, the rules for the legal treatment of children in the event of a crisis in the relationship between their parents, whether married or not, had been unified, and the new rule common to all cases, whether concerning children conceived in or out of wedlock, had been that of shared custody of children by both parents. At an interpretative level, then, it could perhaps be said that Italian law had already begun to recognise other forms of family in addition to the traditional one founded on marriage. Only with the reform of filiation, however, was this process, although still perfectible today, completed. In fact, by absolutely separating the legal protection of filiation from the protection granted to marriage, the Italian legal system recognises that marriage is no longer the only legal foundation of the family.

Another peculiarity that deserves to be highlighted is that the Italian legal system achieved this evolution in a different and completely peculiar way compared with any other system in the Western legal tradition. In the latter tradition, the law has gradually introduced, over the last few decades, new titles founding the family in a legal sense, through the introduction of laws on registered partnerships and civil unions.[9] In Italy, this change occurred temporally before any legal regulation of cohabitations and civil unions, and in a different way;[10] that is, through the reform of filiation.

In fact, through the full legal protection of filiation, both inside and outside marriage, Italian law recognises, for all intents and purposes, that filiation can, in itself, constitute a basis for effective and full legal protection, which until now had been limited only to the matrimonial family unit. Starting with the filiation reform, the legal consequences of the equalisation introduced by the law have gone well beyond the express scope of the legislation and now extend fully to the single-parent family formed by one or more children and a single parent. This last nucleus, even without any previous marriage of the parent to a third party, is a family in a legal sense for all intents and purposes. Since the protection is directed towards filiation, and from filiation, the legal relationships today extend by law to the entire branch of the parent's relatives; the single-parent family is a legal family protected, for all purposes, as much as a matrimonial one.

---

[9] On this point, allow me to refer to F. Giardini, 'The Concept of "Legal Family" in Modern Legal Systems: A Comparative Approach' in L.D. Wardle and C.S. Williams, *Family Law: Balancing Interest and Pursuing Priorities*, William S. Hein & Co., Inc., 2007, pp. 73 ff.

[10] The Italian regulatory framework regarding civil unions and cohabitations has, in fact, intervened, only after the reform of filiation, with Law 20 May 2016, no. 76, which entered into force on 5 June 2016. On this point, see section 7 below.

7. THE PROTECTION OF COHABITATION AND THE HOMOSEXUAL FAMILY IN ITALIAN LAW: THE INTRODUCTION OF THE 2016 LAW ON CIVIL UNIONS

The Law of 20 May 2016, no. 76, the so-called Cirinnà law, introduced the institution of civil unions, reserved for the protection of cohabitation between people of the same sex, into the Italian legal system. The law has provided that, in order to ensure the protection of the rights and the fulfilment of the obligations deriving from the civil union between persons of the same sex, the provisions relating to marriage and those containing the words 'spouse' or 'spouses' or equivalent terms, where they occur in laws, will also apply to the parties to a civil union between people of the same sex.

A civil union is established by two adults of the same sex with a declaration made to the civil registrar in the presence of two witnesses. The officer ensures the registration of civil union documents in the civil status archive. The parties, with a declaration to the civil registrar, can indicate a common surname by choosing it from their surnames, and may place their own surname before or after the common surname, if different.

Generally speaking, the forms of protection provided for marriage have been extended to civil unions. Those united civilly acquire the same rights and mutually assume the same duties as married couples. They are required, each in proportion to their assets and capacity for professional and domestic work, to contribute to the common needs of the union. From the civil union derives the mutual obligation to provide moral and material assistance and cohabitation. However, unlike marriage, there is no obligation of loyalty or mutual collaboration.

Like spouses united in marriage, the parties agree on the direction of family life and establish their common residence. Each party has the power to implement the agreed direction. The property regime of a civil union, in the absence of a different property agreement, is – as for marriage – that of community property. A civil union also gives couples inheritance rights.

The dissolution of a civil union will take effect immediately, without any period of separation. Civil unions can, therefore, be dissolved more quickly than marriages. Separation need not be initiated; it is sufficient for the partners to communicate their intention to dissolve their relationship to the civil registrar, even if they do not both join the action. Once three months have passed, the couple can apply for divorce; that is, the dissolution of the civil union. Divorce regulates the partners' property division, with the possibility of recognising the economically weaker party's right to alimony and the assignment of the house in which the couple established their residence.

Italian law also extends protection orders against family abuse to civil unions.

In the event of one civil partner's death at work, the other partner is entitled to the payment of all indemnities provided for by law. In the event of dissolution of the civil union, a partner is entitled to 40 per cent of any severance pay received by their ex-partner in the years in which the bond was in existence, provided that there has been no subsequent marriage or new civil union. The law provides that civil unions are subject to the provisions on conjugal leave; dismissal during marriage; leave for bereavement, for particular events, or to assist the disabled spouse; and also on specific economic treatments to assist a person with a verified disability, priority transformation of the employment relationship from full-time to part-time in the event that there is a need to assist a partner suffering from cancer.

As regards criminal law precisely in order to protect civil unions in the same way in which the law protects marriage, the legislature has introduced a provision similar to that with which, in the civil context, the spouse is equated with the of civil union. In fact, it has been established that, for the purposes of criminal law, the term 'marriage' is considered equivalent to the establishment of a civil union between persons of the same sex.

The aforementioned Law of 20 May 2016, no. 76, in addition to establishing civil unions, which are reserved for homosexual couples, also regulates cohabitation between people regardless of their sex, so that they can formally regulate their coexistence from an economic and legal point of view (Article 1, paras. 36 to 69).

8. THE SO-CALLED CARTABIA REFORM AND NEWS REGARDING FAMILY LAW

The Legislative Decree of 10 October 2022, no. 149 – the so-called Civil Reform Cartabia – takes its name from the former minister of justice of the Draghi government, Marta Cartabia, and has the aim of speeding up civil trials, intervening both on some aspects of procedural process and providing for a progressive increase in the digitalisation of trials. It modifies, in general terms, the civil process, but also affects all special processes that concern minors and the family.

The reform falls within the obligations assumed by Italy towards the EU in the National Recovery and Resilience Plan (PNRR), following the COVID-19 pandemic. It is a general reform of the civil process, which involves every phase and level of judgment. In the context of those innovations introduced by the reform which concern family law, the legislator seems, perhaps for the first time (compared with recent decades), to have adopted an organic vision of the system to be reformed as a whole, to try to overcome that series of interpretative, applicative but simultaneously organisational difficulties for the judicial offices, and for the parties involved in trials, caused by the most recent reforms, since those reforms intervened on the single issue sporadically and not organically.

The reform introduces the figure of a single judge with jurisdiction over all family and minor disputes, thus eliminating the problems relating to the previous system of division of competences between the different courts. The aim, ultimately, is to create a uniform model of civil procedure in the matter of persons, minors and families, applicable to all procedures which have as their object the rights of the person, minors and families (Article 473-*bis et seq.* of the Civil Procedure Code). The institution of listening to minors in proceedings concerning them has been strengthened significantly by the reform, to the point of becoming decisive. Taking into account the minor's age and level of maturity, the minor has the right to express their thoughts in proceedings that concern them. The reform has also defined the cases in which the appointment of a special guardian for the minor is mandatory (for example, where there has been a request for revocation of parental responsibility, formulated by the public prosecutor or the other parent; where foster care of the minor has been arranged outside the family of origin; or where a situation of serious harm to the minor has emerged, in terms of procedural representation), distinguishing these from cases in which the appointment of the minor's special guardian is optional.

The concrete implementation of the reform was planned to take place gradually and in individual phases. For example, starting in March 2023, a new procedure called 'procedure regarding persons, minors and families' came into force, which applies to everyone – both spouses and cohabitants. Before the reform, there were two different procedures. Now, there is one uniform procedure for everyone; that is, for those who are separating, for those who are divorcing, for those who are dissolving a civil union, and for those who are terminating a cohabitation.

The new procedure can be joint – that is, based on the agreement between the two parties – or judicial; where the parties disagree on one or more financial or personal matters relating to minor children, it is mandatory to attach the so-called 'parental plan' provisions from the introductory document – a document in which parents must indicate their children's commitments and daily activities relating to school, extracurricular activities, usual attendance and holidays. With the new procedure, it is possible to request separation and divorce in the same document, but it is not yet possible, in general, to divorce without first separating.[11] The establishment of the single court for individuals, minors and families is expected in December 2024, unifying the skills that

---

[11] The Court of Cassation, with order no. 28727/2023, issued following a preliminary ruling made by the Court of Treviso, admitted the cumulation of requests for separation and divorce also in consensual proceedings, i.e. those proposed on the joint request of the parties (Art. 473-*bis*, 51 civil procedure code).

are currently distributed between the Ordinary Court, the Juvenile Court and the guardianship judge at the Ordinary Court. At the same time as all this, the legislature wanted to strengthen the alternative dispute resolution tools. In this context, the guarantees of impartiality and independence of arbitration have been strengthened, and the scope of assisted negotiation and mediation has been extended. As regards assisted negotiation, already introduced in 2014, it is possible to use this procedure to find a consensual solution between parents on many of the issues that usually cause disputes in the courts. Specifically, this refers to issues concerning custody and maintenance of minor children born out of wedlock, and particularly the methods of maintenance of non-economically self-sufficient adult children born out of wedlock and the modification of the conditions already determined, for the determination of the maintenance allowance requested from parents by the economically non-self-sufficient adult child, and also the determination of maintenance itself. Important innovations have also been introduced regarding the institution of mediation. In fact, the law provides that, with the decree setting the first hearing, the judge is required to inform the parties of the possibility of making use of mediation, with the exception of cases involving gender violence or domestic violence.

9. CONCLUSIONS: FORMATION OF THE LEGAL RULE, ROLE OF THE JUDGE AND NEED FOR REFORMS

The evolution of Italian law in recent decades, particularly in the field of family law, has been characterised more and more clearly by an intervention of the Italian courts as a function of the actual creation of the legal rule. The phenomenon now belongs to what can be defined, without reservation, as 'usual' relationship dynamics between the two formants – the legislative one and the jurisprudential one. The jurisprudence, primarily that of the Supreme Court of Cassation, but also the so-called jurisprudence of merit, is no longer limited to the traditional interpretative work, even of a nomopoietic nature, which for decades has characterised its action within the system, but acts as a true creative source of the rule of law.

The reason behind the phenomenon is that the legal rule, which in its classic explication in a codified system of law like the Italian one is that of the ordinary law of a parliamentary source, is often lacking. It appears incomplete and/or imperfect, barely intelligible, technically perfectible both from a formal point of view – that is, considered in and of itself – and in a broader way, from a systematic point of view. Today, the dynamics of development and implementation of the system of sources of the legal rule require not only – as in the past – to adapt quickly to changed economic and social needs, but also require skills in the formation of the rule, and in the preparation of the correct mechanisms for its implementation, which are clearly unprecedented.

Even the recent Cartabia reform, which from the outset seemed to have a unitary project – an overall consideration of the legal system in which to insert functional changes for the shortening of civil proceedings and the disposal of existing backlogs in the courts – has, unfortunately, created, since the early stages of its entry into force, coordination and application problems that have not yet been resolved.

Private law, and more particularly that sector of private law which perhaps best provides the magnifying glass for knowledge of the relationship not only between policy and the rule of law, but more broadly between society and law, and between institutions (using a civil law expression) and needs – that is, family law, a subject perhaps today more correctly described as 'families law' – is in fact in itself a privileged observation ground for these dynamics.

Even the recent Cartabia reform did not affect the methods of formation of the legal rule as it should have done. It follows that the judge (in the Supreme Court, first of all) often creates a new rule because an existing rule is completely missing, or is inadequate because it does not coordinate with other rules of a substantial and/or procedural nature which are highlighted in the specific case. Jurisprudence fills the gap in the law or makes up for the technical deficiency of the new regulatory provisions.

Consider, among others – but only by way of example – the fact that the reform has introduced the possibility of cumulating the request for separation and divorce in the same proceeding, but only in cases in which the proceeding is contentious, while nothing has been said regarding the consensual procedure; that is, the procedure established on the basis of a joint appeal by the parties. This circumstance, after the jurisprudential conflict that had arisen, forced the Court of Cassation to 'integrate' the scope of the new legislation, clarifying that the cumulation in the proposition of separation and divorce is also applicable to the case of consensual proceedings.[12] This is just one of the many examples of imperfection in the law that could be cited.

The dismantling of the system of sources to which the highlighted phenomenon necessarily leads, from a legal perspective – such as the Italian one, of Roman-Germanic origin and of a civilistic imprint – has been present in the family sector for several decades now. Entire areas of family law are still regulated by jurisprudence today. One of these, a matter with great social impact – that of divorce maintenance – is still, in fact, regulated by the Supreme Court. The divorce settlement story is too well known to be explored here.

---

12 The intervention of the Supreme Court of Cassation was carried out in October 2023, with order no. 28727/2023, above n. 11.

It saw the Supreme Court of Cassation express its opinion in 1990, in the United Sections,[13] and specifically dictate the new criteria underlying the attribution and quantification of the allowance. The subsequent legal events led to a sentence with which the same Court of Cassation, in 2017, seemed to express, albeit in a simple section, the new regulations.[14] In the context of the contradictions and uncertainty dictated by the contrast between decisions necessarily followed in the Courts of Appeal, but also in the lower ones, the legislative attempt to regain control of the matter was wrecked through the approval of a statute which did not pass overall parliamentary scrutiny, as it stalled after approval in one of the two chambers. And this situation continued until the subsequent ruling of the United Sections of the Supreme Court, in 2018,[15] which in fact still regulates the matter today.

The problem of the quality of the legal rule can no longer be treated as a secondary issue. Legal certainty and economic investments are factors that base their implementation on the technical quality of the legal rule, and the technical quality of the rule is a *sine qua non* for its correct application, and for a procedural model that allows its rapid implementation. The formation process of the legal rule is today based, in an almost essential way, on soft law studies, having a historical-comparative basis, which allow the impact of the rule to be predicted in detail *ex ante* (and not 'suffered' *ex post*) in the system, as the socio-economic cost of its future application. On the contrary, the inadequacy of the traditional mechanisms of formation of the legal rule have repercussions in a constant and systematic way in every area in which they claim to have an impact, and today more than yesterday in the area of protection of personal rights. Legal comparisons also suggest the need to contribute to the process of correct formulation of the legal rule through the creation of a constitutional body whose activity is institutionally preordained to create model laws in the various sectors of the legal system, which can then be adopted by the legislative body. The English Law Commission, which has been operating – as is known – since the 1960s, and which is a type of organism present in many common law realities, is certainly a model from which to draw inspiration.[16] In a time of constitutional reforms, such as the one that seems to be appearing in Italy today (at least on the forms of government), in reality, and perhaps before anything else, it seems no longer possible to put off the fact of technically pondering the introduction of a change in the procedure of law formation, in order to bring the systems that require it – and the Italian one is certainly

[13] SS.UU. 11490/1990.

[14] Cass, sez. I, n. 11504/2017.

[15] SS.UU. 18287 of 2018.

[16] https://lawcom.gov.uk.

among them – into the new millennium. Legal roots and comparative law have, in fact, long been a functional combination also available to the legislature in the process of forming a legal rule, and this combination is technically qualified in a way that is suited to the complex needs that contemporary society expresses today.

PORTUGAL

CHILDREN'S PARTICIPATION RIGHT IN PORTUGAL

An Overview of the Last Fifty Years

Rosa Cândido Martins

Résumé

Le plus emblématique des droits de l'enfant est celui de participer aux procédures judiciaires et administratives qui affectent sa vie.

Malgré la consécration juridique progressive du droit de l'enfant à participer aux procédures de droit de la famille dans le droit portugais, la mise en œuvre effective de ce droit n'est pas encore conclue.

Dans le présent chapitre, l'histoire et la culture du système juridique portugais sont analysées afin de comprendre les fondements de ce droit de l'enfant et ainsi permettre de justifier la nécessaire reconnaissance de ce droit en tant que droit substantiel. Les raisons pour lesquelles ce droit n'est pas encore pleinement garanti sont également analysées, en gardant à l'esprit sa nature procédurale.

La Constitution portugaise de 1976 offre un cadre interprétatif au soutien de ce droit de l'enfant à participer aux procédures le concernant, ce qui, en tant que tel, est un réel argument contre toute résistance à l'octroi de ce droit. Depuis l'adoption de la Convention internationale des droits de l'enfant, de grandes avancées ont vu le jour en ce qui concerne le droit de participation de l'enfant. La Loi sur la protection des enfants et des jeunes en danger a renforcé la reconnaissance de ce droit. Le Régime général de tutelle civile a permis de considérer le droit de l'enfant à participer comme un outil d'autonomisation.

Cependant, des obstacles à la mise en œuvre effective de ce droit subsistent. Ce chapitre analyse les progrès effectués et soulève des nouvelles questions. Celles-ci sont relatives à la participation des enfants dans les procédures judiciaires et administratives, au soutien dont ils ont besoin pour parvenir à un exercice concret de ce droit, mais aussi à la signification et au poids qui devraient être accordés aux perspectives des enfants dans les procédures familiales ainsi qu'à leur status dans ces procédures.

1. INTRODUCTION

The awareness, in contemporary societies, of children as active and competent in shaping their own lives, influencing the lives of those around them, and even the societies in which they live, has led to important changes in their legal status.

Nowadays, children are, at international, European and national level, afforded general human rights as well as specific ones. The most iconic of children's right is the right to participate in judicial and administrative proceedings affecting their lives. Family law proceedings are considered to be the ones that have most impact on children's lives. However, the conviction that children have participatory rights that allow them to express their perspectives about family life matters, as well as to be active participants in decision-making process about those matters, has had to overcome some resistance[1] in judicial and administrative practices in family law proceedings.[2] Despite the acknowledgement of children's agency and the progressive legal enshrinement in Portuguese law of children's right to participate in family law proceedings, the effective implementation of this right is yet to be achieved.

This chapter addresses the question whether or not children in Portugal are granted an effective right to participate in family law proceedings. Answering this question requires a thorough analysis of the Portuguese legal system's history and culture, in order to ascertain the basis of this particular children's right and its legal recognition and implementation.

An argument running through the chapter is that the theoretical model sustaining the position that, in Portugal, children hold the right to participate in judicial and administrative proceedings affecting their lives has its roots in Portuguese constitutional law after the 1974 revolution.

As a matter of fact, the text of the Constitution of the Portuguese Republic (CPR) of 1976 started with an important statement: that Portugal is a republic grounded in 'the dignity of the human person'.[3] This initial declaration sustains an interpretative framework which enables the granting of fundamental rights to children. However, the demand for children's rights was not a primary concern for the Constitutional Assembly that passed and decreed the CPR of 1976, nor for Portuguese society at the time. Accordingly, that interpretation was not defended by legal scholars in general back then.

The acceptance that children have rights confronts basic social beliefs, philosophical considerations and moral and legal values. This discussion implies a cultural change regarding society's attitude towards children, which

---

1 E.E. Sutherland, 'Listening to the Child's Voice in the Family Setting: From Aspiration to Reality' (2014) 26(2) *Children and Family Law Quarterly* 157–62.

2 Charlotte Moll sates that children and children's lives are often at the centre of family law proceedings, and defines such proceedings, for the purpose of her study, as proceedings regarding 'parentage, adoption, parental responsibilities, custody, access, international child abduction and child protection or care proceedings'. The same definition is used here. See C. Moll, *The Child's Right to Participate in Family Law Proceedings: Represented, Heard or Silenced?*, Intersentia, 2022, pp. 12–13.

3 See Art. 1 Constitution of the Portuguese Republic, 2005, at: https://www.parlamento.pt/sites/EN/Parliament/Documents/Constitution7th.pdf.

is grounded on the perception of children, and on their role in that society at a given time.[4] Indeed, Portuguese society at the time was not yet ready to infer all the consequences that the CPR of 1976 brought to children's legal status.

Since then, there has been an enormous evolution of the Portuguese legal system concerning the recognition and implementation of children's right to participate. The adoption and ratification of the UN Convention on the Rights of the Child[5] boosted awareness of this particular children's right among the public and legal professionals.

Great efforts have been made to grant children their right to participate in judicial and administrative proceedings affecting their lives. Despite this, there is still a long way to go to effectively afford children that right.

2. THE FIRST STEPS IN THE CHILDREN'S PARTICIPATION RIGHT IN PORTUGUESE CIVIL LAW BEFORE THE UN CONVENTION ON THE RIGHTS OF THE CHILD

2.1. THE CONSTITUTION OF THE PORTUGUESE REPUBLIC

Even though Portugal ratified the UN Convention on the Rights of the Child on 26 January 1990, the child's right to participate in family matters had already been recognised to some degree in the Portuguese legal system.

Prior to that date, the influence of the children's rights movement in the 1970s, as well as the new constitutional order after the 1974 revolution, introduced a different legal image of children and established the basis for an ongoing recognition of children's rights.

The 1974 revolution aimed to replace a dictatorial regime with a democratic one, allowing a 'new beginning' for Portuguese society, through the 'restoration of the fundamental rights and freedoms of Portuguese people'.[6] Therefore, the CPR declares that 'Portugal is a sovereign Republic based on the dignity of the human person' (Article 1 CPR).[7] This enshrinement is the basis for fundamental rights. The new Constitution established and strengthened the protection

---

4 J. Fionda, 'Legal concepts of childhood: an introduction' in J. Fionda (ed.), *Legal Concepts of Childhood*, Hart Publishing 2001, pp. 4–5; A. James, *Constructing Childhood*, Palgrave Macmillan, 2004, pp. 12–13.

5 See the UN Convention on the Rights of the Child at: https://www.ohchr.org/en/instruments-mechanisms/instruments/convention-rights-child.

6 See the Preamble of the 1976 Constitution of the Portuguese Republic at https://www.parlamento.pt/sites/EN/Parliament/Documents/Constitution7th.pdf.

7 See Art. 1, at https://www.parlamento.pt/sites/EN/Parliament/Documents/Constitution7th.pdf.

of fundamental rights of the human person with the purpose of building a society inspired by the 'common values' of freedom, justice and solidarity (Article 1 CPR).

2.1.1. *The Recognition of Inherent Dignity of the Child*

At the time of the new Constitution, the social and legal image of the child was the result of a negative conception of childhood. Childhood was seen as a phase of human life without much value, because children had not yet developed the physical, intellectual, moral, emotional and social skills to be able to 'govern their own person and manage their own property'[8] on their own. Children were not considered active and competent actors in social and legal life. However, the enshrinement of the principle of human dignity as the basis for the constitutional order opened up the path (still being followed nowadays) to the acknowledgement of children as human beings endowed with an inherent and inviolable dignity. The recognition of the child as a human being with inherent dignity could already be drawn from the interpretation of Article 1 of the Universal Declaration of Human Rights, which stated: 'All human beings are born free and equal in dignity and rights'.[9] The principle of human dignity is grounded in the moral and juridical concept of personhood. Thus, the acknowledgement of children's human dignity enables their consideration as persons.[10] This line of reasoning is reinforced by the statement that 'everyone has the right to recognition everywhere as a person before the law' (Article 6 of the Universal Declaration of Human Rights).

The awareness that children are persons, and have the same dignity as adults, permitted the later acceptance of children as holders of fundamental rights, and will hopefully, in the future, permit their perception as citizens.[11]

---

8 See Art. 130(1) of the Portuguese Civil Code *a contrario*: 'Those who reach the age of 18 acquire full capacity to exercise their rights and are entitled to govern their own persons and manage their own property.'

9 When interpreting constitutional principles, and the constitutional fundamental rights enshrined in the Constitution, the recognition and protection of human rights at international level that followed the Universal Declaration of Human Rights must be borne in mind. That is the reason why reference is made to some Articles of that Declaration.

10 Before the 1976 Constitution of the Portuguese Republic, civil law recognised legal personhood in children. Although, regarding children as subjects of rights, it stressed children's legal incapacity, grounded on their lack of rationality and autonomy. This notion of children hindered their full consideration as persons by depriving them of certain personal rights.

11 On the need to redefine the concept of citizenship in light of the status of children in contemporary society, see J. Roche, 'Children: Rights, Participation and Citizenship' (1999) 6(4) *Childhood* 475. Affirming that children had attained a status of social citizenship, see S.M. Cretney, J.M. Masson and R. Bailey-Harris, *Principles of Family Law*, 7th ed., Sweet & Maxwell, 2002, p. 491.

2.1.2. *Children and the Building of a Democracy Based on the Rule of Law*

The 1976 Portuguese Constitution also mentions other fundamental principles of the Portuguese Republic that have consequences in the field of children's rights. Article 2 states that Portugal is 'a democratic state based on the rule of law … the respect and the guarantee of the effective implementation of fundamental rights and freedoms … with the view to achieving economic, social and cultural democracy and deepening participatory democracy'.[12]

These fundamental principles are of great importance to the interpretative framework of fundamental rights granted by the Constitution, in terms of their extension to children and their consideration of citizens. The implementation of fundamental rights and freedoms will only be effective if these fundamental rights and freedoms are also bestowed on children.

Moreover, building a participatory democracy will encompass the recognition of children's right of participation in all matters affecting their lives. Children are the future; therefore, to forge a truly democratic society and political regime implies that children should learn how to participate in a responsive way in societal and political matters, especially those affecting their lives. Indeed, to accomplish that constitutional command, it is important to include children's perspectives, views and wishes in the discussion of public policies, as well as recognising their 'agency and competence to be active participants in policy processes that concern not only their present, but also their future'.[13] Children should be engaged in citizenship practices, and this will reinforce the value of democracy not only in our present society but also in the future.[14]

2.1.3. *Principle of Universality and Children's Fundamental Rights*

Accepting children as bearers of rights, and specifically as holders of fundamental rights laid down in the 1976 Constitution, was not a purpose of the members of the Constitutional Assembly that passed and decreed the Constitution.

The extension of those rights to children is an outcome of an interpretation of the Constitution based on the principle of universality, stated in Article 12

---

12 See Art. 2 of the 1976 Constitution of the Portuguese Republic at https://www.parlamento.pt/sites/EN/Parliament/Documents/Constitution7th.pdf.

13 A.N. de Almeida, A.S. Ribeiro and J. Rowland, 'Children, citizenship and crisis: towards a participatory agenda' in M.C. Lobo, F.C. da Silva and Z.P. Zúquete (eds.), *Changing Societies: Legacies and Challenges, vol. II: Citizenship in Crisis*, Imprensa de Ciências Sociais, 2018, p. 114.

14 A.N. de Almeida, A.S. Ribeiro and J. Rowland, 'Children, citizenship and crisis: towards a participatory agenda' in M.C. Lobo, F.C. da Silva and Z.P. Zúquete (eds.), *Changing Societies: Legacies and Challenges, vol. II: Citizenship in Crisis*, Imprensa de Ciências Sociais, 2018, pp. 114.

CPR, as a general principle of the regime of fundamental rights and duties that the Constitution enshrines: 'Every citizen enjoys the rights and is subject of the duties enriched in the Constitution.'[15]

This principle rests in the acknowledgement of 'all citizens' – of 'all persons', because of their 'human condition' – as having the status of holders of fundamental rights (and duties). On that account, this recognition must necessarily embrace both adults and children. The Constitution's 'message' seems to be that 'children have, as a rule *(prima facie)*, the same rights as adults', and that 'exceptions should only be admitted – especially regarding the rights' exercise – when the legitimacy of these restrictions can be found in the very nature of the fundamental right in question, through the proper interpretation method of those rights'.[16]

2.1.4. *Children and the Equality Principle*

Children born out of wedlock cannot be subject to any kind of discrimination for that reason (Article 36(4) CPR).[17] Legislature, public authorities and private institutions are obliged to abstain from using discriminatory language when referring to them. This is an implementation of the general principle of equality: 'All citizens possess the same social dignity and are equal before the law' (Article 13(1) CPR). Nevertheless, childhood or minor age is not expressly considered a possible factor of discrimination; that is to say, there is no reference to *age* in Article 13(2) CPR.[18] A formal consideration of this constitutional provision could lead to a wrong conclusion, as children, as such, are not protected against all forms of discrimination affecting them, but only against those foreseen in constitutional provisions regarding children, such as the one stated in Article 36(4) CPR.[19]

---

15 See Art. 12(1) of the 1976 Constitution of the Portuguese Republic at https://www.parlamento.pt/sites/EN/Parliament/Documents/Constitution7th.pdf.

16 J.J. Gomes Canotilho and V. Moreira, 'Anotação ao artigo 12.º CRP' in *Constituição da República Portuguesa Anotada, vol. I*, Coimbra Editora, 2007, pp. 331–32.

17 See Art. 36(4) CRP at https://www.parlamento.pt/sites/EN/Parliament/Documents/Constitution7th.pdf.

18 'No one may be privileged, favoured, prejudiced, deprived of any right or exempt from any duty for reason of ancestry, sex, race, language, territory of origin, religion, political or ideological beliefs, education, economic situation, social circumstances or sexual orientation.' See Art. 13(2) of the 1976 Constitution of the Portuguese Republic at https://www.parlamento.pt/sites/EN/Parliament/Documents/Constitution7th.pdf.

19 The prohibition of any form of discrimination against children born out of wedlock does not cover all forms of different treatment. However, non-identical legal treatment is only justified if based on the different conditions of birth. For example, children born out of wedlock cannot receive a different portion, compared with children born within marriage, in the partition of their parents' inheritance. Also, there cannot be a different regime regarding the entitlement and exercise of parental responsibilities. The fact that a child's birth was

The original version of the CPR, as well as the ones that followed it, did not include age as a discrimination factor. This absence did not motivate, and still has not motivated, a thorough social or political debate. Even among academics, the inclusion of such a factor, in order to assure the protection of children against all forms of discrimination, is not discussed. However, it is possible to sustain an interpretation of Article 13 that includes age as a discrimination factor.

First, Article 13(2) CPR states a non-exhaustive list of discrimination factors. Indeed, some discrimination factors were added in later versions of the CPR. Second, people can be discriminated against on grounds of their age, and the Portuguese Constitution recognises this in other constitutional provisions. In reality, the Constitution acknowledges three phases of human life: childhood, adulthood and old age. Bearing in mind the vulnerabilities of the first and third of these, the Portuguese Constitution takes on the task of protecting and promoting social, economic and cultural rights. This being so, Article 69 (1) of the Portuguese Constitution grants children 'the right to be protected by society and state, especially from all forms of abandonment, discrimination, and oppression and from the inappropriate exercise of authority in the family or any other institution'.[20] Society and the State must respect and ensure children's social, economic and cultural rights, and the State must undertake appropriate legislative measures in order to prevent any discrimination against children on the grounds of their minor age in the implementation of those rights by public authorities or private institutions. According to a new human rights method of interpretation, social, economic and cultural rights should not be seen as a category of fundamental rights under a different legal regime of civil and political rights and freedoms set forth by the Constitution. Thus, there is no reason to exclude age from the factors of discrimination recognised by the Portuguese Constitution. Third, there is an international law argument: since 2009, Portugal, as a Member State of the European Union, is bound to the Charter of Fundamental Rights of the European Union. The Charter also recognises children's rights, through its Article 24. The insertion of Article 24 in Title III of the Charter, which concerns 'equality', reveals that the principle of equality (Article 20) and the principle of non-discrimination (Article 21) expressly apply to children.[21] The non-restrictive list of factors according to which all discrimination should be banned expressly includes age (Article 21). This being so, age should also be

---

outside or within marriage has no implications on these matters. Nonetheless, that is not the case when establishing legal paternity. In fact, children whose parents are married benefit from a legal presumption that the mother's husband is the father (Art. 1826, Portuguese Civil Code), taking into account the legal duties of fidelity and cohabitation of spouses (Art. 1672, Portuguese Civil Code).

20 See Art. 69 of the 1976 Constitution of the Portuguese Republic at https://www.parlamento.pt/sites/EN/Parliament/Documents/Constitution7th.pdf.

21 G. Passagnoli, 'I diritti del Bambino nella Carta Europea' in G. Vettori (ed.), *Carta Europea e Diritti dei Privati*, CEDAM, 2002, p. 328.

considered a discrimination factor at national level, and, consequently, children should not be discriminated against on grounds of their minor age.

2.1.5. *Children's Right to Constitute a Family*

The Constitution, in its original version, granted to all citizens the fundamental rights to life (Article 25 CPR) and to personal integrity (Article 26 CPR). The second and third amendments made some significant changes, and Article 26 CPR, under the heading 'other personal rights', began to provide for the right to personal identity, the right to one's image, freedom of speech, and the right to privacy of one's personal and family life.

These fundamental rights, as shown above, are also afforded to children, as subjects of fundamental rights. Hence, children have the right to a personal identity that encompasses the right to constitute a family (Article 26(1) CPR),[22] and thus the right to establish their maternity and paternity. In general, the child has the right to establish their maternity and/or paternity through a judicial proceeding filed by them, if they have legal and judicial capacity. In other cases, the child's right is protected by their legal representative. If the latter does not file the judicial proceeding, the child's right will be promoted by the Public Prosecution Service, within its official activity, or as general representative of people who lack capacity (Articles 1814, 1807, 1869 and 1864, Portuguese Civil Code).

2.1.6. *Children's Right to be Raised by Both Parents and the Right not to be Separated from Them*

The Portuguese Constitution also grants to the child the right to be raised by both their parents, grounded on both parents' fundamental right to assume common and equal responsibilities for their child (Article 36(3) and (5) CPR). Furthermore, the Portuguese Constitution ensures the child's right not to be separated from their parents, unless they do not fulfil their fundamental duties towards the child. There must always be a court decision supporting the necessity of such separation (Article 36(6) CPR).

2.1.7. *Children's Protection by Society and the State and their Right to Participate*

Article 67(1) CPR[23] not only recognises family as a group, but also recognises its importance to family members, and on this basis acknowledges the family's

---

22 See Art. 26 of the 1976 Constitution of the Portuguese Republic at https://www.parlamento.pt/sites/EN/Parliament/Documents/Constitution7th.pdf.

23 See ibid., Art. 67(1), at https://www.parlamento.pt/sites/EN/Parliament/Documents/Constitution7th.pdf.

significance to society. This Article states that family is a 'fundamental element in society'. Family is considered to be a group essential to 'enable family members to achieve personal fulfilment'; this especially applies to children. Indeed, as was stated later, in the UN Convention on the Rights of the Child, family is considered to be 'the natural environment for the growth and well-being of all its members and particularly children'.[24] On that account, family should benefit from the protection of society and the State, in order to fully accomplish its responsibilities within society.

The reference to the family in terms of enabling its members to achieve personal fulfilment (in Article 67(1) CPR) is relevant for the argument that the Portuguese Constitution promoted, from the beginning, the acknowledgement of children's right to participate. The Portuguese Constitution was concerned about children's personal fulfilment. In order to achieve this personal fulfilment, children should be given the opportunity to express their views and wishes, and therefore to influence decisions about their lives. This being so, Article 67(1) CPR contributes to the line of reasoning that, in some ways, children's right to participate was already recognised.

Under the same line of reasoning, Article 69(1) CPR reflects the concern about children's personal fulfilment by declaring that they were entitled to the protection of society and the State, 'with a view to their integral development'.[25] The Constitution identifies the protection and promotion of children's rights[26] as the central element of the intervention of society and the State in children's lives, and establishes that such protection and promotion should be oriented towards children's full development of their physical, cognitive, emotional, moral and social abilities.

Another contribution to this reasoning is the statement in Article 70(2) CPR that 'the development of young people's personality' must be among the primary purposes of youth policy.[27]

This means that, in the present author's opinion, the first version of the Portuguese Constitution was aware of the importance of ensuring full development of children's personalities.

---

24 See the Preamble of the UN Convention on the Rights of Children at https://www.ohchr.org/en/instruments-mechanisms/instruments/convention-rights-child.

25 See ibid., Art. 69, at https://www.parlamento.pt/sites/EN/Parliament/Documents/Constitution7th.pdf.

26 Some contemporary legal authors argue that this provision underlies the recognition of children as holders of fundamental rights, and that it implies the acknowledgement of children's right to participate in the decision-making process about matters affecting their lives: J. Miranda and R. Medeiros, *Constituição Portuguesa Anotada, vol. I*, 2nd ed., Universidade Católica Editora, 2017, p. 999.

27 See Art. 70 of the 1976 Constitution of the Portuguese Republic at https://www.parlamento.pt/sites/EN/Parliament/Documents/Constitution7th.pdf.

2.1.8. *The Right to Fully Develop One's Personality and Children's Right to Participate*

The constitutional amendment of 1997 brought to light another personal fundamental right: the fundamental right to the full development of one's personality, which was expressly accorded by Article 26(1) CPR. The recognition of this particular fundamental right is of great significance to the discussion of children's right to participate.

The right to fully develop one's personality, anchored in the principle of human dignity, encompasses the freedom of one's personality formation. This freedom reflects the right to be protected against State intervention in the process of one's personality formation. Therefore, the State, among other things, must not impose models of personality.

This is especially important when it comes to children, taking into account that childhood is the stage of human life when the main and essential traits of one's personality are shaped. Thus, children should be granted the conditions to develop their personalities. The development of a child's personality requires that they be afforded a gradual autonomy in making choices and decisions about their life. The children's right to participate is the legal instrument that reflects that need. This being so, the fundamental right to fully develop one's personality demands and supports the enshrinement of children's right to participation.

2.2. THE CHILDREN'S PARTICIPATION RIGHT AND 1977 REFORM OF THE PORTUGUESE CIVIL CODE

In the late 1970s, Portuguese society started to look at children in a different way. Children were still seen as an 'object of protection' from adults. Nevertheless, there was an almost invisible recognition of children's right to participate in family matters in several legal rules of the Portuguese Civil Code, reviewed in 1977 in order to meet the new constitutional requirements regarding family issues.

The concept of childhood adopted by the 1977 reform was based on the idea that children were human beings in progressive development, gradually acquiring physical, cognitive, emotional, moral and social abilities. Therefore, the 1977 reform provided children with several ways of participating in family matters, although there was not a clear reference to children's right to participate in family law proceedings, despite the interpretative framework provided by the Portuguese Constitution. Some examples follow below.

2.2.1. *Parental Responsibilities*

Reflecting the spirit of the 1976 Constitution, the family, in the 1977 reform, was thought to be the best environment for full development of the personality of each of its members. Family was considered to be the place for personal fulfilment, bearing in mind the existential needs of the human being for belonging, togetherness, affection and solidarity. The new family was characterised by its new structure. It was no longer based on a patriarchal, hierarchical structure, subject to the authority of the 'head of the family' – the husband and father – but on an egalitarian structure, grounded on the values of affection, solidarity, mutual respect and cooperation between its members. Hence, the legal regime of parental responsibilities underwent several changes in 1977.

Parental responsibilities[28] became exercised by both father and mother on an equal basis. The 1977 reform abolished the sole exercise of these by the father. This was an application of the constitutional principle of equality between spouses (Article 36(3) CPR). Additionally, children were no longer submitted to the sole authority of their father. They should obey their parents, but parents should protect them and promote their autonomy, always respecting the children's personality.

2.2.1.1. Children's Opinions about Important Family Matters

The concept of parental responsibilities was conceived as the collection of rights and duties attributed by the law to both parents until their child reaches the age of majority, so that they can look after the child and their property in their child's best interests, which has become the guiding principle for parents when exercising parental responsibilities. The rights and duties included in parental responsibilities should not be exercised in an authoritarian way. According to the child's level of maturity, parents should take into account the child's opinions about important family matters. Moreover, always bearing in mind the child's level of maturity, parents should grant their child autonomy in the organisation of their life (Article 1878(2). This legal regime remains in force today.

2.2.1.2. The Right to be Heard when Parents Disagree about Matters of Special Importance to the Child's Life

Article 1901(1) of the Portuguese Civil Code, following the 1977 reform, stated that, during marriage, the exercise of parental responsibilities belonged to both

[28] This terminology was adopted in 2008, by Law 61/2008, 31 October.

parents. In the event of parental disagreement about a matter of particular significance for their children's lives, either of them could go to court and ask for a decision. First, the judge should try to make the parents reach an agreement, because they were the people best placed to know the best option for their child. However, if that was not possible, the child, if over the age of 14, should be heard by the judge before the judge made a decision, unless there were circumstances advising otherwise (Article 1901(2) of the Portuguese Civil Code, according to the 1977 reform). This being so, children's right to be heard in family law proceedings concerning relevant matters of their own lives had been recognised. In 2008, Law 61/2008 established no age limit. Now, the court must always hear the child's voice before deciding (Article 1901(3), Portuguese Civil Code).

2.2.1.3. Religious Upbringing

The Portuguese Civil Code, in its Article 1886, as amended by the 1977 reform, established that parents should decide about the religious upbringing of their children under the age of 16. This was a new provision with content that was quite new. The law recognised the progressive development of children's abilities and, consequently, of their autonomy, specifically in matters related to the development of their personalities. Religion is one such matter. For that reason, parents should decide about the religious education of their children according to the parents' evaluation of the children's best interests. Nevertheless, respect for the personalities of children, and awareness of their progressively increasing abilities to make decisions about their present and future lives, dictated that, from the age of 16, children would be able to decide autonomously about religious matters. This legal regime remains in force today.

3. THE UN CONVENTION ON CHILDREN'S RIGHTS AND THE 'LAW ON PROTECTION OF CHILDREN AND YOUNG PEOPLE IN DANGER'

Despite the legal framework provided by the Portuguese Constitution and Civil Code, the right of the child to participate in judicial and administrative family law proceedings had little impact on children's lives. Only with Portugal's signature and ratification of the UN Convention on the Rights of the Child, in 1990, did that right begin to become a topic of discussion. Indeed, this Convention represented an important 'milestone in the history of the child'[29] by enshrining

[29] M. Freeman, 'Introduction: Children as Persons' in *Children's Rights: A Comparative Perspective*, Dartmouth, 1996, p. 1.

a 'participatory model' rooted in a new conception of the child. Children were perceived as active participants in the construction of their futures, and were granted the right to participate in the decision-making processes of matters affecting their lives. Children were no longer seen as 'objects of rights', but as 'equal and privileged subjects of rights'.[30] The children's participation right is the most significant children's right foreseen by the UN Convention.[31] It relies on a mostly new image of children, and reflects a very different social and legal concept of childhood.

According to Article 12(1) of the UN Convention, children capable of forming their own views are granted the right to express those views freely in all matters affecting them. Moreover, children's views should be taken into account by adults when deciding about those matters, in accordance with the children's age and maturity. In order to enhance this right, Article 12(2) upholds children's right to be heard in all judicial and administrative proceedings affecting them.[32]

The adoption of the UN Convention on the Rights of the Child sparked debate about children's right to participate, among portuguese legislative bodies, courts, administrative authorities, public and private welfare institutions, and legal scholars. As an outcome from this debate, the Law on Protection of Children and Young People in Danger (Law No. 147/99, of 1 September) came into force, and enshrined, as one of its guiding principles, the right of children to be heard, and to participate in matters affecting their lives. Moreover, this law foresaw as mandatory the child's right to be heard, and their right to participate in judicial and administrative proceedings concerning the promotion and protection of their rights, without reference to age limits (Article 4 (j)).[33]

This law, inspired by the UN Convention, aimed to protect children 'against all forms of physical or mental violence, injury or abuse, neglect or negligent treatment, maltreatment or exploitation, including sexual abuse',[34] and to

---

30 M.-T. Meulders-Klein, 'Droits des enfants et responsabilités parentales. Quel juste équilibre?' in *La personne, la famille et le droit (1968–1998). Trois décennies de mutations en Occident*, Bruylant/LGDJ, 1999, p. 345.

31 M. Freeman, *Understanding Family Law*, Sweet and Maxwell, 2007, p. 354.

32 For a thorough analysis of Art. 12 of the UN Convention on the Rights of the Child, see C. Moll, above n. 2, pp. 24–44. See also S. Detrick, *A Commentary on the United Nations Convention on the Rights of the Child*, Martinus Nijhoff Publishers, 1999.

33 Or Art. 4 (i), according to the first version of Law on Protection of Children and Young People in Danger. There was no reference to the child's age or maturity. Art. 4 (i): 'hearing and participation – children and young people – whether separately or accompanied by their parents or by a person of their choice – as well as their parents, legal representative or guardian have the right to be heard and to participate in the acts and in the definition of the measure of protection and promotion of children's rights'.

34 See Art. 19 (1) of the UN Convention on the Rights of the Child at https://www.ohchr.org/en/instruments-mechanisms/instruments/convention-rights-child.

promote their rights. Among these rights, special attention should be paid to children's participation right. The Law on Protection of Children and Young People in Danger foresaw ways of exercising this right in several of its legal provisions when regulating administrative and judicial proceedings regarding the protection and promotion of children's rights.

For instance, the above-mentioned law made the intervention of several entities,[35] aiming a child in danger protection, dependent on whether that child opposes the intervention or not.

In reality, the intervention of those entities and institutions would only take place in relation to children aged 12 or over if those children do not oppose it (Article 10(1)). Furthermore, objections by children under 12 to such intervention had also to be taken into account if the child was considered capable of understanding the reasons for the intervention (Article 10(2). Additionally, the child – if over the age of 12, or under 12, where their ability to understand the meaning of the intervention made this advisable – had the right to be heard by the Commission for the Protection of Children in Danger, or by the court, about the circumstances that led to the intervention, and about the application, review or termination of a certain measure of promotion and protection[36] (Article 84, in its original version).

If the intervention was promoted by the Commission for the Promotion of Rights and the Protection of Children and Young People, the child, if over 12 years old, had the right to participate in the agreement about the measure of promotion and protection to be adopted, as well as to give their consent to the implementation of that agreement (Articles 5 (f), 55(1)(c) and 98(3), in its original version).

Another example of the recognition of the children's right to participate, foresaw by the above-mentioned Law is the child's right to request investigations and offer evidence in the context of a judicial proceeding to determine the measure of promotion and protection (Article 104.º, in its original version).

4. GENERAL REGIME OF CIVIL TUTELAGE

Although the Law on Protection of Children and Young People in Danger was a very important step in the path towards the full acknowledgement, in Portugal,

35 These are public and private entities and institutions that are, by virtue of their functions, in contact with children – namely schools, units of health system, social security services, non-governmental organisations (NGOs) (Art. 7) as well Commissions for the Promotion of Rights and the Protection of Children and Young People (Art. 8).

36 These measures seek to remove the danger children are in; provide them with the conditions to protect and promote their safety, health, training, education, well-being and integral development; ensure the physical and psychological recovery of children and young people, who are victims of exploitation or abuse (Art. 34).

of children's right to participate, this law did not regulate the real conditions and procedural rules to ensure that this right was respected effectively in family law proceedings.

As a result, legal scholars, judges, public prosecutors, social workers and other professionals working with children were involved in a debate about how to ensure that children were able to participate in judicial and administrative procedures regarding their present and future lives, in particular family law proceedings.

Over the past few decades, there has been a major awareness of children as human beings who are in a process of development that gradually enables them to form their perspectives, views and opinions autonomously. There is now a greater awareness that children are able to provide valuable information about their lives, needs, problems and worries. Children can, if they are allowed to do so, be active participants in contributing to the decisions of family disputes affecting them.

Given this shift of attitude towards children, and under the influence of international and European human rights instruments, a considerable evolution of the concept of children's participation in family law proceedings took place. In this context, in 2015, the General Regime of Civil Tutelage (Law No. 141/2015, of 8 September) came into force and established specific procedural rules for some family law judicial proceedings involving children and their relationships with their parents, legal guardians or carers.

Similarly to the Law on Protection of Children and Young People in Danger, this law grants to children who are capable of understanding the issues under discussion, taking into account their age and maturity, the right always to be heard on the decisions that concern them. This is as a guiding principle of the law (Article 4(1)(c)). Moreover, the law specifies that there should, preferably, be assistance given by the court's technical advice services when judicial authorities are listening to the child (Article 4(1)(c)). The child is also afforded the right to be assisted by an adult of their choice whenever they require it, unless the judge presents a reasoned refusal (Article 4(1)(c)). Article 4(2) states that the judge shall evaluate, on a case-by-case basis, the child's real ability to understand the matters discussed in that specific proceeding. In order to do so, the judge can ask for the assistance of the court's technical advice services. This could lead to the impression that the General Regime of Civil Tutelage imposes no age limits on the exercise of the child's right to be heard. However, Article 35(3) establishes that a child who is over 12, or is under that age but considered capable of understanding the matters at stake, having reference to their age and maturity, should be heard by the court in custody proceedings.

In addition, and for the first time, this law contained rules concerning by whom, how and when the child should be heard. Article 5 of the General Regime of Civil Tutelage highlights a concern about how to implement the children's right to participate in some family law proceedings. Although this was not a new question, it had not been clearly addressed under the Portuguese legal system.[37] Indeed, the Portuguese Civil Code did not contain specific provisions regarding the participation of children in family law proceedings.

Article 5(1) affords children the rights to be heard and to have their opinions taken into account by judicial authorities in the determination of their best interests. The other provisions under this Article reflect the legislature's concern about the conditions in which the child is heard. Adults involved should bear in mind that being listened to in family law proceedings is a right granted to the child, and does not involve a duty being imposed on the child.[38] In this sense, the judge shall promote the necessary judicial procedures for the child to be heard, which may take place at a specially scheduled official hearing (Article 5(2)). Before being heard, the child must be given clear and proper information on the meaning and scope of this procedure. This information must be provided according to the child's age and maturity (Article 5(3)).

Special attention must also be given to the environment where the child is going to be heard. The space must be chosen carefully in order not to be intimidating, hostile or inappropriate for the child's age, maturity and personal qualities (Article 5(4)(a)). Moreover, the law requires that the judicial operators (judges, public prosecutors, lawyers, clerks) that may be present when the child is being heard have special training in matters relating to children (Article 5(4)(b)). Article 5(5) also states that, preferably, judges, public prosecutors and lawyers should not wear their professional clothing. Nevertheless, listening to the child in some family law and in civil tutelage proceedings can assume another form and scope. Always bearing in mind the child's best interests, the judge, on request or *ex officio*, may hear the child at any stage of the proceedings, so that their statements can subsequently be used as evidence in the trial (Article 5(6)). Article 5(7) provides special procedural rules so that the child's statements can be considered as a means of proof, namely that the child's interview shall occur in a child-friendly environment; the child shall be assisted by a specially trained non-legal professional, probably one of the professionals working in the court's technical advice services, previously appointed for this purpose; the questions shall be asked by the judge, although the public prosecutor and the lawyers may also ask additional questions; and the child's statements shall be recorded by means of audio or audiovisual recording.

Most remarkable, in terms of promoting children's participation right, are Article 17(1), which, for the first time, grants a child over 12 years old

---

37 P. Guerra, 'Anotação ao artigo 5.º' in C. Araújo Dias, J.N. Barros and R. Martingo Cruz (coords), *Regime Geral do Processo Tutelar Cível Anotado*, Almedina, 2021, p. 101.

38 M. Santos Pais, 'Child participation', *Documentação e Direito Comparado*, 81/82, 2000, 93.

the procedural right to commence litigation in family law and in civil tutelage proceedings covered by the referred law, and Article 18(2), which accords the child with sufficient maturity the right to ask the court to nominate a lawyer to represent them, besides the cases where such nomination is mandatory; that is, where there is a conflict of interests between the child and of their parents, legal representative or de facto guardian.

5. CONCLUSION

Great progress has been made with regard to the child's right to participate in family law proceedings. However, there still are multiple questions and doubts about the best method to improve children's participation and make it effective.

Nowadays, achieving the best solutions for children, in their best interests, according to the circumstances of the case, has become the ultimate goal of all the professionals who have contact with children in such proceedings. Deciding on children's best interests implies (not always, but most of the time) respect for children's right to participate in family law proceedings. In reality, involving children in the decision-making process, by listening to their voices and granting them the opportunity to participate in other ways, allow adults to know the children better – their personalities, their own truths, their feelings, their perspectives, their opinions and their real situations. Thus, granting them the right to participate in family law proceedings is also a significant instrument to better determine their best interests.[39] Children's best interests are not uniquely determined by adults; children themselves are also able to contribute in an important way to that determination. Notwithstanding the awareness that giving a child the opportunity to participate in family law proceedings allows judges to achieve better decisions in such proceedings, children's right to participate must not be considered an instrumental right for reaching that goal.

Children's right to participate must be considered autonomously as a children's human right. There are currently no serious doubts about its substantive nature. As stated above, the Portuguese Constitution supports the idea that children are human beings in the process of development. Additionally, despite admitting that children are particularly vulnerable, and thus guaranteeing their protection by society and the State for that reason, the Portuguese Constitution allows the understanding of children as people going through a process of development

---

[39] P. Parkinson and J. Cashmore, 'Children's Participation in Decisions about Parenting Arrangements' in J.G. Dwyer (ed), *The Oxford Handbook of Children and the Law*, OUP, 2020, p. 846.

of their skills and abilities. The premises for attributing to children a right to participate in matters affecting their lives, and particularly in family law proceedings concerning them, were already established in the Constitution of 1976.

The Law on Protection of Children and Young People in Danger reinforced the acknowledgement of children's right to participate in family law proceedings, and the General Regime of Civil Tutelage enabled the consideration of that right as an instrument of children's empowerment. Children's right to participate reflects the perception of children as active participants in shaping their own futures. Therefore, the recognition of the substantive nature of children's right to participate is embedded in Portugal's society and legal system.

Nevertheless, the recognition of that right as a substantive right is not enough. The children's participation right also has a procedural nature that cannot be overlooked if the right is to be fully respected in its substantive dimension.

There are still several questions to be answered. Should the child's right to participate be identified with their right to be heard? Are there several other ways of listening to children's voices besides hearing them?[40] How should the child be heard? How should the child's interview be conducted? Are specific communication skills required? What is the relevance of hearing the child, and what are the consequences of not hearing them? What does it mean to be able to understand the issues under discussion? How many times should the child participate in the family law and civil tutelage proceedings? How should children's voices be understood? What is the procedural status of children when they are heard?

[40] Ibid., p. 835.

TAIWAN

FROM STATUS TO CONSENT

A Feminist Critique of Fifty Years of Family Law Reform in Taiwan

Chao-ju CHEN

Résumé

La légalisation du mariage entre personnes de même sexe à Taïwan en 2019 a été saluée par la communauté internationale, consolidant la position du pays en tant que leader régional de l'égalité des genres en Asie de l'Est. Depuis près d'un demi-siècle, le droit de la famille taïwanais n'a cessé d'évoluer vers l'égalité des sexes, le combat juridique féministe ayant joué un rôle déterminant. Considérée comme une pierre angulaire du mouvement féministe et un produit de la démocratisation de Taïwan, la réforme du droit de la famille est un élément essentiel dans la recherche d'une société égalitaire pour Taïwan. Cependant, cela ne représente que la moitié de l'histoire. Commencée juste avant la fin de la loi martiale en 1987, la réforme du droit de la famille a remis en question le patriarcat, tout en facilitant sa « préservation par la transformation ». Elle a également renforcé la suprématie maritale. Ce chapitre passe en revue l'évolution du droit de la famille au cours des cinquante dernières années en mettant l'accent sur les changements relatifs à l'égalité des sexes, en discutant de la stratégie et du rôle des mouvements féministes et LGBTQ, et en présentant un bilan de la réforme sous l'angle du féminisme.

1. INTRODUCTION

In 2017, the announcement of Taiwan's Constitutional Court's decision recognising same-sex couples' right to marry immediately garnered international attention and recognition, and was widely celebrated as a remarkable step towards further marriage equality. Two years later, a law was passed to legalise the registration of same-sex marriages, solidifying Taiwan's position as a regional leader for gender equality in East Asia. For nearly half a century, Taiwanese family law[1] has continuously evolved towards gender equality, with feminist legal advocacy playing an instrumental role. Widely celebrated as a cornerstone of the feminist movement and a product of Taiwan's democratisation, family law reform has been a vital component of Taiwan's quest for a free and equal society. However, this tells only half the story. The process began just before the end of martial law in 1987. Family law reform has dismantled patriarchy, while simultaneously facilitating its transformation. It has also reinforced marital supremacy. This chapter reviews the last 50 years of the development of family law in Taiwan, with a focus on changes regarding gender equality, discussing the strategy and role of feminist and LGBTQ legal advocacy, and providing a radical feminist assessment of reform, beginning with an introduction of the three stages and three trends in family law reform, followed by a critique of the status-to-consent family law story and the reinforcing of marital supremacy.

---

1 In this article, family law is defined narrowly as Part IV (Family) (親屬編) and Part V (Succession) (繼承編) of the Civil Code of the Republic of China (中華民國民法) (hereinafter referred to as the 'Civil Code'), and broadly as all laws regulating family relationships, with a focus on the former. Drafted and enforced in China in the 1920s and 1930s, the Civil Code took effect in Taiwan in 1945 – the end of Japanese colonial rule in Taiwan. It should also be noted that laws of procedure are beyond the scope of this chapter.

2. THREE STAGES OF FAMILY LAW REFORM

Taiwan has been through three stages of family law reform over the past five decades. The first stage began under martial law and ended with the revision of the Civil Code in 1985, two years before the lifting of martial law. Feminist family law reform, beginning in 1990, marked the second stage of family law reform, centred on the heterosexual marital family, resulting in a series of legal changes in the 1990s and 2000s. The rise of the LGBTQ movement in the 2010s paved the way for the third stage of family law reform, through which same-sex marriage was legalised.

2.1. THE FIRST STAGE (1972–85): TOP-DOWN MODERATE REFORM

The first round of reforms began when the authoritarian Kuomintang (KMT or Nationalist Party (國民黨) government announced a legal reform project to amend the Civil Code in 1974, leading to a milestone revision in 1985.[2] As the KMT government declared martial law in 1949, which remained in place until 1987, family law reform was a product of authoritarian reform implemented in a top-down fashion with limited input from civil society and little influence from the New Feminism movement (新女性主義運動),[3] which advocated for more radical reform.[4] The revision of the Civil Code was passed in 1985 by a legislature that had not been fully re-elected since 1947.

Initiated and dominated by the authoritarian KMT government, the family law reform project aimed to update the law to meet the needs of society,[5] an approach that reflected the view that took law as 'the mirror of society'.[6]

---

2 It was also the first revision of the Civil Code, which had already been in effect in Taiwan for nearly three decades without any formal revisions.

3 Taiwan's first wave of post-war feminism, called 'New Feminism', emerged in the early 1970s, and was suppressed in the late 1970s, when its main leader, Annette Hsiu-lien Lu (呂秀蓮), was convicted and jailed for her involvement in anti-government activities. The movement advocated liberal feminist thinking, under the slogan 'first be a person, then be a man or a woman' (先當人，再當男人或女人).

4 People still managed to voice their opinions regarding the family law reform project by sending petitions to the legislature. Despite the difficulties in legislative lobbying under the KMT's authoritarian rule, the New Feminism movement sought to change public opinion, hoping for indirect influence on the legislature. See 陳昭如C. Chen, 父姓的常規，母姓的權利：子女姓氏修法改革的法社會學考察 ('Patronymic Norm and the Right to Use the Maternal Surname: A Social-legal Study of the Legal Reform of Children's Surname Law') (2014) 42臺大法學論叢 *(NTU Law Journal)* 271–380.

5 司法行政部民法研究修正委員會 (The Civil Code Amendment Research Committee of the Judicial Ministry), 中華民國民法制定史料彙編（下）('Collection of Materials regarding the Making of ROC Civil Code Part II'), The Judicial Ministry, 1976, p. 979.

6 The 'law-as-mirror-of-society' or the 'mirror thesis' is the assumption that the law reflects and mirrors society, which finds one of its best representations in legal sociologist and historian

Equality between men and women was considered in regard to three issues addressed in the government's reform proposal: (1) whether or not to abolish uxorilocal marriage (招贅婚) (a form of marriage through which the husband enters into the wife's household);[7] did this type of marriage entail male dependency because the husband becomes a subordinate in the family, or does it facilitate equality between men and women because it is the reverse of a marriage in which the wife enters the husband's household? (2) whether or not to revise the provision (Article 1059) that required a child to assume their father's surname; should the law be revised to allow parental agreement to pass the mother's surname to the child? (3) whether or not to adopt the principle of economic independence in the statutory marital property regime; should the law be revised to respond to the social reality of the increasing number of dual-income families?[8]

After a decade-long deliberation, the Civil Code was revised in 1985. Uxorilocal marriage remained a legal form of marriage. The provision regarding the child's surname (Article 1059) was revised to allow the parents to pass the mother's surname to the child through mutual agreement, on the condition that the mother did not have a brother. The statutory marital property regime (法定財產制), originally characterised by a married man's monopoly over marital property, was moderately revised to grant married women more entitlements to, and control over, marital property without eliminating their disadvantaged economic position.[9] The freedom to divorce was expanded by

---

Lawrence Friedman's words: '[l]egal systems do not float in some cultural void, free of space and time and social context; necessarily, they reflect what is happening in their own societies.' See L. Friedman, 'Borders: On the Emerging Sociology of Transnational Law' (1996) 32 *Stanford Journal of International Law* 72.

7 In an uxorilocal marriage, a man, the 'called-in husband' (贅夫), enters the family of his wife (usually a woman without brothers), and at least one of the couple's children assumes the mother's surname. Anthropologist Margery Wolf named the 'called-in husband' a 'male bride': M. Wolf, *Women and the Family in Rural Taiwan*, Stanford University Press, 1987, p. 194.

8 Civil Code Amendment Research Committee, above n. 5, pp. 982–83.

9 The statutory marital property regime (the most common regime) under the pre-1985 law permitted a married woman to hold her own property, including keeping her earnings separate from the joint property, but it vested most rights and power over the marital property in her husband while also holding her responsible for her husband's debts. Although the husband's earnings were considered part of the joint property, he was presumed to be the owner of the joint property and invested with the right to manage the property. This marital property regime resembled the Blackstonian doctrine of marital unity, and was constantly denounced as unequal treatment that rendered the marital property the husband's property. The 1985 revision modestly corrected married men's dominance over marital property, but simultaneously and significantly brought in new forms of discrimination against married women. Married men no longer had presumed ownership over property registered under their wives' titles or any property that could not be proven to be owned by either of them, and creditors could no longer claim the value of a married man's debts from this property. However, the 1985 revision took a step backwards by granting a married man control over his wife's earnings, by considering the earnings part of their joint holdings.

adding a general clause that entitled either spouse to apply for judicial divorce where there had been a grave incident that rendered the maintenance of marriage impossible (unresolved differences),[10] and extending a married man's right to pursue judicial divorce if he had been ill-treated by his wife's lineal ascendants (a right previously reserved for an abused wife) (Article 1052). The revision also changed the assignment of minor children's legal domicile from the father's to the parents' (Article 1060).

2.2. THE SECOND STAGE (1990s–2010): FEMINIST LEGAL REFORM OF THE MARITAL FAMILY

Not long after the 1985 revision of the Civil Code, democratisation and the lifting of martial law in 1987 paved the way for the second stage of family law reform, launched by the feminist movement in 1990, leading to a series of family law revisions that extended from 1995 to 2010. Adopting an incremental approach,[11] the feminist movement pursued a free and equal society in which women would not be subordinated to men in and through the family unit. Unlike the authoritarian legal reform project that sought to mirror society in the law, the feminist project aimed to make change through the law, and considered the revision of family law a priority and a necessity. Its reimagination of the family presented a picture in which marriage was no longer a cage for women and the family was a place where parents were equals. A dual strategy of lobbying and litigation was adopted, resulting in several Constitution Court decisions[12] that ruled gender-specific Civil Code provisions unconstitutional, and the revision of the Civil Code in a piecemeal fashion, sometimes in response to the Constitutional Court's decisions and at other times through independent acts of the legislature. The revision of the children's surname law, in 2007 and 2010, can be considered 'the final act' of the second stage of family law reform, centring on equal treatment between women and men.

The achievements of the second round of family law reform were remarkable. Uxorilocal marriage was no longer a legally recognised form of marriage. Legal patrilocality, the restriction on women's remarriage, and the ban on the marriage of two persons who had engaged in an extramarital affair were abolished.

---

10 If one spouse was responsible for the unresolvable differences, only the other spouse could file for judicial divorce. The Constitutional Court, in *Judgment 112-Hsien-Pan-4* (112年憲判字第4號) (2023), declared it unconstitutional to deny the spouse at fault the right to seek judicial divorce on the grounds of unresolved differences, and gave the legislature two years to amend the law.

11 To be precise, the feminist legal reform movement adopted this incremental approach not as a deliberate choice, but out of necessity, due to the legal and political dynamics.

12 See below n. 27.

The statutory marital property regime dramatically changed the schema of marital property, from a union in which two became one to a partnership that portrayed a married couple as two independent individuals, while at the same time stressing the value of household labour. The new regime celebrates separate ownership and property management while also taking into account spousal contributions to the marital property as a whole.[13] Rather than presuming that a wife will prefix her husband's surname unless she opts out, a married person can choose whether or not to prefix their spouse's surname (Article 1000). As the last act of the second stage of family law reform, the revision of Article 1059, in 2007, replaced the presumption that a child will take their father's surname with a choice of the father's or mother's surname made by parental agreement. A subsequent revision of Article 1059, in 2010, further revised the requirement for the change of a child's surname, making it easier for a parent to do so with court approval,[14] while also allowing adults to change their own surnames at will by removing the parental consent requirement.

Legal changes towards a freer and more equal family were not limited to the Civil Code. For instance, the Family Violence Prevention Act (家庭暴力防治法) was passed in 1998, to provide protection orders for victims of family violence and to mandate criminal punishment of family violence. The Criminal Code (刑法) was revised in 1999 to explicitly outlaw marital rape, although it remains an offence chargeable only upon complaint. The Nationality Act (國籍法) was revised in 2001 to abolish automatic marital naturalisation for women and the paternal rule of *jus sanguinis*, making the right to apply for marital

13 Adopting the new categories of 'premarital property' (婚前財產) and 'property acquired during marriage' (婚後財產), the new law stipulates that all property belonging to the spouses at the time of marriage becomes their 'premarital property'; all property that a spouse acquires during marriage, and as a result of the fruits of that spouse's premarital property, becomes their 'property acquired during marriage'; and any property that cannot be proven as belonging to a specific spouse is also presumed to be 'property acquired during marriage' jointly owned by the couple (Art. 1017). These two kinds of property should be held separately and managed by the husband and wife (Art. 1018), respectively. To further prevent a spouse from concealing or engaging in deceit with respect to their financial situation, the new law also mandates that the husband and wife are under a mutual obligation to report the state of their respective 'property acquired during marriage' (Art. 1022) to one another. The new law also acknowledges the value of housework by entitling a couple to make an agreement in which one spouse gives a certain amount of money (so-called 自由處分金 – literally, 'money to be freely used'), which should not be included in household expenses, to the other spouse, to be used at their discretion (Art. 1018-1). As a compromised reification of the 'wage-for-housework' argument, the law advisedly avoids terms like 'allowance' or 'wage', so as to avoid the suggestion that such payments are pocket money, and to dodge controversy over whether a spouse's labour in the home should be legally rendered a form of paid work.

14 The 2007 law made it a requirement for the court to examine whether or not the change of a child's surname would lead to a disadvantageous influence on the child. The 2010 law replaced the disadvantageous influence requirement, instead considering the interests of the child.

naturalization the same for male and female foreign spouses and granting nationality to children born to citizen mothers and foreign fathers. The Gender Equality in Employment Act (性別平等工作法),[15] which was passed in 2001, and which entered into force in 2002, provides parental and family leave. All in all, new laws revoked many male privileges and improved women's legal status, reframing the family as a domain where sameness is the norm and difference the exception. It should also be noted that the second stage of family law reform centred not only on equality between women and men, but also on children's rights. The custody law reform introduced the best interests of the child doctrine, replacing prioritised custody rights for the father. The best interests of the child doctrine also guides the courts' adoption decisions (Article 1079-1). The children's name law reform made the interests of the child the guiding principle for the courts in reviewing a parent's request to change their child's surname (Article 1059). A child's right to know the identity of, and be cared for by, their parents has also become a constitutional right.[16]

2.3. THE THIRD STAGE (2010s–): THE LEGALISATION OF SAME-SEX MARRIAGE

Same-sex marriage came to the fore of the family law reform debate in the 1990s. As the second stage of family legal reform to pursue equality between women and men had reached the point where many of the laws disadvantaging women had either been abolished or replaced by gender-neutral rules, the time was ripe for LGBTQ equality to move in from the margins. The third stage of family law reform made its official debut in the legislature in 2012, when two legislators introduced bills to legalise same-sex marriage and introduce other forms of legal recognition of non-heterosexual family relationships, against the background of rising demands from the LGBTQ movement to recognise diverse forms of family, in particular same-sex marriage.[17] In the meantime, a counter-movement emerged and grew rapidly in opposition to the legalisation of same-sex marriage. The heated battle within and outside the legislature continued until the Constitutional Court took up two cases regarding the constitutionality

---

15 The original title of the law enacted in 2002 used the term 'two genders' (兩性). This term was subsequently replaced by 'gender' (性別), in 2008, when sexual orientation was added as a prohibited ground for discrimination.

16 In *Judicial Yuan Interpretation No. 587* (司法院釋字第587號解釋) (2004), the Constitutional Court ruled that the child's right to know their genetic origin and confirm their paternity was constitutionally protected. Art. 1063 of the Civil Code was subsequently revised to allow the child to challenge the marital presumption in court, which further enabled the child to establish a legal relationship with their biological father.

17 In 2006, a bill entitled 'The Same-sex Marriage Act' (同性婚姻法) was introduced in the legislature. It was, however, a proposal with no hope of proceeding at that time.

of the same-sex marriage ban, in 2017. In the same year, the Constitutional Court announced its decision, *Judicial Yuan Interpretation No. 748*, ruling it unconstitutional to deny same-sex couples the freedom to marry. Although the counter-movement had been successful in a 2018 referendum, in which the majority stated their disapproval of the legalisation of same-sex marriage via a revision of the Civil Code, the success in the Constitutional Court secured the LGBTQ movement's demand of recognising same-sex couples' right to marry. In May 2019, just before the Court's two-year deadline to comply with the decision, the legislature passed the Enforcement Act of the Judicial Yuan Interpretation No. 748 (司法院釋字第七四八號解釋施行法) (hereinafter the 748 Act) and legalised same-sex marriage. As a pivotal step towards formal equality between same-sex couples and opposite-sex couples, the passage of the 748 Act marks the highlight of the third stage of family law reform.

The 748 Act is a product of compromise. It requires a same-sex couple to effect their union by marriage registration at the Household Administration Bureau (Article 4); however, the statutory language of the 748 Act does not refer to the registered same-sex union as 'marriage' and the term 'spouse' is not used to refer to either party in the same-sex union, indicating a legislative attempt to respond to the counter-movement's objection to recognising same-sex unions as 'marriages'. The 748 Act reiterates many, but not all, of the legal consequences of marriage contained in the Civil Code, including the legal consequences of unlawful marriage, marital property regimes, post-divorce relationships (custody, alimony and the division of marital property), spousal support, spousal inheritance, the duty to cohabit, etc., with some revisions. It also stipulates that laws, other than the Civil Code, concerning couples, spouses and marriage shall apply *mutatis mutandis* (準用) to registered same-sex unions unless otherwise specified. There are a few differences between Civil Code marriage and the 748 Act's legal regulation of same-sex unions, for instance the non-recognition of in-laws, a narrower category of unmarriageable kin, the lack of a prima facie rule for the couple's legal domicile, step-parent adoption being the only form of adoption available for married same-sex couples, etc.[18] In 2023, the 748 Act was revised to permit a married same-sex couple to apply for joint adoption, eliminating one of the Act's differences in treatment between married same-sex couples and opposite-sex couples.[19]

---

18 For a critical review of the 748 Act prior to its revision in 2023, see C. Chen, 'A Same-sex Marriage that is Not the Same: Taiwan's Legal Recognition of Same-sex Unions and Affirmation of Marriage Normativity' (2019) 20 *Australian Journal of Asian Law* 59–68.

19 The administration has also changed its policy to recognise all international same-sex marriages except a same-sex union between a citizen of Taiwan and a citizen of the People's Republic of China. Prior to 2023, it did not allow a Taiwanese citizen to register a same-sex marriage with a foreigner from a country where same-sex marriage is not legal.

Of particular note is the continued endeavour to eliminate remaining differential treatment on the basis of gender. In 2021, Articles 973 and 980 of the Civil Code were revised to make the ages of consent for marriage (結婚年齡) and getting engaged (訂婚年齡) the same for both men and women, and in 2023 the revision took effect.[20] Previously, the age of consent for marriage was 16 for women and 18 for men, and the age of consent for getting engaged was 15 for women and 17 for men. The gender age differences were based on the assumption that men were ready to enter into marriage after they had finished a certain degree of education and were able to serve as breadwinners, whereas women were thought ready as soon as they were capable of reproduction.[21] The new law mandates the age of consent for getting engaged at 17 for both genders, and the age of consent for marriage at 18, which presumably subverts the gendered assumption of an ideal marriage being composed of a breadwinner husband and a caretaking housewife. However, the law of marital presumption (婚生推定), which defines the status of a child in accordance with the mother's marital status,[22] remains in place, meaning that maternity is presumed, whereas paternity needs to be established. The issue of whether the law of marital presumption should apply to married same-sex couples also remains a controversy.

3. THREE TRENDS OF FAMILY LAW REFORM

Over the last 50 years, family law reform in Taiwan has been characterised by three trends: the shift towards gender-neutrality, the expansion of family autonomy and the constitutionalisation of family law. The first two trends demonstrate the prevailing acquiescence to formal equality and individualism, whereas the last trend indicates the Constitutional Court's pivotal role in reshaping family law.

3.1. THE MOVEMENT TOWARDS GENDER-NEUTRALITY

The replacement of gender-specific rules with gender-neutral ones is hard for any observers to miss. Gradually, laws that specifically privileged men and

---

20 As part of a revision of the Civil Code that lowered the age of adulthood from 20 to 18.

21 Civil Code Amendment Research Committee, above n. 5, 585.

22 A 'marital child' (婚生子) is one who was conceived by a mother who was, at the time of conception, married to a man, who is presumed to be the child's father. A 'non-marital child' (非婚生子) is one who was conceived by a woman who was not married at the time of conception or whose mother's husband has been proven not to be the child's biological father. A 'non-marital child' can be legitimised and acquire the status of a 'marital child' through the marriage of the mother and the biological father (準正) or the biological father's de facto or *de jure* acknowledgement (認領).

disadvantaged women have become history. In their quest for gender equality in family law, feminists in Taiwan, like their counterparts in other countries, prioritised the fight against differential treatment based on gender. Family law reform was at the top of the feminist agenda because various differential legal treatments of the family rendered women subordinate to men. The dominant line of thinking presumes differential treatment to be discrimination. Pursuing equality, therefore, requires the replacement of differential treatment with equal treatment unless the differential treatment is based on justified differences. The same logic requires the law to make no distinction between same-sex and opposite-sex couples unless the differential treatment can be justified by the differences between same-sex and opposite-sex couples.

This line of thinking would suggest that the mandatory requirement for a wife to take her husband's domicile as her legal domicile is both differential treatment and discrimination. So, too, is the requirement that a child take their father's surname, the disqualification of married daughters from inheritance, and the ban on same-sex couples marrying in the same way as opposite-sex couples. To make things equal, a wife should have the same right to determine her legal domicile as her husband has, as well as the same right to pursue divorce in the courts when unable to secure a consensual divorce. A mother should have the same right to determine the surname of her child as a father has. So, too, should a daughter have the same rights as a son when it comes to inheritance. The development of family law over the last 50 years has resulted in the same treatment of women and men in many respects: a married woman is treated the same as a married man, a mother the same as a father, and a daughter the same as a son. Equality between women and men can be called 'equality 1.0'. The legalisation of same-sex marriage, moreover, takes a further step by treating same-sex couples in a very similar, if not exactly the same, way to opposite-sex couples. Equality between gay and straight people can be called 'equality 2.0'.

Indeed, the achievement of equality 1.0 paved the way for equality 2.0. Gender-specific language has mostly been replaced by gender-neutral language. The terms 'husband' (夫) and 'wife' (妻) have either been replaced by the gender-neutral term 'spouse' (配偶) or used together (husband(s) and wife/wives) (夫妻), to implement gender-neutrality. Since there is no gender-neutral term for parents in Chinese, the terms 'father' and 'mother' are used together (father(s)/mother(s)) (父母) to denote gender-neutrality. The choice to pass a new law (the 748 Act) rather than applying the Civil Code to same-sex couples reflects more the legislature's intent to comply with the counter-movement's demands and less a legal necessity, due to the inapplicability of the Civil Code to same-sex couples.[23]

---

23 It is also argued that new legislation (as opposed to a revision of the Civil Code to legalise same-sex marriage) was necessary due to the results of the referendum in 2018. There were

3.2. THE EXPANSION OF FAMILY AUTONOMY

The movement towards gender-neutrality has been accompanied by the expansion of family autonomy in the form of contractualisation. The replacement of gender-specific rules with gender-neutral rules, and status rules with contract rules, are two of the basic themes of the development of family law in Taiwan. As family law is also called 'the law of status' (身分法), this development can also be understood as the contractualisation of 'the law of status'.[24] The old family law featured status rules that reflected and constituted male supremacy: a married man's authority in determining the location of the married couple's domicile and control over marital property, the father's privileged status in the assignment of custody and children's surnames, and the privileged status of paternal lineage, to name but a few. The new family law, celebrated as an achievement of the liberal feminist legal reform project launched in the 1990s, is dominated by gender-neutral status rules and contract rules that privilege private negotiation between free individuals, although such contractual freedom is not absolute, and is still subject to legal regulation. The adoption of contract rules has expanded the autonomy of a family to determine its own affairs. Married couples are entitled to decide the location of their domicile together, and children's surnames are also subject to parental negotiation. The institution of marriage has opened the door for same-sex couples to enter into a marriage contract. The liberalisation of divorce has made it easier for those who are unable to engage in contracts to achieve consensual divorce to pursue judicial divorce, particularly on the grounds of irreconcilable differences.[25]

---

three referendum questions with regard to same-sex marriage. The referendum on 'the definition of marriage in the Civil Code shall be a union of a man and a woman' and the referendum on 'protecting same-sex couples' right to establish a permanent conjugal life relationship in forms other than the chapter on marriage in the Civil Code' were approved by the majority of voters. The referendum on 'protecting same-sex couples' right to marry by amending the Civil Code' failed. According to the Referendum Act (公民投票法), the legislature is legally bound to make its legislative decision in accordance with the result of the referendum. However, the legislature is also entitled to seek the Constitutional Court's guidance if a constitutional question arises from the enforcement of the adopted referendum. Legally speaking, the legislature, in exercising its power, can argue that the adopted referendum on excluding the legalisation of same-sex marriage by amending the Civil Code was a potential violation of the Constitution, and seek the Constitutional Court's opinion by having more than one-third of the legislators petition the Court. Regrettably, the legislators did not pursue this approach to resolve the controversy, and instead considered themselves constrained by the adopted referendum in making their legislative choices.

24 This is not to suggest that the State has retreated completely from the family regime, but rather to emphasise the law's growing recognition of private ordering. As a global phenomenon, family law's movement towards contract in traditional family formations has been accompanied by the State's regulation of new family formations. See F. Swennen (ed.), *Contractualisation of Family Law – Global Perspectives*, Springer, 2015.

25 Consensual divorce, which does not have to go through the courts, accounts for the vast majority of divorces in Taiwan. In 2023, 85.11% of all divorces were achieved by agreement.

3.3. THE CONSTITUTIONALISATION OF FAMILY LAW

Together, the shift towards gender-neutrality and the expansion of family autonomy facilitate the liberal feminist vision of the family as one in which individuals are equals, capable of making choices and reaching agreement. The constitutionalisation of family law since the 1990s[26] has played a paramount role in this process, thanks to feminist constitutional activism which submitted sex-specific laws for judicial review, and the dual strategy of lobbying and litigation.[27] In a series of decisions, the Constitutional Court developed its jurisprudence on gender equality and marital status discrimination in the domain of the family, declaring differential treatment of married women, mothers and married daughters unconstitutional.[28] Remarkably, the very first Constitutional Court

---

See 離婚對數按離婚方式 ('the number of divorce in accordance to the way of divorce'), available at https://www.ris.gov.tw/app/portal/346. The percentage of divorce cases granted on the ground of irreconcilable differences increased from 68.86% in 2013 to 87.64% in 2022. In 2022, out of 4,892 divorce cases filed in district courts, 2,891 cases resulted in judgments in favour of the plaintiffs. See 司法院統計處 (Department of Statistics, the Judicial Yuan), 司法統計年報 *(Judicial Statistics Yearbook)*, The Judicial Yuan, 2023.

26 Li-ju Lee has argued that the Constitutional Court's intervention in the regulation of the family since the 1990s has resulted in the constitutionalisation of Taiwanese family law, which has steered family law in the direction of gender equality. Specifically, the Constitutional Court has recognised the family as a constitutionally protected institution; the application of individual rights and the principle of gender equality to family law; and a growing group of fundamental rights regarding marriage and family. See L. Lee, 'The Constitutionalization of Taiwanese Family Law' (2016) 11 *National Taiwan University Law Review* 273–332.

27 Feminist constitutional activism in the early 1990s advocated for a 'Women's Constitutional Charter' (婦女憲章), which resulted in partial success with the passage of a Constitutional amendment in 1992 that stipulated that '[t]he State shall protect the dignity of women, safeguard their personal safety, eliminate sexual discrimination, and further substantive gender equality'. The passage of a new Constitutional amendment was by no means the end of a social movement which has endeavoured to pursue its goal through the mobilisation of law. Questions remain as to how feminist activism can help carry out the textual promises inherent in the Constitution and serve as a catalyst for further changes in constitutional culture. After the partial success of feminist constitution-making, feminists turned to different battlefields – the judiciary and the legislature – while the Constitution continues to serve as a source of authority and an enabling framework that facilitates legal changes. A constitutional litigation movement was launched to bring cases to the Constitutional Court for judicial review, in the hope that the justices would invoke the gender equality clause to invalidate laws discriminating against women, which in turn would force the legislature to amend laws. This feminist constitutional activism put women's lives front and centre by using female plaintiffs – married women, mothers and daughters – a strategy that marked a stark contrast with the approach Ruth Bader Ginsberg pursued when she directed the women's rights project at the American Civil Liberties Union, which primarily made use of male plaintiffs to persuade male-dominated courts.

28 *Judicial Yuan Interpretation No. 410* (司法院釋字第410號解釋) (1996) (declaring it unconstitutional that the Enforcement Law for Part IV (Family Law) of the Civil Code (民法親屬編施行法) sustained the husband's dominant rights over the community property after the 1995 revisions of the Civil Code, and upholding Art. 16, subpara. 11 of the Estate

decision to rule a statute unconstitutional on gender equality grounds, *Judicial Yuan Interpretation No. 365* (1995), was a decision regarding family law and a positive response to a feminist test case featuring two mothers whose exercise of parental rights had been denied by the courts because the law explicitly privileged fathers (Article 1089 of the Civil Code). Premised on the 'law-as-mirror-of-society' thesis, the Court announced that the law granting the father superior parental rights over the mother – a status rule that determined one's rights and duties in accordance with one's gender – was no longer a proper reflection of the society it was based on, and offered a solution to 'seal the gap'; that is, it acknowledged the fact that, nowadays, women's competence as legal guardians of their children is no different to that of men. This landmark decision depicted a feudal past with cultural traditions and social circumstances that justified women's disqualification in the family, and contrasted it with a modern society where women are entitled to the same educational and employment opportunities as men, which proves their de facto competence and provides legitimacy for their *de jure* equal treatment.[29] The decision led to a revision of the Civil Code in 1996, abolishing the paternal supremacy rule and assigning to the

and Gift Tax Act (遺產及贈與稅法), which stipulated that the total amount of the inherited property excluded the surviving spouses' and heirs' separate property or contributed property officially registered or recorded by deed); *Judicial Yuan Interpretation No. 452* (司法院釋字第452號解釋) (1998) (invalidating Art. 1002 of the Civil Code, which stipulated that a married woman should take up her husband's residence and the 'called-in' husband should take up the wife's residence unless otherwise agreed); *Judicial Yuan Interpretation No. 457* (司法院釋字第457號解釋) (1998) (invalidating 'the Regulation for the Handling of Government-Owned Housing and Farmlands Vacated by Married Veterans after their Hospitalization, Retirement or Death' (本會各農場有眷場員就醫、就養或死亡開缺後房舍土地處理要點), on the basis of gender and marital status discrimination, because it denied a veteran's married daughter the right to inherit her father's leasing privileges from the government); *Judgment 112-Hsien-Pan-1* (112年憲判字第1號) (2023) (ruling it unconstitutional to use gender and marital status classification in the determination of the qualification of successors of ancestor worship guilds (祭祀公業)).

29 The Court said that '[Article 1089 of the Civil Code] was … a product of the cultural traditions and social structure at that time. However, with widespread education and more equal access to education between men and women as well as more equal opportunities for women in employment, such provision granting final decision-making authority to fathers would render different results today …; In cases of unsettled disagreements, the said provision nevertheless grants the final decision-making authority to fathers, without taking into account the positions of mothers. Such result will violate the principle of equal protection between men and women and be incompatible with the actual status of women in current family life.' The same line of argument can also be found in the Constitutional Court's subsequent decision regarding a married couple's domicile, *Judicial Yuan Interpretation No. 452* (司法院釋字第452號解釋) (1998), in which the Court ruled legally mandated patrilocality (Art. 1002 of the Civil Code) unconstitutional. Following the statement that, '[g]iven that education is very common nowadays and men and women have almost the same opportunity to make career choices, the workplace of the husband and the wife may not be the same', the Court continued to reason that the denial of the other party's right to choose the residence was in violation of constitutional equality.

courts the responsibility to make decisions in accordance with the best interests of the child in cases where there is a disagreement between parents. Not only has the decision triggered the substitution of gender-specific rules with gender-neutral rules, but it has also provided the standard of review for constitutional gender equality, which defines gender equality as referring to equal treatment unless there are biological differences or biologically based social differences that can justify differential treatment. This standard of review remains dominant in the court's equality jurisprudence.[30]

The Court's family law cases have played a pivotal role in shaping its jurisprudence on discrimination based on gender and marital status. It has recognised gender and marital status discrimination as a violation of constitutional equality in cases involving denying married daughters the right to inheritance.[31] After the turn of the new millennium, the Court developed

30 The Constitutional Court further specified the standard of review in *Judicial Yuan Interpretation No. 807* (司法院釋字第807號解釋) (2021), a case in which the Constitutional Court declared the ban on women working night shifts unconstitutional. The standard requires heightened scrutiny for differential treatment based on gender distinctions when immutable characteristics or historical or systematic gender stereotypes serve as the basis for such a distinction.

31 In *Judicial Yuan Interpretation No. 457* (司法院釋字第457號解釋) (1998), a decision widely recognised as upholding a married daughter's right to inheritance, the Court ruled that the government's discriminatory treatment of veterans' daughters, which disqualified them from 'inheriting' their deceased fathers' benefits (government-distributed farmland and houses) when they had a brother or were married, was unconstitutional. However, the Court deliberately dodged addressing whether the distributed farmland was inheritable, stating that there was no need to address the inheritance issue since the case already involved discriminatory treatment against a specific group of women based on sex and marital status. The decision was widely celebrated for repudiating the traditional idea that 'daughters who marry out of the family are like spilled water'. However, years later, *Judicial Yuan Interpretation No. 728* (2015) reversed course on the previous rejection of treating married daughters as outsiders. *Judicial Yuan Interpretation No. 728* involved the qualification of successors to ancestor worship guilds. The petitioner was a married woman who had been denied the status of successor to her natal family's worship guild, which was worth tens of millions of New Taiwan (NT) dollars. She contested the constitutionality of the law in question, which respected the self-governance of a worship guild and recognised the exclusion of women set forth in their charters. Rather than ruling against the self-governance of worship guilds, the Court viewed ancestor worship guilds as rooted in 'history and tradition' and deemed the law constitutional in the name of protecting property rights and the autonomy of private law, and thus hesitated to rule it unconstitutional. In a recent development, the Court reverted to its position on the status of married women as set forth in *Judicial Yuan Interpretation No. 457*. *Judgment 112-Hsien-Pan-1* (2023) partly overturned *Judicial Yuan Interpretation No. 728*, and instead aligned with *Judicial Yuan Interpretation No. 457* in denouncing differential treatment based on gender and marital status. The petitioners were married women and their children, who claimed their rights to be recognised as successors to the ancestor worship guilds of their birth families. The Court ruled that the exclusion of married women was unconstitutional differential treatment based on gender and marital status, reasoning that the traditional practice of limiting the qualification of successors to unmarried female descendants in the absence of male descendants was manifestly discrimination based on gender and a distinction

its equality jurisprudence further, considering discrimination based on sexual orientation in the area of family law by issuing *Judicial Yuan Interpretation No. 748*, in the renowned same-sex marriage case, which ruled that the constitutional protection of gender equality includes the equality of 'gender, gender identity, and sexual orientation' and declared that the standard of heightened scrutiny should be applied to distinctions based on sexual orientation. In doing so, the Court embraced formal equality between same-sex and opposite-sex couples by arguing that there is no difference between same-sex and opposite-sex couples in respect of their need, willingness and ability to create a permanent union of an intimate and exclusive nature. The Court also identified sexual orientation as an immutable characteristic and homosexuals as a 'discrete and insular minority' in society.

Given the Constitutional Court's adherence to the anti-classification principle, which centres on the permissibility of classification and differential treatment, it is unsurprising that the Constitutional Court has a poor record in responding to gender-neutral family law provisions that have contributed to women's inequality. In cases involving statutes that are facially gender neutral but have a disparate impact on women, the Constitutional Court has often refused to rule them unconstitutional. *Judicial Yuan Interpretation No. 372* (1995) exemplifies how formal equality fails to adequately address and combat gender inequality when it comes to domestic violence. *Judicial Yuan Interpretation No. 372* tackled a notorious precedent which denied a mistreated spouse the right to judicial divorce in a case where 'the other party temporarily loses control and overreacts to misconduct'. The petitioner to the Constitutional Court was an abused wife whose claim to judicial divorce, on the grounds of having suffered unbearable mistreatment from her husband, was turned down by the courts because her husband's acts of physical violence were deemed 'temporary overreactions', not unbearable mistreatment. Rather than condemning the prevalence of domestic violence as a form of discrimination against women and an indication of the husband's unbridled power over his wife, the Constitutional Court rejected the petitioner's argument that the precedent at issue endorsed a husband's right to chastise his wife,[32] considered the abuse to consist of neutral acts that could be committed by either party against the other, and deemed the precedent constitutional.

---

based on historical gender stereotypes, and hence an unjust difference in treatment of the excluded female descendants.

32 The wife's petition argued that the precedent the courts had invoked was a sign of the State's tolerance of a husband's violence against his wife, as long as he considers that she has misbehaved, and that this, in effect, invested the husband with the power to discipline his wife, excused by her alleged misconduct – a violation of the constitutional guarantee of gender equality and people's basic freedoms and rights.

The Constitutional Court has also repeatedly denied requests to revoke the exclusion of women as successors designated in ancestor worship guild charters (祭祀公業規約). Female offspring, particularly daughters who have 'married out', have historically been excluded from succession in ancestor worship guilds, specifically through guild charters. The disputed provisions of the Act for Ancestor Worship Guild (祭祀公業條例) involve two forms of regulation, a gender-neutral one and a gender-specific one. The Act stipulated that: (1) in cases where there is a guild charter, the successors shall be decided by the charter; (2) in the absence of a guild charter, the successors shall be the male offspring of the family, or their unmarried female offspring when there are no male offspring. In *Judgment 112-Hsien-Pan-1* (112年憲判字第1號) (2023), the Court struck down, as discrimination based on gender and marital status, the gender-specific provision that privileged male offspring, but refused to declare the gender-neutral provision that honours the guild's charter unconstitutional.[33] Again, the constitutionality of gender-neutral family law with disparate impacts on women was sustained. *Judgment 112-Hsien-Pan-4* (112年憲判字第4號) (2023), which deems Section 2, Article 1052 of the Civil Code's strict ban on an at-fault spouse seeking judicial divorce on the grounds of irreconcilable differences a violation of the constitutional protection of marriage freedom, is an exception. The Court, however, does not consider the constitutionality of the judicial divorce requirement to be an issue of gender equality.

4. FROM STATUS TO CONSENT: THE RADICAL FEMINIST FAMILY LAW STORY

The development of family law over the last half-century has re-envisioned the family as a unit formed of equal individuals, honouring children's rights and welfare rather than treating them as the belongings of their parents (particularly their father). The institution of marriage has been reconstructed in law as one that celebrates individual freedom and mutual agreements, and is no longer a union dominated by the husband. However, gender inequality in the family remains a reality in contemporary Taiwan, despite the achievements of family law reform over the last 50 years. The gender gap in post-divorce custody assignments has narrowed significantly, and mothers have gradually begun to outnumber fathers in getting custody.[34] However, women still inherit less property than men,

---

33 *Judgment 112-Hsien-Pan-1* (112年憲判字第*1*號)(2023) partly overturned *Judicial Yuan Interpretation No. 728*. See above n. 31 for further discussion.

34 A recent study claims that the genders, occupations and economic resources of parents are no longer determining factors in the courts' custody decisions. See H.-L. Shao, R.B. Leflar and S.-C. Huang, 'Factors Determining Child Custody in Taiwan after Patriarchy's Decline:

although the gender gap is slowly narrowing.[35] The common practice of children taking their fathers' surnames endures, with only 2.89 per cent of all newborns in 2022 being given their mothers' surnames through parental agreement.[36]

Equality advocates in Taiwan who subscribe to the liberal legal ideology of individualism and formal equality are inclined to consider existing inequality in family formation and relationships a matter of culture rather than law, except where differential treatment exists under the law. For them, legal reforms towards gender equality are incomplete for two main reasons. Firstly, there remains differential treatment under the law that needs to be changed, in particular the remaining differences between the legal status of same-sex marriage and opposite-sex marriage. Secondly, patriarchal cultural traditions are considered the main obstacle to the implementation of equality in family law, and pursuing cultural change is seen as the key to making equality laws work. From this point of view, patriarchy and heterosexual supremacy have survived family law reforms due to the law's limited ability to realise the ideal 'republic of choice' to which equality advocates aspire.

This view of equality law and social change is a matter of controversy. Featuring individualism, gender-neutrality, and private ordering through mutual agreements,[37] the development of Taiwanese family law over the last 50 years seems to tell a story of a shift from status to contract – a shift echoed in many other countries. As a narrative of modernity, this status-to-contract story facilitates Taiwan's self-identification as a modern state that has departed from its

---

Decision Tree Analysis on Family Court Decisions' (2023) 18 *Asian Journal of Comparative Law* 272–88.

35 One of the key mechanisms to disinherit women, in particular daughters, is the exercise of individual freedom of property through various forms, which include: (1) the writing of wills; (2) the act of gift-giving; and (3) the signing of a waiver. The preferences of testators might not be a crucial factor because testamentary succession is not common. Gift-giving and the signing of waivers play a more significant role in the exclusion of daughters. There have been persistent but narrowing gaps between the numbers of women and men who paid gift taxes, or who waived their rights to inheritance. In 2022, 59.2% of individuals subject to gift tax were male, while 40.8% were female, yielding an 18.4 percentage point gender gap, down from 24.2 points in 2012. Over the past decade, changes in the gender ratio of gift recipients have been minimal. Additionally, among those who waived their inheritance rights in 2022, 45.1% were male and 54.9% were female, resulting in a gender gap of 9.8 percentage points, a decrease from 14.6 points in 2012. This trend reflects a declining proportion of women relinquishing their inheritance rights over the last ten years. Department of Gender Equality, Executive Yuan, *Gender at a Glance in R.O.C. (Taiwan)* (2024), Executive Yuan, p. 33.

36 內政部 (The Ministry of the Interior), 全國姓名統計分析 ('An Analysis of National Statistics of Names, Ministry of the Interior'), 2023, p. 236.

37 To be precise, private ordering (individuals setting rights and obligations through mutual agreements) has long been part of Taiwanese family law, as exemplified by the legal option of consensual divorce outside court. Family law reform has expanded the public recognition of private ordering.

backward past, and as a society that fits Henry Maine's definition of 'progressive societies' rather than being one of the 'stationary societies', as Maine categorised most non-Western societies. In what may be called the liberal feminist version of Taiwan's family law story, the road from status to contract is preferred and revolutionary, but the journey remains incomplete. This status-to-contract story, which shows a progression from patriarchy to freedom,[38] is popular in what Jill E. Hasday called 'family law canons' in the US, which she finds to be problematic on both factual and normative grounds.[39] Identifying with Maine's 'status-to-contract' thesis ('the movement of the progressive societies has hitherto been a movement from Status to Contract')[40] may serve Taiwan's need to be recognised as a progressive democracy. However, this recognition is being purchased at the cost of double blindness: blindness to the Orientalism embodied in Maine's thesis,[41] and blindness to the contribution of contract rules in sustaining inequality.

4.1. FROM 'PATRONYMY BY STATUS' TO 'PATRONYMY BY CONSENT'

The children's surname law serves as a textbook case for examining the 'status-to-contract' story and the liberal feminist view of equality law and social change. Patronymic naming systems are dominant in many societies, of which Taiwan is one.[42] Such systems are a product of both law and culture. In countries where it is legally required that children take their father's surname, patronymy is a legal norm that both constitutes and reflects the culture of patronymic naming. In countries where the law makes it a parental decision to choose their child's surname, the 'cultural' practice of patronymic naming is sustained by personal

---

38 Carole Pateman considers what Maine called 'status' as patriarchy, and 'contract' as freedom: C. Pateman, *The Sexual Contract*, Stanford University Press, 1988, pp. 9–10.

39 J.E. Hasday, *Family Law Reimagined*, Harvard University Press, 2014, pp. 95–158. Hasday defines 'family law canons' as 'the dominant narratives, stories, examples, and ideas that judges, lawmakers, and (to a less crucial extent) commentators repeatedly invoke to describe and explain family law and its governing principles' (ibid, p. 2).

40 H.S. Maine, *Ancient Law*, Henry Holt and Co., 1906, p. 136.

41 For a critique of Orientalism in Maine's theory, see V. Corcodel, *Modern Law and Otherness: The Dynamics of Inclusion and Exclusion in Comparative Legal Thought*, Edward Elgar, 2019.

42 The patronymic naming system requires that a child be named after their father, and that a married woman adopt her husband's surname. A discussion on women's marital names and a comparison with children's surnames is beyond the scope of this chapter. For the same reason, the naming of indigenous people in Taiwan, who have various naming systems distinct from those of Han people, is not be discussed in this chapter. For a discussion of intersectionality and a comparison of marital names and children's surnames, see C. Chen, 'Becoming "Outsiders Within": A Feminist Social-Legal Study of Surname Inequality as Sex, Race, and Marital Status Discrimination in Taiwan' (2018) 18 *Journal of Korean Law* 1–58.

'choices', acknowledged by law. In either case, law is both constitutive and reflective of patronymy.

The relationship between law and patronymy may differ in accordance with the ways in which the law regulates naming. There is a huge difference between legal bars on giving children their mother's surname and legal endorsement of parental choices over children's surnames. In the latter situation, parents are entitled to reach an agreement over their child's surname, and this entitlement provides an opportunity to practice non-conventional naming, which holds the potential to challenge patronymy; that is to say, the right to choose children's surnames through parental agreement can serve as a form of empowerment. It can, however, also serve to legitimise patronymy. The development of Taiwan's children's surname law is, on its face, a movement from status to contract, but in reality a movement from 'patronymy by status' to 'patronymy by consent'.

Article 1059 of the Civil Code, prior to its revisions in 1985 and 2007, provided that a child should assume the surname of their father, and where the husband marries into the wife's household, the child should assume the surname of the mother, unless another agreement had been reached. Article 1059 endorsed the notion that a child was assumed to continue the paternal line, be it on the husband's side or the wife's. When children take their father's surname, they take their descent from their father; when they take their mother's surname, they take their descent from their maternal grandfather. In this way, women are interpreted as bearing children for men (fathers), regardless of whether the father in question is *her own* father or *her children's* father. Patronymy is, indeed, as Omi Morgenstern Leissner puts it, 'a classic example of a "double bind"'.[43]

The law was revised in 1985 to enhance the probability of children taking their mother's surname, officially easing the State's strict and direct control of children's surnames. Article 1059 was amended to permit a wife in a patrilocal marriage to pass her surname to her child through mutual agreement, provided that she had no brother. In 2003, the Name Act (姓名條例) was revised, making it possible for a divorced parent who had custody of the child to change the child's surname so that the mother and child shared the same surname. A divorced mother was, therefore, entitled to give her child her own surname.

The revolutionary revision of Article 1059, in 2007, made it a requirement that children's surnames be determined by mutual agreement between the parents in writing. This was a hard-won success for the feminist movement, which had advocated the abolition of patronymy for almost four decades. Celebrated as a landmark achievement of the women's movement,[44] the new

---

43 O. Morgenstern Leissner, 'The Problem That Has No Name' (1998) 4 *Cardozo Women's Law Journal* 258.

44 Nevertheless, many feminist groups were critical of the new legislation, despite their support for the newly adopted principle of private negotiation. One of the critiques condemned the

children's surname law substitutes the State's direct enforcement of patronymy (status) for private negotiation (contract), by stating that parents shall agree in writing, before filing the child's birth registration, which surname (the mother's or the father's) the child will assume. Parents are not allowed to combine their surnames[45] or choose a surname other than their own. This legislation should not be considered a form of 'deregulation' because: (1) private negotiation is made possible by law; (2) in the event that parents fail to reach a consensus, the law decides how the child's surname shall be determined; that is, through the drawing of lots.[46]

The celebration of feminist achievement soon turned into a (foreseeable) disappointment. Since the new law took effect, official statistics consistently show that very few women have exercised this hard-won right by reaching an agreement with their husbands to give their child their own surname. From 2007 to 2022, only 1.93 per cent of all parents of newborns, on average, mutually agreed to give their child the mother's surname.[47] The extremely low percentage of children taking their mothers' surnames is often understood as an unfortunate gap between law and social norms, and demonstrates the incapability of law to effectively change social norms, although there is an alternative explanation for this phenomenon.

National surveys show that the new surname law has been accompanied by a change in attitudes toward choosing children's surnames, with a growing approval rate for matronymic practices. Gender and socio-economic status play a significant role when it comes to people's attitudes toward children's surnames: women as a whole are more likely than men to support matronymic

---

new law's lack of recognition of an individual's right to determine their own surname, while the Constitutional Court had ruled that the right of an individual to select their name was a constitutionally protected right in Judicial Yuan Interpretation No. 399 (司法院釋字第399號解釋) (1996). The 2007 revision required parental permission for a child who had reached adulthood to change their surname. The law was revised again, in 2010, to remove the requirement of parental permission.

45 In Taiwan's legal naming system, the last name (surname) is placed before the first name, with the exception of indigenous people's naming traditions. This naming system enables some parents to circumvent the legal ban on combining both parents' surnames by incorporating one of their surnames into their child's first name.

46 In Taiwanese law, the drawing of lots as a method of random selection is required in certain situations, but not in family law matters, except in the case of a child's surname. Against the government's proposal that the court intervene, in the absence of parental agreement, to determine a child's surname according to the child's best interests, the legislature chose the drawing of lots (proposed by feminist legislators and feminist advocacy groups) as the legal solution. The drawing of lots to determine a child's surname is also a legal solution once recommended by the German Federal Constitutional Court, in a 1991 decision in which it ruled that the German Civil Code's privileging of the husband's surname was a violation of the German Basic Law. It was, ultimately, rejected by the Bundestag in 1993, which passed a law giving the guardianship court the power to decide. See S. Jeleff (ed.), *The Gender Perspective (Debates/Parliamentary Assembly)*, Council of Europe, 1995, p. 61.

47 The Ministry of the Interior, *An Analysis of National Statistics of Names*, above n. 36, p. 21.

naming; men are significantly more likely than women to support patronymic naming; respondents with a higher level of education and non-manual workers seem to be more flexible in their approach to bestowing children's surnames – the more 'privileged' a woman is (in terms of education level and occupation), the more likely it is that she will challenge patronymy and have a positive influence on her husband, or be supported by him.[48]

Indeed, those who get more in life get more in law. Formal equality in law usually reflects, rather than effectively challenges, inequality in life. While women in general are more supportive of matronymic naming, those who successfully negotiate a surname contract to give their child their own surname are a small minority. This confirms the radical feminist thesis that liberal feminist law reform towards formal equality benefits mostly 'the privileged few'.[49] The idea that the new surname law is incapable of radically changing the status quo is also demonstrated by the fact that men are more supportive of patronymic naming. Maintaining a system of exclusive patrilineal surnames confers multiple benefits on men as a group.[50] Men are inclined to maintain the status quo because they enjoy a patriarchal dividend. The new surname law gives men the legal right to maintain patronymy; that is, the father's right to 'negotiate' with the mother. A woman cannot give the child her surname unless the child does not have a legal father or the legal father agrees to this. This means that she has to get his permission, and that he has a right to say no. The fact that the random solution (drawing lots at the household registration office when parents fail to reach an agreement) is rarely sought in practice[51] also demonstrates the constrained autonomy of mothers and the de facto power of fathers.

While, in law, the surname contract is supposed to be built on mutual agreement between the parents, there is reason to believe that, in many if not all cases, the 'agreement' to give the child the father's surname is not something that comes into being, but already exists. More often than not, the agreement is 'assumed' rather than 'reached'. As Catharine A. MacKinnon has forcefully argued, consent tends to be presumed in the private sphere, and the problem is 'getting anything private to be perceived as coercive'.[52] A national survey

---

48 See C. Chen, Y. Peng and C. Chang, 'Women's (No) Naming Right under the Shadow of Patronymy: Changes in the Public Attitudes in Taiwan between 2002 and 2012' (2017) 138 *Survey Research – Method and Application* 57–97.

49 C.A. MacKinnon, *Feminism Unmodified: Discourses on Life and Law*, Harvard University Press, 1987, p. 24.

50 C. Nugent, 'Children's Surnames, Moral Dilemmas: Accounting for the Predominance of Fathers' Surnames for Children' (2010) 24 *Gender & Society* 499–525.

51 From 2007 to 2022, only 0.02% of newborns, on average, were given their surnames based on the drawing of lots: The Ministry of the Interior, *An Analysis of National Statistics of Names*, above n. 36, p. 21.

52 C.A. MacKinnon, *Toward a Feminist Theory of the State*, Harvard University Press, 1989, p. 190.

conducted in 2019 revealed that 89.8 per cent of parents interviewed had not had a discussion to decide their children' surnames, and 75.3 per cent decided their children's surnames in accordance with social conventions ('following what the majority of people do').[53] A mother's consent to name the child after the father is the presumption, although it may be legally rebuttable. This indicates a tendency to maintain custom, and patronymy is the custom – the default rule. The law endorses this tendency by affirming the 'choice' to practice patronymy, and allows for non-conformity mostly for a privileged few. In most cases, the mother will 'consent'.

Consent has replaced the blunt status rule that functioned to sustain patronymy, updating the ways in which patriarchy operates.[54] It demonstrates what Reva Siegel terms 'preservation through transformation';[55] that is, preserving male supremacy in children's naming through the transition from status rules to contract rules. It also offers an illustration of MacKinnon's critique that '[c]oercion legitimated becomes consent'[56] and Carole Pateman's critique that '[c]ontract is the specifically modern means of creating relationships of subordination, but, because civil subordination originates in contract, it is presented as freedom'.[57] Although a few women do manage to negotiate the

---

53 The Legal Culture and Social Change Survey (2019), https://srda.sinica.edu.tw/datasearch_detail.php?id=3546. It is a nationwide, face-to-face survey of 2,052 samples.

54 Another textbook example of inequality perpetrated through consent is the practice of daughters signing waivers to give up their rights of inheritance. The freedom of waiving one's right of inheritance, recognised by the law under certain legal conditions (Art. 1174 of the Civil Code), has led to the disinheritance of daughters by consent. It should be noted, however, that while the signing of waivers is sometimes an act that demonstrates the daughter's compassion for the unity and harmony of the family, it can also be a part of a bargain through which the daughter receives some compensation in exchange for her consent. A waiver of inheritance in exchange for compensation can be seen as a bargain that serves multiple purposes, including reducing the legal risks of disinheriting daughters who are legally entitled to inherit, and facilitating a balance between economic interests and harmonious family relations. Whether or not the daughter agrees to sign the waiver, and the price of her consent, are core issues to be resolved for an inheritance bargain, and the daughter's legal right to inherit serves as a powerful bargaining chip for her. The gender politics of signing the waiver thus reveals the paradox of rights: exercising one's right while simultaneously relinquishing one's right. It is politics surrounding a woman's consent that has empowered her as a legal subject capable of, and entitled to give, consent, but which also subordinates her as a woman deemed ineligible to inherit. See 陳昭如 (C. Chen), 在棄權與爭產之間——超越被害者與行動者二元對立的女兒繼承權實踐 ('Bargaining with Patriarchy: Daughter's Right of Inheritance in Practice') (2009) 38臺大法學論叢 *(NTU Law Journal)* 133–228.

55 R. Siegel, 'Why Equal Protection No Longer Protects: The Evolving Forms of Status-Enforcing State Action' (1997) 49 *Stanford Law Review* 1111–48.

56 Above n. 52 at 238. MacKinnon has challenged the very concept of consent by arguing that consent is essentially an unequal concept: C.A. MacKinnon, 'Rape Redefined' (2016) 10 *Harvard Law & Policy Review* 440.

57 C. Pateman, *The Sexual Contract*, above n. 38, p. 127. Pateman contends that consent is given to something which already exists, whereas contract 'brings new relationships into being': C. Pateman, 'Afterword' in M. Shanley, I. Young and D. O'Neill (eds.), *The Illusion of Consent: Engaging with Carole Pateman*, Penn State University Press, 2008, p. 238.

surname contracts that pass their surnames to their children, their partial agency does not invalidate the very structure that subordinates women. The problem lies not only in the unequal conditions under which contracts are entered into and consent is given, but also in the very ideas of contract and consent themselves. A radical legal reform that moves beyond formal equality and the contract model is needed to challenge patronymic norms in law and life.

4.2. THE FREEDOM TO MARRY AND MARITAL SUPREMACY

While family law remains a status-based system, the contractualisation of family law has expanded the space in which people can make choices and form contracts irrespective of their gender, which is often perceived as the best solution that the law can offer. The 'status-to-consent' family law story reveals the myth of liberal feminist legal reform. The case of children's surnames is a testament to how formal equality in law and contractual rules serves to legitimise, rather than overturn, the normalisation of male dominance as a way of life. The same-sex marriage controversy serves as a further example of how the privileging of the choice to marry, in family law reform, has enshrined the supremacy of marriage. Firstly, the marriage equality movement came to embrace 'marriage' as the only option to recognise same-sex unions, after a series of interactions with their counter-movement, diverging from the movement's original goal of pursuing diverse forms of legal recognition by highlighting the right to marry as the paramount right necessary for LGBTQ equality.[58] Secondly, same-sex marriage was legalised through the 748 Act, an unprecedented piece of legislation in both name and nature which, despite domestic and international plaudits, denies same-sex relationships an official designation. Although the 748 Act grants same-sex couples the right to register marriages, it refers to the relationship of a registered same-sex couple as an 'Article 2 Relationship',[59] the legal consequences of which partially differentiate it from Civil Code marriage. It affirms marriage normativity by mimicking heterosexual marriage as prescribed in the Civil Code, with some differences, creating a dual-track system that confirms the superiority of opposite-sex marriage (regulated by the Civil Code) over same-sex marriage (regulated by the 748 Act, in which marriage is *not* the statutory name for the same-sex union).

---

58 For a critique of the marriage equality movement and the Constitutional Court's decision to embrace equality and marital supremacy, as well as of the marriage equality movement's interactions with the counter-movement, see C. Chen, 'Migrating Marriage Equality without Feminism – *Obergefell v. Hodges* and the Legalization of Same-sex Marriage in Taiwan' (2019) 52 *Cornell International Law Journal* 65–107.

59 Art. 2 stipulates: 'Two persons of the same sex may form a permanent union of an intimate and exclusive nature for the purpose of living a common life.'

A critical look at the 748 Act would find that, while recognition of same-sex unions does challenge heterosexual normativity by recognising same-sex family formation, it reinforces marriage normativity. Using Civil Code marriage as a template, it extends many marital status-based privileges to same-sex couples who are willing to enter into the institution of marriage, while leaving behind LGBT singles and unmarried couples. The recognition of same-sex co-parents, for instance, is premised on marriage; members of a same-sex couple cannot become legal co-parents unless they are married. Prior to its revision in 2023, the 748 Act did not permit same-sex joint adoption, which was reserved for opposite-sex married couples only,[60] and provided that the only option for the recognition of same-sex co-parenthood was step-parent adoption of the spouse's biological child (Article 20); that is to say, only married same-sex couples with biological children could pursue legal recognition of their co-parenthood. They were required first to register their marriage, then to petition the court to approve the spouse's adoption of the parent's biological child, as a step-parent. This legal solution to same-sex co-parenting affirmed parentage through marriage and the supremacy of 'natural parenthood', and provided a poor fit for same-sex family formation.[61] A revision of Article 20 of the 748 Act, in 2023, removed the requirement of biological parentage, and applied the Civil Code *mutatis mutandis* to married same-sex couples, to allow joint adoption and step-parent adoption. Consequently, the legal recognition of same-sex co-parenthood has been expanded, but is still premised on marriage. The Civil Code's privileging of marital parenthood has been extended to the 748 Act, so as to make same-sex marriage equal to opposite-sex marriage. The extremely low rate of non-marital births (roughly 4 per cent) in Taiwan is a testament to how closely parenthood is still entangled with marriage, and how prevalent the stigma of illegitimacy is. The legalisation of same-sex co-parenthood confirms the supremacy of marriage, making the choice to marry the precondition to the choice to co-parent.

5. CONCLUSION

After half a century of family law reform, members of the millennial generation in Taiwan enjoy more equality and freedom under the law than their forebears. Their freedom to marry is constitutionally recognised and legally protected irrespective of gender, despite the dual-track system of marriage. The legal institution of marriage that they may choose to enter into is, by and large, a formally equal one which protects their individual rights, requires their mutual

---

60 Art. 1074 of the Civil Code.

61 See S.L. Friedman and C. Chen, 'Same-sex Marriage Legalization and the Stigmas of LGBT Coparenting in Taiwan' (2023) 48 *Law & Social Inquiry* 660–88.

support of one another, recognises their contribution to the union, and allows them to decide certain family affairs through mutual agreement, all irrespective of gender. Their freedom to get divorced is also protected, with the possibility of court interventions to equalise the division of marital property, and to decide custody of any children in accordance with the children's best interests. However, from a radical feminist point of view, gender-neutrality and the replacement of status rules by contract rules do not guarantee equality. Despite the progress made through the shift from status to contract, the status-to-consent family law story reveals a subtle form of male dominance legitimised by consent. Despite its contribution in recognising the right of same-sex couples to form families, the legalisation of same-sex marriage has reinforced marital supremacy. For family law reform to protect the vulnerable and promote autonomy with equality, lessons must be learned from the status-to-consent story, and the needs of single and unmarried people must be moved from the margins to the centre ground. Redirecting the trajectory of family law is a necessary step to advance equality for all.

UNITED STATES

FIFTY YEARS OF FAMILY LAW FEDERALISM

June CARBONE*

Résumé

Depuis cinquante ans, soit approximativement de la fin de la Seconde Guerre mondiale jusqu'au milieu des années 90 environ les différents États des États-Unis ont vu leurs dispositions juridiques relatives au droit de la famille converger. Au cours de cette période, les cinquante États ont démantelé le divorce pour faute

* Robina Chair in Law, Science and Technology, University of Minnesota Law School. I would like to thank Zara Abassi for her research assistance.

au profit d'options sans faute, transformé les systèmes opposés de *common law* et régime matrimonial de communauté en modèles de partenariat similaires, remplacé l'attribution préférentielle de la garde des enfants à la mère par des principes de garde partagée, promulgué des mesures fédérales qui incitent à des efforts plus importants en matière d'exécution des décisions relatives aux pensions alimentaires, reconnu le droit constitutionnel des pères non mariés à la reconnaissance d'enfant et rationalisé les procédures d'établissement de la paternité. La combinaison des actions des États, des garanties constitutionnelles, de la pression du Congrès pour pousser les États fédérés à réformer leur droit, de l'adoption d'actes uniformes a contribué à nationaliser le droit de la famille sans pour autant réduire le rôle principal joué par les États fédérés dans la gouvernance et l'administration du droit de la famille.

Les forces qui ont poussé à une plus grande uniformité dans le droit de la famille pourraient cependant être en train de s'affaiblir. Les clivages culturels et la polarisation politique accrue font, aujourd'hui, du droit de la famille un terrain de division qui rappelle les conflits ayant précédé ce demi-siècle de convergence. Des questions très médiatisées, telles que l'avortement et les soins en lien avec les questions de genre, divisent désormais les États. En outre, les différences plus marquées en termes de richesse régionale et de subventions publiques augmentent les différences entre les familles, même lorsque le traitement juridique est théoriquement similaire. En l'absence d'efforts nationaux importants, les États conservateurs reculent dans la reconnaissance des familles et des couples de même sexe, tandis que les États libéraux expérimentent de nouvelles réformes.

Ce chapitre décrit comment le système fédéral américain fait face à la convergence et à la divergence des systèmes des États fédérés en matière de droit de la famille, en fonction des besoins et des conflits liés aux différentes époques.

1. INTRODUCTION

For a 50-year period that started during the 1940s, fully took hold during the 1970s, and continued into the 1990s, the United States underwent a remarkable degree of family law convergence. During that period, the 50 states eliminated fault as the sole basis for divorce, transformed what had been divergent common law and community property systems into much more similar partnership models, replaced fault-based and maternal custody preferences with shared custody principles, enacted federal measures that incentivised greater child support enforcement efforts, granted unmarried fathers' a constitutional right to recognition, and streamlined paternity establishment procedures. The combination of coordinated state actions, constitutional guarantees, Congressional impetus for state reforms, the adoption of Uniform Acts, and full faith and credit guarantees have helped nationalise family law without dislodging the primary role of the states in governing and administering it.[1]

The forces that compelled greater uniformity in family law may, however, be fraying. Greater cultural divisions and political polarisation make family law a site of division today in ways that resemble the conflicts that preceded the half-century of convergence. High-profile issues such as abortion and gender-affirming care now divide the states. In addition, greater regional differences in economic prosperity and the sources of family disruption such as opioid abuse, increase the practical differences among families even when the legal treatment on the books is similar. And without strong national efforts, conservative states are backsliding on recognition of same-sex couples' families while liberal states are experimenting with further reforms.

This chapter describes how the federal system in the United States manages the convergence and divergence of state-based family law systems in accordance with the needs and conflicts of different time periods. The chapter first considers the nature of the federal system, then describes the era of family law convergence, goes on to consider the current era of state law divergence, and ends with a reflection of the forces that can contribute to convergence and manage divergence within a federal system.

2. FAMILY LAW FEDERALISM

In the United States, the family and family law has been said to be the 'quintessential symbol of localism'.[2] The US Supreme Court has observed that the '"regulation of domestic relations" is "an area that has long been regarded as a virtually exclusive province of the States"'.[3] And the Court recognises 'a judicially invented "domestic relations exception" prohibiting federal courts from exercising jurisdiction over divorce, alimony, and custody decrees'.[4]

---

1 See, e.g. V.M. Mather, 'Evolution and Revolution in Family Law' (1993) 25 *St. Mary's L.J.* 405, 406 (observing that, in the middle of the twentieth century, family law became more uniform throughout the United States, and that the uniformity is due to a combination of federal statutes, voluntary state adoption of Uniform Acts, and Supreme Court constitutional decisions). The National Conference of Commissioners on Uniform State Laws drafts proposed laws ('Uniform Laws') and the American Law Institute (ALI) summarises legal developments across the 50 states and proposes reforms, but such measures become law only if adopted by individual states.

2 J.E. Hasday, 'Federalism and the Family Reconstructed' (1998) 45 *UCLA L. Rev.* 1297, 1297.

3 *United States v. Windsor*, 570 U.S. 744, 766 (2013) (citing *Sosna v. Iowa*, 419 U.S. 393, 404 (1975)).

4 H.K. Gerken, 'Federalism and Nationalism: Time for a Détente?' (2015) 59 *St. Louis U. L.J.* 997, 1018.

Family law has been treated as a state matter since the adoption of the US Constitution at the end of the eighteenth century, a time when the federal government had limited powers. The states disagreed from the beginning on essential elements of family law. Perhaps most fundamentally, they disagreed on the status of the enslaved. Southern, pro-slavery states treated the bonds 'between master and slave as a domestic relation', and thus as a matter of family law entrusted to the states, while the Northern states, which did not recognise slavery as a legal status at all, treated the children of the enslaved who lived in the North as members of their birth families.[5] In addition, the New England colonies, dating back to the seventeenth century, granted the courts the ability to grant divorces, while the Southern colonies followed the British ecclesiastical practice and, until after the Civil War, required an Act of the legislature to dissolve marital bonds.[6]

The differences among the states created what Ann Estin has termed the 'evils of migratory divorce', as couples might be divorced in one state but still married in another state. To address the divorce problem, legislation 'to enact a constitutional amendment was introduced in almost every session of Congress from 1884 until the late 1940s'.[7] The Supreme Court eventually resolved the issue through a series of cases in the 1940s that held that the states had to give 'full faith and credit' to *ex parte* divorces in other states.[8] Starting after World War II, however, American family law entered a remarkable period of convergence.

3. FEDERAL LAW CONVERGENCE

3.1. DIVORCE REFORM

In the middle of the twentieth century, the grounds for divorce served as a major point of controversy for family law federalism. The Industrial Revolution and the greater emancipation of women had increased the pressure for divorce reform by the turn of the twentieth century, with a 1908 report confirming the steady increase of divorce rates over the preceding 40 years, 'despite the best efforts of conservative reformers'.[9] Those rates would double again over the next half-century, and increase further in the period following World War II.[10]

5 J.E. Hasday, above n. 2, 1326.

6 A.L. Estin, 'Family Law Federalism: Divorce and the Constitution' (2007) 16 *Wm. & Mary Bill Rts. J.* 381, 383–84.

7 Ibid., 390.

8 Ibid., 395–96.

9 A.L. Estin, 'Family Law Federalism', above n. 6, 393.

10 W. Buss and E. Buss, 'Escaping the American Blot? A Comparative Look at Federalism in Australia and the United States Through the Lens of Family Law' (2015) 48 *Cornell Int'l L.J.* 105, 116, fn. 57.

The states served as 'laboratories for experimentation', with Nevada, Indiana, and North and South Dakota taking the lead in liberalising divorce laws, and by 1950, roughly half the states allowed divorce when a couple had lived apart for a lengthy period.[11]

The 'divorce revolution',[12] however, took hold in 1969, when the California legislature adopted the first true 'no-fault' divorce law. California abolished consideration of fault for all purposes at divorce, substituting 'irreconcilable differences' for fault-based grounds such as adultery, and allowing one party to secure a divorce even if the other spouse opposed it.[13] By 1985, almost every state had adopted some version of no-fault divorce, though the states continued to differ in whether they also retained fault grounds, and in how long a period of separation they required before a spouse could obtain a divorce over the objection of the other.[14]

The speed with which no-fault divorce swept the country was in many ways remarkable. The Catholic Church had opposed liberalising divorce laws, and had blocked reform in large urban states; indeed, New York did not adopt a true unilateral divorce law until 2010, due to the opposition of 'powerful Catholics, moralizing conservatives, paternalistic post-Progressive liberals, and faint-hearted politicians'.[15] Bible Belt states like Tennessee, dominated more by evangelical Protestants who, in the middle of the twentieth century, had little in common with Catholics, also opposed liberalised divorce.[16] The speed with which the reforms were adopted may have reflected the pent-up demand for divorce. Indeed, once the new laws had been adopted, the incidence of divorce rose dramatically, peaking in the late 1970s, soon after the adoption of more liberalised divorce procedures.[17]

---

11 Ibid., 117.

12 L.J. Weitzman, 'The Divorce Revolution: The Unexpected Social and Economic Consequences for Women and Children in America', The Free Press, 1985, p. 6.

13 J.L. Grossman and L.M. Friedman, *Inside The Castle: Law and the Family in 20th Century America*, Princeton University Press, 2011, pp. 176–77.

14 W. Buss and E. Buss, above n. 10, 117.

15 J.H. DiFonzo and R.C. Stern, 'Addicted to Fault: Why Divorce Reform Has Lagged in New York' (2007) 27 *Pace L. Rev.* 559, 561–62, 564–70. In 1966, however, New York had liberalised its divorce laws to allow a couple who had lived apart for a year or more, pursuant to an agreement, to obtain a divorce. The Domestic Relations Law required that husband and wife live pursuant to a written agreement of separation filed either with the county clerk or with the court for at least one year. See G.L. Zborovsky, 'Baby Steps to "Grown-Up" Divorce: The Introduction of the Collaborative Family Law Center and the Continued Need for True No-Fault Divorce in New York' (2008) 10 *Cardozo J. Conflict Resol.* 305, 312.

16 A.L. Estin, 'Family Law Federalism', above n. 6, 425–26 (describing Tennessee bigamy prosecutions of couples who obtained out-of-state *ex parte* divorces in the 1940s).

17 W. Buss and E. Buss, above n. 10, 116, fn. 57.

3.2. MARITAL PROPERTY REFORM

With the adoption of no-fault divorce – and the corresponding increase in divorce rates – the 50 American states also modernised their marital property regimes. Before the divorce reform era, the vast majority of states, following the English common law tradition, recognised a title system in which the spouse who held title to property during marriage was awarded the property at divorce.[18] While wives had gradually acquired greater rights over property titled in their own names, and while married couples often held property such as the family home under both names, the system reflected the husband's superior earning power and the Blackstonian tradition that treated the husband as the head of the household.[19] At divorce, a dependent wife received alimony rather than an ownership share in the assets accumulated during the marriage, which were often held in the husband's name alone.[20]

However, eight of the fifty American states (Arizona, California, Idaho, Louisiana, Nevada, New Mexico, Texas and Washington) – states that had originally been colonised by Spain and France – had community property systems. Within these systems, all property acquired during marriage as a result of the labour of either spouse was treated as jointly owned. These states differed among each other in the use of alimony, with California having awarded spousal support on terms similar to the common law states since the nineteenth century, while Texas barred alimony altogether, once the property division had become final, until the 1990s.[21]

With the adoption of no-fault divorce, all of the common law states abandoned the title system in favour of either a marital property regime (which awards separate property, such as inheritances or gifts, to each spouse, and then equitably distributes the marital property accumulated through the labour of either party during the marriage) or an equitable distribution system, which gives the courts the power to distribute all property held by either spouse at the time of the divorce.[22] The Uniform Marriage and Divorce Act,[23] although

---

18 B.R. Turner, *Equitable Distribution of Property*, 2nd ed., Shepards/McGraw-Hill, 1994, §1.02, 4; L. Harris et al., *Family Law*, Little, Brown & Co., 1996.

19 D.H. Bell, 'Family Law at the Turn of the Century' (2002) 71 *Miss. L.J.* 781, 822.

20 Ibid. In most states, alimony terminated on remarriage and in some states, a 'guilty wife' might not be entitled to alimony at all. In contrast, property awards constituted final judgments. See D.H. Bell, 'Equitable Distribution: Implementing the Marital Partnership Theory Through the Dual Classification System' (1997) 67 *Miss. L.J.* 115, 119–20.

21 See J.W. Paulsen, 'The history of alimony in Texas and the new "spousal maintenance" statute' (1998) 7 *Tex. J. Women & L.* 151. See also J.T. Oldham, 'United States: The Surprising Continuing Lack of Consensus Under U.S. Law for the Award of Spousal Support After Divorce' in R. Fretwell Wilson and J. Carbone (eds.), *International Survey of Family Law 2022*, Intersentia, 2022.

22 See J.T. Oldham, *Divorce, Separation and the Distribution of Property*, Law Journal Press, 2005, §3.03. And Wisconsin adopted a community property system; V.M. Mather, above n. 1, 112.

23 Unif. Marriage and Divorce Act §307 (amended 1973), 9A U.L.A. 238–39 (1987).

not widely adopted, proposed two alternative marital property regimes – a community property system and an equitable distribution system – and 'sparked a national debate that resulted in the passage of equitable distribution statutes in almost all states'.[24] Some states adopted specific statutory regimes, while, in other common law states, the courts simply confirmed that divorce courts had the power to divide the property accumulated over the course of the marriage.[25] In most common law states, title still determined ownership and decision-making power over assets during the marriage, but at divorce the courts could divide the couple's estate, taking marital contributions and post-divorce needs into account, while generally favouring a roughly equal division of marital assets. Mississippi became the last state to abandon the title system, in the 1990s.[26]

As with no-fault divorce, the transformation of the common law property systems occurred in a relatively uniform fashion across the 50 states within a matter of decades. Virtually every state embraced the partnership theory of marriage, recognising the increased status of women and adopting a presumption that each spouse made equal contributions to the marriage.[27] The result was a remarkable degree of convergence. Community property and common law states both became more likely to split property at divorce more equally, with all of the common law states giving divorce courts the ability to distribute property independently of title.[28] During this period of convergence, the two property systems, despite their very different origins, both modernised in a similar fashion across the 50 states, and came to produce produce relatively similar property divisions at divorce, even though the state systems continued to differ in their legal formulations.

3.3. SHARED CUSTODY

Child custody has been described as 'ground zero in the gender wars'[29] – a more controversial sticking point in managing increasing divorce rates than the move toward equalising property divisions. While every American state had adopted

24 D.H. Bell, 'Equitable Distribution', above n. 20, 174, fn. 35.

25 J.T. Oldham, 'Changes in the Economic Consequences of Divorces, 1958–2008' (2008) 42 *Fam. L.Q.* 419, 428–29.

26 D.H. Bell, 'Equitable Distribution', above n. 20, 127–30.

27 Ibid.

28 Ibid., 130. Some community property systems during this period changed from a 50–50 division of marital property to the use of equitable distribution principles, in part to allow use of a higher property award in lieu of alimony, while California did the opposite and moved from equitable distribution to a 50–50 division of community property.

29 J. Carbone, *From Partners to Parents: The Second Revolution in Family Law*, Columbia University Press, 2000, p. 20.

the best-interest-of-the-child standard to determine custody by the middle of the twentieth century,[30] the critical factor in the administration of the best interests test has always been state presumptions of what served children's best interests, and these presumptions changed over the second half of the twentieth century. The two principle factors in a best-interest analysis had been fault – a parent found guilty of adultery, for example, might be viewed as morally unfit to take custody[31] – and a maternal presumption for children of 'tender years', generally presuming that young children belonged with their mothers. The courts also favoured award of custody to a single parent, fearing that splitting custody between two parents would only invite conflict.[32] Between 1970 and the end of the century, every state would move away from fault-based and gendered custody presumptions, and as they did, virtually every state would embrace some form of shared custody, albeit in accordance with widely varying statutory prescriptions.

The impetus started with constitutional challenges to the maternal presumption; that is, a presumption that the best interests of children of 'tender years' lay with a custody award to their mothers. Many states, starting in the 1970s, viewed continuation of the presumption as constitutionally untenable, and by 1990, every state had moved away from the maternal presumption.[33]

The second factor, which followed the increase in divorce, was the growth in a fathers' rights movement that fought for and won greater custody rights.[34] Women initiate the vast majority of divorces, and many fathers wanted greater contact with their children following a break-up.

These considerations contributed to a wholesale shift in custody decision-making. A family law report concluded, in 2014, that '[t]he most significant trend in contemporary child custody law is toward greater active involvement by both parents in post-separation childrearing'.[35] By 2012, 47 states and the District of Columbia had enacted statutes authorising joint legal or physical custody awards, and the other three were making such awards as a matter of case law.[36] In addition, almost all states now have statutes

---

30 V.M. Mather, above n. 1, 413.

31 J. Carbone, *From Partners to Parents*, above n. 29, p. 181.

32 J.H. DiFonzo, *From the Rule of One to Shared Parenting: Custody Presumptions in Law and Policy* (2014) 52 *Fam. Ct. Rev.* 214, 215.

33 J. Carbone, *From Partners to Parents*, above n. 29, pp. 181–82.

34 See D. Dinner, 'The Divorce Bargain: The Fathers' Rights Movement and Family Inequalities' (2016) 102 *Va. L. Rev.* 79, 131 (observing that fathers' rights activists 'fought for a legislative presumption that joint custody served the best interest of the child *in all cases*') (emphasis in original).

35 M.K. Pruett and J.H. DiFonzo, 'Closing the Gap: Research, Policy, Practice and Shared Parenting' (2014) 52 *Fam. Ct. Rev.* 152, 156.

36 D.R. Fait et al., 'The Merits and Problems with Presumptions for Joint Custody' (Feb. 2012) 45 *Md. Bar J.* 12, 14. See also J.H. DiFonzo, above n.32, 217 (describing the three states that lack such statutes).

identifying children's best interest with 'frequent and continuing contact with both parents'.[37]

These changes primarily came into existence in the last 20 years of the twentieth century. More than 30 states had adopted joint custody statutes of some kind by the early 1990s.[38] Moreover, even without a presumption in favour of joint custody, a large number of states adopted presumptions in favour of custody awards to the parent most likely to encourage the continuing involvement of the other parent.[39] State custody statutes are many and varied, but the move from 'the rule of one' to promotion of the continuing involvement of both parents, as an important factor in custody decision-making, is close to universal.

The 50 states have achieved even greater uniformity with respect to child custody jurisdiction. Congress passed the Parental Kidnapping Prevention Act of 1980,[40] which required state authorities to give full faith and credit to a child custody determination of another state with jurisdiction over the matter. In addition, every state but Massachusetts has adopted the Uniform Child Custody Jurisdiction Act, which determines which state has jurisdiction of custody determinations when the parents or the child move from one state to another.[41]

3.4. PATERNITY ESTABLISHMENT AND CHILD SUPPORT

In the middle of the twentieth century, determinations of parenthood were tied to marriage.[42] The woman who gave birth was automatically treated as a parent and, if she was married, her husband was presumed to be the father, without the need for either parent to take action to receive recognition.[43]

---

37 Ibid., 216 (observing that, '[a]s a matter of public policy, the phrase "frequent and continuing contact with both parents" appears in most state statutes with nearly mechanical regularity').

38 V.M. Mather, above n. 1, 413.

39 See J. Carbone and N. Cahn, 'Parents, Babies, and More Parents' (2017) 92 *Chi.-Kent L. Rev.* 9, 37.

40 Parental Kidnapping Prevention Act of 1980, Pub. L. No. 96-611, §§6–10, 94 Stat. 3568–3573 (codified at 28 U.S.C. §1738A).

41 J. Booth, 'Applying the UCCJEA in Family Law' (2021) 43 *Fam. Adv.* 17 (American Bar Association, 10 May 2021).

42 Indeed, in a draft opinion, Chief Justice Burger wrote: 'Unmarried fathers are not recognized, they are given no rights, and they are burdened with no responsibilities. … This has been the pattern of society's dealing with the support and paternity of illegitimate children for centuries and never challenged until now.' See S. Mayeri, 'Foundling Fathers: (Non-)marriage and Parental Rights in the Age of Equality' (2016) 125 *Yale L.J.* 2292, 2323.

43 C. Huntington, 'Postmarital Family Law: A Legal Structure for Nonmarital Families' (2015) 67 *Stan. L. Rev.* 167, 178 (observing that a married father does not need to take an additional step to establish parental rights over his child.).

Most births took place within marriage and the marital presumption was relatively hard to rebut, making determinations of parenthood certain and routine.[44] Determinations of parents' financial responsibility for their children largely took place in the context of divorce proceedings, and were either secondary to, or included as part of, alimony proceedings providing support for custodial mothers.[45]

The Supreme Court initiated greater recognition of non-marital fathers when, in 1972, it held an Illinois statute unconstitutional that treated Peter Stanley, an unmarried father, as a stranger to his young children, and removed them from his custody when their mother (with whom Stanley had been living) died. The Illinois statute did not recognise unmarried biological fathers like Stanley as parents, even though he had lived with the children since their birth, and had jointly raised them with their mother.[46]

Over the course of the next 17 years, the Court decided a series of cases[47] that held that:

> The significance of the biological connection is that it offers the natural father an opportunity that no other male possesses to develop a relationship with his offspring. If he grasps that opportunity and accepts some measure of responsibility for the child's future, he may enjoy the blessings of the parent-child relationship … If he fails to do so, the Federal Constitution will not automatically compel a state to listen to his opinion of where the child's best interests lie.[48]

In 1989, however, the Supreme Court upheld the constitutionality of the marital presumption, on the basis of a case in which both the biological father and the mother's husband had established relationships with the child. Thereafter, the Court left the matter to the states.[49]

The Supreme Court decisions prompted, both directly and indirectly, a wholesale reconsideration of determinations of paternity. The states began to expand their recognition of unmarried fathers, with the 1973 Uniform Parent

---

44 J. Carbone, 'The Legal Definition of Parenthood: Uncertainty at the Core of Family Identity' (2005) 65 *La. L. Rev.* 1295, 1307 (observing that the standard necessary to rebut the marital presumption was high, and that common law courts had precluded evidence of the mother's infidelity, making the presumption effectively irrebuttable in the era before reliable paternity tests).

45 J. Carbone, *From Partners to Parents*, above n. 29, p. 154.

46 S. Mayeri, above n. 42, 2309.

47 See *Quilloin v. Walcott*, 434 U.S. 246 (1978); *Caban v. Mohammed*, 441 U.S. 380 (1979); *Lehr v. Robertson*, 463 U.S. 248 (1983).

48 *Lehr v. Robertson*, 463 U.S. 248, 262 (1983).

49 *Michael H. v. Gerald D.*, 491 U.S. 110, 123 (1989). See S. Mayeri, above n. 42, 2301 (commenting that, '[a]fter 1989, the Court largely withdrew from the constitutional regulation of nonmarital fathers' parental rights, leaving states to go their own way.').

Act (UPA) seeking to extend recognition 'equally to every child and to every parent, regardless of the marital status of the parents'.[50] Yale law professor Doug NeJaime concludes that the lawmakers read the Court's constitutional decisions 'as requiring pathways to parentage for unmarried fathers'.[51] The states differed more on the role of fathers in newborn adoptions, an intrinsically difficult issue because of the direct conflict between mothers who wanted to place a child for adoption and fathers who opposed it, but even in the adoption context, the states generally moved to 'enforce "biology plus"';[52] that is, to extend fathers greater rights where they were prepared to assume custody at birth, and had assumed responsibility for the support of the mother and child during pregnancy.[53] Mississippi became the last state to deny notice of adoption to unmarried fathers altogether, when its statute was struck down as unconstitutional in 1998.[54]

The bigger change, however, came as Congress incentivised the states to adopt streamlined paternity procedures, in an effort to spur greater child support collection efforts.[55] Federal child support legislation required all states, as a condition of eligibility for certain federal benefits, to adopt 'voluntary acknowledgments of paternity (VAPs)', which allow mothers and fathers to sign an acknowledgement attesting to the father's status as the biological father and file it with the state.[56] VAPs, which go by different names in different states, have the legal effect of a judgment of paternity, and can be challenged only in limited circumstances.[57] As a result of the Congressional legislation, all states today have VAPs, and they have become the principal method for establishing paternity outside of marriage.[58]

---

50 Unif. Parentage Act §2 (Unif. Law Comm'n 1973).

51 D. NeJaime, 'The Constitution of Parenthood' (2020) 72 *Stan. L. Rev.* 261, 380.

52 L. Oren, 'The Paradox of Unmarried Fathers and the Constitution: Biology "Plus" Defines Relationships; Biology Alone Safeguards the Public Fisc' (2004) 11 *Wm. & Mary J. Women & L.* 47, 107.

53 J. Carbone, *From Partners to Parents*, above n. 29, pp. 170–72 (describing the states as falling into four categories, all of which gave unmarried biological fathers, at least as of 1998, a right to receive notice that their children were being placed for adoption, but differing in their determinations of the circumstances, if any, in which fathers' consent to the adoption was a requirement).

54 Ibid., 170.

55 See Personal Responsibility and Work Opportunity Reconciliation Act of 1996, Pub. L. No. 104–193, tit. III, §331, 110 Stat. 2105, 2227 (codified as amended at 42 U.S.C. §666(a)(5) (2018)); Family Support Act of 1988, Pub. L. No. 100–485, tit. I, §111, 102 Stat. 2343, 2348–50 (codified as amended in scattered sections of 42 U.S.C.); 45 C.F.R. §§302.70(a)(5)(iii), 303.5 (2019).

56 42 U.S.C. §666(a)(5)(C) (2006).

57 D. NeJaime, above n. 51, 302.

58 L.J. Harris, 'Reforming Paternity Law to Eliminate Gender, Status, and Class Inequality' (2013) *Mich. St. L. Rev.* 1295, 1296, 1318.

The changes in paternity establishment complemented an increased federal emphasis on child support enforcement.[59] The most significant change involved federal requirements, again as a condition of eligibility for federal funding, that the states adopt quantitative child support guidelines that made child support amounts more consistent (and higher than in the pre-guideline period), with the biggest improvement in state performance occurring after further changes in the 1990s.[60] In addition, Congress, which provided funds to facilitate enforcement efforts, also required that states enact the Uniform Interstate Family Support Act, in 1996, which included mandates for automated state data processing systems, streamlined proceedings in certain enforcement contexts, and procedures to revoke occupational, professional, recreational and driver's licences for non-compliance with support orders.[61]

While the child support system has been criticised as unnecessarily punitive, especially with respect to 'dead broke' fathers who cannot afford to pay the child support orders levied against them, federal legislation prompted a national change in the treatment of unmarried fathers, facilitating paternity establishment, securing consistent and predictable support orders, and providing greater assistance with enforcement actions.

3.5. CONCLUSION

The period from 1970 to the mid-1990s produced a significant degree of family law convergence without displacing the primary role of the states as family law administrators. This convergence happened for a number of reasons.

Perhaps most significantly, all of the states had to face a transformation in the family, with women achieving greater economic independence, and thus greater ability to leave unhappy unions;[62] the dismantling of traditional gender

[59] Congress initially created the federal Office of Child Support Enforcement in 1974, convinced that more women were seeking welfare benefits because fathers were failing to support their children. The legislation 'provided that states must establish support enforcement programs to continue receiving full AFDC funding. Aid recipients were required to assign their child support rights to the states and to cooperate in efforts to establish paternity and secure support orders.' See A.L. Estin, 'Sharing Governance: Family Law in Congress and the States' (2009) 18 *Cornell J.L. & Pub. Pol'y* 267, 283. Congress also required, as a condition of eligibility for AFDC funding, that the states to establish child support enforcement programmes to assist both AFDC recipients and others with outstanding unpaid child support orders (ibid).

[60] Ibid., 298.

[61] Ibid.

[62] See M.F. Brinig and D.W. Allen, '"These Boots Are Made for Walking": Why Most Divorce Filers Are Women' (2000) 2 *Am. L. & Econ. Rev.* 126, 128 (indicating that women initiate approximately two-thirds of divorces).

roles as the foundation of marriage;[63] and changing patterns of family life, including a dramatic increase in non-marital relationships and childbearing.[64]

The changes in women's status most thoroughly remade the family roles of elite women; that is, women's greater college attendance rates and college graduate women's greater workforce participation contributed to the demand for divorce reform, more egalitarian gender roles, and ultimately, at least for white college graduates, a stabilisation in family formation practices.[65] Elite family changes thus created support for family law reform and guided its implementation.

In addition, the two major political parties overlapped to a greater degree than they do today, allowing many of the reforms to be adopted on a bipartisan basis.[66] The 1973 Supreme Court decision in *Roe v. Wade*, for example, which recognised a constitutional right to abortion access, was a 7-2 decision, with Republicans and Democrats in both the majority and the dissent; abortion, while always contentious, did not become a partisan issue until decades later.[67] And even the divisive, partisan issues of the time, such as the purported relationship between federal welfare aid and the black marital birth rate, increased bipartisan support for measures such as paternity establishment for unmarried fathers, with liberals favouring greater legal recognition of unmarried parents generally and conservatives accepting such recognition as a necessary measure to increase private support for children.[68]

These factors strengthened the role of national measures that guided the state realignment. They made possible bipartisan support for Congressional action that tied federal funding of programmes such as Aid for Families with Dependent Children (AFDC) to streamlined paternity establishment, and enactment of Uniform Acts providing interstate recognition of state child orders.

---

63 See, e.g. A. Cherlin, *Love's Labor Lost: The Rise and Fall of the Working-Class Family in America*, Russell Sage Foundation, 2014 (describing the prosperity in the mid-twentieth century that set the stage for changes in family law and the subsequent destabilisation of these conditions).

64 See, generally, N. Cahn and J. Carbone, *Red Families v. Blue Families: Legal Polarization and the Creation of Culture*, OUP, 2010 (describing changing gender roles and the accompanying changes in family formation).

65 See J. Carbone and N. Cahn, *Marriage Markets: How Inequality Is Remaking the American Family*, OUP, 2014, for a summary of these changes.

66 See, e.g. N. Cahn and J. Carbone, *Red Families v. Blue Families*, above n. 64 (describing the increasing political polarisation at the end of the twentieth century).

67 *Roe v. Wade*, 410 U.S. 113 (1973). See J. Carbone and N. Cahn, 'Embryo Fundamentalism' (2010) 18 *Wm. & Mary Bill Rts. J.* 1015, for a discussion of the political trends.

68 For a summary of the debate, see, e.g. M. Eichner, 'The Privatized American Family' (2017) 93 *Notre Dame L. Rev.* 213, 255–58; J. Carbone and N. Cahn, *Marriage Markets*, above n. 65, 29–31 (describing the misguided public belief that the expansion of welfare benefits caused the changes in the family).

They also strengthened the role of the US Supreme Court in setting a floor for the recognition of rights, prompting state reconsideration of gender-specific laws and practices, more equal treatment of non-marital children, and, in 2015, recognition of a right to marriage equality, which will be discussed in greater detail below. Still, a large part of the shift was neither mandated by federal courts nor guided by Congress. Instead, state legislatures and family courts, acting on their own, modernised family law by looking at the examples from other states. In some cases, proposed uniform laws influenced new legislation, but the majority of the changes took place in state legislatures acting on their own. Indeed, the highest-profile uniform laws on the substantive reforms were not widely adopted; instead, the most consequential uniform Acts, such as the Uniform Child Custody Jurisdiction and Enforcement Act (UCCJEA), coordinated state exercises of jurisdiction over family law disputes. Certainty in the determination of family rights and responsibilities, though procedural mechanisms securing state-based authority and guaranteeing recognition for the resulting decrees in other states, has proved to be an important factor in systematising state family law across the United States.

While these changes have occurred across the United States, and have created a new foundation for family administration, they do not extend to all aspects of family law. Instead, as the next section will demonstrate, a number of issues on the horizon pose the risk of greater divisions going forward.

4. FAMILY LAW DIVERGENCE

If the period from the middle of the twentieth century through to the mid-1990s was one of convergence, the period from the mid-1990s onwards has been one of increasing conflict between the states. To some degree, this has been true because the nature of the interests at stake have changed. The convergence described above, which followed the adoption of no-fault divorce, involved a wholesale shift to a new system that reflected women's increased economic independence, and that system remains largely in place. Indeed, challenges to the no-fault system, such as Louisiana's adoption of covenant marriage, which allows couples to opt into marriages with greater divorce restrictions, have been widely viewed as a failure, with very few married couples opting into the regime.[69] Instead, many of the most widespread recent reforms have been procedural.[70]

---

[69] See, e.g. S.L. Nock et al., 'Covenant Marriage Turns Five Years Old' (2003) 10 *Mich. J. Gender & L.* 169, 170 (observing that fewer than 2% of married couples in Louisiana opt into covenant marriages).

[70] See, e.g. J.C. Murphy, 'Rethinking the Role of Courts in Resolving Family Conflicts' (2020) 21 *Cardozo J. Conflict Resol.* 625, 629 (describing procedures); J. Murphy and J. Singer, *Divorced from Reality*, New York University Press, 2015, ch. 3 (critiquing their limitations).

Most states, for example, now encourage family law litigants to use mediation or other alternative dispute resolution mechanisms, and while relatively few states mandate such procedures, many subsidise them and promote their availability.[71] The result is less focus on substantive family law reforms and greater attention to court procedures that resolves disputes without litigation, with the procedural reforms often taking place one state or courthouse at a time.

The exceptions to this account of doctrinal stability and incremental procedural reform have been the issues that have become flashpoints in the culture wars that fuel political polarisation. The intensity of the conflict over these issues has been fed by entrepreneurial politicians seizing on intrinsically divisive issues and using them as political markers that attract attention and lock in political identities. In the context of its federal system, the United States resolves these issues at the state level, with state-level conflicts sometimes serving to diffuse the issues by allowing different resolutions in different parts of the country. The results, however, often create interstate conflicts that reproduce the tensions that existed before the adoption of no-fault divorce.

This section will review the issues recreating the conflicts that today dominate American family law, looking specifically at abortion, gender-affirming care, LGBT family recognition, and child support reforms. The section emphasises that federal mechanisms, such as Supreme Court guidance and federal legislation, remain possibilities, but that the justices and Congress have either become less inclined to use these mechanisms to resolve the conflicts or less able to do so in the face of deep-rooted political division.

4.1. ABORTION

Abortion is an intrinsically divisive issue. Those who believe, as a matter of religious faith, that life begins at conception, see abortion as murder of an unborn child,[72] while those who favour abortion rights see such decisions as essential to women's equality.[73] Despite this, abortion was not a partisan issue at the time it was legalised as a result of the US Supreme Court decision in

---

71 C.J.A. Beck et al., 'Intimate Partner Abuse in Divorce Mediation: Outcomes from a Long-Term Multi-cultural Study 11' (2011), https://www.ojp.gov/pdffiles1/nij/grants/236868.pdf (describing mediation process in high-conflict cases).

72 See, e.g. *Planned Parenthood of Se. Pennsylvania v. Casey*, 505 U.S. 833, 940–41, (1992), overruled by *Dobbs v. Jackson Women's Health Org.*, 597 U.S. 215 (2022) (describing different positions on abortion and characterising the position of those opposed as being that 'a woman considering whether to terminate a pregnancy is entitled to no more protection than adulterers, murderers, and so-called "sexual deviates"').

73 *Planned Parenthood of Se. Pennsylvania v. Casey.*, 853 (describing competing view).

Roe v. Wade[74] in the 1970s.[75] This was true, at least in part, because it was seen as a Catholic issue at a time when many fundamentalist Protestant groups were still anti-Catholic.[76] The issue became a partisan one in the 1990s, as a result of what has been described as a deliberate political strategy to 'describe abortion as murder, define an uncompromising stance as the only moral stance one could take, get the 30 percent of Americans with the least tolerance for ambiguity on moral questions to the polls, and let the Democrats offer dozens of different positions'.[77] Since then, the partisan lines have hardened. Public opinion polls indicate that, while 61 per cent of Americans believe that abortion should be legal in all or most cases, 60 per cent of Republicans – and 72 per cent of those who identify as 'conservative Republicans' – believe that abortion should be illegal in all or most cases. In contrast, 80 per cent of Democrats and 90 per cent of 'liberal Democrats' believe that abortions should be legal in all or most cases.[78]

As a result, when the Supreme Court overturned the right to abortion, in 2022,[79] and returned the issue to the states, the states adopted sharply divergent legislation that entrenches abortion-restrictive versus abortion-supportive approaches. Since the Supreme Court decision, 14 states have effectively banned abortion,[80] 11 states have adopted restrictive laws hostile to abortion, 11 states

74 *Roe v. Wade*, 402 U.S. 941 (1971).

75 See A. Gelman, D. Park, B. Shor and J. Cortina, *Red State, Blue State, Rich State, Poor State*, Princeton University Press, 2008, p. 118 (describing increasing partisan polarisation on abortion); L. Greenhouse and R.B. Siegel, 'Backlash to the Future? From *Roe* to *Perry*' (2013) 60 *UCLA L. Rev. Discourse* 240, 244 ('Polling on the eve of *[Roe]* showed that ... [m]ore than two-thirds of self-identified Republicans–more Republicans than Democrats–and 56 percent of Catholics told Gallup that "[t]he decision to have an abortion should be made solely by a woman and her physician." Three major surveys conducted in the immediate aftermath of *Roe*–Harris, Field, and NORC–all showed that the decision did not reduce but rather consolidated these broad levels of popular support.').

76 See R. Post and R. Siegel, '*Roe* Rage: Democratic Constitutionalism and Backlash' (2007) 42 *Harv. C.R.-C.LN. L. Rev.* 373, 412–23 (describing political shift); E.G. Carmines and J. Woods, 'The Role of Party Activists in the Evolution of the Abortion Issue' (2002) 24 *Pol. Behav.* 361 (finding that abortion views have become more highly correlated with party voting, and exploring the role of party activists); S. Collitt and B. Highton, 'The Policy Polarization of Party Activists in the United States' (2021) 49 *Am. Pol. Rsch.* 386, 391 (noting that the pace of polarisation on abortion 'picked up considerably' after the 1970s).

77 D. Westen, *The Political Brain: The Role of Emotion in Deciding the Fate of the Nation*, PublicAffairs, 2007, p. 178.

78 H. Hartig, 'About six-in-ten Americans say abortion should be legal in all or most cases', *Pew Resarch Center*, 13 June 2022, https://www.pewresearch.org/fact-tank/2022/06/13/about-six-in-ten-americans-say-abortion-should-be-legal-in-all-or-most-cases-2 [https://perma.cc/FDH5-5V97].

79 *Dobbs v. Jackson Women's Health Org.*, 597 U.S. 215 (2022).

80 Center for Reproductive Rights, 'After *Roe* Fell' (2024), https://reproductiverights.org/maps/abortion-laws-by-state/.

protect access to abortion, and another 11 states have expanded access.[81] In short, the gulf among the states has become enormous.

What will happen in the future is open to debate, precisely because of the partisan polarisation on the issue. The federal government has tried to provide at least a minimum level of protection by authorising the use of abortion pills[82] and guaranteeing access to emergency room treatment for pregnancy complications that threaten women's health, but these efforts are currently subject to judicial challenges.[83] When the issue has been presented at the polls, even voters in relatively conservative states such as Kentucky, Kansas and Ohio have supported abortion rights.[84] Despite the broad-based public support, however, entrenched partisan positions make compromise difficult. Instead, what lies ahead is continued conflict about the right to travel to different states, with some states criminalising assistance in cross-border travel to access abortion, outlawing possession and use of abortifacients, and threatening to prosecute medical providers who in any way facilitate abortions.[85] Given the role of abortion as a political marker and the 6-3 anti-abortion majority on the Supreme Court, these differences are likely to remain entrenched at the state level unless one party or the other effects a long-term political realignment at the national level. Both parties have proposed national legislation either guaranteeing abortion rights or banning abortion entirely. Enacting such legislation would require, as a practical matter, that a single party controls the presidency and both houses of Congress

---

81 Ibid. See the chapter by R. Fretwell Wilson in this book: 'Abortion after Dobbs: Navigating a Tangle Of State Restrictions'.

82 See *All. for Hippocratic Med. v. FDA*, 668 F. Supp. 3d 507 (N.D. Tex. Apr. 7, 2023), aff'g in part and vacating in part, 78 F.4th 210 (5th Cir. 2023), cert. granted *sub nom Danco Labs. LLC v. All. for Hippocratic Med.*, 144 S. Ct. 537 (2023). The Supreme Court reversed the lower court decisions on standing grounds. *Food & Drug Admin. v. All. for Hippocratic Med.*, No. 23-235, 2024 WL 2964140 (U.S. June 13, 2024).

83 See *United States v. Idaho*, 623 F. Supp. 3d 1096 (D. Idaho 2023), 82 F.4th 1296, aff'd (9th Cir. 2024), cert. pet. granted, 144 S. Ct. 541 (Jan. 5, 2024). The district court, which upheld the federal regulations, noted: 'Back to the pregnant patient in the emergency department. The doctor believes her EMTALA obligations [federal regulations] require her to offer that abortion right now. But she also knows that all abortions are banned in Idaho. She thus finds herself on the horns of a dilemma. Which law should she violate?' (ibid., 1102). The Supreme Court dismissed the grant of certiori as improvidently granted in a per curium decision. *Moyle v. United States*, 603 U. S. —— (June 27, 2024).

84 'Tracking Abortion Bans Across the Country', *New York Times*, 1 May 2024, https://www.nytimes.com/interactive/2024/us/abortion-laws-roe-v-wade.html.

85 B. Pierson, 'Abortion battles shift to medical emergencies, travel', *Reuters*, 27 December 2023, https://www.reuters.com/legal/abortion-battles-shift-medical-emergencies-travel-2023-12-27/; J. Bogage and C. Rowland, 'Chasm Opens Between States on Abortion Pills and Out-of-State Care', *Washington Post*, 25 June 2022; Memorandum from J. Bopp, Jr. (Nat'l Right to Life Comm. Gen. Couns.), C.T. Milbank and J.D. Maughon to National Right to Life Committee re: NRLC Post-*Roe* Model Abortion Law, 15 June 2022, p. 3, https://www.nrlc.org/wp-content/uploads/NRLC-Post-Roe-Model-Abortion-Law-FINAL-1.pdf [https://perma.cc/BB5Z-25CF].

with sufficient majorities to pass the legislation. And it is possible that the US Supreme Court, currently controlled by conservatives appointed at least in part because of their opposition to abortion, would declare federal abortion rights unconstitutional, while a more moderate future Court might be sceptical of a national ban.[86] Therefore, without a significant national resolution of current partisan divisions, the states are likely to remain deeply divided about abortion access, affecting not only the availability of abortion, but potential parental liability for assisting minors in obtaining abortions, the availability of divorce during pregnancy, husbands' participation in abortion decision-making, and other family law issues.

4.2. GENDER-AFFIRMING CARE

The question of the appropriate authorisation of gender-affirming care for minors is a complex issue, involving, among other issues, disputes about the appropriate age at which minors should be able to make their own decisions; questions about the degree of deference to be accorded to parental decision-making; and evolving medical science about the standard of care involving use of puberty blockers, sexual reassignment surgery and psychological counselling. Unlike abortion, therefore, it is not an all-or-nothing issue.[87] Nonetheless, it has become a subject of deep division among the 50 states, precisely because it has been used as a political issue that reinforces partisan identities and divisions, undermining the possibility of national consensus on the issue.

As with abortion, the political parties are deeply divided about the issue. Among Republicans in 2022, 47.9 per cent supported legislation that would prohibit various sorts of gender-affirming medical care for minors, while only 21.8 per cent opposed such legislation. Among Democrats, by contrast, 56.5 per cent opposed such legislation, while 31.9 per cent supported it.[88]

---

86 See, e.g. R.A. Levy, 'No constitutional authority for a national abortion law', *The Hill*, 11 July 2022, https://thehill.com/opinion/congress-blog/3552965-no-constitutional-authority-for-a-national-abortion-law/ (arguing that Congress has no authority to enact a national guarantee of abortions rights); I. Somin, 'A Conservative Constitutional Argument Against a National Abortion Ban', *Reason: The Volokh Conspiracy*, 29 August 2023, https://reason.com/volokh/2023/08/29/a-conservative-constitutional-argument-against-a-national-abortion-ban/ (arguing that Congress lacks the power to enact a national abortion ban).

87 See, e.g. E. Coleman et al., 'Standards of Care for the Health of Transgender and Gender Diverse People, Version 8' (2022) 23 *Int'l J. Transgender Health* S1, S76 (explaining the different possible responses to gender dysphoria and how they may vary for different individuals).

88 D. Lewis et al., 'American Attitudes Toward Transgender Rights', *Gender Policy Report*, 15 November 2023, https://genderpolicyreport.umn.edu/american-attitudes-toward-transgender-rights/.

In accordance with these political divisions, conservative legislators, viewing trans rights as a 'wedge issue' that divides Democrats,[89] have introduced 593 bills, in 42 states, that would restrict trans rights.[90] As of May 2024, 25 states have banned gender-affirming care for minors, affecting 39 per cent of trans youth nationally.[91] This legislation is under legal attack in many states on various grounds, including interference with parental rights to seek appropriate medical care for their children.[92] These attacks on trans care had, by May 2023, persuaded five states – Colorado, Illinois, Maryland, New Mexico and Minnesota – to pass bills 'designed to shield transgender health care through legal protections, health care coverage and access'.[93] In addition, at least 11 states had declared themselves to be 'sanctuary states', protecting medical providers who provide gender affirming care for residents of other states.[94]

Prohibition of medical care for minors suffering from gender dysphoria has been an effective 'wedge' issue that unites conservatives and splits opposing parties, precisely because it affects relatively few people, and a large part of the public is relatively uninformed about the issue. The legal resolution of challenges to the new legislation, however, may prompt reconsideration of the constitutional basis and scope of parental rights to determine medical care for their children (and, in more liberal states, children's rights to have a say in their own care), and such reconsideration may ultimately lead to a redefinition of family decision-making power. For the present, however, these issues are deeply controversial, and national convergence is unlikely.[95]

---

89 See A. Nagourney and J.W. Peters, 'How a Campaign Against Transgender Rights Mobilized Conservatives', *New York Times*, 16 April 2023, https://perma.cc/2Y2H-K24Y (describing the efforts of conservative groups, such as the American Principles Project and the Alliance Defending Freedom, to deploy anti-trans arguments as a wedge issue, and put it under the banner of parental rights).

90 Trans Legislation Tracker, '2024 anti-trans bills tracker', 2024, https://translegislation.com/.

91 Human Rights Campaign, 'Map: Attacks on Gender Affirming Care by State', 2024, https://www.hrc.org/resources/attacks-on-gender-affirming-care-by-state-map.

92 See, e.g. N. Cahn, 'The Political Language of Parental Rights: Abortion, Gender-Affirming Care, and Critical Race Theory' (2023) 53 *Seton Hall L. Rev.* 1443, 1446 (describing the role of parental rights in the debate).

93 D. Ferguson, et al., 'Minnesota to join at least 4 other states in protecting transgender care this year', *NPR*, 21 April 2023, https://www.npr.org/2023/04/21/1171069066/states-protect-transgender-affirming-care-minnesota-colorado-maryland-illinois.

94 A. Hernández, 'More blue states declare themselves sanctuaries for transgender health care', *Stateline*, 22 June 2023, https://stateline.org/2023/06/22/more-blue-states-declare-themselves-sanctuaries-for-transgender-health-care/.

95 For a discussion of these issues, see C. Huntington, 'Parental Rights: Rhetoric Versus Doctrine' (2024) 91 *U. Chi. L. Rev.* 503; J. Quinter and C. Markowitz, 'Judicial Bypass and Parental Rights After *Dobbs*' (2023) 132 *Yale L.J.* 1908, 1969. The *Dobbs* decision, overturning the right to abortion, arguably calls into question the entire line of cases that include the foundation for parents' constitutional protection. Commentators, however, disagree on the implications, and the Court has yet to take up cases that might shed light on the issue.

4.3. REDEFINING PARENTHOOD

The major revolution taking place in American family law today is redefining the basis for parenthood. These changes involve three different groups, each challenging traditional definitions of parental status, but with different political, policy and doctrinal implications. The first group involves LBGT couples, who are struggling to incorporate LGBT community norms underlying family formation into family law; this group would recognise parentage based on a couple's intent at the time of a child's conception, independently of marriage, biology or adoption.[96] The second group involves the growing number of unstable families who incorporate intimate partners into child-rearing roles, either within marriage as step-parents, or outside marriage. These individuals, who typically were not present at the time of the child's conception or birth, seek recognition on the basis of their assumption of a parental role within the context of an intimate relationship.[97] The third group consists of dysfunctional families, who, particularly with growing rates of substance abuse,[98] may include grandparents, friends and neighbours, or collateral relatives who have taken over parental roles, typically because of the legal parent or parents' death or incapacity.[99] In these cases, the adults often step in on an emergency basis, with or without the legal parent's consent, and become, as a practical matter, the child's only adult guardian(s).[100] What the three groups have in common

---

Compare J. Bowes, 'Opinion: Overturning *Roe* Could Threaten Rights Conservatives Hold Dear', *Washington Post*, 24 June 2022, https://www.washingtonpost.com/outlook/2022/06/24/overturning-roe-could-threaten-rights-conservatives-hold-dear, with M. Toth, 'Opinion: Parental Authority Gets a Boost from *Dobbs*', *Wall Street Journal*, 27 July 2022, https://www.wsj.com/articles/parental-authority-gets-a-boost-from-dobbs-justice-alito-glucksberg-unenumerated-rights-history-tradition-education-meyer-pierce-11658941498.

96 See, e.g. D. NeJaime, above n. 51; C.G. Joslin, 'The Gay Rights Canon and the Right to Nonmarriage' (2017) 97 *B.U. L. Rev.* 425, 438.

97 See, e.g. J. Feinberg, 'Whither the Functional Parent? Revisiting Equitable Parenthood Doctrines in Light of Same-Sex Parents' Increased Access to Obtaining Formal Legal Parent Status' (2017) 83 *Brook. L. Rev.* 55, 72 (describing the most important elements in these doctrines as the requirements that 'the petitioner assum[e] … the obligations of parenthood and form … a parent-child bond with the child'.).

98 See, e.g. C.G. Joslin and D. NeJaime, 'How Parenthood Functions' (2023) 123 *Colum. L. Rev.* 319, 433, fn. 334 (observing that 'between 2009 and 2016, the incidence of parental alcohol or other drug use as a contributing factor for children's out-of-home placement rose from 25.4 to 37.4 percent' (citations omitted)).

99 Ibid.

100 These adults often assume parental roles because of the legal parent's death, incarceration or incapacitation because of drug use, and in many of these cases obtaining the legal parent's consent may be difficult, if not impossible. See, e.g. P. Span, 'As Families Grieve, Grandparents Step Up', *New York Times*, 12 April 2022, https://www.nytimes.com/interactive/2022/04/12/well/family/covid-deaths-parents-grandparents.html (describing grandparents who assumed custody following their children's deaths from COVID-19).

is the importance of function as the basis for a claim of legal parentage: in each case, different adults have assumed parental roles and established an emotional bond with the child outside of the traditional doctrines that once made marriage, adoption and biology the exclusive bases for the determination of legal parentage. This section will first discuss a point of convergence – the recognition of married LGBT spouses as parents – and then turn to the evolving incorporation of function into parenthood determinations across the 50 states.

4.3.1. *Marriage Equality and National Convergence*

Twenty years ago, marriage equality was as divisive an issue as abortion or trans rights.[101] Indeed, President George W. Bush encouraged battleground states to place on their ballots referenda blocking adoption of marriage equality, in an effort to boost voter turnout during his re-election campaign in 2004; the measures passed overwhelmingly.[102] By the time the Supreme Court recognised a constitutional right to marriage for same-sex couples in 2015,[103] however, public opinion had shifted and a majority of the American public supported same-sex marriage.[104] Public support increased further after the decision, and the right to marriage equality enjoyed 71 per cent support in 2023,[105] with at least a plurality supporting it in every state.[106] The right to same-sex marriage is, thus, likely to remain available across the 50 states, with more division about the terms for recognition of parental rights.

Despite the broad public support, however, constitutional protection for the right of same-sex couples to marry is uncertain today because of the *Dobbs* decision, which reversed the right to abortion. That case called into question the right to privacy on which both abortion rights and marriage equality had been based, with one justice calling for the reversal of the entire line of substantive due process cases that includes *Obergefell*.[107] To protect existing marriages, Congress passed the Respect for Marriage Act, in 2022,[108] requiring 'interjurisdictional recognition of same-sex and interracial marriages lawfully

---

101 See N. Cahn and J. Carbone, *Red Families v. Blue Families*, above n. 64, p. 134.

102 J. Carbone, 'What Does Bristol Palin Have to Do with Same-Sex Marriage?' (2010) 45 *U.S.F. L. Rev.* 313, 340 (noting that every measure passed, with, on average, 70% support).

103 *Obergefell v. Hodges*, 576 U.S. 644, 666 (2015).

104 J. McCarthy, 'U.S. Same-Sex Marriage Support Holds at 71% High', *Gallup*, 5 June 2023, https://news.gallup.com/poll/506636/sex-marriage-support-holds-high.aspx.

105 Ibid.

106 Public Religion Research Institute surveys, 'Same-Sex Marriage, 2023', https://ava.prri.org/#lgbt/2023/States/lgbt_ssm/2 9 (showing that, in 2023, marriage equality enjoyed at least 50% support in every state except Arkansas, where it enjoyed 49% support).

107 *Dobbs*, 597 U. S. 215 (2022) (Thomas, J.) (concurring, slip. op. 1-7).

108 Respect for Marriage Act, Pub. L. 117–228, 136 Stat. 2305 (2022).

entered into in another state'.[109] As a practical matter, this means that, even if the Supreme Court were to reverse the right to marriage equality and some states then refused to perform same-sex marriages, all states would still be required to recognise marriages valid at the time and place they were performed. This both protects existing marriages and allows couples who could not marry in their home states to marry elsewhere.[110]

After granting same-sex couples the ability to marry, the Supreme Court also ruled, shortly thereafter, that the states could not discriminate against same-sex spouses in the determination of parentage.[111] The Court, however, has never ruled that the marital presumption of paternity, which assumes that the husband is the father of a child born to his wife, automatically applies to same-sex spouses, who, by definition, do not ordinarily have a genetic connection to the child.[112] Instead, the Court's decision was limited to circumstances where the particular state would recognise a husband without a genetic tie to a child as a legal parent, typically in cases where the husband had consented to his wife's use of artificial insemination by a donor. The Court thus required equal treatment of same-sex and different-sex couples in circumstances where the different-sex spouse also lacks a genetic or adoptive tie to the child.

In the intervening years, state courts have generally required that the marital presumption be applied to same-sex couples, either directly or because most states have legislation that recognises husbands as parents where they consent to their wives' use of donor sperm.[113] Despite what appears to be a broad consensus

---

109 D. Laycock, T.C. Berg, C.H. Esbeck and R. Fretwell Wilson, 'The Respect For Marriage Act: Living Together Despite Our Deepest Differences' (2024) *U. Ill. L. Rev.* 511, 513.

110 Ibid., 520 (explaining that, 'as long as at least one of the fifty states does license and perform same-sex marriages, same-sex couples will be able to travel to that state, get married, and have the marriage recognized back in their home state').

111 *Pavan v. Smith*, 582 U.S. 563, 565, (2017) (observing that, under Arkansas law, 'the requirement that a married woman's husband appear on her child's birth certificate applies in cases where the couple conceived by means of artificial insemination with the help of an anonymous sperm donor', and that the state was, therefore, required also to place the name of the wife of a woman who conceived the child through use of a sperm donor on the child's birth certificate).

112 The exception involves women who donate an egg to a partner, who gives birth, in which cases both partners can be said to have a 'biological' relationship to the child, with one woman giving birth and the other woman contributing the egg that supplied the child's maternal genetic inheritance. See, e.g. *K.M. v. E.G.*, 117 P.3d 673 (Cal. 2005).

113 See, e.g. Me. Stat. tit. 19-a §1923 (2016) (Any 'person who consents to assisted reproduction by a woman … with the intent to be the parent of a resulting child is a parent of the resulting child'). Cf. Ala. Code §26-17-201 (West 2008); Ala. Code §26-17-703 (West 2008); Ala. Code §26-17-704 (West 2008); Tenn. Code Ann. §68-3-306 (West 1977) ('A child born to a married woman as a result of artificial insemination, with consent of the married woman's husband, is deemed to be the legitimate child of the husband and wife.'). The latter statutes limit the application of the donor insemination provisions to married couples where the husband consented to the insemination. See also J. Carbone and N. Cahn, 'Jane the Virgin and Other Stories of Unintentional Parenthood' (2017) 7 *U.C. Irvine L. Rev.* 511, 532–37;

on this issue, some states, however, continue to resist application of the marital presumption to married same-sex couples. Idaho, an outlier, provides a notable example. In *Gatsby v. Gatsby*, a married couple, Linsay and Kylee, used a known donor to conceive a child. Linsay performed the insemination on Kylee in their home. After the child was born, Kylee identified Linsay as a parent and, on that basis, the state issued a birth certification recognizing Kylee and Linsay as legal parents.[114] When the couple split up after a physical altercation, Linsay had sole custody for six months because Kylee had been arrested for domestic assault, and then the couple shared custody for an additional year. Despite this, the lower court granted sole custody to Kylee, finding that Linsay was not a legal parent. In affirming the lower court ruling, the Idaho Supreme Court first found that the state's artificial donor statute, and not the marital presumption, controlled the outcome.[115] Second, the court held that, under a strict construction of the artificial insemination statute, Linsay did not qualify as a parent. She had signed the wrong consent form; Linsay had downloaded a sperm donor agreement from the Web, identifying Linsay and Kylee as 'recipients' of the sperm donation, rather than a form specifically consenting to her spouse's insemination. The couple also did not use a doctor in performing the insemination, as the statute stipulated, and no one filed the consent form with the appropriate Idaho agency.[116] Finally, after acknowledging that no couple in the state using artificial insemination had ever fully complied with the statute, the court refused to retroactively apply legislative reforms dispensing with the registration requirement.[117] The US Supreme Court refused to review the case.[118]

The *Gatsby* case is unusual because the Idaho artificial insemination statute was particularly strict, requiring use of a particular form (as opposed to simply an indication of consent to the insemination), and also had a trap for the unwary – a little-known requirement that the forms be filed with the state (a requirement that the legislature had repealed by the time of the case). The dissent insisted that the outcome would have been different had Linsay been a man, and that the result violated Idaho's policy of promoting the legitimacy of children born within marriage.[119]

Idaho is a particularly conservative state, with some of the most extreme abortion restrictions in the country, and the opinion has been seen, as the dissent

L.J. Harris, '*Obergefell*'s Ambiguous Impact on Legal Parentage' (2017) 92 *Chi.-Kent L. Rev.* 55 (describing the impact of marriage equality on the law of parentage); J.L. Grossman, 'Parentage Without Gender' (2016) 17 *Cardozo J. Conflict Resol.* 717, 737–41 (discussing the application of the marital presumption to same-sex couples).

114 *Gatsby v. Gatsby*, 495 P.3d 996 (Idaho, 2021).

115 Ibid., 999.

116 Ibid., 1003–04.

117 Ibid., 1006–08.

118 *Gatsby v. Gatsby*, 142 S. Ct. 2709 (2022).

119 Ibid., 1016.

suggested, as a refusal to recognise the parental standing of same-sex couples. Nonetheless, the case also illustrates the continued variations in state family law. Artificial insemination statutes do vary by state, and the strictness of the Idaho statute made the result possible without blatantly violating equal protection mandates. And while many states use estoppel to recognise two parents in cases where the initial legal parent welcomed her spouse's participation in the child's life, equitable estoppel is a discretionary doctrine used differently in different states.[120] Nonetheless, the dissent is almost certainly right that the court used technicalities to deny the parentage of a same-sex spouse in circumstances where it would have been more reluctant to do so in the case of a husband who had consented to his wife's use of artificial insemination by a donor to conceive a child. Particularly with a more conservative Supreme Court unwilling to enforce the rights of same-sex couples, greater state variation remains possible.

4.3.2. Functional Parenthood

The looming controversy, however, is less about the rights of married couples than about the determination of parentage among unmarried couples. Recognition of the rights of unmarried same-sex couples is the next battlefront in LGBT recognition. Doug NeJaime of Yale Law School and Courtney Joslin of the University of California at Davis, in particular, have argued that, just as unmarried fathers have won recognition as parents outside marriage, so too should same-sex couples be entitled to recognition as coequal parents in non-marital relationships, particularly where the couples jointly arranged for the child's conception and birth with the intention of raising the child together.[121] The fight to expand the bases for parental recognition also coincides with the increased number of non-marital births, which are now approximately 40 per cent of all US births,[122] and the more fragile nature of American families, as step-parents, non-marital partners (with and without a biological connection to the child), grandparents and other collateral relatives have taken on parental roles.[123] These groups do not fit neatly into the conventional parental categories defined by marriage, biology and adoption, and the law in different states has evolved to provide greater recognition, albeit in different ways.

---

120 See *McLaughlin v. Jones in & for Cnty. of Pima*, 401 P.3d 492, 501 (Ariz. 2017).

121 See, e.g. D. NeJaime, above n. 51; C.G. Joslin, above n. 96, 438.

122 ChildStats: Forum on Child and Family Statistics, 'Births to Unmarried Women', https://www.childstats.gov/americaschildren/tables/fam2a.asp [https://perma.cc/7KPS-8UYF] (noting that, in 2019, approximately 40% of births were to unmarried women).

123 See C.G. Joslin and D. NeJaime, above n. 98. Joslin and NeJaime describe the largest category receiving recognition as functional parents – more than a third of the total – as relatives, particularly grandparents. The other large groups are step-parents, unmarried different-sex partners and unmarried same-sex partners (ibid., 356–57).

Joslin and NeJaime report that 34 of the 50 American states provide some form of recognition of parenthood on the basis of function.[124] These doctrines include both express statutory provisions and common law doctrines, such as equitable estoppel, *in loco parentis*, de facto parentage, psychological parentage and other state-specific doctrines, which the courts in some states have adopted without express legislation.[125] In addition, some categories, such as de facto parentage, may be the product of either express legislation or common law adoption, and the terms of such recognition may vary from one state to another.[126] Overall, the states can be described in terms of three categories. The first group of 15 states recognises functional parents as legal parents without requiring marriage, a biological tie or adoption.[127] A second group of 24 states do not recognise functional parents as legal parents but nonetheless grant them standing to seek custody or visitation.[128] Four of these state statutes, however, permit non-parents to seek only visitation.[129] A third group of 16 states either provide no recognition or have not addressed the issue. Joslin and NeJaime list some states, such as Colorado, New Hampshire, New York and Pennsylvania, in both of the first two categories, because they have multiple bases for recognition that may operate in different ways, and the authors acknowledge that some of the states they list in category two could be placed in category one because the doctrines cited are sometimes used to grant functional parents 'the same rights and responsibilities as a legal parent'.[130] In short, even among those states recognising functional parents, the doctrines vary widely, and even doctrines with the same names, such as 'de facto parentage', vary in the prerequisites they require for recognition, and the rights and responsibilities that follow from such recognition. The law of parentage is thus very much a work in progress.

The variation in the states with respect to these doctrines is likely to continue. Scholars advocating greater protection of LGBT families have pushed for greater recognition of unmarried partners without a biological tie to the child,[131] and the

---

124 Ibid., 345.

125 Ibid., 323.

126 Ibid., 423–27, App. A. The State of Washington's de facto parentage legislation, for example, provides that a de facto parent 'stands in legal parity with an otherwise legal parent' (ibid., 323). By contrast, 'Wisconsin's doctrine, which is based on a frequently cited de facto parent case, yields standing merely to seek visitation' (ibid., 340).

127 Ibid., 350, fn. 183 (California, Colorado, Connecticut, Delaware, Kansas, Maine, Massachusetts, Michigan, New Hampshire, New Mexico, New York, Pennsylvania, Rhode Island, Vermont and Washington).

128 Ibid., 351, fn. 184 (Alaska, Colorado, District of Columbia, Georgia, Hawaii, Indiana, Kentucky, Maryland, Montana, Nebraska, New Hampshire, New Jersey, New York, North Carolina, North Dakota, Ohio, Oklahoma, Pennsylvania, South Carolina and West Virginia).

129 Ibid., 351, fn. 187 (Arkansas, Massachusetts, Minnesota and Wisconsin).

130 Ibid., 351.

131 See, e.g. D. NeJaime, above n. 51; C.G. Joslin, above n. 96.

current version of the Uniform Parentage Act contains a variety of mechanisms for recognition, including making voluntary acknowledgements of parenthood available to intended parents without a biological tie to the child.[132] States, like Idaho, that have resisted greater recognition of same-sex families are unlikely to adopt such measures. And while Idaho does have a 'de facto custodian' statute, it limits standing under the statute to individuals 'related to [the] child within the third degree of consanguinity'.[133]

On the other hand, two-thirds of the states recognise functional parenthood in some form, precisely because family courts are confronted with children who would otherwise lack any legal parent, or who would be cut off from an adult who had been a significant source of emotional and material support in their lives. California, for example, initially expanded its interpretation of its parentage statutes in the context of a dependency case where the mother had been imprisoned and the only adult prepared to care for the child was the mother's unmarried former partner, who had long acted as the child's father.[134] California's functional parentage doctrine was only later extended to same-sex couples.[135] Similarly, Kentucky, a relatively conservative state, has a large number of functional parent cases, primarily brought on the basis of its de facto custodian statute, which applies to a person who has been 'the primary caregiver for, and financial supporter of, a child' and has lived with the child for a certain period of time.[136] Recognising such functional parents has been particularly important for Kentucky because it has been hit hard by the opioid epidemic; Joslin and NeJaime note that, '[i]n one community in Appalachian Kentucky, "local school staff in the region estimate that as many as 40 percent of students are being raised by a relative caregiver"'.[137] And Minnesota, which has a relatively restrictive third-party visitation statute, has interpreted the statute to grant standing to seek visitation to de facto parents where 'visitation is in the best interests of the child and that visitation will not interfere with the custodial parent's relationship with the child',[138] effectively giving the courts discretion to

---

132 See, e.g. S. Hazeldean, 'Illegitimate Families' (2024) 59 *Harv. C.R.-C.L. L. Rev.* 157, 168 (noting that 'Maryland is one of eleven states to allow LGBTQ parents to execute a Voluntary Acknowledgment of Parentage, an administrative process used to establish legal parentage' that results in both partners' names being placed on the child's birth certificate).

133 Idaho Code §32-1703(1)(a) (2022).

134 *In re Nicholas H.*, 46 P.3d at 933–34 (2002). See J. Carbone, 'From Partners to Parents Revisited: How Will Ideas of Partnership Influence the Emerging Definition of California Parenthood?' (2007) 7 *Whittier J. Child. & Fam. Advoc.* 3 (for a description of the evolution of California's functional parentage doctrine, which favours at least two parents for every child, and gives more weight to function than marriage or biology in determining parentage).

135 J. Carbone, 'From Partners to Parents Revisited', above n. 134.

136 C.G. Joslin and D. NeJaime, above n. 98, 352.

137 Ibid., 433 (citations omitted).

138 *SooHoo v. Johnson*, 731 N.W.2d 815, 823 (Minn. 2007).

recognise former partners who had lived with the child for over two years and established a parent-like relationship with the child. Judicial decrees granting custody and visitation rights pursuant to these provisions are generally entitled to full faith and credit in other states, creating little need for consistent laws across the 50 states. Rather, within each state, the disputes involve the legal needs of children who risk the loss of contact with an adult who has assumed a parental role versus the authority of the initial legal parents, who may not have realised that living with an unmarried partner might mean granting that partner rights as a coequal parent.[139] These doctrines are likely to continue to evolve on a state-by-state basis.

4.4. CHILD SUPPORT ENFORCEMENT REFORM

Federal efforts guided a national movement towards more uniform efforts at child support enforcement. Today, those efforts have been subject to withering critiques to the effect that publicly initiated child support efforts trap low-income men into debt that they cannot escape.[140] Courts often impose unrealistic child support orders on parents with very limited incomes, who often cannot pay the amounts ordered.[141] This occurs, in part, because courts impute income to non-custodial parents based on assumptions of what they could earn, and make it difficult to alter the amounts when the parents, in fact, cannot earn the imputed incomes. In addition, while middle-class fathers often trade the greater assumption of custodial responsibilities for lower child support amounts, fathers caught up in public action have less or no ability to effect such trades.[142]

---

139 See, e.g. G. Strauss, 'What Role Remains for De Facto Parenthood?' (2019) 46 *Fla. St. U. L. Rev.* 909 (observing that these 'parents consented to help, not to transfer their parental rights'); See also R. Fretwell Wilson, 'Undeserved Trust: Reflections on the ALI's Treatment of De Facto Parents' in R. Fretwell Wilson (ed.), *Reconceiving the Family: Critical Reflections on the American Law Institute's Principles of the Law of Family Dissolution*, CUP, 2006, pp. 90, 100 ('[O]ne can easily imagine that the rights the ALI seeks to confer on Ex Live-In Partners could be exploited not as an opportunity to stay in the children's lives, but as an opportunity to control a child or her mother.'); K.K. Baker, 'Quacking Like a Duck? Functional Parenthood Doctrine and Same-Sex Parents' (2017) 92 *Chi.-Kent L. Rev.* 135 (observing that open-ended embraces of functional parenthood allow courts to determine parentage, often over the objections of established legal parents).

140 See, e.g. T.L. Brito, 'The Child Support Debt Bubble' (2019) 9 *U.C. Irvine L. Rev.* 953, 954.

141 Approximately 70% of the outstanding child support debt is owed by men with annual incomes below $10,000. See ibid., 954. The system has particularly harsh effects for the incarcerated. Imprisonment makes it impossible to hold a job, but in most states incarceration does not automatically suspend child support obligations. See L. Haney, 'Incarcerated Fatherhood: The Entanglements of Child Support Debt and Mass Imprisonment' (2018) 124 *Am. J. Soc.* 22.

142 See C. Huntington, 'Postmarital Family Law', above n. 43; J. Carbone and C. Huntington, 'Fatherhood, Family Law, and the Crisis of Boys and Men', *Columbia L. Rev.* (forthcoming 2024).

And state-initiated actions often use the funds collected to reimburse the state for expenses or public benefits rather than for the well-being of the custodial parent and the children.[143]

The states have begun to address these abuses. At least six states – California, Illinois, Michigan, New Mexico, Vermont and Wyoming – have adopted recent reforms to their child support enforcement laws to pass through more of the money collected to custodial parents,[144] with Colorado passing through the entire amount to custodial parents.[145] In addition, California amended its child support statutes, in 2022, to suspend the accrual of obligations while a parent is incarcerated,[146] and to give courts greater flexibility in determining ability to pay.[147] There is growing bipartisan recognition that the child support enforcement programme is counterproductive,[148] and Congress has considered federal efforts to reform the system, but, to date, changes are occurring one state at a time.

5. CONCLUSION

The American federal system, while entrusting family law to the states, has robust mechanisms for producing convergence when there is the will to engineer such results. The Supreme Court decision in *Obergefell v. Hodges*, for example, broke through determined minority opposition to marriage equality, ushering

143 D.L. Hatcher, *Injustice, Inc.*, University of California Press, 2023 (observing, for example, that in California, 40% of child support debt is owed to the state).

144 E. Hager, 'More States Are Allowing Child Support Payments to Reach Children', *ProPublica*, 3 May 2024, https://www.propublica.org/article/more-states-allow-child-support-to-reach-children#:~:text=Since%20a%20ProPublica%20investigation%20found,states%20have%20changed%20their%20policies; see also N.Y.C. Hum. Res. Admin., Dep't of Soc. Servs., *Child Support Handbook for Noncustodial Parents* (2016), p. 9, https://www.nyc.gov/assets/hra/downloads/pdf/services/child_support/noncustodial_parents.pdf (explaining that, in New York State, the maximum child support order is $25 a month for a non-custodial parent whose earnings are below the federal poverty level, and that arrearages are capped at $500).

145 Nat'l Conf. of State Legislatures, 'Child Support Pass-Through and Disregard Policies for Public Assistance Recipients', 30 May 2023, https://www.ncsl.org/human-services/child-support-pass-through-and-disregard-policies-for-public-assistance-recipients (describing the pass-through legislation in roughly half of the states, but also noting that many states allow only a limited pass-through amount, such as $50, and that Colorado is the only state that allows 100% of the child support payment to go to a Temporary Assistance to Needy Families recipient).

146 Cal. Fam. Code §§4007.5, 4054 & 4058(b)(3) (2024).

147 Ibid., §4058(b)(1).

148 The legislation, introduced into Congress in 2023, proposed greater pass-through of child support to families rather than the state. See Women's Cong. Pol'y Inst., 'House Approves Child Support Reform and Fatherhood Package', https://www.wcpinst.org/source/house-approves-child-support-reform-and-fatherhood-package/.

in same-sex marriage in all 50 states. In contrast, some issues, such as changes in the determination of functional parentage, are slowly gaining ground without yet crystallising into consensus-based national proposals. Individual courts, faced with the exigencies of the families before them, have expanded longstanding equitable doctrines and the Uniform Parentage Act, and the American Law Institute proposals for de facto parenthood have created models for states that wish to adopt such legislation, increasing the likelihood that some form of functional parenthood will eventually be recognised in most of the country. Other issues, such as abortion, remain the subject of intense contestation because they have become identity markers associated with the political polarisation that divides the states. The convergence in family law in the middle of the twentieth century occurred at a time of greater economic equality and greater confidence in American institutions. At a time of intense political divisions at the national level, incremental family change at the state level produces a basis for more constructive reforms today.

PART IV

DEVELOPMENTS IN FAMILY LAW

GLOBAL PERSPECTIVES

RETHINKING THE LINKS BETWEEN THE CHANGING FAMILY, LAW, AND GENDER

Ursula Basset

Résumé

Le féminisme a (du moins en apparence) exercé une influence considérable sur la pensée juridique. Il s'agit certes d'un sujet important, mais aussi d'un sujet politiquement incontournable. Qui a peur de ne pas être féministe de nos jours ? La pensée féministe se traduit par des textes et des cadres juridiques qui visent à assurer l'égalité des femmes dans l'accès à la justice, l'égalité avec les hommes dans tous les domaines, l'égalité des salaires et des chances au travail, la réglementation des soins, de la famille et de la vie personnelle. Ce discours « politiquement correct » impose un certain langage, une formulation inclusive et une représentation des femmes dans tous les domaines.

Les progrès sont en partie réels. Dans la plupart des pays occidentaux, la situation des femmes est meilleure qu'elle ne l'a jamais été au cours de l'histoire. Cependant, certaines améliorations restent à faire et, ce qui est plus grave, certaines discussions théoriques dans le féminisme contemporain et certaines politiques sociales et lois conçues initialement en faveur des femmes se sont retournées contre elles. La cause de ce renversement de situation est probablement l'approche de la pensée féministe elle-même.

Le présent chapitre étant le résultat d'une recherche de quatre ans sur les nouvelles discriminations à l'égard des femmes et, plus récemment, sur les discriminations structurelles et symboliques, notre objectif est de présenter très brièvement certaines des conclusions auxquelles nous parvenons relativement : (a) aux discussions théoriques actuelles au sein des mouvements féministes et aux conséquences pratiques de l'évolution de la conjugalité, de la parentalité et de la prise en charge des enfants ; (b) et aux éléments à prendre en compte dans le cadre de futures orientations.

1. THE STARTING POINT

Feminism has had a widespread influence on legal thought.[1] Women's rights are not only a relevant topic, but also a politically correct one.[2] Who is *not* afraid of *not* being feminist?

Feminist thought has been translated into legal wordings and legal frames that aim at equality for women in access to justice; equal pay and opportunities at work; regulations for care, family, and personal life;[3] and equal standing with men in any domain. Political correctness impels a certain discourse, inclusiveness in wording and representation of women in any setting.

These advancements are real improvements in women's quality of life. Women are better off in most Western countries than at any other time in history.[4] However, there are still some improvements to be made. And, worst of all, some of the current theoretical discussions in contemporary feminism, and some of the social policies and laws advanced in the name of feminism, have generated

1 C.R. Sunstein, 'Feminism and legal theory' (1988) 101(4) *Harvard Law Review* 826–48: 'The women's movement is the most powerful contemporary development of this sort; feminism provides its theoretical foundation" (even if the author recognises that women's voices are sometimes downplayed).

2 J. MacLeod Heminway, 'Corporate Management Should All Be Feminists' (2022) 40(2) *Law and Inequality: Journal of Theory and Practice* 409–32.

3 See R. West and C. Grant Bowman, *Research Handbook on Feminist Jurisprudence*, Edward Elgar, 2019.

4 E. Todd, *Où en sont-elles? Une esquisse de l'histoire des femmes*, Seuil, 2022.

a backlash, and the cause of the backlash is probably the very approach of some feminist thought.[5]

As this chapter is the result of a four-year research project on new forms of discrimination against women and more recent research on structural and symbolic discrimination, it aims at showing very briefly some of the findings on the theoretical discussions in feminism and the practical consequences in the changing conjugality, parenthood and care constellations. The chapter will conclude with possible future lines of work.

2. SOME OF THE CURRENT THEORETICAL DISCUSSIONS IN FEMINISM AND THEIR IMPACT ON FAMILY LAW

Many histories of feminist thought have been written, and most of them agree in dividing feminism into waves. There is also a vast consensus asserting that the first wave of feminism dealt with political rights, while the second wave dealt initially with economic and social rights, and then with symbolic and cultural issues. Some speak of a third-wave feminism, or even of a post-feminism.[6]

2.1. FIRST- AND SECOND-WAVE LIBERAL FEMINISMS

First- and second-wave feminism were concerned with advancing women's citizenship in quite practical domains. It was undoubted that feminism was concerned with the rights of women because of the unequal legal standing women had in society compared with men. Hence, the Universal Declaration of Human Rights, due to Hansa Mehta's contributions to the preparatory works, deliberately and explicitly refers to 'man and woman'.[7] Discrimination on the basis of sex is generally prohibited in every human rights treaty.

---

5 S.J. Kenney, 'Backlash Against Feminism: Rethinking a Loaded Concept' in D. Brake, M. Chamallas and V.L. Williams (eds.), *The Oxford Handbook of Feminism and Law in the United States*, online ed., Oxford Academic, 9 June 2021, https://doi.org/10.1093/oxfordhb/9780197519998.013.19. But see also the classic book by S. Faludi, *Backlash: The Undeclared War Against American Women*, Crown Publishing, 1991.

6 D. Llewellyn, "Talking in Waves: A Generational and Secular Metaphor" in *Reading, Feminism and Spirituality*, Palgrave Macmillan 2015, pp. 31–64. B.G. Smith and N. Robinson (eds.), *The Routledge History of Feminism*, Routledge, 2022; M. Walters, *Feminism: A Very Short Introduction*, OUP, 2005; S. Budgeon, *Third Wave Feminism and the Politics of Gender in Late Modernity*, Palgrave Macmillan, 2011.

7 For more information, see R. Adami, *Women and the Universal Declaration of Human Rights*, Routledge, 2018. See also the UN Website: 'Women who shaped the Universal Declaration on Human Rights', available here: https://www.un.org/en/observances/human-rights-day/women-who-shaped-the-universal-declaration.

The initial anti-discrimination provisions were designed to give access to equality to women, defined by their biological sex, who had been excluded in categorical ways from many of the rights enjoyed by men. Over time, the need for protection and guarantees of full inclusion have called into question not just distinctions between men and women per se, but also a variety of considerations linked to gender; that is, traits and behaviours associated with the stereotypically masculine and feminine. The relationship between sex and gender, and the construction of treaty protections and anti-discrimination law, are subject to ongoing evolution in theory and practice.

In the case of gender, this is usually construed as an interpretation from the open clause found at the end of each anti-discrimination clause of every human rights treaty. To illustrate, Article 2 of the Universal Declaration of Human Rights states:

> 'Everyone is entitled to all the rights and freedoms set forth in this Declaration, without distinction of any kind, such as race, colour, sex, language, religion, political or other opinion, national or social origin, property, birth or other status.' Sex is explicitly prohibited as a discrimination ground, while gender is omitted, and has to be construed from the wording 'or other status'.

The unfolding of humanity in men and women is to be found in human rights in areas where the discrimination was more explicit, such as 'men and women. have the right to marry', 'men and women [have the right] to the enjoyment of all economic, social and cultural rights set forth in the present Covenant' (Covenant on Economic, Social and Cultural Rights), and 'equal pay for equal work' (also in the Covenant on Economic, Social and Cultural Rights). These wordings were later reflected in the internal legal systems of the signatory parties.

2.2. THE CONVENTION ON THE ELIMINATION OF ALL FORMS OF DISCRIMINATION AGAINST WOMEN (THE RELEVANCE OF THE BASIS OF SEX AS A PROTECTIVE CATEGORY)

The separate enunciation of women and men in international treaties expresses a specific concern about the unequal standing of women with regard to certain rights. This is also reflected in the Convention on the Elimination of All Forms of Discrimination Against Women (CEDAW), adopted in 1979. The CEDAW approach is an integrative one: it aims to include women in every sphere of society. Women are not seen as being in a clash of rights with men. A more liberal and inclusive approach prevails.[8]

---

8 S. Zwiegel, *Translating International Women's Rights: The CEDAW Convention in Context*, Palgrave Macmillan 2014, pp. 2–3.

To attain this goal, the CEDAW offers a holistic approach, granting individual rights for women, asking the ratifying states to support women in their endeavours, and proposing an evolutionary cultural framework concerning the representation of women in societies.[9] The CEDAW goes far beyond formal and substantial equality, aiming also to eliminate structural and systemic discrimination in society.[10]

It is necessary to underscore, however, that the CEDAW prohibits all discrimination based on sex. Women are undeniably the reason why the CEDAW was conceived, as this is stated in Article 1, which leaves no doubt on the scope of its protection:

> 'For the purposes of the present Convention, the term "discrimination against women" shall mean any distinction, exclusion or restriction made on the basis of sex which has the effect or purpose of impairing or nullifying the recognition, enjoyment or exercise by women, irrespective of their marital status, on a basis of equality of men and women, of human rights and fundamental freedoms in the political, economic, social, cultural, civil or any other field.'

Moreover, Article 5 of the CEDAW reinforces sex-based anti-discrimination principles when underlining 'maternity as a social function'.

As recently pointed out in a position paper – bound to be controversial – by the UN Special Rapporteur on Violence against Women,[11] the CEDAW protects 'biological sex':

- 'While not addressing or defining the terms "sex" or "gender", many foundational human rights treaties, and declarations, including CEDAW, enshrine a prohibition of discrimination based on sex which can only be taken to mean as referring to biological sex. In General Recommendation No. 28, the CEDAW Committee reiterated that "the objective of the Convention is the elimination of all forms of discrimination against women on the basis of sex.'
- 'Building on the implicit understanding that the word "woman" refers to biological females, the CEDAW Committee's reference to lesbian women can only be understood to mean biological females that are attracted to biological females. Such a conclusion can be inferred from its description of the term "lesbian" as reflected in the Committee's view under article 7(3)

---

9 R. Holtmaat, 'The CEDAW: A holistic approach to women's equality and freedom' in A. Hellum and H. Sinding Aasen (eds.), *Women's Human Rights: CEDAW in International, Regional and National Law*, CUP, 2013, pp. 95 ff.

10 Ibid.

11 R. Alsalem, 'Position paper on the definition of "woman" in international human rights treaties, in particular the Convention on the Elimination of All Forms of Discrimination Against Women Special Rapporteur on violence against Women, Special Rapporteur on violence against women and girls, Reem Alsalem', available at https://www.ohchr.org/sites/default/files/documents/issues/women/sr/statements/20240404-Statement-sr-vawg-cedaw-convention.pdf.

of the Optional Protocol concerning communication No. 134/2018, which refers to "same sex sexual activity." In expressing its view, the Committee mentions lesbian women as one of the groups of women that experience discrimination (in addition to bisexuals, transgender, intersex, and others).'

However, these clear statements are slightly watered down in the next paragraph, where the same position paper states: 'Based on this intersectional approach, the CEDAW Committee, in its jurisprudence, has highlighted that discrimination against women was inextricably linked to other factors that affect their lives and which include "being lesbian, bisexual, transgender, or intersex."'

This succinct depiction shows the internal tensions between an originalist interpretation of the CEDAW and the trends tending to stretch sex towards gender.

2.3. THE INTER-AMERICAN HUMAN RIGHTS SYSTEM: DISCRIMINATION BASED ON GENDER (TOWARDS THE IRRELEVANCE OF GENDER AS A PROTECTIVE CATEGORY)

The Inter-American system of human rights, in the Convention of Belem do Pará (CBP) on the Prevention, Punishment, and Eradication of Violence against Women, has adopted a completely different wording. Article 1 states: 'For the purposes of this Convention, violence against women shall be understood as any act or conduct, based on gender, which causes death or physical, sexual or psychological harm or suffering to women, whether in the public or the private sphere.' We should not get carried away by this wording; the CBP protects women in contexts of gender-based violence.

The scope of this Convention is not to protect women's rights, but to protect women's rights against violence. Because of violence, women are perceived to be in a more vulnerable situation than they are in the context the drafters of the CEDAW had in mind.

There is also another difference from the framework of the CEDAW. The CBP embraces an approach to feminism closer to radical feminism than to the liberal feminism on which the CEDAW seems to be modelled.[12] For instance, Articles 6 and 8 CBP address a 'pattern of subordination' of women.[13]

12 Liberal feminism is usually understood as the second-wave feminism that gave way to equality between women and men within the frame of liberal democracy and human rights, through political and legal reform. Radical feminism is a perspective within feminism that calls for a radical reordering of society in which male supremacy is eliminated in all social and economic contexts. See, for instance, B.G. Smith and N. Robinson (eds.), *The Routledge History of Feminism*, Routledge, 2022. M. Walters, above n. 6; S. Budgeon, above n. 6.

13 C. O'Connell, 'Women's Rights and the Inter-American System' in N. Reilly, *International Human Rights of Women*, Springer Singapore, 2019, p. 142.

The Inter-American Court of Human Rights has done the rest. Picking up on the inclusion of gender as a trope of the Inter-American human rights system, the Court has gone on to predicate gender as a protective category applicable to every human being. In its Advisory Opinion 24, gender is understood as consisting of 'socially constructed identities, attributes and roles for women and men and society's social and cultural meaning for these biological differences'.[14] This means that gender is no longer associated exclusively with women; it can be used to protect both women and men, even if, in the context of the CBP, it addresses women only, in the biological sense.

In the case *Fornerón v. Argentina*, the Inter-American Court understood that stereotypes might apply to men. See, for instance, the following passage:

> The considerations of the first instance judge also reveal a preconceived idea of what it is to be a single parent, because Mr. Fornerón's capacity and possibility of fulfilling the role of father was questioned and conditioned on the existence of a wife. The single status of Mr. Fornerón, compared by one of the judges to 'the absence of biological family,' used as grounds for legally depriving him of performing his role as a father, constitutes the denial of a basic right based on stereotypes about the capacity, qualities or attributes required to exercise single parenthood, without considering the specific characteristics and circumstances of the father who wishes, alone, to fulfill his role as a father.[15]

This opinion broke new ground in its willingness to protect men from gender stereotypes asserting that single fathers, unlike single mothers, could not be adequate parents.

Now, if the main category to think of in terms of impermissible discrimination is no longer sex but gender, and gender includes socially constructed identities for women and men, neither sex nor gender seem to be relevant as a protective category. A category that includes all human beings, male and female, might, as such, be redundant.

2.4. THE TROPE OF SEX/GENDER DIFFERENCE AS A TOOL TO ACHIEVE EQUALITY

Since the liberal approach to second-wave feminism (the wave that fought for social and economic rights), there has been a deep discussion on how to deal with discrimination: should feminism seek to eliminate references to 'men

14 IACtHR, Advisory Opinion 24, available at https://www.corteidh.or.cr/docs/opiniones/seriea_24_eng.pdf.

15 IACtHR, *Fornerón v. Argentina*, 2012, para. 96. But see also paras. 97–98. Available at https://www.corteidh.or.cr/docs/casos/articulos/seriec_242_ing.pdf.

and women' – given that such language assumes that biological differences define individuals – in favour of universal language referring to 'human rights' or 'the rights of each human being'? The advantages of the undifferentiated approach are conveyed by the fact that there is no difference in dignity or in recognition of humanity. The original preference for language that included 'women' in the wording of the legal texts had the advantage of enhancing specific protective devices for women and making them visible. In international treaties, this theoretical discussion was resolved by including women in the general enunciation of rights (trying, when possible, to avoid the generic masculine), and the difference between men and women, and the equal rights of both were preferred when it came down to applicable issues (family, work, etc.).[16]

Theory was more complicated. Feminists were convinced that women had to work side by side with men, and that no difference should be made between them. However, as Judith Lorber pointed out in her book, *Paradoxes of Gender*, since total equality was not attained, corrections still needed to be made.[17] And, of course, some will remember the change of heart of Betty Friedan, the renowned American feminist, once her daughter had tried to fulfil her liberal ideas about women competing in a world of men. If, in the beginning, she was all for gender-neutrality, in her book *The Second Stage* she realised the need to value feminine traits in society.[18]

Thus, the language should not be gender-neutral. Women should be visible, to boost equality. This brings us to a discussion that comes not from liberal feminism, but from radical second-wave feminism. Radical feminists are mostly concerned with the symbolic and structural dimensions of gender. Yet, it is the belief of many of the representatives of this movement that our current societies have come to understand gender more as a spectrum of sexual self-perceptions[19] than as the classical meaning we find in international documents by the CEDAW Committee, relating it to the concept of woman. And there is, of course, transfeminism and the question of the place of trans women in the feminist debate.[20]

---

16 J. Lorber, 'Using gender to undo gender: A feminist degendering movement' (2000) 1(1) *Feminist Theory* 79 ff. Available here: https://bpb-us-e2.wpmucdn.com/sites.middlebury.edu/dist/7/1905/files/2017/12/LorberUsingGendertoUndoGender.pdf.

17 J. Lorber, *Paradoxes of Gender*, Yale University Press, 1994. An updated and revised look at the same matters can be found in J. Lorber, *The New Gender Paradox: Fragmentation and Persistence of the Binary*, Polity Press, 2021.

18 B. Friedan, *The Second Stage*, Summit Books, 1981.

19 J. Lorber, *The New Gender Paradox*, above n. 17, ch. 2, p. 19 (Kindle ed.).

20 See K.T. Bartlett, 'Gender Law: After Twenty-Five Years' (2020) 27 *Duke Journal of Gender Law & Policy* 1–23.

2.5. THE TROPE OF 'DEGENDERING LAW' TO ACHIEVE EQUALITY

Due to activism to achieve the recognition of diversity of sexual orientations and self-perceived identity, the word 'woman' has increasingly been erased from our legislation, being substituted by the word 'gender', which now sometimes includes any gender, since all of them are believed to be social constructs. The concept of woman has been watered down or simply removed completely from our legal texts.

The relationship between sex and gender is challenging. Judith Lorber, in her book, *Gender Paradox*, points out, citing Wallach Scott, that it is 'an inevitable feminist paradox that to fight to erase the effects of gender differences, you must invoke them: To the extent that it acted for "women," feminism produced the "sexual difference" it sought to eliminate.'[21] If the sexual difference is fully erased, no protective devices are possible.

A harsher critique comes from other feminists, who hold that gender-neutrality is a new form of patriarchy imposed upon women to erase them.[22] Nancy Dowd, for instance, has put it this way: 'So, for example, gender neutrality, while persuasive in theory, hides asymmetrical realities, such as the disproportionate caretaking responsibilities of women or women's disproportionate victimization from sexual assault and domestic violence.'[23] As a matter of fact, this is happening in family law: the regulation of divorce has had a negative impact on women in many countries, mostly because it is neutered[24] and based upon a presumed equality that does not really happen in most cases.[25] Many of the presentations at the Antwerp ISFL World Conference on Family Law dealt with the disproportionate impact of marital breakdown on women caused by laws that presume an equal standing between men and women. In this case, indirect and structural discrimination are partially based on symbolic violence.

When the discussion comes down to how to deal with the gender-neutral rules of filiation in countries that have legalised same-sex parenthood by Artificial Reproductive Techniques or change of sex in a registry, the discussion

---

21 J. Lorber, *The New Gender Paradox*, above n. 17, p. 68 (Kindle ed.).

22 R. Barrett, *Female Erasure*, Tidal Times Publishing, 2016; J. Acker, 'Hierarchies, jobs, and bodies: A theory of gendered organizations' (1990) 4 *Gender & Society* 139–58; M. Becker, 'Patriarchy and Inequality: Towards a Substantive Feminism', *University of Chicago Legal Forum*: Vol. 1999 (Issue 1, Art. 3), available at http://chicagounbound.uchicago.edu/uclf/vol1999/iss1/3.

23 N.E. Dowd, *The Man Question: Subordination and Privilege*, New York University Press, 2010, p. 2.

24 M.A. Fineman, *The Neutered Mother, The Sexual Family and Other Twentieth Century Tragedies*, Routledge, 1995.

25 Susan Faludi, discussing sex-neutral norms in divorce, states that patriarchy did not disappear, but just changed its ways of presenting itself: S. Faludi, above n. 5, p. 40.

is not only about how to create blind rules to establish parenthood, but also a new invisibility of a series of costly involvements by women in the procreation, engenderment and nursing of children.[26] Eliminating references to women will necessarily make invisible the enormous importance and risks of giving birth to a child. This threat was noted by the American feminist Professor Martha Fineman almost 30 years ago, in her book *The Neutered Mother*.[27] Instead of valuing the contribution women are making to society, we might neutralise them.

2.6. WHAT TO MAKE OF THIS?

This discussion eventually echoes in other anti-discrimination topics: should there be a quota for women or is the quota undignifying? Further, should gender perspectives in access to justice always apply (meaning that women are always more vulnerable) or is it offensive nowadays to say that women are *always* and, in *any* respect, more vulnerable than men? If women are more vulnerable, should there be a standard protective approach (risking paternalism) or should the protective approach be applied on a case-by-case basis?

Many of these issues are addressed in CEDAW's General Recommendation No. 33 on women's access to justice. This document underscores the obstacles to achieving equality in terms of structural and systemic discrimination. It highlights crucial issues such as lack of credibility and negative stereotypes associated with women, and calls for a greater consciousness of gender bias. However, do these considerations apply to every woman? Are there some women who are more believed than others?

As stated by Claire Dalton, 'the equality route had as one of its chief disadvantages the suppression of the concrete ways in which women's lives tend to be shaped differently from men's'.[28]

2.7. ESSENTIALISM AND WOMEN'S RIGHTS? DOES IT WORK?

These questions are of great importance, and have a quite practical bearing. Characterising women as always being vulnerable (a vulnerable group by definition) may perpetuate stigmatising stereotypes. Take, for instance, the

---

26 S. Frelich Appleton, 'How Feminism Remade the American Family Law' in R. West and C. Grant Bowman, above n. 3, pp. 427 ff.

27 M. Fineman, *The Neutered Mother*, Routledge, 1996. See also M. Fineman, *Mothers in Law*, Routledge, London, 1995.

28 C. Dalton, 'Where We Stand: Observations on the Situation of Feminist Legal Thought' (1987) *Berkeley Women's Law Journal* 1–13, 5.

recurrent example of treating women with leniency in penal law or even in family disputes: does this, as Mahatma Gandhi once hinted, disrespect them?[29]

In the end, essentialism is a prejudice that allows for new forms of paternalism towards women. If essentialism entails that all women will act the same way, freedom of choice is taken away from women,[30] and with it differences between and among women. When women are construed as archetypes ('subordinated sex', 'mother'), the theoretical approach risks dissolving individual identities and self-determination into essentialist categories.

Much of these discussions can be seen in the way women victims of violence are treated: in many respects, it is presumed that their will is not completely free. Much the same has happened with other protective devices. Let us take, for example, the case law of the Inter-American Court of Human Rights. In the case *IV v. Bolivia*, the Court stated that a woman's consent to sterilisation is not completely free when given while she is giving birth:[31] 'In the Court's opinion consent cannot be considered free if a woman is asked to provide it when she is not in a condition to take a fully informed decision because she is in a situation of stress and vulnerability, inter alia, such as, during or immediately after giving birth or undergoing a caesarean section.' Note the use here of 'inter alia'.

The same line of reasoning was put forward in a recent case, *Britez Arce v. Argentina*, from 2022.[32] What implications does this have for reproductive rights? Or for other choices made during pregnancy or after birth? What implications would it have for surrogacy? To dismantle patriarchy did we engage in a new paternalism?

Another topic related to this is the rhetorical question about women being serial killers. This topic comes from the commonplace notion that when someone says 'serial killer' it is a man that comes to mind and not a woman.[33] Some feminists understand this as a belittling stereotype. The paradox is that

---

29 'To call woman the weaker sex is a libel; it is a man's injustice to woman. If by strength it is meant moral power, then woman is immeasurably man's superior. Is she not more self-sacrificing, has she not great powers of endurance, has she not greater courage? Without her, man could not be.'

30 See M. Nussbaum, 'Aristotle, Feminism, and Needs for Functioning' (1992) 70(4) *Texas Law Review* 1019–28.

31 IACtHR, *IV v. Bolivia*, 2016, para. 183.

32 IACtHR, Arce v. Argentina, 2022, para. 84: *'La Corte recuerda que, durante o inmediatamente después del parto o de una cesárea las mujeres se encuentran en una situación de especial vulnerabilidad. En esa medida, el estado de ansiedad, angustia y estrés al que fue sometida la señore Brítez Arce, sumado a la vulnerabilidad en que se encontraba, llevó a que fuera víctima de un trato deshumanizado. Sobre este asunto, la Corte encuentra que el peritaje elaborado por la Universidad Católica de Córdoba sostuvo que "se perdió de vista [a] la paciente por hacer diagnóstico de feto muerto."'*.

33 B. Simpson, 'Murder, Prostitution and Patriarchy: Why serial killing is a feminist issue' (2001) 26(6) *Alternative Law Journal* 278–80, https://doi.org/10.1177/1037969X0102600603.

this belittling comes from a supposed praise of women. But how many other belittling stereotypes disguised as praise are there? For instance, a woman is always a good defenceless mother, and the father a man that wants to harm her by taking her children away from her? Are women innocent by definition?

This relates to the very discussion of 'parental alienation' strongly resisted by some groups of feminists. It was feared that new forms of patriarchy would jeopardise the credibility of women and their claims of child abuse carried out by fathers.[34] Women do not lie? Authors like Naomi Wolf and Katie Roiphe claim that second-wave feminists (such as Andrea Dworkin, Catharine MacKinnon and Adrienne Rich) are guilty of focusing 'on female victimization at the expense of social agency'.[35] Depriving women of their capability of making morally or legally wrong choices in life deprives women of their moral agency, which is a defining trait of human dignity.

But then we come back to the other topic of feminism: are women angels or demons?[36] Probably neither; sometimes they are angels, sometimes they are ill-natured, sometimes somewhere in the middle – just like any human being. Sometimes it is the theoretical approach to women that makes women less equal, and thus partly invisible.

3. WHAT TO LOOK AT AND POSSIBLE FUTURE WORKING LINES

To sum up, feminists have proposed either protective, empowering or neutralising approaches with different theoretical frames. As we have seen, many of these approaches have driven great advancements in women's rights, and yet sometimes entail paradoxes and negative side effects. In many cases, the side effects come from an absolutisation of a certain theoretical frame that loses sight of the totality of the implications involved.

---

34 See, for instance, N. Jaffe-Geffner, 'Gender Bias in Cross-Allegation Domestic Violence-Parental Alienation Custody Cases: Can States Legislate the Fix?' (2021) 42(1) *Columbia Journal of Gender and the Law* 21–107.

35 N. Wolf, *Fire with Fire*, Random House, 1993, p. 212: 'The focus of some feminists, like Andrea Dworkin, Catharine MacKinnon, and Adrienne Rich, on female victimization at the expense of female agency, derives from conditions that once applied more than they do now. During the early 1970s women were indeed overwhelmingly silenced and negated but the genderquake means that the rationale of this kind of feminism is becoming obsolete. Virtually every woman's political organization, and most grassroots groups, seek power-feminist goals. But the language of victim feminism often dominates discussion of the movement in the mass media.'

36 J.L. Stephens, 'Subverting the demon-angel dichotomy: Innovation and feminist intervention in twentieth-century drama' (1989) 9(1) *Text and Performance Quarterly* 53–64, https://doi.org/10.1080/10462938909365912.

Possible lines to move on from here could include some of the following considerations:

1. How might the visibility of the category of 'women' be preserved in laws with gender-neutral language? Does the language of inclusiveness include women as an explicit and not only implicit legal category?
2. Anti-discrimination law risks eliminating protected categories on behalf of a rhetoric of empowerment of the very same categories it was bound to protect. In a way, this shows a trouble in naming: i.e. naming disabilities; naming women; naming trans people; naming, or treating, children as children. It might be that this trouble in naming is hiding an implicit thought that these categories should not be named, because naming them is unworthy or somewhat shameful. Is it so? It is precisely the opposite: dignity shines the most in vulnerability. Why would we need to silence the differences? Being vulnerable and asking for varied protective devices is not less dignified. To ask why differences should be silenced is an issue to address when researching on anti-discrimination law.
3. There is also trouble with the concept of autonomy and agency when applied to women. Women are perceived as simultaneously vulnerable and subordinate by systemic discrimination and patriarchy. Do these views favour essentialism? Do they reproduce stereotyping patterns? How should this be addressed in research?
4. How should indifference or negligence in due diligence and protection duties towards women be avoided?
5. How should overprotective approaches be avoided? On the other hand, there is radical and overprotective feminism that would want women to always be right and to get all they ask for. Does this approach do justice to women's studies?
6. What if the future of feminism were less theoretical and more concerned with its practical impact? An extremely theoretical feminism ends up watering down concrete women in the anonymity of theories. How can the leading roles of feminism be restored to concrete women?
7. What if we subsumed gender perspective in a general comprehension of human vulnerability theory and empathy? After all, we are a 'band of brothers' as it was beautifully put by Shakespeare;[37] or, as was said by Paul Ricoeur, the others are not others but other 'me'.[38] Empathy in our commonality and diverse vulnerabilities is a more human approach to dealing with discrimination.

---

[37] Henry V, Act 4, Scene 3.

[38] P. Ricouer, *Soi même comme un autre*, Seuil, 1990.

POLAND

PROTECTION OF MINOR UKRAINIAN CITIZENS

War Refugees Residing in Poland

Małgorzata Balwicka-Szczyrba and Anna Sylwestrzak

Resumé

L'invasion de l'Ukraine par la Russie en février 2022 a provoqué une grande vague de migration de citoyens ukrainiens vers la Pologne. On estime que plus de 15 millions de réfugiés ont franchi la frontière polonaise depuis le début de la guerre et qu'il y a actuellement plus d'un million de réfugiés sur le territoire polonais. Parmi les réfugiés, de nombreux enfants privés de leurs parents ont été protégés par des dispositions légales spéciales. La loi du 12 mars 2022 sur l'assistance aux citoyens ukrainiens dans le cadre du conflit armé sur le territoire de ce pays a introduit un certain nombre de dispositifs visant à protéger les intérêts des réfugiés et à stabiliser leur situation juridique en Pologne. L'article présentera deux d'entre eux : la mise en place d'un tuteur temporaire pour les mineurs ukrainiens résidant en Pologne et la création, sur la base de la loi polonaise, d'une réglementation spéciale pour les familles d'accueil ukrainiennes qui prennent en charge un enfant ukrainien. Si ces deux types de mesures de protection des enfants sont décidés par le tribunal, leur réglementation présente de nombreuses différences avec les mesures ordinaires de prise en charge des enfants qui sont régies par le code polonais de la famille et de la tutelle. L'article se propose d'évaluer la mise en place et l'efficacité de ces nouveaux dispositifs, ainsi que d'analyser les principes visant à renforcer la protection des mineurs réfugiés.

1. INTRODUCTION

Russia's (the Russian Federation's) invasion of Ukraine began on 24 February 2022.[1] The attack carried out in February 2022 was an escalation of the hybrid war that had been going on since 2014, when Russia's seizure of Ukraine's Crimea region took place, sparking further conflict.[2] The actions of Russia, both in 2014 and, above all, in relation to the ongoing war with Ukraine, have significantly affected the security environment in Europe,[3] and Ukraine has received both military and humanitarian assistance on an unprecedented scale from many countries and organisations. More than 4.2 million people from Ukraine currently benefit from the temporary protection mechanism in the European Union,[4] and the total number of Ukrainian refugees in Europe has already exceeded 6 million people.[5]

The migration of people related to the war in Ukraine has had many social, economic and legal consequences. One such consequence is the separation of families associated with the need for men to remain in Ukraine. Single-parent families arriving in other countries required, and still require, support and assistance adapting to different living conditions. A significant problem has been the provision of care for children orphaned from soldier parents, as well as for children who arrived in other countries in the custody of persons other than their parents, including grandparents. The phenomenon of the arrival of whole groups of children from Ukrainian 'orphanages' was also observed, which created the need to integrate them into the childcare system. The increased migration of Ukrainian children has led to further social consequences, including problems fulfilling compulsory education requirements, assisting language learning and securing adequate housing.

Poland is one of the European countries that has accepted the largest number of refugees from Ukraine. Government figures show that 1,719,257 Ukrainian

---

1 Wikipedia: https://pl.wikipedia.org/wiki/Inwazja_Rosji_na_Ukrain%C4%99.

2 See, more broadly, A. Zyguła, 'International Effects of the Conflict in Ukraine – Reaction of the International Community to the Hybrid War in Eastern Ukraine, Defense', *Zeszyty Naukowe*, 2018, no. 3(27), 252.

3 See P. Krzykowski, 'Consequences of the War in Ukraine in the Food, Economic and Energy Dimensions' (2022) 14 (50) *Social Science Chronicle* 93.

4 Statistics on refugees from Ukraine in the European Union are available at the website: https://www.consilium.europa.eu/pl/infographics/ukraine-refugees-eu/ (last access: 10.09.2024).

5 Data on the global situation of Ukrainian refugees are available at the website: https://data.unhcr.org/en/situations/ukraine (last access: 10.09.2024).

citizens have legal residence in Poland and war refugee status, with 35.8 per cent of the refugees under the age of 18. Statistics from the Ministry of Education and Science show that the largest number of Ukrainian students are being educated in Polish secondary schools (over 19,000), post-secondary schools (almost 39,000), with another 32,000 in primary schools. In kindergartens in Poland, there are about 42,000 Ukrainian children, of whom 28,000 are refugees.[6]

The subject of this chapter will be an analysis of the tools for the protection of underage Ukrainian citizens – war refugees residing on the territory of the Republic of Poland.

2. LEGALISATION OF THE STAY OF UKRAINIAN REFUGEES IN POLAND

Such a large migration of people from Ukraine to Poland required the enactment of specific legal regulations dedicated to this group of war migrants. The basic legal Act relating to the assistance of the Ukrainian community in Poland is the Act of 12.03.2022 on Assistance to citizens of Ukraine in connection with the conflict on the territory of that country (the 'Act on Assistance').[7] It primarily sets out specific rules for the legalisation of the stay of Ukrainian citizens, including Ukrainian children, who have arrived in the Republic of Poland from Ukraine in connection with the hostilities, as well as the rights of Ukrainian citizens on Polish territory and the related obligations of State and local authorities. Article 2(1) stipulates that, if a Ukrainian citizen arrived legally on the territory of the Republic of Poland in the period after 24 February 2022 and declared their intention to stay in the Republic of Poland, their stay is deemed legal until 30 September 2025. However, it is stipulated that the departure of a Ukrainian citizen from the territory of the Republic of Poland for a period exceeding 30 days deprives them of this entitlement. The Act, therefore, provides a legal basis for recognising the stay of a Ukrainian citizen, which occurs *ex lege*; that is, without the need for an administrative decision in this regard.

Registration obligations are associated with the legalisation of the stay of Ukrainian citizens, including Ukrainian children. A PESEL number[8] is assigned to a Ukrainian citizen whose stay on the territory of the Republic of Poland is considered legal. It is assigned on the basis of an application submitted to any executive body of a municipality in the Republic of Poland, which is done

6 https://www.rp.pl/edukacja/art39462041-ile-dzieci-z-ukrainy-jest-w-polskich-szkolach-i-przedszkolach-poznalismy-dane.
7 Journal of Laws 2023, item 1234.
8 The numer of Universal Electronic System of Population Registration.

in a simplified administrative procedure.[9] The application must be submitted on a form which has been published, in Polish and Ukrainian, in the Public Information Bulletin of the minister responsible for information technology.[10] An application on behalf of a minor is submitted by their parent, guardian, custodian, temporary custodian or person having actual custody of the child. However, the child must also appear in person at the municipality if they are over the age of 12, due to the need to be fingerprinted.

It needs to be emphasised that Ukrainian citizens who obtain a PESEL number, including Ukrainian children, enjoy rights equal to those of Polish citizens in many spheres of social life: in terms of social assistance, including in obtaining appropriate benefits, employment and self-employment; and in health care, including the possibility of obtaining medical services or psychological support. Ukrainian children can attend Polish nurseries and kindergartens, and are subject to compulsory education on Polish territory. Pursuant to the amended Ordinance of the Minister of Education and Science of 21 March 2022 on the organisation of education, upbringing and care of children and youth who are citizens of Ukraine,[11] compulsory schooling, including the entitlement for Ukrainian children to take eighth grade and matriculation examinations, was extended for the year 2023/2024.[12]

The Act also contains a regulation on the legalisation of the residence of Ukrainian children born in Poland (Article 2(1) of the 'Act on Assistance'). The Act of 28.11.2014 Law on Civil Status Records, which makes the registration of foreigners on the territory of Poland compulsory, also applies to children born in Poland. This rule also applies to the children of refugees, and therefore the drawing up of birth certificates of such children takes place according to the general rules. However, since the birth certificate of a Ukrainian refugee child will indicate the Ukrainian origin of the child's mother, the 1993 Bilateral Convention on Legal Assistance and Legal Relations in Civil and Criminal Matters, concluded between the Republic of Poland and Ukraine, will apply.[13] In accordance with the Convention, both the child's origin and their name will be governed by Ukrainian law (Article 28 in conjunction with Article 25 of the Convention), regardless of the nationality of the child or the child's father.

---

[9] See more detailed commentary on Art. 4 of the Act on assistance to citizens of Ukraine in connection with the conflict on the territory of this country, *Commentary with patterns regarding residence, access to the labor market, social benefits, education and health care* (P. Drembkowski (ed.), 2022).

[10] https://www.gov.pl/web/gov/karty-uslug--uslugi-dla-uchodzcow.

[11] Journal of Laws 2023 r., item 2094.

[12] See, more broadly, M. Paradowski, 'Population register of refugees from Ukraine in the perspective of administrative law norms', *Metryka* 2022, no. 1–2, 124.

[13] Agreement of 24 May 1993 between the Republic of Poland and Ukraine on legal assistance and legal relations in civil and criminal matters, concluded in Kiev, Journal of Laws of 1994, No. 96, item 465 (the 'Bilateral Convention').

Finally, it needs to be emphasised that Ukrainian citizens, including children, arriving on the territory of Poland are provided with a wide range of support measures, which result from the general regulations as well as the 'Act on assistance'. Special entitlements to receive social assistance, resulting from Article 12 of the Act, deserve to be highlighted. Under the terms of this Article, the provincial governor may provide assistance to Ukrainian citizens, consisting of accommodation, provision of collective meals on a daily basis, provision of transport to places of accommodation, financing of travel by means of public transport, and provision of cleaning and personal hygiene products and other products. Assistance may also be provided by other public administrations, units subordinate to or supervised by public administrations, units of the public finance sector, and other public authorities.

It is estimated that, in 2022 alone, Poland has spent a total of around PLN 35–40 billion on assistance to Ukraine.[14]

3. TEMPORARY CUSTODIANS

The norms of private international law in the relations between Poland and Ukraine, regulated by the above-mentioned bilateral agreement, were established in 1993; that is, in peacetime, before the annexation of Crimea by Russia, and at a time when mass migration of Ukrainian citizens to the territory of Poland was not anticipated.[15] After February 2022, the sudden and enormous influx of refugees, including underage children, arriving in Poland in life-threatening circumstances triggered the need to urgently normalise the legal situation of these children. Ordinary legal measures proved insufficient for this; it was necessary to create a new tool, dedicated to this extraordinary situation, which would make it possible to quickly and effectively legalise the status of the Ukrainian children's legal representatives, as well as to introduce appropriate supervision to safeguard the children's welfare. This objective has been fulfilled by the new institution of a temporary guardian, hitherto unknown in the Polish legal system, regulated in Article 25 of the Act on Assistance, and intended for minor Ukrainian citizens residing on the territory

---

14 https://www.infor.pl/prawo/nowosci-prawne/5635962,Polska-pomoc-dla-Ukrainy-2022-ile-kosztowala.html.

15 Pursuant to Arts. 28 and 31 of this Treaty, parental authority over a Ukrainian child living in Poland is subject to Ukrainian substantive law, which is applied by Polish authorities adjudicating the relations between parents and children. In turn, with regard to the care and guardianship of Ukrainian children residing in Poland, the applicable law is, in principle, Ukrainian law; however, the Polish authorities may take the necessary measures in cases of urgency. The competent Ukrainian jurisdiction may transfer the exercise of care or guardianship to a Polish authority, which will henceforth apply Polish law.

of Poland without the care of adults responsible for the child in accordance with Polish law.

This institution is, therefore, not intended to replace or duplicate properly functioning institutions in the field of custody and representation of minors, but comes into play where such institutions are lacking or do not function properly, or where the fate of the child's legal representatives is unknown. Therefore, it does not apply where a child remains in the custody of at least one parent (in a typical situation, Ukrainian children stay in Poland with their mothers while their fathers are engaged in the war) or where a child under 14 years of age is in the custody of a legal guardian appointed by a Ukrainian court. In the latter case, the Ukrainian decision establishing the guardian is subject to recognition in Poland without any additional proceedings.[16] However, if, under Ukrainian law, the guardianship has been established by an administrative decision issued by a public administration body (the procedure for establishing guardianship by administrative decision is not known to Polish law), the effectiveness of the guardianship will be subject to judicial recognition in Poland.[17]

Under Ukrainian law, however, the institution of guardianship applies only to younger children who have not yet reached the age of 14, while for older children (14–18 years) deprived of parental custody, curatorship is established (Article 243 of the Ukrainian Family Code), with guardianship being transformed by law into curatorship as soon as the ward reaches the age of 14. In contrast, Polish law provides for a uniform guardianship institution for all children, regardless of age. The discrepancy between the systems of guardianship institutions in Poland and Ukraine means that a Ukrainian teenager over the age of 14 in the custody of a curator (regardless of whether the curator was appointed by a Ukrainian court or a Ukrainian administrative authority) will not be properly represented in Poland, so it is necessary in such a situation to apply, in Poland, for the appointment of a temporary guardian. This also applies if the child's previous guardian's status automatically changed to curator when the child turned 14. To sum up, a temporary guardian is an institution intended for Ukrainian refugee minors staying in Poland who are neither under the custody of their parents nor under the custody of a guardian, so that, for example, they stay under the actual custody of other

16 Art. 48, Bilateral Convention, above n. 12. The doctrine states that, compared with the long-term recognition procedure, obtaining a temporary guardian is faster, and therefore it may be a more favourable option for Ukrainian refugees, and should be recommended to them: A. Kwaśniewska-Sadkowska, in A. Klaus (ed.), *Act on assistance to citizens of Ukraine in connection with an armed conflict on the territory of this country*, Wolters Kluwer Polska, 2022.

17 The procedure is regulated by Arts. 50–53 of the Bilateral Convention, above n. 12.

persons (often relatives or friends of their parents) or under the custody of a curator appointed in Ukraine.

A temporary guardian is appointed by the guardianship court with jurisdiction over the minor's place of residence, applying the preference criteria indicated in Article 25(5)–(6) of the Act on Assistance, which are, however, only of an auxiliary nature, as the choice of the guardian should be dictated primarily by the welfare of the child. In the first instance, the court takes into account the child's relatives and affinities, as well as other persons giving a guarantee of the proper performance of the guardian's duties. This may, therefore, be a person from outside the child's family circle, and under whose de facto custody the child currently resides, which is quite common in the case of refugees. It should be noted that there is no citizenship criterion here, so a guardian may either be a citizen of Ukraine or a citizen of Poland. However, a candidate for a temporary guardian must not exhibit any of the disqualifying features of a guardian enumerated in Article 148 of the Family and Guardianship Code,[18] which should also be applied to a temporary guardian.

If there are no candidates for a temporary guardian, the guardianship court asks the social welfare unit to identify such a candidate within 48 hours. In contrast to the ordinary guardianship regulation in the Civil Code, the preference for temporary guardians designated by the child's father or mother (provided that the parents have not been deprived of parental authority) has been omitted. One can guess that this omission is due to the assumption that a temporary guardian will often be appointed in the absence of parents whose fate is not known, as well as for evidentiary reasons, as proving the will of the parents could be difficult, and at the same time could leave room for abuse. However, it should be borne in mind that many de facto guardians have received notarised authorisation from the child's parents in Ukraine to travel abroad with the child, and to take care of the child. Under Polish law, the granting of such authorisations does not result in the acquisition of the status of a legal guardian in Poland; however, the court should consider the Ukrainian authorisation as part of the totality of circumstances taken into account in the selection of a temporary guardian, especially if the person indicated in the authorisation currently has actual custody of the child. If there is no conflict of interests between minors, they may have a joint guardian; in the case of siblings, joint guardianship is the rule (Article 25(7) of the Act on Assistance).

The provisions of the Act on Assistance do not explicitly regulate the relationship between the guardian's temporary custody and the parental authority of the parents who have remained in Ukraine, and who still have

---

18 These are: lack of full legal capacity, deprivation of public rights, deprivation of parental authority, or conviction for one of the crimes listed in Art. 148 §2 of the Family and Guardianship Code.

parental authority. However, it can be inferred from the wording of Article 25 (1) and (2) of the Act that, as a general rule, full custody and representation of the child will be vested exclusively in the temporary custodian, disregarding the parents. This kind of full custody is particularly suitable for children whose parents are unknown, have disappeared, or are not exercising their parental authority (for example, because they are involved in the fighting). However, the guardianship court setting up a temporary guardianship may define the scope of the rights and obligations of the temporary guardian differently – for example, by limiting the scope of care – but the law does not indicate what this difference should consist of, leaving it for decisions in individual cases to be tailored in practice. For example, in a situation where the parents residing in Ukraine have parental authority, the guardianship court could, when shaping the powers of the guardian, take into account the participation of the parents in decision-making concerning the child (for example, by obliging the guardian to consult the parents on certain matters concerning the child).

However, application of such limitations should only apply where parents have been identified who are interested in the child, and want to have an impact on the child's fate and maintain regular contact with the guardian and child. In addition, this type of divided authority should be limited to cases where the child is residing in Poland under the custody of another person because of war-induced concern for the safety of the child combined with the parents' need to stay in Ukraine (for example, due to conscription in the army) on a temporary basis. The flexibility of the scope of temporary guardianship distinguishes it from the ordinary guardianship for minors, regulated in the Polish Family and Guardianship Code, the scope of which is rigidly defined by law. This flexibility makes it possible to adapt this tool to the diverse social and family situations in which refugee minors find themselves, and is a great advantage.

The mechanism for verifying the proper functioning of temporary custody is twofold, as it is divided between the guardianship court and social welfare authorities, which makes temporary custody for Ukrainian minors different from the Polish ordinary custody institution regulated by the Family and Guardianship Code, as the latter is entirely subject to court supervision. In the case of temporary guardianship, the guardianship court grants permits in all important matters concerning the minor's person or property and, in turn, the day-to-day supervision of temporary guardianship is exercised by the social welfare centre or social services centre, which is an organisational unit of a municipality. The task of the supervising authority is primarily to oversee the provision of adequate conditions of care and upbringing for minors (Article 25, s. 3bb of the Act on Assistance), and in the course of exercising this task, the supervising authority may request necessary information, enter the premises where the children are staying, observe the children, conduct individual interviews with the children, and inspect residential facilities (Article 28a, s. 4 of the Act on Family Support and the System of Foster Care).[19]

Proceedings for the appointment of a guardian *ad litem* may be initiated either *ex officio* or on application,[20] and are intended to be a fast and effective tool. This is supported by a three-day time limit for the examination of the case, determined from the date of receipt of the application or receipt of information on the need to appoint a temporary guardian. A closed session may be held, during which only documentary evidence is taken, unless the circumstances of the case raise doubts as to the proper exercise of custody and such proceeding limited by evidence would not compromise the minor's welfare. It is rightly suggested in the doctrine that the court should readily dispense with the need for other evidence (in particular, the hearing of the candidate for temporary guardianship) because of the risk of harm to the welfare of the child from delay.[21] In proceedings for the appointment of a provisional guardian, there are no fees, and the expenses are to be borne by the State Treasury.

The regulation of the institution of temporary guardianship contained in the Act does not specify the relation of this form of guardianship to the institution of guardianship regulated in the Family and Guardianship Code, apart from indicating that Article 148 of the Family and Guardianship Code, enumerating obstacles to the appointment of a guardian, also applies to the temporary guardian. At the same time, it should be noted that the institution of temporary guardianship has not been standardised in an exhaustive manner: for example, there is no indication whether the guardianship may be joint or held only by one person, whether the legal actions taken by the temporary guardian on behalf of the child are unacceptapble if there is a risk of conflict with the interests of the ward, whether the temporary guardian may claim remuneration from public funds, or, finally, whether the guardian may claim, from the court, an exemption from providing care. Most of the aforementioned dilemmas can be resolved through the application of the guardianship provisions of the Civil Code, and this is the direction to be advocated. From a theoretical point of view, however, it will still not be clear whether the provisions of the Civil Code apply directly to temporary guardianship (this would be the case if temporary guardianship is treated as a specialised variety of guardianship) or only by analogy (if temporary guardianship is determined to be a separate institution from 'ordinary' guardianship).

---

19 Act of 9 June 2011, uniform text: Journal of Laws of 2024, item 177.

20 The right to submit an application is granted to, among others, the person having actual custody of the minor, the border guard, the prosecutor, the police and the heads of social welfare organisational units.

21 A. Kwaśniewska-Sadkowska, above n. 16.

However, due to the specificity of the application of the provisions of the Polish Family Code to refugee minors, not all of the norms of this Code turn out to be adequate, and some issues would require separate rules. For example, in the case where, in Poland, the temporary guardian of a child relinquishes the actual custody of the child to the child's parent, who under Ukrainian law has parental authority, it is not clear whether the temporary guardianship terminates by operation of law (such an effect could be achieved by a corresponding or analogous application of Article 170 of the Polish Family and Guardianship Code, according to which the guardianship terminates by operation of law when parental authority is restored over the minor), or whether a court order must be revoked in order for it to terminate. The consideration of the protection of the rights of the parents, as well as the temporary nature of the guardianship, would support the first option; however, in order to avoid confusion, this matter requires the intervention of the legislature.

4. FOSTER CARE FOR UKRAINIAN REFUGEE MINORS

The avalanche of underage Ukrainian refugees in need of placement in foster care within Poland has necessitated involving Ukrainian citizens as widely as possible in the exercise of this care. This direction is appropriate not only because the number of children in need exceeds the capacity of the Polish foster care system, but above all because of the desire to preserve the children's sense of ethnic belonging to the Ukrainian nation, and to bring them up in that spirit. For this reason, Polish courts are obliged to respect Ukrainian foster care, so if a refugee minor has already been placed in foster care on Ukrainian territory before their arrival in Poland, and has arrived in Poland together with the person in charge of this care, the court will establish this person as a temporary guardian for that minor (Article 25(7) of the Act on Assistance).

In other cases, where there is a need to place a minor in foster care and there is no existing Ukrainian foster care, the court may entrust this function to a Ukrainian citizen, with the proviso that, if this citizen has crossed the Polish border as a result of the war, they will enjoy a special privilege consisting of exemption from the training required for candidates to become foster parents, as well as from the training required to be eligible to run a family foster home. These exemptions make it easier for Ukrainian refugees to quickly obtain the status of a foster family or family foster home. However, such a privilege is not enjoyed by other Ukrainian citizens (for example, persons who came to Poland for work purposes before the war), which is probably due to the assumption that Ukrainians who came to Poland before the outbreak of hostilities enjoy greater opportunities to undergo appropriate training.

However, the consequences of the war, and the mass emigration of Ukrainian nationals to Poland, took everyone by surprise, including Ukrainian nationals already residing in Poland, who often did not anticipate that the need would suddenly arise to take care of the children of their relatives and loved ones who had arrived in Poland. The requirement that they undergo training on an equal footing with Polish citizens, therefore, did not meet the needs of society, and in particular the needs of the many children in this emergency situation. It should be noted that the function of a foster family may also be entrusted to a Polish citizen, but if they have not undergone adequate training and are not an ascendant or a sibling of a minor (ascendants and siblings are exempt from training), they are obliged to make up for this lack of training within six months.

The efficiency of the institutional foster care system, in view of the massive influx of Ukrainian children, required an urgent increase in the supply of Ukrainian citizens willing to work in this area.[22] The legislature met these expectations by exempting Ukrainian citizens applying for the position of a tutor or a childcare supervisor in a foster care institution from the requirements of having the education specified by the law. However, this exemption applies only to those Ukrainian citizens who have crossed the Polish border due to the war, and their employment requires the consent of the appropriate government administration authority (the voivode, the starost or the voivodship marshal).

The large number of Ukrainian children in need of custody made it necessary to lower the standards concerning the number of children who can be placed in a foster family (the rules in Poland specify a maximum of three children placed in a foster family, unless there are more siblings; a maximum of eight children placed in a family foster home; and a maximum of fourteen children placed in a specialised care and educational centre).[23] In the case of minors who are Ukrainian citizens, the limits in force in Poland do not apply, but the Act on Assistance does not indicate any limits in this respect, and the control over the proper functioning of foster care is exercised by the voivode, head of district, starosta or voivodship marshal, by giving consent for each time a child is admitted to foster care (Article 27, s. 3 of the Act on Assistance).

The relaxation of the standard requirements for persons providing foster care, as well as the abolition of quantitative limits for children placed in foster

---

22 Ibid.

23 These limits were introduced by the Family Support Act of 9 June 2011, uniform text: Journal of Laws of 2024, item 177, in order to ensure the quality of foster care.

care, enabled a large number of children to be quickly placed in foster care, and was necessary during the initial wave of Ukrainian migration to Poland. However, it should be noted that this is associated with an increased risk of harming the well-being of children, who may be under the care of unqualified people, often in less than comfortable educational conditions. Since more than two years have passed since the outbreak of the war, and the situation of war refugees in Poland has stabilised somewhat, it should be time to consider the validity of maintaining the above-mentioned regulations in their current form. Perhaps it would be advisable, instead of giving up the standard requirements, to adapt them to the needs of Ukrainian citizens, for example by introducing a requirement that Ukrainian citizens undergo training, or by restricting the possibility of exceeding the quantitative limits applicable in Poland for children placed in foster care only to particularly justified cases covered by special control.

5. SUMMARY

The two-year-long war in Ukraine, related to the Russian invasion of that country, has had a significant impact on the security environment in Europe. It has also been the basis for numerous activities supporting the Ukrainian State and its citizens fleeing the war. The enormous scale of war migration gave rise to the need to provide protection and support to war refugees, a significant proportion of whom were children. Poland is one of the European countries that accepted the largest number of refugees from Ukraine.

This chapter addresses the issue of tools for protecting minor Ukrainian citizens – war refugees staying in the territory of the Republic of Poland. Tools legalising their stay in Poland were presented, including registration rights related to obtaining a PESEL number, as well as the wide range of aid rights granted to Ukrainian citizens residing in Poland, including Ukrainian children. The most important of these include the possibility of obtaining social benefits for children; support in accommodation; access to health care, nurseries and kindergartens; and the possibility of completing compulsory schooling in Poland.

The chapter also discusses special aid tools. Due to the need to provide care for Ukrainian children, the institution of a temporary guardian was introduced into the Polish legal system, and applies where there are no legal guardians of the child, or where these guardians do not act properly, or the fate of the child's legal representatives is unknown. Foster care for Ukrainian children was also regulated in a special way, in order to promote the inclusion of Ukrainian refugees in the provision of this care in the widest possible way.

It should be emphasised that the scale of the support measures provided by Poland to Ukrainian citizens, including Ukrainian children, was unprecedented. The enormous help provided to them by both State and local authorities, and – what should also be emphasised – by ordinary citizens, proves the great solidarity of the Polish and Ukrainian nations.

SERBIA

(NO) IMPACT OF THE EUROPEAN COURT OF HUMAN RIGHTS CASE LAW ON LGBT RIGHTS IN SERBIA

Melanija Jančić Mihić

Resumé

Dans de nombreux pays européens, les changements législatifs relatifs à l'orientation sexuelle, spécialement en matière de discrimination, trouve leur origine dans l'évolution de la jurisprudence de la Cour européenne des droits de l'homme de Strasbourg. Une grande majorité de la population LGBT+ a été confrontée à divers types de discrimination et a dû lutter pour l'égalité de diverses manières, mais il s'agissait toujours d'obtenir légalement une égalité de droits et de traitement sans égard pour l'orientation sexuelle. Dans ce chapitre, l'auteur analyse la jurisprudence de la Cour européenne des droits de l'homme en matière de discrimination liée à l'orientation sexuelle et de droits des personnes LGBT, en mettant l'accent sur la Serbie, et donne ainsi un aperçu détaillé de l'évolution de la reconnaissance des droits des personnes LGBT dans certains États membres du Conseil de l'Europe. Cette analyse devrait, en outre, montrer si la jurisprudence de la Cour européenne des droits de l'homme a un impact sur le droit serbe en matière d'orientation sexuelle et de droits des personnes LGBT. L'évolution et le développement de la jurisprudence de la Cour européenne des droits de l'homme en matière de discrimination fondée sur l'orientation sexuelle ont donné lieu à une initiative du législateur Serbe : revoir le Code civil serbe en incluant beaucoup plus précisément l'interdiction des discriminations fondées sur l'orientation sexuelle dans le droit positif. Bien que l'orientation sexuelle figure déjà parmi les critères liés à l'interdiction des discriminations et qu'une telle discrimination soit interdite par la Constitution, la loi antidiscrimination et de nombreux autres textes juridiques, le travail sur le Code civil était censé donner plus de poids à la réglementation en faveur des droits des personnes LGBT. Ce travail a duré plus d'une décennie, mais sans véritable résultat, si ce n'est qu'il a fait l'objet de nombreuses citations dans les médias. La loi sur l'union homosexuelle a par la suite été élaborée pour réglementer plus précisément certains droits des personnes LGBT, mais malgré le vif espoir de voir cette loi promulguée, la communauté LGBT n'a rien obtenu du tout.

1. INTRODUCTION: DEFINING SEXUAL ORIENTATION

Worldwide, people are subject to persistent human rights violations because of their actual or perceived sexual orientation and gender identity.[1] Since the main focus of this chapter will be sexual orientation, as part of LGBT+ rights, and not gender identity, it is necessary to define and clarify the concept precisely. According to the American Psychological Association, sexual orientation refers to an enduring pattern of emotional, romantic and/or sexual attractions to men, women or both sexes, and to a person's sense of identity based on those attractions, related behaviours, and membership in a community of others who share those attractions.[2] Sexual orientation has, recently, been closely associated with a person's identity,[3] right to privacy and right to have a choice in the selection of a sexual partner.

In 2006, in response to well-documented patterns of abuse, a distinguished group of international human rights experts met in Yogyakarta, Indonesia, to outline a set of international principles relating to sexual orientation and gender identity, resulting in the Yogyakarta Principles.[4] These are a universal guide to human rights, describing sexual orientation as each person's capacity

---

1 M. O'Flaherty, 'Sexual Orientation and Gender Identity' in D. Moeckli et al. (eds.), International Human Rights Law, 3rd ed., OUP, 2018, p. 296.

2 American Psychological Association, 'Understanding sexual orientation and homosexuality', https://www.apa.org/topics/lgbtq/orientation, 10 January 2024.

3 S. Jaswal, 'The Evolution of Sexual Orientation Discrimination Laws' (2022) 5(2) *International Journal of Law, Management and Humanities* 1684.

4 The Yogyakarta Principles on the Application of International Human Rights Law in Relation to Sexual Orientation and Gender Identity (2007), available at: https://yogyakartaprinciples.org/.

for profound emotional, affectional and sexual attraction to, and intimate and sexual relations with, individuals of a different gender or the same gender, or more than one gender.[5] This definition is grounded in the jurisprudence of human rights courts and treaty-monitoring bodies.[6]

This chapter examines the case law of the European Court of Human Rights (ECtHR) and its evolving reasoning regarding sexual orientation and same-sex partnerships, and argues that the margin of appreciation[7] used is quite flexible and balanced. Bearing in mind that the case law of the ECtHR is based on the European Convention of Human Rights and Fundamental Freedoms (1950) ('ECHR' or 'Convention'),[8] it is important to remember that sexual orientation is neither explicitly incorporated into the Convention's provisions and rights nor specified as a ground for discrimination. However, despite its non-regulation, sexual orientation has been accepted as a basis for legal protection before the ECtHR. This analysis shows how the evolutionary path in judgments addressing sexual orientation falls under the scope of Article 8 of the ECHR, which guarantees the right to respect for private and family life.

This chapter reviews the existing state of LGBT rights in Serbia. While there are international and national guarantees that prohibit discrimination on the basis of sexual orientation, not all countries enforce these requirements effectively, with the result that discrimination still exists in many countries, including Serbia.

Finally, this chapter concludes with a discussion of the importance of case law in understanding the issues of sexual orientation and evaluating the impact of the ECtHR and its jurisprudence on shaping human rights laws at national level.

---

5 Ibid., Preamble.

6 M. O'Flaherty, above n. 1, p. 297.

7 The term 'margin of appreciation' refers to the space for manoeuvre that the Strasbourg organs are willing to grant national authorities in fulfilling their obligations under the ECHR (S. Greer, *The Margin of Appreciation: Interpretation and Discretion under the European Convention on Human Rights*, Council of Europe, 2000, p. 5). The margin of appreciation is a doctrine developed by the ECtHR in its case law. It describes the degree of discretion the Court affords states when taking measures at the national level that would otherwise limit or interfere with rights afforded by the ECHR. In cases where the Court gives states a wide margin of appreciation, it will not engage in a complete review of the substance, but will generally accept the choices made by domestic authorities. (D. Stanculescu, 'Subsidiarity and the Margin of Appreciation in Protocol 15 of the ECHR: Substantial or Symbolic Change?', *PILPG*, July 2021, https://www.publicinternationallawandpolicygroup.org/lawyering-justice-blog/2021/7/5/subsidiarity-and-the-margin-of-appreciation-in-protocol-15-of-the-echr-substantial-or-symbolic-change).

8 The European Convention of Human Rights and Fundamental Freedoms, Council of Europe Treaty Series 005, Council of Europe, 4 November 1950, available at: https://www.echr.coe.int/documents/d/echr/convention_eng.

2. SEXUAL ORIENTATION ISSUES BEFORE THE EUROPEAN COURT OF HUMAN RIGHTS

Many sexual orientation-related issues have arisen before the ECtHR, including criminalisation of private homosexual[9] activity, recognition of same-sex partnerships, succession rights of same-sex partners, and adoption of children by persons in same-sex relationships. For the purposes of this chapter, the analysis will include a few of the most significant cases in order to provide an insight into whether the jurisprudence of the European Court of Human Rights has any influence on the legislation of the Council of Europe member states, including Serbia.

The early claims with regard to sexual orientation were decided by the European Commission of Human Rights in the 1950s. These first claims met with no success, and their subject matter was far from the wide range of LGBT rights[10] recognised nowadays. At that time, as illustrated by *W.B. v. the Federal Republic of Germany*,[11] criminalising homosexual acts was not considered a violation of Convention rights – not even a breach of the right to respect for private life guaranteed by Article 8 – because the main justification for the state's interference was the protection of public health or morality.[12] The European Commission of Human Rights, in *X. v. UK*,[13] similarly upheld the state's claim that the prosecution of the applicant, who was in a homosexual relationship, had a legitimate aim of protecting the rights and freedoms of others, and was necessary in a democratic society.[14]

However, in 1981, the ECtHR was the first international body to rule that laws criminalising sexual orientation violate human rights, namely the right to respect for private and family life.[15] The first successful LGBT case dealing with sexual orientation and homosexual activity was initiated before the Strasbourg

---

9 For more on homosexuality and homosexual behaviour, see R. Green, 'Human Sexuality and Law: Three Decades of Transition' in A. Kales et al. (eds.), *The Mosaic of Contemporary Psychiatry in Perspective*, Springer, 1992, pp. 36–43. See also J. Drescher, 'Out of DSM: Depathologizing Homosexuality' (2015) 5 *Behavioral Science* 565–75.

10 For more about this topic, see M. Fichera, 'Same-Sex Marriage and the Role of Transnational Law: Changes in the European Landscape' (2016) 17(3) *German Law Journal* 389.

11 *W.B. v. the Federal Republic of Germany*, no. 104/55, Commission decision, 17 December 1955.

12 M. Fichera, op. cit.

13 *X. v. UK*, no. 7215/75, Commission decision, 7 July 1977.

14 P. Johnson, *Homosexuality and the European Court of Human Rights*, Taylor & Francis, 2013, p. 39.

15 Council of Europe, '*Dudgeon v. the United Kingdom*, 22 October 1981: The 40th anniversary of a key European Court of Human Rights case that led to the decriminalisation of homosexuality – a turning point for LGBTI persons', 22 October 2021, available at https://www.coe.int/en/web/sogi/-/40th-anniversary-of-a-leading-european-court-of-human-rights-case-that-led-to-the-decriminalisation-of-homosexuality-a-turning-point-for-lgbti-persons.

Court. In *Dudgeon v. UK*,[16] the Court extended privacy protection to such conduct, producing a leading precedent for further development of international human rights law. This groundbreaking judgment led to the decriminalisation of homosexuality in Northern Ireland, in 1982, and the United Kingdom and Europe at large, as any law criminalising homosexual behaviour between consenting adults in Council of Europe Member States would subsequently be considered a violation of Article 8; the judgment thereby recognised the human rights of millions of people.[17] In its decision in *Dudgeon v. UK*, the ECtHR agreed with the applicant that the existence, in the criminal law in force in Northern Ireland, of various offences capable of relating to male homosexual conduct, and the specific police investigation in January 1976, constituted an unjustified interference with his right to respect for his private life, in breach of Article 8.[18] However, the Court found it unnecessary to examine the case under Article 14,[19] taken in conjunction with Article 8.

A few years later, in 1988, as in the *Dudgeon* case, the ECtHR reaffirmed its opinion in *Norris v. Ireland*,[20] ruling that Irish legislation criminalising homosexual conduct between consenting adults capable of valid consent violated Article 8 of the Convention. Specifically, in this case, the Court noted that there was a better understanding and increased tolerance of homosexual behaviour, and that it could no longer be necessary or appropriate to apply the sanctions of the criminal law to the homosexual activities in question.[21] Retaining such legislative provisions unamended could lead to detrimental effects on the life of a person of homosexual orientation, like the applicant, who gave evidence of having suffered deep depression and loneliness on realising that any overt expression of his sexuality would expose him to criminal prosecution, which no longer had any proper justification.[22] The great influence of the ECtHR's case law became evident when, in June 1993, Ireland officially enacted legislation that decriminalised homosexuality.[23] In 1993, the same legal matter was discussed in *Modinos v. Cyprus*, which ended with the ECtHR ruling in favour of the applicant

---

16 *Dudgeon v. the United Kingdom*, no. 7525/76, 22 October 1981.

17 Council of Europe, '*Dudgeon v. the United Kingdom*', above n. 13.

18 *Dudgeon*, above n. 14, para. 34.

19 Article 14 of the European Convention prescribes the prohibition of discrimination: 'The enjoyment of the rights and freedoms set forth in this Convention shall be secured without discrimination on any ground such as sex, race, colour, language, religion, political or other opinion, national or social origin, association with a national minority, property, birth or other status.'

20 *Norris v. Ireland*, no. 10581/83, 26 October 1988.

21 Ibid., para. 46.

22 Ibid.

23 For more about the history of the battle for LGBT rights in Ireland, see H. Halpin, 'Here's a Short History of the Battle for LGBT Rights in Ireland', *The Journal*, June 2018, available at: https://www.thejournal.ie/history-lgbt-rights-ireland-4078424-Jun2018/.

that the existence of the prohibition of male homosexual activity continuously and directly affected the applicant's private life,[24] and thus constituted a violation of Article 8.

The case of *Sutherland v. UK*[25] is very interesting, as criminal law provisions regarding homosexual conduct were amended during the proceeding before the ECtHR, therefore making it easier for the Court to strike the application. Specifically, the applicant feared criminal prosecution because he was in a fulfilling relationship with another man, who was 16 years of age. Such a relationship was considered a criminal offence under the law, so long as a person had not attained the age of 21. In 1994, the House of Commons accepted the amendment to reduce the minimum age to 18, but the applicant complained that fixing the minimum age at 18 rather than 16 – as for heterosexual activities – was a violation of his right to privacy, guaranteed by Article 8 of the Convention, and was discriminatory. In 2000, the law was amended to equalise the age of consent for homosexual acts between consenting males to 16.

The ECtHR, in 1999, continued the practice of protecting the right to respect for the private lives, including sexual lives, of homosexuals, in the cases of *Smith and Grady v. UK*[26] and *Lustig-Prean and Beckett v. UK*,[27] dealing with the military recruitment ban on homosexual persons. In both cases, the Court held that there was a violation of Article 8, but not of Article 14, which guarantees the prohibition of discrimination.

All these cases addressed the same legal matter: criminalisation of homosexual acts in private, and unjustified State interference in breach of the right to respect for private life under Article 8 of the Convention. Privacy rights were put in the foreground as a fundamental issue, but later the right to respect for family life under Article 8 was brought into focus before the Court, requiring the Court to interpret the notion of family, family life and family members in the context of same-sex relationships. This case study shows that the jurisprudence of the ECtHR went from considering the family solely in its traditional heterosexual sense to extending the interpretation of family life to include same-sex couples.

For example, despite the modern evolution of attitudes towards homosexuality, the European Commission of Human Rights, in 1986, in *S. v. United Kingdom*,[28] a case regarding the succession of tenancy rights by a same-sex partner, interpreted family life as a traditional family unit, and refused to recognise a stable homosexual relationship between two men as a family that

---

24 *Modinos v. Cyprus*, no. 15070/89, 22 April 1993, para. 24.
25 *Sutherland v. UK*, no. 25186/94, 27 March 2001.
26 *Smith and Grady v. UK*, nos. 33985/96 and 33986/96, 27 September 1999.
27 *Lustig-Prean and Beckett v. UK*, nos. 31417/96 and 32377/96, 27 September 1999.
28 *S. v. UK*, no. 11716/85, 14 May 1986.

would fall within the scope of the right to respect for family life. Therefore, the Commission declared the application inadmissible. In 2001, the ECtHR made the same decision, declaring the application inadmissible, in *Mata Estevez v. Spain*,[29] where the applicant had complained of the difference in treatment between de facto homosexual partners and married couples with respect to eligibility for a survivor's pension. The Court explained that, in spite of the growing tendency in some European countries to legalise de facto homosexual partnerships, a long-term homosexual relationship between two men did not fall within the scope of the right to respect for family life protected by Article 8 of the Convention, leaving to Member States a wide margin of appreciation. Therefore, the Court refused to grant protection of the right to respect for family life to same-sex couples.

The ECtHR overturned these decisions in *Karner v. Austria*,[30] a 2003 judgment decided on the matter of succession to tenancy rights by family members, including life companions of the same sex. The applicant, Mr. Karner had been in a homosexual relationship with Mr. W., and after the death of his partner, the landlord brought a proceeding for the termination of the tenancy which belonged to Mr. W., and the case ended up at the Austrian Supreme Court, which granted the landlord's appeal and concluded that the legislature's intention was not to include same-sex partners in succession to tenancy rights. Although the aim of the law was to provide surviving cohabitants with social and financial protection from homelessness, the Austrian Supreme Court interpreted the provision very restrictively, protecting the family only in its traditional heterosexual sense. The European Court stated:

> The aim of protecting the family in the traditional sense is rather abstract and a broad variety of concrete measures may be used to implement it. In cases in which the margin of appreciation afforded to States is narrow, as is the position where there is a difference in treatment based on sex or sexual orientation, the principle of proportionality does not merely require that the measure chosen is in principle suited for realising the aim sought. It must also be shown that it was necessary in order to achieve that aim to exclude certain categories of people – in this instance persons living in a homosexual relationship – from the scope of application of section 14 of the Rent Act. The Court cannot see that the Government have advanced any arguments that would allow such a conclusion. Accordingly, the Court finds that the Government have not offered convincing and weighty reasons justifying the narrow interpretation of section 14(3) of the Rent Act that prevented a surviving partner of a couple of the same sex from relying on that provision. Thus, there has been a violation of Article 14 of the Convention taken in conjunction with Article 8.[31]

---

29 *Mata Estevez v. Spain*, no. 56501/00, 10 May 2001.

30 *Karner v. Austria*, no. 40016/98, 24 July 2003.

31 Ibid., paras. 41, 42, 43.

In 2010, the question of re-examining the right of homosexual partners to marry was brought to the Court, and was unsuccessfully challenged in *Schalk and Kopf v. Austria.*[32] The applicants, who were a same-sex couple, referred to the breach of Article 12[33] and Article 14 taken in conjunction with Article 8 of the Convention, complaining that rejecting same-sex couples' access to marriage or another form of legal recognition was discriminatory. Although it is often emphasised in the Court's case law that the Convention is a living instrument which is to be interpreted in light of present-day conditions, and even though the Court has recognised the major social changes to the institution of marriage (such as in *Christine Goodwin v. UK*),[34] it still noted in *Schalk* that there was no European consensus[35] regarding same-sex marriage.[36] Furthermore, the Court 'would no longer consider that the right to marry enshrined in Article 12 must in all circumstances be limited to marriage between two persons of the opposite sex. Consequently, it cannot be said that Article 12 is inapplicable to the applicants' complaint. However, as matters stand, the question whether or not to allow same-sex marriage is left to regulation by the national law of the Contracting State.'[37] Thus, the Court did not impose on the respondent state any positive obligation to provide a satisfactory legal framework. Before the Court delivered its judgment, the Registered Partnership Act had entered into force in Austria, on 1 January 2010, giving legal effect to same-sex relationships, so that the applicants had already obtained the opportunity to enter into a registered partnership by the time of the decision. However, the Court needed to examine whether the respondent state should have provided the applicants with an alternative means of legal recognition of their partnership any earlier than it did.[38] It is somewhat puzzling that the Court found that this case fell within the scope of Article 8, 12 and 14, and within the notion not only of private life, but also of family life, but was overruled by the state's wide margin of appreciation, holding that there was no violation of the aforementioned provisions.

---

32 *Schalk and Kopf v. Austria*, no. 30141/04, 24 June 2010. For a detailed analysis of this case, see L. Hodson, 'A Marriage by Any Other Name? *Schalk and Kopf v Austria*' (2011) 11(1) *Human Rights Law Review* 170–79, available at https://www.ilga-europe.org/sites/default/files/a_marriage_by_any_other_name_-_schalk_and_kopf_v_austria_www.pdf.

33 Article 12 of the European Convention on Human Rights refers to the right to marry: 'Men and women of marriageable age have the right to marry and to found a family, according to the national laws governing the exercise of this right.'

34 *Christine Goodwin v. UK*, no. 28957/95, 11 July 2002, para. 100.

35 For more about the concept of the European consensus, see G. Alves de Faria, 'Sexual Orientation and the ECtHR: what relevance is given to the best interest of the child? An Analysis of the European Court of Human Rights' Approach to the best interest of the child in LGBT parenting cases', *Family & Law*, April 2015, available at: https://www.familyandlaw.eu/tijdschrift/fenr/2015/04/FENR-D-15-00002.pdf, 12.

36 *Schalk and Kopf*, above n. 29, paras. 46, 57, 58.

37 Ibid., para. 61.

38 Ibid., para. 104.

The issue of the interpretation of the notion of family life and introducing same-sex partnership by drafting legislation extending the scope of civil unions to include same-sex couples was successfully challenged in *Vallianatos and Others v. Greece.*[39] Specifically, in its 2013 judgment, the Court noted that sexual orientation is a concept covered by Article 14, and that difference in treatment based on sexual orientation is unacceptable under the Convention, giving the state a narrow margin of appreciation.[40] The issue of reinterpreting Article 12 was questioned again in a 2015 case, *Oliari and Others v. Italy*,[41] in which the ECtHR confirmed its views, as in *Schalk and Kopf v. Austria*, that Article 12 of the Convention does not impose any positive obligation on the respondent state to grant same-sex couples access to marriage.[42] However, the Court noted that, while the aim of Article 8 is to protect individuals against arbitrary interference by public authorities, it may impose on a respondent state positive obligations, such as a need to adopt measures to secure respect for privacy or family life, even in the sphere of relations of individuals between themselves. The Court also ruled that being unable to marry and have access to a legal framework that would recognise their status and rights[43] was a violation of Article 8. The difference between the *Oliari* and *Vallianatos* cases is that, in *Oliari*, the Court set out the principle of legal recognition of same-sex unions, whereas *Vallianatos* affirmed a right to equal access to civil unions outside marriage for all couples, regardless of their sexual orientation.[44]

In *Fedotova and Others v. Russia*, the Court, in its 2023 judgment, confirmed that there is a positive obligation under Article 8 for Member States to provide a legal framework for recognition of same-sex couples.[45] The lack of a legal framework that would allow same-sex couples to enter into marriage or any other type of civil union was also an issue of sexual orientation discrimination in a case against Ukraine. In 2023, in *Maymulakhin and Markiv v. Ukraine*,[46] the Court delivered a judgment in favour of the applicants' complaint of discriminatory treatment and violation of Article 14 taken in conjunction with Article 8. The Court took into consideration that protection of a traditional family is a weighty and legitimate reason to justify a difference in treatment on the basis of sexual orientation, but stated that it cannot be accepted as a valid public interest,

---

39 *Vallianatos and others v. Greece*, nos. 29381/09 and 32684/09, 7 November 2013.

40 Ibid., para. 77.

41 *Oliari and Others v. Italy*, nos. 18766/11 and 36030/11, 21 July 2015.

42 Ibid., para. 192.

43 Ibid., paras. 159, 167.

44 F. Edel, *Case law of the European Court of Human Rights relating to discrimination on grounds of sexual orientation or gender identity – Second Edition*, 2019, p. 150, available at https://hal.science/hal-04262898/document.

45 *Fedotova and Others v. Russia*, nos. 40792/10, 30538/14 and 43439/14, 17 January 2023, para. 178.

46 *Maymulakhin and Markiv v. Ukraine*, no. 75135/14, 1 June 2023.

because legal recognition of same-sex couples in stable relationships certainly cannot be understood as harmful to traditional families.[47] Exactly the same issue was initiated before the Court in *Buhuceanu and Others v. Romania*, in which the lack of legal recognition of same-sex relationships was considered a violation of Article 8, since the state had failed to comply with its positive obligation to secure the applicants' right to respect for their private and family lives, and had overstepped its margin of appreciation.[48]

There are a few same-sex parental custody and adoption cases. The adoption of children by same-sex couples is an area of discrimination in which the ECtHR was not eager to rush into a decision that Convention rights had been violated.[49] In 2000, the Court found a violation of Article 8 taken in conjunction with Article 14, and an unacceptable difference in treatment, in *Salgueiro da Silva Mouta v. Portugal*,[50] in which the applicant complained that his sexual orientation was the only reason why Portuguese national authorities had made a decision to award parental responsibility for their daughter to his ex-wife. This case is of great importance, since the Court set a legal precedent that sexuality ought not to be a factor in determining whether a parent should be granted custody over their own child, since such a consideration would amount to unlawful discrimination.[51] The issue of same-sex adoption was considered in *Frette v. France*,[52] in which the applicant complained that the rejection of his application for authorisation to adopt was based exclusively on an unfavourable prejudice about his sexual orientation, violating Article 14 of the Convention taken in conjunction with Article 8. Having in mind that there was no consensus among Contracting States or the scientific community on this matter, especially on the potential impact on a child's psychological development of being adopted by an adult who openly affirmed his homosexuality, the main reason to justify the difference in treatment was the protection of the best interest of a child,[53] as one of the most important principles in family law matters. The Court, therefore, accepted that national authorities were acting within their margin of appreciation. A few years later, the Court, in *E.B. v. France*, held that 'in rejecting the applicant's application for authorisation to adopt, the domestic

47 Ibid., paras. 75, 76.

48 *Buhuceanu and Others v. Romania*, no. 20081/19 and 20 others, 23 May 2023.

49 M. O'Flaherty, above n. 1, p. 302.

50 *Salgueiro da Silva Mouta v. Portugal*, no. 33290/96, 21 March 2000.

51 H. Jakobien Liesker, 'Caught in a Balancing Act: The European Court of Human Rights and the Road to Recognition for Sexual Minorities' (2017) 4(3) *Oslo Law Review* 182, available at https://www.researchgate.net/publication/321845373_Caught_in_a_Balancing_Act_The_European_Court_of_Human_Rights_and_the_Road_to_Recognition_for_Sexual_Minorities.

52 *Frette v. France*, no. 36515/97, 26 February 2002.

53 Ibid., para. 36.

authorities made a distinction based on considerations regarding her sexual orientation, a distinction which is not acceptable under the Convention', and therefore found a breach of Article 14 of the Convention taken in conjunction with Article 8.[54]

According to its case law, it is evident that the Court gradually shifted focus not only from private to family matters, but also from the LGBT individual to the LGBT couple.[55]

3. SEXUAL ORIENTATION AND LGBT RIGHTS IN SERBIAN LAW: A GROUND OF DISCRIMINATION OR FAKE EQUALITY?

In Serbia, sexual orientation is not explicitly a part of constitutional anti-discrimination provisions, but it is a part of the Anti-Discrimination Act protections and other Acts as well. The Serbian Constitution, enacted in 2006, grants equality before the constitution and law to everyone, and prohibits all direct or indirect discrimination based on any ground,[56] listing some of the grounds in particular, but not including sexual orientation among them. Since the list of constitutionally protected categories is not exhaustive, the constitutional provisions could be interpreted to cover sexual orientation indirectly.[57]

Serbia enacted the Anti-Discrimination Act in 2009, giving a legal definition of the notion of discrimination, but not of sexual orientation. Therefore, there is no legal definition of sexual orientation as such, but the Act prescribed that sexual orientation is a private matter, and that no one can be called on to publicly declare their sexual orientation, but that everyone has a right to declare it, and being discriminated against because of such a declaration is prohibited.[58] As far as specific LGBT rights granted to individuals are concerned, there is no legislation at all – not even on civil unions, not to mention same-sex marriage and adoption. Regardless of some attempts at legal recognition of at least same-sex civil unions, this has not yet happened.

---

54 *E.B. v. France*, no. 43546/02, 22 January 2008, para. 96, 98.

55 H. Jakobien Liesker, above n. 47, 182.

56 The Constitution of the Republic of Serbia, *Official Gazette of the RS*, no. 98/2006, Art. 21.

57 M. Jančić, *Zabrana diskriminacije na osnovu seksualne orijentacije i rodnog identiteta – teorija i praksa (The Prohibition of Discrimination on Grounds of Sexual Orientation and Gender Identity – Theory and Practice)*, Novosadski humanitarni centar i Fakultet za pravne i poslovne studije dr Lazar Vrkatić, Univerzitet Union (Novi Sad Humanitarian Centre and The Faculty of Law and Business Studies Dr Lazar Vrkatić, University Union), 2020, p. 68.

58 Anti-Discrimination Act of the Republic of Serbia, *Official Gazette of the RS*, no. 22/2009 and 52/2021, Art. 21.

In 2005, a procedure before the Constitutional Court of Serbia challenged the constitutionality and legality of Article 4 of the Family Act (2005), a provision on extramarital unions and cohabitation that is limited to heterosexual persons. The applicant complained that the provision discriminates against same-sex couples by prohibiting their entry into civil unions, and thus is incompatible with the constitutional principle of equality, and the anti-discrimination provision of Article 14 of the ECHR.[59] The Court, in 2010, decided that this provision of the Family Act was not incompatible with the Constitution and ratified international conventions, and that the legislature had an objective and reasonable justification for limiting civil unions to heterosexual cohabitants. Specifically, the justification was the protection of the traditional family and family relationships, which means that it is founded on either marriage or an extramarital union between a man and a woman, despite the fact that the ECtHR cases described above ruled in favour of same-sex couples who had contested Member States' failures to recognise their families and their right to enter into State-created statuses such as civil unions. Analysis of this case leads to the conclusion that there has been no significant impact of the ECtHR's case law on either Serbian legislation or jurisprudence.

The legal concepts of marriage and extramarital unions adopted in Serbia are traditional ones, having in mind that only heterosexual couples have access to these. According to the constitutional provision, marriage is concluded on the basis of freely given consent of a man and a woman before the State's authority, and an extramarital union is equal to marriage.[60] The Family Act (2005) defines a marriage as a union for life between a man and a woman, regulated by the law, and an extramarital union as a longer lasting union for life between a man and a woman, who have the rights and obligations of spouses under the conditions prescribed by this law.[61] Thus, the legislature has firmly opted for the heterosexual nature of marriage and civil union: a very traditional family law regulation cherishing traditional family values and stereotypical gender roles.

In the following years, there were attempts to create a basis and conditions for legal regulation of same-sex unions, making minimal improvements to the legal status of LGBT persons. Specifically, the Commission to draft a Civil Code of Serbia was established in 2006,[62] and there was a proposal to address family law

---

59 Decision of the Constitutional Court of the Republic of Serbia, no. IУ-347/2005, available in Serbian at http://www.ustavni.sud.rs/page/predmet/sr-Latn-CS/6916/?NOLAYOUT=1.

60 Constitution of Serbia, above n. 52, Art. 62.

61 The Family Act of the Republic of Serbia, *Official Gazette of the RS*, no. 18/2005, 72/2011 – another law and 6/2015, Arts. 3 and 4.

62 Decision of the Government of the Republic of Serbia on establishment of the Commission for drafting the Civil Code, *Official Gazette of the RS*, no. 104/06 and 110/06.

issues concerning same-sex couples. Although the members of the Commission retained the traditional definition of marriage, the Commission, according to the Pre-Draft Civil Code, proposed to change the definition of extramarital unions, which had previously been available only to different-sex couples. Defining extramarital union as a more permanent union of life between two persons of the opposite or the same sex (Art. 2119 of the Pre-Draft)[63] would, for the first time, leave room for potential detailed legal regulation and recognition of LGBT rights. However, in July 2019, the government decided to terminate the work of the Commission,[64] and so the years of effort and work by legal experts failed to produce any results.

Furthermore, in February 2021, the Ministry of Human and Minority Rights and Social Dialogue began its work drafting the Same-Sex Unions Act, which was to regulate legal status and all issues regarding same-sex relationships, except the rights to conclude marriage and to adopt children. The work was finished and the draft law was prepared. When it seemed that the draft would be proposed to the Parliament, and that it had enough support to enter the parliamentary procedure of enactment, and was expected to be successfully adopted, the whole work was aborted in 2023, and no further efforts have been undertaken since the work on the draft was finished. The Council of Europe had given its expert opinion on the draft law, in which it stated that, by creating a specific legal framework recognising same-sex unions, Serbia would have been in compliance with the ECtHR case law by granting a number of core rights to couples in stable and committed relationships.[65]

Although the enactment of the Anti-Discrimination Act is considered a positive step towards possible legal recognition of LGBT rights in Serbia, the government has been slow to implement and apply the law,[66] denying the evolving changes in societal and moral attitudes towards same-sex persons and their relationships and human rights.

---

63 Prednacrt Gradjanskog Zakonika Republike Srbije (Druga verzija – radni tekst), Stvarno pravo, Porodični odnosi i Nasledjivanje (The Pre-Draft Civil Code of the Republic of Serbia (Second version – working text), Property Law, Family Relationships and Succession), published in *Branič – Časopis za pravnu teoriju i praksu Advokatske komore Srbije (Branič – The Journal of Legal Theory and Practice of Bar Association of Serbia)*, Belgrade, May–June 2019, p. 149.

64 Decision of the Government of the Republic of Serbia on termination of work of the Commission for drafting the Civil Code, *Official Gazette of the RS*, no. 51/2019.

65 Council of Europe, 'Expert Opinion on the Draft Law on Same-Sex Unions of Serbia', Strasbourg, May 2021, p. 4, available at https://rm.coe.int/opinion-same-sex-unions-serbia/1680a2b5b3.

66 Regional Center for Minorities et al., 'The Violations of the Rights of Lesbian, Gay, Bisexual, and Transgender Individuals in Serbia – A Shadow Report', March 2010, p. 2, available at https://www.boell.de/sites/default/files/assets/boell.de/images/download_de/LGBT_ICCPR_Shadow_Report_Serbia.pdf.

4. THE IMPACT OF THE ECtHR ON LGBT RIGHTS IN SERBIA

A very difficult task put before the ECtHR is to create and implement a uniform rule regarding sexual orientation-related discrimination issues, bearing in mind that there are many Council of Europe Member Countries which are not at the same or a similar developmental level, in terms of legal, economic and social development and level of awareness of sexual orientation-related discrimination. Still, there is a certain level of compliance with the rule of law and the right to equality that needs to be protected and respected in the same or similar cases regardless of the state against which the application is filed. There are standards of respect for rights established by the Council of Europe and its conventions and other legal Acts. To minimise the impact of developmental problems and absence of European consensus[67] when making a decision and delivering a judgment, the ECtHR introduced a margin of appreciation,[68] which can be really wide in some cases, especially with regard to sexual orientation, as quite a delicate issue. The margin of appreciation is, therefore, not a creation of the ECHR, but rather of the ECtHR.

The analysis of the case law of the ECtHR has shown that the margin of appreciation has been reduced significantly when it comes to affording same-sex couples the possibility of legal recognition and protection. As the Court acknowledges in its judgment in *Norris v. Ireland*, national authorities do enjoy a wide margin of appreciation, but not an unlimited one.[69] In *Dudgeon*, the Court stated that not only the nature of the aim of the restriction but also the nature of the activities involved will affect the scope of the margin of appreciation, and since that case concerned a most intimate aspect of private life, there must exist particularly serious reasons before interference on the part of the public authorities can be legitimate for the purposes of Article 8(2).[70] The Court explained in *Oliari and Others v. Italy* that the margin will be wider when there is no consensus within the Member States of the Council of Europe, either as to the relative importance of the interest at stake or

---

67 For a very interesting point of view with regard to the European consensus, see J.T. Theilen, 'The Future of Sexual Orientation and Gender Identity in Human Rights: Where Will European Consensus Take Us?', *Völkerrechtsblog*, 9 February 2023, available at https://voelkerrechtsblog.org/the-future-of-sexual-orientation-and-gender-identity-in-human-rights/.

68 For more about different concepts of the margin of appreciation, see G. Letsas, 'Two Concepts of the Margin of Appreciation' (2006) 26(4) *Oxford Journal of Legal Studies* 705–32. See also T.A. O'Donnell, 'The Margin of Appreciation Doctrine: Standards in the Jurisprudence of the European Court of Human Rights' (1982) 4(4) *Human Rights Quarterly* 474–96.

69 *Norris*, above n. 17, para. 45.

70 *Dudgeon*, above n. 14, para. 52.

the best means of protecting it, particularly where the case raises sensitive moral or ethical issues.[71]

As far as the impact of the ECtHR's jurisprudence on Serbian legislation is concerned, it remains unknown why there have been no cases against Serbia and complaints to the ECtHR on this matter. There have been many cases against Serbia with regard to other issues and Articles of the Convention, especially the right to a fair trial, but for the time being, with regard to sexual orientation issues and LGBT rights, there are none. Possible reasons could be various, from financial ones, or ignorance of rights and legal mechanisms available to LGBT persons, to lack of confidence in legal ways of fighting for equality. Although the ECHR and other ratified international treaties have a priority, after the Constitution, in the hierarchy of legal Acts on the national level, domestic judges are rarely eager to implement them or to refer to the conventional provisions or jurisprudence of international bodies, especially of the ECtHR. While there has been a growing tendency to refer to the ECtHR's case law in the practice of domestic courts, in particular the Constitutional Court of Serbia, in the last ten years,[72] there is no great judicial pressure on the legislature to make important changes in the lives of LGBT persons, and public discourse on this issue is at a very low level.

Every time work on legislation addressing LGBT issues seems about to come to fruition, there appears to be no political will to enact the legislation and grant LGBT people the same rights that members of heterosexual population have, establishing conditions where LGBT people can live without daily fear of discrimination.

5. CONCLUSION

This chapter has examined the jurisprudence of the ECtHR in relation to sexual orientation discrimination and other related issues in respect of Articles 8 and 14 of the ECHR. Thus, this chapter has shown the impact of the Court's case law on national legislation with regard to sexual orientation and LGBT rights within the Member States of the Council of Europe, with special reference to Serbia.

The analysis demonstrated that, on one hand, there are some legal issues which the law has addressed and resolved before the majority of the population even became aware of the existence of the issues and the problems they create

[71] *Oliari*, above n. 37, para. 162.

[72] L. Milutinović, I. Krstić and B. Čučković, *Kvalitativna studija o uticaju presuda Evropskog suda za ljudska prava na jurisprudenciju sudova u Republici Srbiji (Qualitative Study on the Impact of ECtHR Case Law on the Jurisprudence of the Courts in the Republic of Serbia)*, Council of Europe, 2016, pp. 136, 137.

for those affected by them. On the other hand, there are specific legal issues of which the population has been aware long before the political will to change the law and extend equal protections to the entire population has come into existence. One of the latter issues, certainly, is sexual orientation.

The ruling in *Dudgeon v. UK* was, certainly, a huge encouragement for other LGBT people combating discrimination and fighting for equal rights, and it paved the way for creating laws in favour of LGBT rights in many Member Countries – but not in Serbia. Nevertheless, lawmakers and judicial authorities in Serbia do not contribute much to the improvement of the legal status of same-sex couples by giving a restrictive and narrow interpretation of the right to equality. Although there are, for now, no rulings of the ECtHR against Serbia in relation to the sexual orientation discrimination issue, it is, as a Member State of the Council of Europe, indirectly, via the jurisprudence of the ECtHR, obliged to follow the Council's established standards and take affirmative steps with regard to sexual orientation issues, and to move towards protection and recognition of LGBT rights, at least to some extent.

Is there any hope for a legal framework for same-sex relationships in Serbia any time soon? Regardless of the European standards established by the case law of the ECtHR on this matter, and Serbia's membership of the Council of Europe and ratification of the ECHR, the present author doubts that any legal change will happen in the near future, because of the negative public opinion and discourse on same-sex issues.

SOUTH AFRICA

EQUITY IN REPRODUCTION DECISION-MAKING

Acknowledging and Safeguarding the Reproductive Rights of Fathers in Abortion Matters

Katlego Mashiane*

Résumé

Historiquement, les questions relatives aux droits reproductifs se sont surtout concentrées sur la protection des droits des femmes, en particulier dans le contexte de l'avortement. Le rôle des pères dans la prise de décision en matière de procréation, notamment en ce qui concerne l'avortement ou la garde de l'enfant, a souvent été négligé. Le système juridique sud-africain actuel oblige les pères à soutenir financièrement leurs enfants, même si le père n'avait pas l'intention d'avoir cet enfant ou si la mère a refusé d'avorter. Cet article examine les méthodes qui peuvent être développées pour protéger les hommes qui expriment explicitement leur désir de ne pas devenir père ou qui demandent à une mère d'avorter dans

* North-West University, South Africa, Lecturer. katlego.mashiane@nwu.ac.za.

un délai acceptable. En outre, il explore des mesures tels que le transfert et la congélation d'embryons, le don d'ovocyte et le don de sperme comme alternatives visant à sauvegarder les droits parentaux de ceux qui choisissent de renoncer à leur autorité parentale et à leurs droits parentaux. Le texte plaide pour une évolution du cadre juridique existant afin de faire progresser et d'atteindre l'égalité des sexes dans la prise de décision en matière de procréation et de protection du bien-être de l'enfant s'il naît.

L'étude utilise une approche qualitative et met en place des résultats qui pourraient être utiles aux décideurs politiques. Elle préconise des recommandations pour atteindre l'équité entre les sexes dans la prise de décision en matière de procréation.

1. INTRODUCTION

The issue of unilateral decision-making powers by women regarding abortion has become a focal point of discussion, particularly within the international community, where gender equality and reproductive autonomy are valued and protected.[1] Abortion is internationally recognised, and is protected in many countries, although some countries prohibit it.[2] Abortion, or termination of pregnancy, is an important aspect of reproductive rights, particularly in family planning.[3] Reproductive rights guarantee a right to decide when and how to assume a parental role.[4]

In South Africa, legislative frameworks such as the Choice on Termination of Pregnancy Act 92 of 1996 ('CTPA') empower women to legally make abortion decisions without consideration of the input of other parties, notably the fathers of their children.[5] This legal framework has sparked concerns about inequality and the disregarding of the potential impact on men of women's decisions whether or not to terminate a pregnancy. Moreover, if a woman chooses to continue the

1 M.K. Eriksson, 'Abortion and Reproductive Health: Making International law More Responsive to Women's Needs' in K.D. Askin and D. Koenig, *Women and International Human Rights*, Brill Nijhoff, 2000, p. 3.

2 K.R. Culwell and M. Hurwitz, 'Addressing Barriers to Safe Abortion' (2013) 121 *International Journal of Gynecology & Obstetrics* 516.

3 See C. Dehlendorf, M.I. Rodriguez, K. Levy, S. Borrero and J. Steinauer, 'Disparities in Family Planning' (2010) 202(3) *American Journal of Obstetrics and Gynecology* 214–20. See also S. Ambast, H. Atay and A. Lavelanet, 'A Global Review of Penalties for Abortion-related Offences in 182 Countries' (2023) 8(3) *BMJ Global Health* 2.

4 See A. Huzaimah, M. Abdillah, N.Q. Laila, M. Tamudin and T.M.P. Astuti, 'Disregarding the Reproductive Rights of Women in Child Marriage in Indonesia' (2023) 7(3) *Samarah: Jurnal Hukum Keluarga Dan Hukum Islam* 1099.

5 Choice on Termination of Pregnancy Act 1996, s.14.

pregnancy despite the father expressing a clear desire not to become a parent, legal obligations are nevertheless imposed upon the father, including parental rights and responsibilities.[6] These disparities prompt an exploration of how the current legal system can be reformed to enable fathers who have explicitly stated their intentions before conception or within the first trimester of pregnancy to relinquish their parental rights over the child.

Legal frameworks such as the Maintenance Act 99 of 1998 and the Children's Act 38 of 2005 legally bind the father to provide financial support for the child, regardless of the father's desire not to assume the parental role or the mother's decision to disregard the father's preference for abortion.[7] Failure to maintain the child or comply with the order of the court to maintain the child can result in imprisonment, raising concerns about whether the legal system penalises the father for decisions made solely by the mother.[8] This chapter delves into the ramifications of the CTPA in perpetuating gender-based inequality in reproductive decision-making. It further scrutinises the legal obligation imposed on individuals upon becoming a parent in South Africa, and explores avenues for protecting fathers from these legal implications, particularly in cases where they explicitly expressed their desire for an abortion, or their lack of interest in fatherhood, during the first trimester of pregnancy.

2. ARTIFICIAL FERTILISATION AND TERMINATION OF PREGNANCY

The termination of pregnancy in South Africa is regulated by the CTPA. This legislation establishes the circumstances and conditions under which a woman's pregnancy can legally be terminated. Under section 2(1) of the CTPA, a pregnancy may be terminated upon a woman's request or in accordance with a medical practitioner's advice. This study focuses on early-stage abortion in the first trimester; that is, the first 12 weeks of pregnancy. Early-stage abortions, typically performed within the first trimester, are associated with lower risks of complications, such as excessive bleeding, infections and uterine perforation.[9]

In cases of assisted reproduction in South Africa, the Regulations Relating to Artificial Fertilization of Persons of 2012 ('the Regulations') govern the process.

---

6 Children's Act 2005, s. 18.

7 Ibid., s. 18(2)(b). See also Maintenance Act 1998, s. 2.

8 Maintenance Act 1998, s. 31(1).

9 O. Miskolci, D. Morley and I. Martin-Loeches, 'Infection During Early Pregnancy and Septic Abortions' in S. Einav, C.F. Weiniger and R. Landau (eds.), *Principles and Practice of Maternal Critical Care*, Springer, 2020, pp. 243–53.

The Regulations define artificial fertilisation as an introduction by other than natural means of a male gamete or gametes into the internal reproductive organs of a female person for the purpose of human reproduction.[10] It includes artificial insemination, *in vitro* fertilization (IVF), gamete intrafallopian tube transfer, embryo intrafallopian transfer or intracytoplasmic sperm injection.[11] The Regulations further define embryo transfer as placing the embryo into the uterus or fallopian tube of the recipient.[12] This definition clarifies the precise method involved in assisted reproductive technologies and surrogacy arrangements. The transfer of embryos to a surrogate requires inclusivity and respectful approaches, to protect reproductive autonomy and choice.[13]

In terms of Regulation 11(1)(b)(iii) of the Regulations, a competent person intending to effect the embryo transfer to a recipient shall, before effecting the embryo transfer, obtain informed consent from the recipient relating to embryo transfer. Regulation 11(1)(b)(ii) underscores an important ethical consideration in the realm of assisted reproduction, and emphasises the need for informed consent before conducting embryo transfer to a recipient. This requirement prioritises the autonomy and dignity of the recipient.

In essence, the Regulations impose an obligation on the competent person intending to effect the embryo transfer to a recipient to have an agreement (pre-conception agreement) to obtain consent. This pre-conception agreement ensures mutual understanding between parties regarding the implications of embryo transfer and associated responsibilities. In cases where parties have prior agreements regarding the disposal of embryos after transfer, and there are disagreements, such disputes should be treated as contractual obligations that need to be upheld. However, in South Africa, such a contract, as long as it limits the rights provided in the CTPA, will be set aside on the grounds of *contra bonis mores*. In *Mort v. Henry Shields-Chiat*, Davis J said that the constitutional values of freedom require parties in contracts to uphold a 'minimum threshold of mutual respect', to promote equality and dignity.[14] This case demonstrates that contracts should be legally and ethically sound in order to be enforceable in a court of law.

Obtaining informed consent promotes the well-being of both the recipient and potential offspring. The Regulations safeguard against coercion and exploitation while fostering trust and transparency in the embryo transfer process. The present writer posits that adherence to the Regulations can foster an ethical framework that respects the rights and choices of people involved in

---

10 Regulation Relating to Artificial Fertilization of Persons of 2012, s. 1.
11 Ibid.
12 Ibid.
13 Ibid., s. 11.
14 *Mort v. Henry Shields-Chiat* 2001 (1) SA 404 (C), para. 475B.

assisted reproduction,in instance where the embryo was created outside human bodies, and the recipient of the embryo is the surrogate or the mother of the child (woman who had her egg fertilised to create an embryo).

The present writer posits that the first trimester of pregnancy can be a safe period for embryo transfer or embryo intrafallopian transfer. This assertion aligns with existing research indicating that, during the first trimester, the maternal environment is relatively stable and supportive of early embryo development.[15] Furthermore, during this period, the risk of pregnancy complications, such as miscarriage or ectopic pregnancy, is generally lower.[16] It is posited that, while the first trimester may offer certain advantages, careful consideration of individual medical histories and risk factors is important to ensure efficacy and safety. Furthermore, research and clinical trials are necessary to validate this hypothesis and establish guidelines for embryo transfer timing, balancing the potential benefit with associated risks. The procedure requires specialised equipment, trained personnel and stringent protocols to ensure the viability and integrity of the embryos during their extraction, storage and potential future use.[17]

The CTPA and the Regulations grant women the autonomy to make decisions regarding their reproductive health and enable them to access safe and legal abortion services during the early stages of pregnancy.[18] By allowing termination of pregnancy within the first trimester, the law aims to protect women's mental and physical health, preventing unsafe abortion practices and promoting reproductive rights. While this chapter acknowledges the importance of women's autonomy over their bodies, it raises questions about the involvement and consent of men in reproductive decision-making. Excluding men from the abortion decision-making process disregards their potential emotional, financial and parental interests in the outcome. Section 5(2) read together with section 2(1) of the CTPA demonstrates the unilateral nature of abortion decisions during the first trimester, highlighting a potential disparity in reproductive rights between men and women. These sections empower a woman, whether the surrogate or the mother of the child, to terminate the

---

15 S. Cai, S. Quan, G. Yang, Q. Ye, M. Chen, et al., 'One carbon metabolism and mammalian pregnancy outcomes' (2021) 65(2) *Molecular Nutrition & Food Research* 2.

16 H.M. Abujledan, A. Mehmood, S. Mughal, A. Mallah and F. Akram, 'Contraceptive Conundrum: Unraveling the IUD's Role in Ectopic Pregnancies – Risk Factors, Causes, and Effective Management' (2023) 6(2) *Annals of Obstetrics and Gynecology* 3. See also N. Lukinovic, E.P. Malovrh, I. Takac, M. Sobocan and J. Knez, 'Advances in diagnostics and management of gestational trophoblastic disease' (2022) 56(4) *Radiology and Oncology* 430–39.

17 A. D'Angelo, C. Panayotidis, A. Alteri, S. Mcheik and Z. Veleva, 'Evidence and Consensus on Technical Aspects of Embryo Transfer' (2022) 4 *Human Reproduction Open* 2.

18 Choice on Termination of Pregnancy Act 92 of 1996, s. 2.

pregnancy without consent from the father. As such, if consent has been obtained in terms of Regulation 11(1)(b)(iii) of the Regulations for embryo transfer, and a pre-conception agreement has been entered into that resulted in pregnancy, the surrogate or the mother of the child is protected by the CTPA should they choose to abort the pregnancy without the consent of the father. By allowing women sole authority over pregnancy termination, the CTPA undermines the principle of equality and shared responsibility. It is posited here that engaging men in reproductive decision-making offers the prospect of fostering mutual understanding, support and shared decision-making, ultimately strengthening familial relationships.

3. DYNAMICS OF EQUITY IN REPRODUCTIVE DECISION-MAKING

The concept of reproductive decision-making includes choices regarding reproductive health, contraception, family planning, pregnancy and parenting.[19] This decision-making process is deeply personal, and is influenced by sociocultural norms, access to health care, education, personal preferences and economic status. Firstly, sociocultural norms play an important role in shaping attitudes towards reproductive decision-making.[20] In addition, cultural beliefs, religious values and societal expectations influence individuals' perceptions of abortion.[21] These factors shape attitudes towards sexuality and morality, impacting on how abortion is viewed within communities.[22] In some cultures and religions, abortion may be stigmatised or considered morally wrong, leading to feelings of guilt, shame or fear of social ostracism for those considering or seeking abortion.[23] Conversely, in more progressive societies, abortion may be viewed as a matter of reproductive rights and bodily autonomy, with societal norms supporting the right to abortion.

---

19 D. Loll, P.J. Fleming, A. Manu, E. Morhe, R. Stephenson, E.J. King and K.S. Hall, 'Reproductive Autonomy and Pregnancy Decision-making Among Young Ghanaian Women' (2020) 15 *Global Public Health* 571–86.

20 V. Mochache, G. Wanje, L. Nyagah, A. Lakhani, H. El-Busaidy, M. Temmerman and P. Gichangi, 'Religious, socio-cultural norms and gender stereotypes influence uptake and utilization of maternal health services among the Digo community in Kwale, Kenya: a qualitative study' (2020) 17 *Reproductive Health* 2.

21 S. Chandrasekaran, K. Key, A. Ow, A. Lindsey, J. Chin and B. Goode, 'The role of community and culture in abortion perceptions, decisions, and experiences among Asian Americans' (2023) *Frontiers in Public Health* 1–11.

22 Ibid., 11.

23 R.J. Cook, 'Stigmatized Meanings of Criminal Abortion Law' in R.J. Cook, J.N. Erdman and B.M. Dickens, *Abortion Law in Transnational Perspective: Cases and Controversies*, University of Pennsylvania Press, 2014, pp. 347–70.

In South Africa, historically, patriarchal structures have conferred greater decision-making authority on men while marginalising women.[24] These powers were often manifested in the unequal decision-making process surrounding abortion, where women's choices may have been disregarded or overridden by male partners, family members and societal expectations.[25] Abortion laws such as the CTPA were enacted to offer women a right in law to have a say in abortion decision-making.

Abortion was first legalised in South Africa through the enactment of the Abortion and Sterilization Act 2 of 1975. Section 2 of this Act prohibited any abortion that was to be procured except in accordance with its provision. In terms of section 3 of this Act, women were granted access to termination of pregnancy under specific circumstances. These circumstances included situations where continuing the pregnancy posed a threat to the life of the woman or could have resulted in serious health complications.[26] The enactment of the CTPA in 1996 marked an important departure throughout the country from the previously restrictive legal framework surrounding abortion. It acknowledged the rights of women to access safe and legal abortion.[27] The CTPA plays an important role in addressing the vulnerability of women and giving them the power to decide whether to keep or terminate a pregnancy without the need to take any person's views or perspectives into account. It is important to note that, despite the legalisation of abortion in South Africa, access to safe and legal abortion services remains limited, particularly for marginalised and vulnerable people.[28] Socio-economic barriers, stigma and inadequate health care infrastructure often hinder the ability of women to access timely and safe abortion care.[29]

The CTPA reinforces the narrative that abortion is solely a women's issue, perpetuating harmful gender norms and undermining efforts to promote gender equality and shared responsibility in reproductive activities. The

24 L.M. Knudsen, *Reproductive Rights in a Global Context: South Africa, Uganda, Peru, Denmark, United States, Vietnam, Jordan*, Vanderbilt University Press, 2006, p. 13.

25 See T.J. Mudau and O.S. Obadire, 'The Role of Patriarchy in Family Settings and its Implications to Girls and Women in South Africa' (2017) 58 *Journal of Human Ecology* 67–72.

26 See Abortion and Sterilization Act 1975, s. 2.

27 See C.G. Ngwena, 'Reforming African Abortion Laws to Achieve Transparency: Arguments from Equality' (2013) 21(3) *African Journal of International and Comparative Law* 398–426. See also C. Pickles, 'Termination-of-Pregnancy Rights and Foetal Interests in Continued Existence in South Africa: the Choice on Termination of Pregnancy Act 92 of 1996' (2002) 15(5) *Potchefstroom Electronic Law Journal/Potchefstroomse Elektroniese Regsblad* 403.

28 N. Solomons and H. Gihwala, 'The Provision of Safe and Legal Abortion Services in South Africa: Expanding Access Through Telemedicine and Lessons Learned During the Covid-19 Pandemic' in O.S. Adelakun and E. Ndoni (eds.), *Reproductive Health and Assisted Reproductive Technologies In Sub-Saharan Africa*, Palgrave Macmillan, 2023, pp. 73–101.

29 R. Dahab and D. Sakellariou, 'Barriers to Accessing Maternal Care in Low-Income Countries in Africa: a Systematic Review' (2020) 17(12) *International Journal of Environmental Research and Public Health* 1.

Constitution of the Republic of South Africa 1996 (the 'Constitution') asserts the principle of equality before the law and the right to equal protection and benefit of the law for everyone.[30] Section 9 of the Constitution provides for full and equal enjoyment of all rights and freedoms, including those related to reproductive decision-making, such as abortion. This section underscores the importance of providing equal protection under the law for individuals seeking abortion, irrespective of factors such as gender. The present author posits that section 5(2) of the CTPA affords women unilateral power to decide on abortion, which may seem to conflict with section 9(1) of the Constitution. Section 9(1) of the Constitution deals with equality before the law and non-discrimination in the enjoyment of rights. Section 5(2) of the CTPA provides unilateral powers exclusively to women without consideration of the rights and interests of men in reproductive decision-making, which is discriminatory and unequal treatment under the Constitution.

It is posited here that section 5(2) of the CTPA violates section 9(1) of the Constitution. The present author notes the importance of the limitation of rights as provided in section 36 of the Constitution, and proposes a balance in protecting societal interests. It is posited that, while women have rights related to abortion decision-making, there should be limitations to ensure that these rights do not infringe upon the rights of men. Section 36 of the Constitution provides that the Bill of Rights may be limited only in terms of law of general application to the extent that limitation is reasonable and justifiable in an open and democratic society based on human dignity, equality and freedom. This section is important in the context of limiting the rights of women to unilaterally decide on abortion without men's consent. There should be a careful balancing act between the right to make decisions regarding reproduction and the potential limitation that may be placed on those rights in the interests of promoting equality and non-discrimination.

It is posited here that section 5(1) of the CTPA should be limited in light of section 36 of the Constitution, and that this assessment should consider whether the limitation serves a legitimate purpose and is proportionate to that purpose. The purpose, in the context of this study, is to prevent imposing parental responsibility and rights on individuals who have intentionally made it clear from the time abortion was feasible that they do not want to become fathers. The limitation of section 5(1) of the CTPA should be consistent with the values of an open and democratic society based on human dignity, equality and freedom. This requires consideration of the broader societal context and the impact of the limitation on the rights and freedoms of all individuals involved. It is argued here that section 5(1) of the CTPA has financial implications for fathers who did not intend to become fathers. If a woman decides to keep a

30 See s. 9 of the Constitution of the Republic of South Africa 1996.

pregnancy after the father has informed her that he does not have the necessary means to support the child, or is not ready to have a child, this may lead to fathers facing financial strain, affecting their ability to pursue other life goals and opportunities. This can exacerbate existing socio-economic disparities and hinder the father's overall well-being. The present author would argue that imposing parental responsibilities on fathers in situations where they did not consent to parenthood may infringe upon their rights and freedoms. This raises the question of fairness and justice, particularly if the father's intention was not taken into account during the reproductive decision-making process. Therefore, in evaluating the limitation of section 5(1) of the CTPA, it is important to weigh all individuals' rights and freedoms, including those of mothers and fathers. While upholding the principles of reproductive autonomy and gender equality, policy-makers should also consider mechanisms to mitigate the financial implications and possible incarceration of fathers, while ensuring that the limitations imposed are fair, justifiable and consistent with the values of an open and democratic society.

The present author would criticise the CTPA for failing to adequately address equity in decision-making regarding abortion. The CTPA primarily focuses on granting women the right to access legal and safe abortion services, without adequately considering the perspectives and rights of men in the decision-making process. This chapter posits that the CTPA, by safeguarding women's rights without explicitly acknowledging men's part in reproduction, perpetuates gender-based power imbalances in abortion decision-making. The failure to acknowledge the rights of men to decide on abortion matters may contribute to social stigma and men raising children they never wanted to have.[31] This leads to situations where men's voices and choices regarding abortion have not been considered or respected, potentially imposing the responsibilities of fatherhood on them without their consent or desire.

Therefore, these shortcomings can be addressed by amending section 5(1) of the CTPA to promote equality in decision-making regarding abortion. The amendment should involve incorporating a provision that recognises and respects men's rights to be involved in the decision-making process, while also providing for support and counselling services for both partners and promoting sexual education that emphasises shared responsibilities and parental rights. Ensuring that people have autonomy to make informed choices about their reproductive lives is important for promoting overall well-being. This study suggests that men are often overlooked and excluded from reproductive decision-making, especially when it comes to abortion. Ensuring equality in decision-making requires the recognition that reproductive rights affect both parties,

31 See C. Shalev, 'A Man's Right to be Equal: The Abortion Issue' (1983) 18(3–4) *Israel Law Review* 381–430.

and the acknowledgement of men's voices. This inclusivity is important for promoting balanced and respectful dialogue, fostering mutual understanding, and ultimately empowering individuals to make informed decisions about reproductive health together. The researcher posits that addressing the neglect of men's input can advance a more equitable approach to reproductive decision-making that values all individuals' perspectives and rights.

4. THE LEGAL IMPLICATIONS OF HAVING A CHILD IN SOUTH AFRICA

4.1. ENSURING THE BEST INTEREST OF THE CHILD

Under section 28(2) of the Constitution, the child's best interests are of paramount importance in every matter concerning the child. This section forms the cornerstone for the protection of children's rights. It mandates that the interests of the child must be given primary consideration in any matter involving a child, including policy decisions and administration action.[32]

The concept of the 'best interest' of the child standard is set out in section 7 of the Children's Act 38 of 2005. In terms of this section, prioritising the interest of the child requires a holistic approach and assessment of various factors that may impact the child's welfare, including their physical, emotional, social and developmental needs. The factors that must be taken into consideration in determining the best interest of the child, in terms of section 7 of the Children's Act, are:

1. The nature of the personal relationship between the child and parents.
2. The attitude of the parents towards the child.
3. The capacity of the parents to provide for the needs of the child, including emotional needs.
4. The environment in which the child is living.

The nature of the personal relationships between children and their parents encompasses various dimensions, including emotional attachment, care, support, communication and overall parental involvement in the children's lives.[33] Children thrive in environments where they feel loved, supported and

---

32 See M. Sormunen, 'Understanding the best interests of the child as a procedural obligation: The example of the European Court of Human Rights' (2020) 20(4) *Human Rights Law Review* 745–68.

33 M.I. Armstrong, S. Birnie-Lefcovitch and M.T. Ungar, 'Pathways Between Social Support, Family Well Being, Quality of Parenting, and Child Resilience: What We Know' (2005) 14 *Journal of Child and Family Studies* 274.

emotionally connected to their caregivers.[34] The present author posits that the situation of fathers raising children they do not want can have a detrimental effect on those children's welfare, including lack of support, emotional neglect, parental resentment, financial strain and psychological impact. Parental involvement extends beyond providing basic needs, to include participation in education and social activities.[35] Parents who are engaged and invested in the interests and achievements of their children foster a sense of belonging. It is argued here that a father who did not want the child may be less invested in providing the necessary support and guidance for the child's upbringing, hindering the child's overall development and future prospects.[36]

On the other hand, if a child were to know that the father did not want them, and had wanted the mother to abort the pregnancy, it might lead to a feeling of rejection or abandonment in the child, which can have long-lasting effects on their self-esteem and mental well-being. Also, the father's resentment towards the child can create a toxic family environment characterised by conflict and tension, compromising the child's mental stability and sense of security. Lastly, raising a child requires financial resources and if the child is not planned, this can result in a child having limited access to basic necessities and opportunities for personal growth. Addressing these challenges requires an approach that aims to ensure that both parties have equal opportunities to consider their circumstances and whether they are ready to become parents. The law should protect those who are ready to become parents and those who are not, irrespective of gender. If a woman does not want to become a parent or a man does not want to become a parent, the law should allow them to relinquish their parental rights and responsibilities if their intentions were made known prior to conception or during the first trimester of pregnancy. The present study notes the importance of protecting the welfare of the child. It also notes that the proposed approach will result in single parenting and socio-economic challenges in raising a child.

---

34 M.B. McMullen and K. McCormick, 'Flourishing in Transactional Care Systems: Caring with Infant and Toddler Caregiver' in D. Narvaez, J.M. Braungart-Rieker, L.E. Miller-Graff and P.D. Hastings (eds.), *Contexts for Young Child Flourishing: Evolution, Family, and Society*, OUP, 2016, pp. 267–87.

35 J.A. Summers, K. Boiler, R.F. Schiffman and H.H. Raikes, 'The Meaning of "good fatherhood": Low-income fathers' Social Constructions of their Roles' in K. Boller and R. Bradley, *The Early Head Start Fathers and Children*, Routledge, 2006, pp. 145–65.

36 See J.D. Gipson, M.A. Koenig and M.J. Hindin, 'The effects of unintended pregnancy on infant, child, and parental health: a review of the literature' (2008) 39(1) *Studies in Family Planning* 18–38.

4.2. PARENTAL RESPONSIBILITY AND RIGHTS IN SOUTH AFRICA

The Children's Act 38 of 2005 outlines key aspects of parental obligations and entitlements in South Africa. The Act provides the duty to care for, maintain contact with, act as guardian of, and contribute to the maintenance of a child.[37] The duty to care includes providing emotional, physical and psychological support, and ensuring the child's well-being and development.[38] Most importantly, a parent should contribute to the maintenance of the child through financial support to meet the child's basic needs.[39] This obligation ensures that children have access to the resources necessary for their growth and well-being.[40] A parent has a legal obligation to support their child until the child can support themselves both mentally and physically.[41] This entails the provision of financial support to ensure the well-being of the child throughout their upbringing. Many jurisdictions hold that the right to support the child belongs to the child, and that neither parent's actions should terminate that right.

In South Africa, in terms of section 15 of the Maintenance Act 99 of 1998, parents bear a responsibility towards their children, which includes providing all necessary support for their well-being and development. This parental duty extends far beyond mere financial support; it encapsulates the holistic nurturing basics for the child's upbringing. Of relevance to this study is that these parental responsibilities are automatically imposed on a parent irrespective of whether the woman has decided to keep the child after the prospective father has advocated an abortion or expressed his desire not to be a parent. This section places a duty on each parent to nurture the child's emotional well-being, offering love, understanding and encouragement. The present author posits that it is likely, when a father assumes parenthood reluctantly or without desire, that it may result in the risk of the child being raised in an environment prone to abuse, thereby jeopardising the child's well-being, particularly where the parents live together or the father is forced to have custody of the child. Under section 15(2) of the Children's Act, any person can approach the court to have either of the parents of the child take care of the child, and this include having the child live with the parent that has the financial means to care for the child. The order of

---

37 Children's Act 2005, s. 18(2). See also Maintenance Act 1998, s.15.

38 See K. Toros, K. Tart and A. Falch-Eriksen, 'Collaboration of Child Protective Services and Early Childhood Educators: Enhancing the Well-being of Children in Need' (2021) 49(5) *Early Childhood Education Journal* 995–1006.

39 M. Hakovirta, C. Skinner, H. Hiilamo and M. Jokela, 'Child Poverty, Child Maintenance and Interactions with Social Assistance Benefits among Lone Parent Families: A Comparative Analysis' (2020) 49(1) *Journal of Social Policy* 19–39.

40 Ibid.

41 Children's Act 2005, s. 18(2)(d).

the court to impose custody on the parent that has the means to care for the child amounts to forceful custody. Forceful custody, in the context of this study, may refer to the custody of the child where one parent in particular – the one who would have opted for abortion – is required to take custody of the child. The parent takes custody of the child because the other parent is legally unfit to have custody of the child, unsafe to live with the child, or refuses to have the child donated.

The present author posits that, in instances where a father never wanted to assume a parental role, there is a heightened likelihood of emotional detachment or outright neglect towards the child. This emotional detachment may manifest in various forms of abuse, whether physical, verbal or emotional, rendering the environment for a child's upbringing detrimental to their overall welfare. Parental responsibilities and rights require biological connection, emotional investment, nurturance and guidance for the child's development.

In South Africa, both parents of a child, whether they are married or unmarried, are legally obligated to support the child.[42] The child's interest in support differs from the child's interest in the custodial right, in that supporting a child does not guarantee custody of the child. Where parents live together, married or unmarried, either parent can apply for a maintenance order in the Maintenance Court because the other parent is failing to maintain or support the child.[43] On the other hand, if married or unmarried parents live separately, any person with the legal right to care for the child, including the parents, may apply for a maintenance order against any parent who fails to support the child.[44] Under section 6(1)(b) of the Maintenance Act 99 of 1998, no one is compelled to apply for maintenance unless one shows that there is a good cause for the court to make a maintenance order.

According to section 31(1) of the Maintenance Act 99 of 1998, any person who fails to comply with a maintenance order shall be guilty of an offence and liable on conviction to a fine or imprisonment. Basically, in the context of this study, if a father fails to pay maintenance in accordance with a maintenance order, he shall be guilty, and be liable on conviction to a fine or imprisonment. This section of the Act deals with the consequences of failing to fulfil parental responsibilities, such as maintaining the child. Notably, this section serves as a deterrent to parents who fail to support their children and underscores the seriousness of parental responsibility and obligation in society. It does not matter whether the father made it clear that he did not want the child during the period in which abortion was feasible; once the child is born alive, the father bears a

42 Maintenance Act 99 of 1998, s. 15.

43 L.K. Vogel, 'Barriers to Meeting Formal Child Support Obligations: Noncustodial Father Perspectives' (2020) 110 *Children and Youth Service Review* 1.

44 Maintenance Act 99 of 1998, ch. 3.

legal responsibility to fulfil his duty of support towards the child. The present author posits that developing a maintenance law to allow fathers to relinquish their parental rights if they expressed their desire not to have a child at a time when abortion was still possible would mark an important shift in the existing legal framework. Such a shift would raise questions about the extent to which individuals should be held accountable for decisions made during the conception and early stages of pregnancy. The proposed shift has the prospect of promoting gender equality by providing men with greater autonomy and control over their reproductive choices. Men would then choose – just as women currently choose – whether or not to assume parental responsibilities. This notion emphasises the importance of recognising the reproductive autonomy of men and reducing the disproportionate burden placed on them in cases where they did not consent to parenthood.

It is posited here that the development of a legal system should allow a father to voluntarily relinquish his parental rights if he expressed his desire not to have a child at a time when abortion was possible. This proposed development might address the situation of imprisoning fathers who never wanted to have a child. Allowing fathers to formally relinquish their parental rights under such circumstances would prevent future disputes or conflicts regarding parental rights and obligations.

5. EXPLORING ALTERNATIVES SUCH AS EMBRYO FREEZING, EGG DONATION AND SPERM DONATION

This part of the chapter seeks to provide perspective on the alternative options to protect and promote equality in reproductive decision-making, particularly abortion. The exploration of alternatives, such as embryo freezing, embryo transfer, egg donation and sperm donation, underscores the deficiency within the current legal framework in safeguarding gender equality in reproductive decision-making, particularly in abortion matters. The present study advocates the exploration of such alternative measures to ensure equitable protection for both women and men where either party does not wish to assume parental responsibilities. The present author posits that the legal system should be developed to allow the transfer of embryos to any person chosen by the man, if a man and woman create embryos through the use of IVF and the woman decides not to become pregnant. Simultaneously, the law should allow a woman to relinquish her parental rights to the child in the event of such a transfer. In this scenario, it is posited that, if a woman relinquishes her parental rights, she should be treated as an embryo donor or egg donor.

If a man expresses a desire not to assume a parental role before implantation of the embryo, and a woman wishes to proceed with a pregnancy using the embryos the man and woman created, the legal system should allow him to relinquish his parental rights and responsibilities. This procedure can work effectively if men and women enter a pre-conception agreement and/or engage in post-conception decision-making. Pre-conception agreements and post-conception decision-making are important aspects of family planning and reproductive rights. A pre-conception agreement is an agreement created by a couple prior to conceiving a child, to establish a clear understanding of the rights and responsibilities of each party concerning the embryo/child. Where there is no pre-conception agreement in place, parties can engage in post-conception decision-making to agree on the future of the embryo/child and potential outcomes and obligations associated with the reproductive process.

The present author posits that discussing and agreeing on matters such as the embryo's future, and who will have rights should anyone decide to relinquish their rights, can assist in avoiding misunderstandings or conflicts. In this instance, the agreement should state that the man should be treated as a sperm donor and give the woman full rights and responsibilities in relation to the embryo.

This proposed paradigm shift seeks to address disparities in reproductive decision-making, offering an equitable parenthood approach.

Therefore, this study delves into the perspective of alternatives, such as embryo freezing, embryo transfer, egg donation and sperm donation. Embryo freezing involves freezing embryos for preservation and future use.[45] Frozen embryos can be used in various ways, such as subsequent transfer and surrogacy.[46] This process of freezing embryos is commonly used when a couple is unsuccessful in achieving pregnancy during IVF.[47] Furthermore, embryo freezing can also be used when women opt to preserve their fertility and reproductive autonomy, whether due to medical reasons, personal circumstances or other factors.[48] Embryo freezing and ownership in South Africa is regulated by regulation 18 of the Regulations Relating to Artificial Fertilization of Persons, 2012.

The present author sees this practice of freezing embryos as a technological advancement that can empower individuals, regardless of gender, to make informed decisions regarding their reproductive futures. Through embryo freezing and embryo transfer, both women and men can plan their families and

---

45 J.L. Dolgin and R. McLeod-Sorjan, 'The Determination of Embryonic Status: Merging Context and Whim' (2021) *Rutgers Journal of Bioethics* 40.

46 Ibid., 41.

47 A. Paffoni, M. Reschini, V. Pisaturo, C. Guarneri, S. Palini and P. Viganò, 'Should Rescue ICSI be Re-evaluated Considering the Deferred Transfer of Cryopreserved Embryos in In-vitro Fertilization Cycles? A Systematic Review and Meta-analysis' (2021) 19 *Reproductive Biology and Endocrinology* 2.

48 M. De Proost and A. Paton, 'Medical Versus Social Egg Freezing: the Importance of Future Choice for Women's Decision-making' (2022) 40(2) *Monash Bioethics Review* 146.

control when and how they have children. This study sees embryo freezing as a crucial tool for women facing medical treatment that may compromise their future fertility, or who do not want to continue with a pregnancy, and men who want to have an embryo kept for future use.[49]

The decision to use a surrogate to transfer an embryo where both parties to the embryo creation intend to have rights and responsibilities towards the child requires consent from all parties involved. On the other hand, where one party to embryo creation intends to relinquish their rights towards the embryo created, the other party should, through a pre-conception agreement or post-conception decision-making, have full rights to, and responsibility for, the embryo.[50] In such cases, where the embryo is transferred to the mother instead of a surrogate, the mother must be allowed to formally relinquish her maternal rights and effectively assume a role akin to an egg donor.[51] The father should make it clear that he desires to be the father, and be granted full parental rights over the child. The present author argues that this process may require legal and ethical considerations to ensure that the rights and responsibilities of all parties involved are clearly delineated and respected. The surrogate must provide informed consent, fully understanding the implications of her role in carrying the pregnancy.[52] Similarly, the woman relinquishing her maternal rights should do so voluntarily without any coercion, and with appropriate legal protection.

In this process, the welfare of the child should remain paramount throughout.[53] It is important to establish measures and structures to address any emotional and psychological challenges that may arise for the woman, including those in relation to the child born as a result of the arrangement. The present author posits that navigating this complex terrain with sensitivity, transparency and legal diligence would make it possible to facilitate a surrogacy arrangement while upholding the autonomy, rights and well-being of the parties involved.

In light of the increasing imprisonment of fathers who fail to support their children, it is important to consider the ramifications of incarcerating a father who explicitly expressed his lack of interest in parenthood from the moment the

---

49 See D.E. Purvis, 'Frozen Embryos, Male Consent, and Masculinities' (2022) 97 *Indian Law Journal* 612–53.

50 See ibid., 626–28.

51 S. Imrie, V. Jadva and S. Golombok, '"Making the child mine": Mothers' Thoughts and Feelings About the Mother–infant Relationship in Egg Donation Families' (2020) 34(4) *Journal of Family Psychology* 469 and 472.

52 See A. Ellenbogen, D. Feldberg and V. Lokshin, 'Surrogacy: A Worldwide Demand. Implementation and Ethical Considerations' (2021) 2 *Gynecological and Reproductive Endocrinology & Metabolism* 66–73.

53 Constitution, above n. 30, s. 28(2).

woman became pregnant.[54] Under the current legal system in South Africa, a father lacks the authority to decide whether the mother should keep or terminate the pregnancy.[55] Consequently, a man who unequivocally expressed his lack of interest in becoming a father can find himself indirectly bound by the mother's decision to proceed with the pregnancy.[56]

The present author contends that the law should be developed to accommodate individuals who, at a time when abortion is still a viable option, voluntarily relinquish parental rights, and treat them as sperm donors rather than fathers. This approach holds the potential to mitigate the incidence of men being imprisoned for failure to fulfil child support obligations for children they never intended to parent. By introducing such legal provisions, society can strive for a balance between reproductive autonomy, parental responsibility and the prevention of unjust imprisonment in South Africa.

6. CONCLUSION

In conclusion, the protection of, and respect for, reproductive rights are important within a democratic society to uphold gender equality in decision-making, particularly in abortion matters. This study sheds light on the imbalance within the current legal system, which permits women to unilaterally make decisions regarding abortion without considering the input of the father. This necessitates developing the current legal system to foster equality in reproductive decision-making. This chapter proposes that parents should have a choice to opt out from or relinquish their parental rights, particularly within the first trimester of pregnancy, when abortion is a viable option. This would enable individuals to make informed choices regarding their involvement in parenthood, mitigating potential conflicts and ensuring autonomy for all parties involved. Furthermore, the chapter proposes limitations on the unilateral termination of pregnancy under section 5 of the CTPA, aiming to foster a more equitable balance of power in the reproductive decision-making process. Policy-makers must develop legal frameworks promoting equality and autonomy in reproductive decision-making.

---

54 See P. Alex, 'Mahikeng businessman jailed for refusing to pay maintenance for 3 children', *News24*, 3 April 2023, https://www.news24.com/news24/southafrica/news/mahikeng-businessman-jailed-for-refusing-to-pay-maintenance-for-3-children-20230403, last accessed 17.03.2024.

55 Choice on Termination of Pregnancy Act 1996, s. 5(1).

56 Maintenance Act 1998, s. 31.

SOUTH AFRICA

EXPLORING MEN'S REPRODUCTIVE INTERESTS IN ABORTION DECISION-MAKING IN SOUTH AFRICA

A Call for Inclusivity

Seroné Stal*

Résumé

Ce chapitre met en lumière l'évolution des discussions relatives au rôle de l'homme dans la prise de décision d'avoir un enfant en Afrique du Sud. Par une évaluation de la jurisprudence locale et étrangère ainsi que de la doctrine, elle vise à souligner la reconnaissance progressive des intérêts des hommes et leur protection lorsqu'une décision relative à un avortement est en cause. La nécessité de prendre en compte et de préserver les intérêts des hommes dans ce domaine a suscité un débat important et croissant. En Afrique du Sud, où les décisions en matière d'avortement appartiennent exclusivement aux femmes, les hommes sont souvent confrontés à de lourdes conséquences, tant émotionnelles que financières. Alors que le discours dominant sur les droits

* SStal@ufh.ac.za.

en matière de procréation est centré sur l'autonomie des femmes, le présent article montre l'importance de la reconnaissance et de la défense des intérêts des hommes dans ces domaines. Il souligne la nécessité d'une approche plus équilibrée, qui reconnaisse pleinement les dimensions émotionnelles et éthiques de l'implication des hommes dans les décisions relatives à l'avortement. Il s'agit de montrer les avantages et les défis potentiels de la prise en compte des intérêts des hommes dans les discussions sur l'avortement. Pour ce faire, la place de la famille, de l'autonomie personnelle et des normes sociétales sont prises en compte. L'analyse s'inspire, en outre, des lexiques juridiques, des articles, des ouvrages et des lois en recourant à une approche qualitative. Elle préconise une approche inclusive de la prise de décision en matière de procréation qui tienne compte du rôle essentiel joué par les hommes dans les discussions relatives à l'avortement. Contribuant au discours actuel sur l'inclusivité et l'égalité des sexes dans la prise de décision en matière de procréation, elle plaide en faveur d'un cadre plus équitable, favorisant une meilleure compréhension, une plus grande empathie et une prise de décision collective dans le domaine de la procréation.

1. INTRODUCTION

Abortion remains an enduring subject of global contention, fraught with intricate moral, ethical, social and legal implications.[1] While seminal cases such as *Roe v. Wade*,[2] *Doe v. Bolton*,[3] *Dobbs v. Jackson Women's Health Organization*[4] and *Planned Parenthood of Central Missouri v. Danforth*[5] have profoundly influenced the contours of the abortion debate in various jurisdictions, the discourse in South Africa is uniquely nuanced by its own cultural and legal intricacies: see, for example, *Christian Lawyers Association v. Minister of Health*.[6] Predominantly, this narrative has been woman-centric, emphasising the emotional and physical burdens women bear in the context of pregnancy and abortion decisions.[7] However, this chapter aims to shift the spotlight toward the frequently marginalised perspective of men, particularly within the South African context.

---

1 W. Chavkin, L. Swerdlow and J. Fifield, 'Regulation of conscientious objection to abortion: an international comparative multiple-case study' (2017) 19(1) *Health and Human Rights* 55.

2 *Roe v. Wade* 410 US 113 (1973).

3 *Doe v. Bolton* 410 US 179 (1973).

4 *Dobbs v. Jackson Women's Health Organization* 19-1392, 597 U.S (2022).

5 *Planned Parenthood of Central Missouri v. Danforth* 428 US 52 (1976).

6 *Christian Lawyers Association v. Minister of Health* 2005 1 SA 509 (T).

7 P. Orner, M. De Bruyn, J. Harries and D. Cooper, 'A qualitative exploration of HIV-positive pregnant women's decision-making regarding abortion in Cape Town, South Africa' (2010) 2 *Sahara J* 45.

The burgeoning discourse on men's reproductive interests vis-à-vis unborn children necessitates this scholarly examination. Legislation such as The Choice of Termination of Pregnancy Act[8] and section 27 of the Constitution of the Republic of South Africa, 1996,[9] primarily foregrounds the reproductive health rights of women, conspicuously omitting the interests of men. Although section 27 of the Constitution codifies health care, inclusive of reproductive care,[10] as a fundamental human right, it remains silent on men's stakes in abortion decisions. Additionally, Myburgh asserted that provisions like those above, which permit the termination of pregnancies due to socio-economic factors,[11] serve primarily to advance women's rights.[12] This lacuna is notable as men confront their own set of emotional, ethical and financial implications,[13] thereby highlighting an evident gap in the prevailing legal schema. The chapter by no means wants to do away with women's reproductive rights, and by no means intends to change the current laws in place; it is merely advocating for men's reproductive interests to be seen as rights, and asking for a rethink of men's current position legally and in society when it comes to abortion decision-making. Consider a situation where a man, despite recognising that exceptional circumstances are justifying an abortion, is so desperate that he appeals to a family court, attempting to persuade the woman to carry the pregnancy to term.

At its conceptual core, this chapter underscores the pressing need to recognise and integrate men's reproductive interests in abortion dialogues. It endeavours to construct a more inclusive discourse that factors in family dynamics, personal autonomy and societal norms. Such inclusion serves three purposes: it expands the scope of shared responsibilities, mitigates gender-centric conflicts and catalyses the development of more comprehensive reproductive health policies. Despite South Africa's ostensibly progressive stance on abortion,[14] the country continues to grapple with lingering challenges, such as cultural taboos, economic disparities and the alarming incidence of unsafe abortions.[15]

---

8 The Choice of Termination of Pregnancy Act 96 of 1996.

9 The Constitution of the Republic of South Africa, 1996, s. 27.

10 Ibid., s. 27(1)(a).

11 The Choice of Termination of Pregnancy Act 96 of 1996, s. 2(1)(iv).

12 G.A. Myburgh, 'Humanity and the Protection of the Unborn' (Doctoral dissertation, University of Free State, 2008), p. 60.

13 A.E. Hirz, J.L. Avila, and J.D. Gipson, 'The role of men in induced abortion decision making in urban area of the Philippines' (2017) 138(3) *International Journal of Gynecology & Obstetrics* 270.

14 R. Kaswa and P. Yogeswaran, 'Abortion reforms in South Africa: An overview of the Choice on Termination of Pregnancy Act' (2020) 62(4) *South African Family Practice* 1.

15 L.S. Touch, 'Black South African Women's Experiences of Integrating Modern and Traditional African Medicine in Promoting Reproductive Health' (Doctoral thesis, University of Johannesburg, 2012), https://www.proquest.com/docview/2486214152?pq-origsite=gscholar&fromopenview=true&sourcetype=Dissertations%20&%20Theses, accessed on 3 January 2024.

It should be noted that the chapter in no way tries to restrict women's access to abortion. Therefore, enriching the dialogue to include men's perspectives promises a more holistic approach to reproductive decision-making. This expansive perspective dovetails with the overarching objective of the chapter to illuminate the often-overlooked role of men in abortion decision-making within the South African landscape and advocate for a more equitable and inclusive paradigm.

The chapter is thoughtfully structured to achieve these aims, with section 2 exploring South African laws and international jurisprudence shaping current abortion policy. The exploration highlights gaps in acknowledging men's reproductive interests and explores the ethical imperatives for their inclusion. Subsequently, section 3 delves into the emotional and financial repercussions experienced by men when they are excluded from abortion decisions, advocating for a more balanced consideration of these factors. Thereafter, section 4 undertakes a critical analysis of the potential advantages and challenges of integrating men's interests into abortion policy frameworks and societal norms, with a particular focus on the relevance of family dynamics, personal autonomy and social mores in crafting more inclusive reproductive health policies.

2. SOUTH AFRICAN LAWS AND INTERNATIONAL JURISPRUDENCE

2.1. SOUTH AFRICAN LAWS

The Choice on Termination of Pregnancy Act 96 is a pioneering piece of legislation in South Africa,[16] and it boldly asserts expansive abortion rights, distinguishing the country from other African nations. However, a critical examination of the Act exposes a significant oversight: it neglects the reproductive interests of men.

While the Choice on Termination of Pregnancy Act 96 places decision-making power solely on the pregnant individual,[17] this approach raises ethical questions. The conspicuous absence of men in these decisions appears incompatible with section 10 of the South African Constitution, which upholds the inviolable dignity of all individuals. The sidelining of men's reproductive interests undermines this principle. Therefore, section 10 of the Constitution needs to be read together with section 9. Section 9 of the Constitution asserts that everyone is equal before the law and that unjust discrimination is prohibited. However, the current legislation, specifically the Choice on Termination of

16 R. Kaswa and P. Yogeswaran, above n. 14.

17 The Choice of Termination of Pregnancy Act 96 of 1996, s. 2.

Pregnancy Act 96, predominantly excludes fathers from decisions related to reproduction, thereby violating this constitutional principle. This discrepancy is not merely legal but societal as well.

Research conducted by Patel and Johns,[18] as well as Patel and Kooverjee,[19] \ substantiates this assertion. Their findings revealed that a significantly higher proportion of men than women believed that the male partner should be informed about the pregnancy and should participate in the abortion decision. They should have the right to prevent the woman from terminating the pregnancy.

These studies also highlighted participants' astonishment at the idea of a woman deciding to terminate a pregnancy without involving her partner in the decision.[20] In the view of these men, the shared responsibility for conception should translate to shared decision-making regarding abortion.[21] The present author acknowledges that shared responsibility is not always complete, and that a man can walk away after making a woman pregnant and limit his emotional, and sometimes financial, responsibility towards the woman. The relationship's equality is questioned if the woman decides on abortion without consulting her partner;[22] equality refers here to equality in decision-making that concerns the household.

Consequently, the current legislation and societal norms directly contradict the constitutional commitment to equality. This issue is further complicated because men's reactions to efforts promoting gender equality are varied and complex, as Connell noted.[23] This indicates that, while some men might feel marginalised from reproductive decisions, others might not consider this a problem, or might even oppose changes that encourage more equality in these decisions. This complexity highlights the necessity for continuous discussion and negotiation in the pursuit of gender equality, especially in matters as intimate and sensitive as reproductive decisions.

There is an urgent need for a thorough re-evaluation and recalibration of South Africa's reproductive jurisprudence. It should strive to reconcile the current legislation with the principle of comprehensive reproductive autonomy. This would necessitate acknowledging and integrating men's emotional, moral and psychological stakes in abortion decisions.

---

18 C.J. Patel and L. Johns, 'Gender role attitudes to abortion: Are there gender differences?' (2009) 49(3) *The Social Science Journal* 493–505.

19 C.J. Patel and T. Kooverjee, 'Abortion and contraception: Attitudes of South African University students' (2009) 30(6) *Health Care for Women International* 550–68.

20 Ibid.

21 Ibid.

22 C.I. Macleod and J. Hansjee, 'Men and talk about legal abortion in South Africa: equality and rights discourses undermining reproductive "choice"' (2013) 15(8) *Culture, Health & Sexuality* 1002.

23 R. Connell, *Confronting Equality: Gender, Knowledge and Global Change*, Routledge, 2020.

By taking a more integrative approach, South Africa's reproductive policy could redress the glaring omission of male reproductive agency and align more closely with the call for inclusivity. The necessary changes to ensure the law treats everyone with dignity and equality should be made.

2.2. INTERNATIONAL JURISPRUDENCE

International jurisprudential standards have, historically, shaped abortion policies worldwide, prominently emphasising the safeguarding of women's rights.[24] At the heart of these standards lie instruments such as the Convention on the Elimination of All Forms of Discrimination Against Women.[25] Their unwavering focus on ensuring women's autonomy and the right to health has substantially influenced the formulation of national abortion statutes.

However, an evolution in these policies and legal instruments has brought to light a conspicuous lacuna: the marginalisation of men's reproductive interests. This lacuna refers to the worldwide gap in the legislation regarding the reproductive interests of men in decision-making processes. While the privileging of women's rights is grounded in rectifying historical and entrenched inequalities, this often results in an inadvertent sidelining of male perspectives, particularly concerning abortion decision-making.

From a more holistic viewpoint, men's reproductive interests, albeit different from the direct physical and emotional intricacies faced by pregnant women, are imbued with significant emotional, moral and psychological ramifications. Despite this, international legal paradigms scarcely address this multifaceted dimension. The resultant ethical conundrum is twofold: while it remains paramount to preserve a woman's autonomy, given the direct implications of pregnancy and abortion, it is equally pertinent to question whether a decision which often arises from mutual consent should be the exclusive domain of one party.

The International Covenant on Civil and Political Rights[26] underscores the principle of equality before the law. When this is extrapolated to the sphere of reproductive rights, a compelling argument surfaces. Although the importance of women's rights in reproductive decisions is uncontested, the marginalisation

---

24 United Nations, 'Women's Rights are Human Rights' (2014), <https://www.ohchr.org/Documents/Events/WHRD/WomenRightsAreHR.pdf>, accessed 10 December 2023.

25 UNITED NATIONS, 'Convention on the Elimination of all Forms of Discrimination against Women (CEDAW)' (1979). Treaty Series Reference No. A/RES/34/180.

26 S. Carlson and G. Gisvold, *Practical Guide to the International Covenant on Civil and Political Rights*, Brill, 2021. International Covenant on Civil and Political Rights adopted 16 December 1966, 999 UNTS 171 (entered into force 23 March 1976).

of male perspectives seems incongruent with this principle. This tension between individual rights and a broader interpretation of equality crafts a complex ethical dialectic.

Examining other jurisdictions further elucidates this dynamic. For instance, in the United States, the *Planned Parenthood of Southeastern Pa. v. Casey*[27] decision asserted a woman's right to make autonomous decisions about her pregnancy. However, the debate significantly intensified due to the minimal recognition of a father's right – specifically, his right to be informed about the pregnancy or a potential abortion. This aspect was a major point of contention. Similarly, in the European context, the European Court of Human Rights, while consistently upholding a woman's autonomy,[28] has yet to venture into the domain of men's reproductive interests.

The discourse on reproductive rights necessitates a broader, more inclusive spectrum of discussion. The ethical underpinnings of reproductive rights mandate a more encompassing dialogue that integrates all stakeholders' emotional and psychological investments.

While global jurisprudence has, commendably, pioneered the advancement of progressive abortion policies, an emergent need is evident: to judiciously reassess and assimilate the often-neglected reproductive perspectives of men. The future of reproductive rights jurisprudence lies in striking this delicate balance without eroding the foundational rights of women.

3. EMOTIONAL AND FINANCIAL REPERCUSSIONS EXPERIENCED BY MEN WHEN EXCLUDED FROM ABORTION DECISIONS

South Africa, a vibrant amalgamation of cultures, is known for its societal structure that often positions men at the helm of significant decisions.[29] However, when the subject is as sensitive as abortion, men are frequently relegated to the sidelines. This exclusion can spark a whirlwind of complex emotions,[30] exacerbated by societal norms that demand stoicism and emotional strength. By stoicism, we refer to the societal expectation for men to display emotional strength and remain composed in the face of sensitive topics like abortion. This expectation is influenced by cultural norms that associate emotional expression with weakness. As a result, men may feel pressured to suppress their emotions

27 *Planned Parenthood of Southeastern Pa. v. Casey* 505 US 833 (1992).

28 R.J. Cook, above n. 26.

29 L.A.E. Booysen and M.W. van Wyk, *Culture and Leadership in South Africa*, Psychology Press, 2007, p. 434.

30 E. Kushner, *Experiencing Abortion: A Weaving of Women's Words, Routledge*, 2013.

and maintain a stoic demeanour. This can further contribute to the complex emotions they experience when excluded from discussions about abortion, as they navigate the clash between societal norms and their personal experiences and feelings.

Consider Ubuntu, the African philosophy that underlines our interconnectedness, mutual respect and shared responsibility.[31] Ubuntu teaches us, 'I am because we are', reminding us that our fates are woven together, and that our actions echo throughout our communities.[32] Therefore, the matter of abortion should not be a solitary burden for women to bear, nor should it be their exclusive right, as it has far-reaching implications for both men and the community at large.

When men are left in the shadows of abortion decisions, they confront a flood of suppressed emotions, from sadness and guilt to confusion and loss. This emotional turmoil is mainly due to a lack of support available for men at clinics, and societal expectations that discourage them from seeking emotional solace.[33] This can lead to internal battles as men navigate how to express their feelings appropriately, or suppress them to maintain a supportive front for their partners.[34]

Additionally, it is important to consider the financial impact on both men, who are often excluded from abortion decisions, and women, who may feel pressured by their families or male partners to continue with an unwanted pregnancy due to cultural norms. This feeling of pressure from family and male partners can force them to give birth to a child they did not intend to have.[35] The economic burden for women in such situations can be staggering. They may have to bear the costs of medical procedures related to pregnancy and childbirth, as well as the long-term expenses associated with raising a child. This financial dependency can create additional challenges for women who may not have been prepared or willing to take on the responsibilities of parenthood at that particular time. Therefore, when discussing the complex issue of abortion, it is essential to recognise and address the financial implications for both the men and women involved.

Men have limited influence over the decision to become parents, yet they can be legally obligated to provide financial support for a child they did not

---

31 D.D. Mucina, 'Ubuntu: A regenerative philosophy for rupturing racist colonial stories of dispossession' (Doctoral dissertation, University of Toronto, 2011).

32 Ibid.

33 C. Bodenner, 'In the Decision Over Abortion, How Much Say Should the Guy Have?' (*The Atlantic*, 2 August 2016), <https://www.theatlantic.com/health/archive/2016/08/how-much-say-should-a-guy-have-with-abortion/623442/> accessed 26 December 2023.

34 S.L. Newton, L.E. Hebert, B.T. Nguyen and M.L. Gilliam, 'Negotiating masculinity in a women's space' (2020) 23(1) *Men and Masculinities* 65.

35 Ibid.

consciously choose to have.[36] The spectre of paternity fraud looms, adding another layer of financial risk with potential demands for child support and other compensations.[37]

It is, however, important to note that, in South Africa, a man has the right to request a paternity test if he either claims to be the father or denies being the father. The Children's Act,[38] which aims to safeguard the best interests of children, regulates this.[39] Consent from all parties involved in the paternity test, including the biological mother (or legal guardian, if the mother is not available) and the putative father, is necessary. In certain cases, such as child support cases, the court may also order paternity testing if there is reasonable doubt that the potential father might not be the father. There is no specific time limit for contesting paternity in South Africa. However, the Children's Act confirms a presumption that a person who had sexual intercourse with the mother at any time when the child could have been conceived will be presumed to be the biological father of the child unless there is evidence to the contrary that raises reasonable doubt.

The financial responsibilities of child-rearing extend beyond mere direct costs to include labour and emotional investment. The debate regarding a man's role in abortion decisions is indeed contentious. Some argue for the inclusion of men's perspectives within committed relationships, while others advocate for the involvement of the broader family community,[40] directly speaking to the Ubuntu principle.

Neglecting men's perspectives can imply that the man's role in the outcome of the pregnancy is inconsequential and distressing to the woman, and that it is unfair for a man to insist on a role in the abortion decision.[41] This viewpoint can be particularly unjust when potential financial implications are considered. For example, a man might be expected to cover the cost of the abortion procedure as well as related medical expenses, such as pre- and post-procedure care. If the decision is made to continue with the pregnancy, the man could also be legally obligated to provide child support, which can have a significant impact on his financial situation. The present author acknowledges that, regarding abortion decision-making, both men and women might experience some sort of potential financial implications which will affect their future financial position.

---

36 M.L. Jackson, 'Fatherhood and the law: Reproductive rights and responsibilities of men' (1999) 9 *Texas Journal of Women and the law* 58. See a different discussion, S. Sheldon, 'Unwilling fathers and abortion: terminating men's child support obligations? (2003) *The Modern Law Review* 178–94.

37 Ibid., 59.

38 Children's Act 38 of 2005.

39 Ibid., s. 28.

40 E.R. Brando, C.S. Cabral, R.L. Azize and M.L. Heilborn, 'Young men and abortion: the male, perspective on unplanned pregnancies' (2020) 36 *Cadernos de Saude Publica* 9.

41 S.L. Newton, L.E. Hebert, B.T Nguyen and M.L. Gilliam, 'Negotiating masculinity in a women's space', above n. 35, 74.

The stark contrast between a woman's right to choose an abortion and the mutual responsibility that accompanies the birth of a child remains a divisive issue.[42] Ideas such as 'financial abortion', whereby men can relinquish financial and emotional responsibilities early in the pregnancy, have been proposed.[43] However, these potential solutions become entangled in a web of legal and ethical complexities.

Abortion, both locally and internationally, is often framed as a matter of women's reproductive rights and bodily autonomy, which complicates the inclusion of men's perspectives.[44] Legal remedies, like those proposed in some countries, present a potential resolution by allowing men to renounce parental responsibilities within a specific time frame. Despite this, the debate remains sharply divided, with some abortion rights advocates insisting that men should have a say only if they support pro-choice positions.

Compounding the issue, societal narratives, misconceptions and stereotypes often cast men in a negative light within the context of abortion. These stereotypes overshadow the actual emotional and financial challenges that men face when they are excluded from abortion decisions.

The ongoing debate is fraught with ethical and legal complexities, but the ramifications of excluding men from abortion decision-making extend far beyond the immediate decision, profoundly impacting on their emotional well-being and financial stability.

As society navigates these sensitive issues, it is crucial to acknowledge and address the diverse effects on everyone involved. The philosophy of Ubuntu provides a guiding light, urging us to recognise our interconnectedness and shared responsibilities. By embracing this philosophy, we may create a more inclusive, compassionate and balanced discourse surrounding the complex issue of abortion.

4. POTENTIAL ADVANTAGES AND CHALLENGES OF INTEGRATING MEN'S INTEREST INTO ABORTION POLICY FRAMEWORKS AND SOCIETAL NORMS

In the context of South Africa, celebrated for its complex societal structures, lies a distinct challenge: the incorporation of men's perspectives into abortion

42 D. Osborne et al., 'Abortion Attitudes: An Overview of Demographic and Ideological Differences' (2022) 43(51) *Advances in Political Psychology* 29.

43 M.T. Tendero, 'Financial abortion: a feminist issue: are we taking a step back from gender equality?' (Bachelor's Degree Final Project, University of Prompeu Fabra, Barcelona 2023).

44 C. Zampas and J.M. Gher, 'Abortion as a human right – international and regional standards' (2008) 8(2) *Human Rights Law Review* 250.

policy frameworks and societal norms. This multifaceted issue, abundant with potential benefits and complications, is bound to the principles enshrined in the South African Constitution.[45]

The inclusion of men's perspectives in abortion policy frameworks could potentially unravel an expanded understanding of reproductive health.[46] Traditionally, reproductive health discourse has been predominantly woman-centric, with men often marginalised.[47] However, this unidimensional perspective is progressively being questioned. The South African Constitution, a paragon of equality and non-discrimination, advocates for including men, in order to foster a more holistic understanding of reproductive health.[48] Such an initiative could nurture more efficacious and comprehensive policies, resonating with the Constitution's principles of human dignity[49] and equality.[50]

Additionally, incorporating men's viewpoints could instigate a shared sense of responsibility. The realms of pregnancy and abortion are not exclusive to women; they significantly affect men as well.[51] Engaging men in these crucial dialogues could stimulate their involvement in family planning, thereby endorsing equality in reproductive decision-making. This strategy is congruent with the constitutional principles of equal rights and non-sexism.[52]

Furthermore, including men could spark discussions about family planning. By deconstructing societal taboos, it could enable individuals to make more informed decisions about family planning and reproductive health. Such openness promotes transparency and reinforces the freedom of expression protected by the Constitution.

Nevertheless, integrating men's viewpoints into abortion policy frameworks presents its challenges. Foremost among these is the potential encroachment on women's autonomy. The South African Constitution ardently protects the right to bodily and psychological integrity, which includes the right to make decisions concerning reproduction.[53] If men's interests were to sway women's choices unduly, it could undermine these constitutional rights.

---

45 Preamble of the Constitution of South Africa, above n. 9.

46 C.I. Macleod, 'Expanding reproductive justice through a supportability reparative justice framework' (2019) 21(1) *Culture, Health & Sexuality* 49.

47 R.E. Mhlanga, 'Abortion: developments and impact in South Africa' (2003) 67(1) *British Medical Bulletin* 115.

48 The Constitution of South Africa, above n. 9, s. 9.

49 Ibid., s. 10.

50 Ibid., s. 9.

51 J. Strong, 'Men's involvement in women's abortion-related care' (2022) 30(1) *Sexual and Reproductive Health Matters*, <https://www.ncbi.nlm.nih.gov/pmc/articles/PMC8956302/>, accessed on 3 January 2024.

52 Ibid.

53 The Constitution of South Africa, above n. 9, s. 27.

Societal norms and entrenched gender roles could also add complexity to the inclusion of men's perspectives. Due to societal norms, men are often excluded from reproductive health matters, and traditional gender roles could lead to situations where men dominate the conversation, potentially marginalising women's voices. This contradicts the Constitution's unwavering commitment to gender equality and non-discrimination.[54]

Therefore, formulating more inclusive reproductive health policies requires careful calibration. While aiming for a comprehensive understanding of reproductive health, shared responsibility and open dialogue, it must also protect women's autonomy and cautiously navigate societal norms and gender roles. These efforts should harmonise with the principles of human dignity, equality, and the advancement of human rights and freedoms, as enshrined in the South African Constitution.

The integration of men's perspectives into abortion policy frameworks and societal norms is a complex issue, but one laden with immense potential. It necessitates scrutiny and a delicate balance to ensure that the rights and needs of all parties involved are respected and addressed in harmony with the principles of the South African Constitution. As we progress, it is essential to engage in open and inclusive discussions about reproductive health, ensuring that both men's and women's perspectives and experiences are recognised and respected.

5. CONCLUSION

Men's input in abortion decisions, while complex, carries emotional and financial implications often overlooked by current reproductive rights legislation. This oversight, which potentially infringes on principles of equality and dignity, calls for an extensive review of reproductive laws in South Africa and globally. Such a review should reconcile the principle of comprehensive reproductive autonomy with men's emotional, moral and psychological interests in abortion decisions.

International jurisprudential standards should also be reconsidered, to include men's reproductive perspectives without undermining women's foundational rights. Moreover, countries like the United States and European countries should contemplate incorporating men's reproductive interests into their legislation, possibly by recognising a father's right to be informed about reproductive decisions.

---

54 Ibid., s. 9.

Continuous dialogue and negotiation are crucial for gender equality, especially in sensitive issues like reproductive decisions. Such discussions should consider men's diverse and complex responses to gender equality initiatives.

On the flip side, men excluded from abortion decisions often grapple with feelings of sadness, guilt, confusion and loss. The lack of support, and societal expectations, usually aggravate these feelings. Financially, these men may face legal obligations to support a child they did not choose to have, and paternity fraud can add another financial risk layer.

The debate over a man's role in abortion decisions is contentious. Some argue for consideration of men's perspectives, especially in committed relationships. The concept of 'financial abortion', allowing men to relinquish responsibilities early in pregnancy, has been proposed. However, the legal and ethical landscape, including men's perspectives, is complicated. Certain jurisdictions have merely proposed legal mechanisms permitting men to relinquish their parental responsibilities within a specified time frame.

Societal narratives and misconceptions can often unfairly represent men in the context of abortion, obscuring the actual emotional and financial challenges they face. The repercussions of excluding men from abortion decisions extend beyond the immediate decision, affecting their emotional well-being and financial stability.

Based on these findings, the following recommendations are proposed:

1. Increase support for men in clinics and challenge societal norms that deter men from seeking emotional support.
2. Encourage open dialogue and consider men's perspectives within committed relationships, possibly involving counselling or mediation services.
3. Explore legal solutions that allow men to renounce parental responsibilities within a specific time frame without compromising the child's rights and welfare.
4. Challenge societal narratives and misconceptions about men in the context of abotion through public awareness campaigns or educational programmes.
5. Acknowledge and address, potentially through comprehensive research and policy-making, the diverse effects on men's emotional well-being and financial stability of excluding them from abortion decisions.

TRINIDAD AND TOBAGO

MIGRANT CHILDREN AND THE INALIENABLE RIGHT TO EDUCATION

A Case Study on Trinidad and Tobago

Damali Nicholls and Kinda Jacob

Résumé

« Vous portez l'avenir de Trinité-et-Tobago dans vos cartables », ces mots ont été prononcés par feu le Dr Eric Williams, Premier ministre, alors qu'il s'adressait aux jeunes de Trinité-et-Tobago. Ce slogan montre le caractère progressiste du système éducatif de Trinité-et-Tobago, où l'éducation est gratuite et obligatoire jusqu'à l'âge de 16 ans. Toutefois, l'éducation est-elle réellement obligatoire et accessible à tous les enfants de Trinité-et-Tobago, et spécialement aux enfants migrants ? C'est à cette question que le présent chapitre s'intéresse.

La première partie de ce chapitre traite de la manière dont les enfants migrants peuvent accéder à l'éducation à Trinité-et-Tobago, en mettant en parallèle la loi sur l'éducation de Trinité-et-Tobago et les règlements sur l'immigration qui prévoit des conditions qui érigent des barrières à l'accès à l'éducation. La deuxième partie du chapitre traite de la question de savoir si l'État est obligé de supprimer les obstacles au droit d'accès à l'éducation des enfants migrants en raison des obligations internationales auxquelles Trinité-et-Tobago est soumis. Enfin, le présent texte tente de formuler des recommandations et se réfère au rapport de la commission mixte du Parlement de Trinité-et-Tobago sur le traitement des migrants, qui comprenait un volet sur le droit à l'éducation.

1. INTRODUCTION

'*You carry the future of Trinidad and Tobago in your school bags*' – these words were uttered by the late Dr Eric Williams, the country's first prime minister, while addressing the youth of Trinidad and Tobago.[1] This mantra set the stage for the progressive nature of the education system in Trinidad and Tobago, where education is free and mandatory up to the age of 16. However, this chapter will explore whether education is, in fact, truly compulsory and accessible for all children in Trinidad and Tobago, with the emphasis placed on the migrant child.

The next section of this chapter will discuss how migrant children can access education in Trinidad and Tobago, and this is juxtaposed with the Immigration Regulations and Education Act of Trinidad and Tobago, which stipulates conditions that erect barriers to access. Section 3 of the chapter will deliberate on whether the State is obligated to remove barriers to migrant children's right to access education, due to Trinidad and Tobago's international obligations. Lastly, this chapter will endeavour to make recommendations; reference will be made to the Trinidad and Tobago Parliament Joint Select Committee report on the treatment of migrants, which included a focus on rights to education.

2. THE MIGRANT CHILD AND BARRIERS TO ACCESS

Dr Williams pioneered radical changes in the education system in Trinidad and Tobago that focused on breaking down barriers to education based on religion, class and wealth. In December 1960, the Concordat was signed. This was an agreement between the State and various denominational school boards, outlining the terms upon which they would run government-assisted schools.[2] With the Concordat in place, all children had the opportunity to obtain a secondary education regardless of their race, colour, economic background or religious persuasion. While this promise of a universal right to education has generally been realised for citizens of Trinidad and Tobago, the same is not true for 'migrant' children. In this chapter, a 'migrant' will be defined as anyone who changes his or her country of usual residence, irrespective of legal status or the reason for migration, and encompasses different categories of persons, including

---

1 Dr Eric Williams addressed a mass gathering of youth at Woodford Square in Trinidad and Tobago on the eve of independence in 1962 (*Reflections on a National Hero, Dr. Eric Eustace Williams – Father of the Nation*, by Dr. Eric Eustace Williams, Government Printery, Trinidad and Tobago, 1982).

2 The Concordat of 1960: Assurances for the Preservation and Character of Denominational Schools as approved by Cabinet.

asylum seekers and refugees, stateless persons and victims of human trafficking.[3] A child, on the other hand, is any person under the age of 18 years old.[4]

The Ministry of Education had posited during the Parliamentary Joint Select Committee on the Treatment of Migrants, held on 26 May 2023,[5] which focused on access to education, that migrant children from 33 nations were, at that time, integrated within the school population.[6] While this may seem impressive, this chapter will explore whether all migrant children, particularly Venezuelan migrants, are catered for.

Since 2016, Trinidad and Tobago has experienced an influx of Venezuelans seeking to escape the deteriorating living conditions in their home country; as of late 2019, there were around 23,400 Venezuelan refugees and migrants living in Trinidad and Tobago.[7] Recent published articles citing the Response for Venezuelans (R4V) have indicated that, as of 2022, there were an estimated 6,900 children in Trinidad and Tobago needing education support as part of the Refugee and Migrant Response Plan (RMRP).[8] The data managed by the R4V reports 2,900 more children than the United Nations High Commissioner for Refugees (UNHCR).[9]

The Education Act prescribes that the compulsory school age is between 5 and 16 years old.[10] Every parent has a duty to ensure that their children of compulsory school age attend school regularly.[11] Any parent who fails to send their children who are of compulsory school age to school commits an offence.[12] On the face of it, the Education Act propagates that the education of children

3 Joint Select Committee on Human Rights, Equality and Diversity, Fifth Session of the Eleventh Parliament (2019/2020), 18th Report.

4 S. 3 of the Children Act No. 12 of 2012 of the Laws of Trinidad and Tobago.

5 15th Meeting of the Joint Select Committee on Human Rights, Equality and Diversity – Treatment of Migrants, 26 May 2023 <https://www.youtube.com/watch?v=6aRSdPB8Cic>. The Ministry admitted that most of the migrant children were from The Caribbean Community (CARICOM) Member States, and indicated that arrangements were in place for migrant children in general to access education, and that information could be obtained from District Offices, the Ministry's head office and school principals. However, none of the information is available in Spanish, nor are there interpreters or bilingual employees to assist.

6 Ibid.

7 UNICEF, 'The Impact of COVID-19 on Migrant Children in Trinidad and Tobago', <https://www.unicef.org/easterncaribbean/media/2096/file/Impact%20of%20COVID-19%20on%20migrant%20children%20in%20Trinidad%20and%20Tobago.pdf>, p. 1.

8 G. Alvarado, 'No school for many Venezuelan migrant children', *Trinidad and Tobago Newsday*, 4 September 2022, <https://newsday.co.tt/2022/09/04/no-school-for-many-venezuelan-migrant-children/>.

9 Ibid.

10 S. 76 of the Education Act Chapter 39:01 of Trinidad and Tobago.

11 Ibid., s. 77 provides that, subject to s. 78, it shall be the duty of the parent of every child of compulsory school age to cause them to receive efficient full-time education suitable to their age, ability and aptitude, by regular attendance at school.

12 Ibid., s. 83.

between the ages of 5 and 16 is mandatory and compulsory, yet barriers exist, and this chapter proposes that, by virtue of a written law, the majority of migrant children are being excluded from the opportunity to be formally educated.

According to the Immigration Regulations:

> No person shall admit to any educational or training establishment in Trinidad and Tobago any person who is not a citizen of Trinidad and Tobago or a resident, unless that person is in possession of a valid Student's Permit issued by the Chief Immigration Officer. A person who admits any such student into an educational or training establishment without there being in force a valid Student's Permit in relation to that admittance in contravention of the provisions of this regulation is guilty of an offence.[13]

The question then arises of how a migrant child can obtain a student permit, and a perusal of the Ministry of Education website shows a process that is exclusionary, tedious and time-consuming. The parent or guardian of the migrant child must first contact the principal of a school who is willing to accept the child, and should the principal agree to the proposed placement, there are a series of applications and approvals that have to be made to the Ministry of Education. It is noted that approval of the issuance of the student permit is predicated on the migrant parent or guardian having legal status in Trinidad and Tobago. There is still a large percentage of migrants who are without legal status in Trinidad and Tobago, and as such, from the first instance, their application for a student permit would be denied.

It should be added that migrant children who do not qualify for a student permit can also be permitted to attend private schools. This will, however, require that the migrant parent or guardian pay a tuition fee, a luxury that most migrant parents or guardians cannot afford on their own. Further, it should be noted that, without a student permit, migrant children remain barred from national assessments such as SEA and CSEC. These are necessary qualifications that are needed for enrolment in tertiary education or the pursuit of gainful employment.

Ironically, the practices outlined above are inconsistent with section 7 of the Education Act, which prohibits discrimination.[14] Venezuelan migrant children, particularly those who may be unaccompanied, or whose parents have an irregular status, cannot access mainstream education in Trinidad and Tobago.

---

13 Reg. 9 (6)(3)(e) of the Immigration Regulations, Trinidad and Tobago before 22 February 2024.

14 S. 7 of the Education Act of Trinidad and Tobago Chapter 39:01 provides that '[n]o person shall be refused admission to any public school on account of the religious persuasion, race, social status or language of such person or of his parent'.

3. OBLIGATIONS OF THE STATE

Aside from requirements under the Immigration Act and the Education Act, the State has also relied on its position that it has never ratified the 1951 United Nations Convention Relating to the Status of Refugees, or its 1967 Protocol, and has no obligations under these instruments.[15] In Trinidad and Tobago, conventions are considered to have become law when they have been incorporated as part of the domestic law through legislation or settled practice.[16]

This chapter will not debate whether the State is accurate in taking this position; instead, it will focus on instruments and legislation that demonstrate beyond a doubt that the State has obligations to migrant children.

The right to education has been understood, over the years, to be a fundamental right enshrined in international human rights law. Core international human rights instruments guaranteeing the right to education include the International Covenant on Economic, Social and Cultural Rights (ICESCR, Article 2.245), the International Convention on the Elimination of All Forms of Racial Discrimination (ICERD, Article 147) and the UNESCO Convention against Discrimination in Education (CADE, Articles 1.148 and 349).[17]

On the surface, the State would argue they have fulfilled their international obligations. Trinidad and Tobago can proudly boast – and rightly so – that, as a small island nation of approximately 1.4 million inhabitants, it has a robust education system that was free and accessible, and that, until recently,

15 C. Bridglal, 'Faris puts refugee policy to the people', *Trinidad and Tobago Newsday*, 20 November 2018, https://newsday.co.tt/2018/11/20/faris-puts-refugee-policy-to-the-people/ Trinidad and Tobago Newsday.

16 *Yohan Jesus Rangel Dominguez v. Minister of National Security and others*, Claim No. CV 2023 – 00767, para. 45: 'This Court recognizes that the concept of "due process of law" is a compendious expression. The rule of law is ultimately framed and fashioned by the Constitution of Trinidad and Tobago and not by international Conventions which have not been incorporated either through legislation or settled practice into this Country's domestic legislative framework.'

17 UNESCO, 'The status of the right to education of migrants: International legal framework, remaining barriers at national level and good examples of states' implementation' (2018), ED/GEMR/MRT/2018/P1/8, <https://www.right-to-education.org/sites/right-to-education.org/files/resource-attachments/RTE_UNESCO_Background_Paper_Migrants_2018_En.pdf > (pp. 14 and 15); UN General Assembly, International Covenant on Economic, Social and Cultural Rights, United Nations, Treaty Series, vol. 993, 16 December 1966, p. 3, https://www.refworld.org/legal/agreements/unga/1966/en/3342; UN General Assembly, International Convention on the Elimination of All Forms of Racial Discrimination, United Nations, Treaty Series, vol. 660, 21 December 1965, p. 195, https://www.refworld.org/legal/agreements/unga/1965/en/1397; UN Educational, Scientific and Cultural Organisation (UNESCO), Convention Against Discrimination in Education, -, 14 December 1960, https://www.refworld.org/legal/agreements/unesco/1960/en/20674.

persons in Trinidad and Tobago enjoyed free education up to the tertiary school level.

However, despite this, at the Human Rights Council's 2022 Universal Periodic Review, Portugal, in their review, suggested that Trinidad and Tobago implement measures to ensure that all children, including migrants, asylum seekers and refugees, have equal access to all levels of education.[18]

Though pressure from the international community and international law can be persuasive, Trinidad and Tobago, having identified itself as a dualist country, has maintained its sovereign right to manage its national affairs as it pleases. The State, however, is obligated to provide access to compulsory education to every child within its jurisdiction. Trinidad and Tobago ratified the United Nations Convention on the Rights of the Child (UNCRC) in 1991 with no reservations, and this entered in to force on 4 January 1992.[19]

Under the UNCRC, Trinidad and Tobago is obligated not to discriminate against any child within its jurisdiction, regardless of their parents' ethnic or social origin, nationality, language or other status. Trinidad and Tobago agreed that, in all decisions involving children, the State would adhere to the best interest of the child as a paramount consideration, that the voice of the child would be respected, and that, within its jurisdiction, children would have the right not just to live but to thrive.[20]

Article 28 of the UNCRC requires State Parties to make primary education compulsory, available and free to all. The obligations outlined in Article 28 apply to all children within a jurisdiction, with no exceptions. Trinidad and Tobago agreed that education should be compulsory, and the state has been bound to this since January 1992. General Comment No. 6 (2005)[21] outlines that the enjoyment of rights specified in the UNCRC are not limited to children who are nationals of a state, but are intended to be applicable to 'all children – including asylum-seeking, refugee and migrant children irrespective of their nationality, immigration status or statelessness'.

Despite not currently permitting all migrant children to access education, as required by the UNCRC, the present authors suggest that the ratification of the UNCRC has played some part in influencing Trinidad and Tobago officials to have open discussions about deficiencies in the law where it relates to access by migrants to formal education. This sentiment can be supported by discussions

---

18 Human Rights Council 49th session, 28 February–1 April 2022, agenda item 6, Universal Periodic Review.

19 Para. 3 of the Committee on the Rights of the Child Consideration of Reports Submitted by States Parties under Article 44 of the Convention Second Periodic Reports of States Parties due in 1999 – Trinidad And Tobago, 29 July 2003.

20 Guiding Principles of the United Nations Convention on the Rights of the Child – Arts. 2, 3, 6 and 12.

21 General Comment No. 6 (2005) of the Committee on the Rights of a Child on Treatment of unaccompanied and separated children outside their country of origin, para. 12.

that were recorded in the National Child Policy. It was recognised that, pending legislative reform, migrant children are unable to access public education unless a student permit is obtained, which is normally contingent on their parents obtaining work permits. It was added that, without a student permit, no system was in place to facilitate their participation in formal education.[22]

The National Child Policy was able to recognise the gaps in the education system for migrant children, but it failed to make recommendations and advocate directly for legislative change.This chapter, however, recognises that legislative change, in particular, must come so that Trinidad and Tobago can fulfil its obligations. In a television news interview, independent senator and attorney-at-law Hazel Thompson-Ahye advocated that Trinidad and Tobago has a responsibility to educate 'everybody whether documented, undocumented, efugee children'. She further stated that the Immigration Regulations are in clear violation of the UNCRC. They are bad law and should be challenged.[23]

4. THE WAY FORWARD

The Joint Select Committee (JSC) on Human Rights' 2020 report examined the treatment of migrant children, with a specific focus on their right and access to education. The report recommended that the Ministry of Education ensure that migrant children face no stumbling blocks with respect to the process for their registration at schools.[24] The second JSC report was laid in Parliament in February 2024, with much the same recommendations, highlighting the fact that there had been little progress.[25] Urgent legislative reform is needed now; these children have been denied a basic right and key requirement of their development, having already faced the trauma of the circumstances that led to their migration.

In 2019, in response to the crisis in Venezuela, the Trinidad and Tobago Government did take the initiative to register Venezuelan migrants, which would allow them to live and work in Trinidad and Tobago. Approximately 2,500 of the registered migrants were children.[26] This registration process was outside the legislative framework detailed in the Education Act, which means that there are, approximately, at least 2,500 children not receiving full-time formalised education in Trinidad and Tobago. When those who would not have been

---

22 Green Paper, National Child Policy, 2020–2030, p. 13.

23 Tv6 Television Interview, 5 August 2023, <https://www.tv6tnt.com/news/7pmnews/senator-on-migrant-education/article_c0cfd2c4-3332-11ee-9ee9-6f24bdb49975.html>.

24 JSC 2019/2020, above n. 3.

25 Joint Select Committee on Human Rights, Equality and Diversity, 4th Session (2023/2024) of the Twelfth Parliament.

26 Ibid.

registered are taken into account, the number will be far higher. While some of these registered parents have the right to work legally in Trinidad and Tobago, their children were granted only the right to live there. The Catholic Church has stated that they have infrastructure in place at their schools to absorb many of these children.[27] Urgent legislative reform is needed in Trinidad and Tobago to remove barriers, including the immigration status of parents or the requirement for work permits, in order for children to attend school.

It is a fact that Trinidad and Tobago is a developing nation and, as such, may struggle to provide for the education of a large migrant child population in addition to its own local student population. However, assistance is available via partnerships with international organisations such as UNICEF and UNHCR.

The positive news is that the State signalled its intention to enact amendments and make provision for migrant children to attend school.[28] Under the Legal Notice No.44 of 2024 Regulation 9(6) of the Immigration (Amendment) Regulations provides that children of Venezuelan nationals whose parents applied for a Minister's Permit and declared the existence of the said children during the 2019 Migrant Registration Framework are entitled to receive formal education.[29] In a Media Release dispatched from the Ministry of Education dated the 21st June 2024, it was announced that Venezuelan migrant children who fell within the framework of the amended Regulations were permitted to attend school with effect from September 2024.[30]

Unfortunately, instead of removing barriers, the amended Regulation created more obstacles. Of the thousands of migrant children waiting to access formal education, only 23 qualified to attend school in September 2024.[31] This should be of no surprise, given that statements made by the former Attorney General suggest that the Government of Trinidad and Tobago is concerned that the country's citizens may be hesitant for their tax dollars to fund migrants.[32] Coupled with this concern, the government has also made strong pronouncements about Trinidad and Tobago not being 'a refugee camp'.[33]

---

27 Ibid.

28 C. Chan Tack, 'Browne: Migrant children may be integrated into local schools', *Trinidad and Tobago Newsday*, 13 July 2023, <https://newsday.co.tt/2023/07/13/browne-migrant-children-may-be-integrated-into-local-schools/>.

29 The Immigration (Amendment) (No. 2) Regulations, 2024 Legal Notice No. 44.

30 Media Release, 21 June 2024 < Media Releases – Ministry of Education <moe.gov.tt)>.

31 S.Douglas, 'Nearly 2,000 migrant children left out: 23 Venezuelans to start school', 20 August 2024 <https://newsday.co.tt/2024/08/20/nearly-2000-migrant-children-left-out-23-venezuelans-to-start-school>.

32 C. Bridglal, 'Faris puts refugee policy to the people', above n. 15.

33 S. Mohan, '"Migrant Registration Framework": Counting Venezuelan Immigrants in Trinidad & Tobago', 1 August 2019; The Honourable Prime Minister Dr Keith Rowley was quoted in a newspaper article, stating that '[t]his country will not allow the United Nations (UN) or any other international body to convert it into a refugee camp': C. Bridglal, 'TT Not Refugee Camp', *Trinidad and Tobago Newsday*, 27 April 2018, https://newsday.co.tt/2018/04/27/tt-not-refugee-camp/.

The 1960 Concordat revolutionised education in Trinidad and Tobago, but the country is yet to truly fulfil its international and constitutional obligations. Any child within the jurisdiction can be left out due to their nationality, status or origin, and be denied compulsory education. Migration has been a key part of Trinidad and Tobago's development, and all children, including migrant children, are part of Trinidad and Tobago's future. Education will not be compulsory for all until all can access it.

UNITED STATES

THE ABSENCE OF A UNIFIED THEORY IN CHILDREN'S FOURTEENTH AMENDMENT JURISPRUDENCE

Catherine SMITH, Tanya WASHINGTON and
Robin WALKER STERLING

Résumé

Trois décisions marquantes de la Cour suprême des États-Unis – *Brown v. Board of Education*, 347 U.S. 483 (1954), *In re Gault*, 387 U.S. 1 (1967), et *Michael H. v. Gerald D.*, 491 U.S. 110 (1989) – mettent en évidence les conséquences induites par une analyse jurisprudentielle erronée des droits de l'enfant. Ces affaires s'appuient sur une fausse dichotomie entre le fondement et la substance des droits de l'enfant, tant en matière civile que pénale, et démontrent la nécessité d'une interprétation uniforme des droits constitutionnels de l'enfant qui serait centrée sur l'enfant en lien avec les éléments découlant de la jurisprudence relative au Quatorzième Amendement. Pour construire ce système centré sur l'enfant, il est nécessaire de reconnaître l'absence de prise en compte des droits de l'enfant dans sa vie quotidienne au sein de son foyer, de l'école et également devant les tribunaux pour mineurs. Il s'agit de trois domaines distincts dans lesquels la Cour a permis des avancées jurisprudentielles vers une reconnaissance des droits constitutionnels de l'enfant, mais a ensuite battu en retraite, laissant les droits de l'enfant insuffisamment protégés et piégés sous un plafond de verre lié à son âge. L'incapacité de la Cour à élaborer un système complet de protection constitutionnelle, c'est-à-dire fonctionnant dans ces trois domaines, conduit à des résultats qui ne sont pas centrés sur les droits de l'enfant ou qui ne les respectent pas.

1. INTRODUCTION

The United States Constitution's Fourteenth Amendment is not only for adults; it also protects young people.[1] Yet, the Supreme Court has failed to provide a unifying framework that centres children's constitutional rights.[2] The first step in constructing a coherent framework is highlighting the absence of children's constitutional rights in their lived experiences in the home, at school and in juvenile court.

2. CHILDREN'S RIGHTS AND THE AGE-TINTED GLASS CEILING

While the Supreme Court has recognised children's Fourteenth Amendment rights, young people encounter an age-tinted barrier to their enforcement.[3] Time and again, the Court's decisions take one step forward and two steps back from recognising children's rights because of a deep-seated judicial bias in favour of adults' rights. This adult bias is especially prominent in contexts that define children's daily lives: their relationships with their parents, in school with their teachers and peers, and in juvenile court with their attorneys, court officials and community stakeholders.

2.1. CHILDREN AND THEIR PARENTS

In their homes or with their families, children have rights. These rights, however, are neither fixed nor clearly defined, due to the fear that children's rights are at

---

1 See *Planned Parenthood of Cent. Mo. v. Danforth*, 428 U.S. 52, 74 (1976) ('Constitutional rights do not mature and come into being magically only when one attains the state-defined age of majority. Minors, as well as adults, are protected by the Constitution and possess constitutional rights.').

2 For a state constitution that recognises children's rights, see Mont. Const. Art. II, §15 (explicitly protecting children under 18). For countries, see South Africa (Constitution of the Republic of South Africa, ch. 2, s. 28) and Angola (Constitution of the Republic of Angola, ch. II, s. I, Art. 35).

3 A.C. Dailey and L.A. Rosenbury, 'The New Law of the Child' (2018) 127 *Yale L.J.* 1448, 1463–64 ('Children's rights … remain relatively limited and qualified despite language in Supreme Court decisions suggesting that children broadly enjoy constitutional rights.').

loggerheads with parental rights. Still, even in early Supreme Court jurisprudence, the shoots of children's constitutional rights are discernible. In 1923, the US Supreme Court ruled, in *Meyer v. Nebraska*, that state laws prohibiting foreign-language instruction in public schools violated teachers' and parents' liberty interests.[4] Though the Court's principle holding was that the '[instructor's] right to teach and the right of parents to engage [the teacher] ... to instruct their children ... [was] within the liberty of the [Fourteenth] Amendment', the ruling acknowledged that the offending statute materially interfered 'with the opportunities of pupils to acquire knowledge'.[5]

Two years later, the Court, citing *Meyer*, reinforced constitutional protections for parental rights. In *Pierce v. Soc'y of the Sisters of the Holy Names of Jesus & Mary*,[6] Oregon required all children between eight and sixteen years of age to attend public school.[7] The Court's decision that the statute violated the Fourteenth Amendment due process clause centred on its determination that parental choice regarding whether to enrol their children in public or parochial schools was a constitutionally protected 'liberty interest'.[8] The unanimous ruling also, importantly, explicitly acknowledged children as more than 'the mere creature[s] of the state' and advanced an interpretation of liberty to inherently 'exclude[] any general power of the State to standardise its children by forcing them to accept instruction from public teachers only'.[9] The Court's reasoning centred, as the foundation of the opinion, the 'liberty of parents and guardians to direct the upbringing and education of children under their control' and protection for parochial schools from government action adverse to their business interests.[10] After *Meyer* and *Pierce*, courts began to selectively cast children's rights as falling within the protective sphere of the Fourteenth Amendment due process clause.[11]

Nearly two decades later, while still favouring parental rights, the Court expressly recognised children's rights as constitutionally protected, in *Prince v. Massachusetts*.[12] In *Prince*, a Massachusetts statute prohibited children from soliciting for religious purposes in public spaces.[13] The Court recognised the relationship between the adult's parental rights and children's rights infringed by the enactment as distinct.[14] In a 5-4 decision, the majority explained, '[t]wo

4 *See Meyer v. Nebraska*, 262 U.S. 390, 398, 399–400, 401, 402, 403 (1923).
5 Ibid., 400–01.
6 *Pierce v. Soc'y of the Sisters of the Holy Names of Jesus & Mary.*, 268 U.S. 510, 530 (1925).
7 Ibid.
8 Ibid., 535.
9 Ibid.
10 Ibid.
11 See *infra* pp. 2–7.
12 *Prince v. Massachusetts*, 321 U.S. 158, 171 (1944).
13 Ibid., 163, fn. 6.
14 Ibid., 164, 165–66.

claimed liberties are at stake. One is the parent's, to bring up the child in the way he should go, which for appellant means to teach him the tenets and the practices of their faith. The other freedom is the child's, to observe these'.[15]

The independence of children's constitutional rights from adults' parental rights was fully articulated by Justice Douglas, nearly 20 years later, in his dissenting opinion in *Wisconsin v. Yoder*.[16] The majority opinion made clear that its ruling, upholding the constitutionality of a Wisconsin statute mandating compulsory education of Amish children through to twelfth grade, did not depend 'on the assertion of the religious interest of the child as contrasted with that of the parents'.[17] The decision emphasised that, '[i]t is the parents who are subject to prosecution here for failing to cause their children to attend school, and it is their right of free exercise, not that of their children, that must determine Wisconsin's power to impose criminal penalties on the parent'.[18]

Justice Douglas' dissent in *Yoder* highlighted the Court's responsibility to recognise and enforce children's rights against a law directly affecting Amish children.[19] His opinion offered a stinging critique of his fellow justices' failure to do so, and an expansive embrace of children's constitutional protections. He reminded his brethren:

> The Court's analysis assumes that the only interests at stake in the case are those of the Amish parents, on the one hand, and those of the State, on the other. The difficulty with this approach is that, despite the Court's claim, the parents are seeking to vindicate not only their own free exercise claims, but also those of their high-school-age children ... Recent cases ... have clearly held that the children themselves have constitutionally protectable interests.[20]

The Supreme Court majority's pattern and practice of selectively recognising and ignoring children's rights reached its zenith in *Michael H. v. Gerald D.*, where, based on the facts, it did not seem possible to subvert the rights of the child at the centre of the legal controversy before the Court.[21] A 5-4 decision, authored by Justice Scalia, managed the impossible.

---

15 Ibid., 164.

16 *Wisconsin v. Yoder*, 406 U.S. 205, 242, 243, 244–45 (1972) (Douglas, J., dissenting).

17 Ibid., 230.

18 Ibid., 230–31. The majority opinion further explained, '[o]ur holding in no way determines the proper resolution of possible competing interests of parents, children, and the State in an appropriate state court proceeding in which the power of the State is asserted on the theory that Amish parents are preventing their minor children from attending high school despite their expressed desires to the contrary. Recognition of the claim of the State in such a proceeding would, of course, call into question traditional concepts of parental control over the religious upbringing and education of their minor children recognized in this Court's past decisions.' (ibid., 231).

19 Ibid., 241.

20 Ibid., 241, 243.

21 See *Michael H. v. Gerald D.*, 491 U.S. 110, 130–31 (1989).

At the heart of *Michael H.* was nine-year-old Victoria – the product of her married mother's adulterous affair with her neighbour, Michael.[22] For a time, the three lived together, and Victoria regarded Michael as her father and called him 'daddy'.[23] There was a 98.07% probability of Michael's biological paternity and the guardian *ad litem* supported the continued relationship between Victoria and Michael, as did Victoria's mother.[24] Michael challenged the constitutionality of a California statute that deprived a biological father who had not established his parental status within two years of a child's birth of a right to a relationship with his child. Victoria asserted a claim that she had a constitutional right to her relationship with her biological father. The Supreme Court ruled that Michael's asserted constitutional rights were not infringed by the statute, and that his rights were subordinate to those of Victoria's stepfather Gerald, to whom Victoria's mother was married. Gerald's status as father was deemed superior to Michael's because Victoria had been born into his existing marriage to Victoria's mother.

In what is arguably one of the most egregious examples of the subversion of children's constitutional rights in the familial context, Justice Scalia, in a plurality opinion, sidestepped Victoria's constitutional protections and interests entirely, and explained that '[w]e have never had occasion to decide whether a child has a liberty interest, symmetrical with that of her parent, in maintaining her filial relationship. We need not do so here'.[25] The opinion issued a cursory dismissal of Victoria's constitutional claim and concluded:

> even if we were to construe Victoria's argument as forwarding the lesser proposition that … she has a liberty interest in maintaining a filial relationship with her natural father, Michael, we find that, at best, her claim is the obverse of Michael's, and fails for the same reasons.[26]

Astonishingly, none of the concurring and dissenting opinions highlighted the plurality opinion's failure to factor Victoria's right to a relationship with her natural father into the constitutional calculus.[27]

In *Michael H.*, even though the child was at the centre of the controversy, the Court declined to determine her right to a relationship with her natural father,

22 Ibid., 114.
23 Ibid., 143–44.
24 Ibid., 114.
25 Ibid., 130.
26 Ibid., 131.
27 T. Washington, 'In Windsor's Wake: Section 2 of DOMA's Defense of Marriage At The Expense of Children' (2014) 48 *Ind. L. Rev.* 1, 39 ('Negating th[e] [parent–child] relationship and its benefits and preventing the child from raising claims and rights related to it infringes her constitutional rights.').

and the Court's holding, as in *Yoder*, defaulted to a focus on adults' rights.[28] Out of concern that recognising children's rights would diminish the scope and substance of adults' parental rights, the Supreme Court's decisions involving children's constitutional rights and parental rights continue to frustrate the development of a coherent children's rights canon.[29]

2.2. AT SCHOOL

While Supreme Court decisions regarding children's constitutional rights in relation to parental rights continued to struggle to find secure constitutional clarity and purchase, *Brown v. Board of Education* took a step towards recognition and enforcement of children's rights by identifying children's rights to an equal education.[30]

Brown v. Board of Education of Topeka, Shawnee Cnty., Kan. (*Brown I*) firmly established children's rights as separate and distinct from their parents' rights.[31] In *Brown I*, the young plaintiffs challenged the constitutionality of the separate-but-equal doctrine in primary and secondary public schools.[32] The Court held that '[s]egregation of children in public schools solely on the basis of race … deprive[s] the children of the minority group of equal educational opportunities'.[33] Importantly, the Court did not focus solely on the young plaintiffs' race; it also took into consideration their youth, providing 'an unprecedented inclusion of the qualities and characteristics of young people in its constitutional analysis'.[34] It explained that, '[t]o separate [black children] from others of similar age and qualifications solely because of their race generates a feeling of inferiority as to

28 Ibid.

29 Ibid.

30 Justice Stevens described the indeterminate nature of children's constitutional rights in the familial context and observed: 'While this Court has not yet had occasion to elucidate the nature of a child's liberty interests in preserving established familial or family-like bonds, it seems to me extremely likely that, to the extent parents and families have fundamental liberty interests in preserving such intimate relationships, so, too, do children have these interests, and so, too, must their interests be balanced in the equation. At a minimum, our prior cases recogniz[e] that children are, generally speaking, constitutionally protected actors' (*Troxel v. Granville*, 530 U.S. 57, 88–89 (2000)).

31 See *Brown v. Board of Education of Topeka, Shawnee Cnty., Kan.*, 347 U.S. 483, 493 (1954) (*Brown I*).

32 Ibid., 487.

33 Ibid., 493; see H.H. Clark, Jr. , 'Children and the Constitution' (1992) *U. Ill. L. Rev.* 1, 3 ('Another case not generally considered a children's rights case, but one which promised great potential benefits for children, was *Brown v. Board of Education*.').

34 C. Smith, '*Brown*'s Children's Rights Jurisprudence and How It Was Lost' (2022) 120 *B.U. L. Rev.* 2297, 2304; *Brown I*, 347 U.S., 493–95.

their status in the community that may affect their hearts and minds in a way unlikely ever to be undone'.[35]

At last, *Brown I* provided a Supreme Court decision recognising children's rights on their own terms. Unfortunately, the acknowledgement was short-lived. Within ten years, *Brown I*'s nascent children's rights precept stalled, as the Court's child-focused doctrine migrated to an almost exclusive focus on adults' rights – White adults' rights. Under the guise of upholding states' rights and parents' rights, the Court suppressed the children's rights gains of *Brown I*.[36] By ordering desegregation with 'all deliberate speed' in *Brown* II, the Court played directly into the hands of segregationists' strategy to deny black young people an equal education:[37] '[a]fter all, free and independent black children ha[d] always been perceived as a significant threat to White supremacy, just as their subjugation ha[d] been one of the most powerful and effective means to uphold it.'[38]

In *Brown I*, children's rights were invoked to challenge state action, and their independent claims did not threaten parental rights (at least the rights of their own black parents); yet, they too were ultimately sublimated to White adults' rights. Despite a stride towards children's constitutional rights, the Court retreated, leaving children's rights underdeveloped and trapped under a deep-seated judicial bias in favour of adults' rights – namely White adults' rights.

35 Ibid., 494.

36 *Brown v. Bd. of Ed. of Topeka, Kan.*, 349 U.S. 294 (1955) (*Brown II*); see R.J. Cottrol, R.T. Diamond and L.B. Ware, Brown v. Board of Education: *Caste, Culture, and the Constitution*, University Press of Kansas, 2003, p. 7; C.J. Ogletree Jr. , 'The Flawed Compromise of "All Deliberate Speed"', *Chronicle of Higher Education*, 2 April 2004, https://www.chronicle.com/article/the-flawed-compromise-of-all-deliberate-speed/ ('At the same time, its decision, though unanimous, contained a critical compromise, which I argue undermined the broad purposes of the campaign to end racial segregation immediately and comprehensively.'); see also D. Bell, 'The *Brown* Decision: "A Magnificent Mirage"', *Education Week*, 19 May 2004, https://www.edweek.org/leadership/opinion-the-brown-decision-a-magnificent-mirage/2004/05 ('A year later, the court, in *Brown II*, reacted to the outraged cries of "never" coming from the South and the absence of support from the executive and legislative branches, and backed away from its earlier commitment. In evident response to the resistance, the court issued a fall-back decision that became a prelude to its refusal to issue orders requiring any meaningful school desegregation for almost 15 years.').

37 *Brown II*, 349 U.S. at 301; C. Smith, above n. 34, 2309.

38 C. Smith, above n. 34, 2299; see Library of Congress, '*Brown v. Board* at Fifty: "With an Even Hand"', https://www.loc.gov/exhibits/brown/brown-segregation.html [https://perma.cc/84RC-4V8J] (documenting how Margaret Douglass, a former enslaver in Virginia, was arrested 'when authorities discovered that she was teaching "free colored children" to read and write'); Va. Code, ch. 198, §32 (1849).

2.3. IN JUVENILE COURT

In *In re Gault*,[39] the Court took a step closer to conceptualising a child-centered Fourteenth Amendment jurisprudence. Procedural due process protections for children accused of crime is one of the few areas in United States law where the Court has recognised that children's developmental differences are both completely disconnected from their parents' influence and constitutionally meaningful. The scope of these r in advancing children's interests, has depended on recognition of children's developmental differences. Those differences, while underlying the Court's initial decision in *In re Gault*, would receive full-throated expression in *Roper*.

Since *Roper v. Simmons*,[40] in which the Court struck down the juvenile death penalty as violative of the Eighth Amendment's prohibition on cruel and unusual punishment, children prosecuted as adults for homicide crimes have benefited from a line of cases that allows that 'children are different' because their brain development makes them 'categorically less culpable'. The Court cited three main developmental hallmarks of youth: increased susceptibility to peer pressure; reduced decision-making capacity, particularly in high-stress, criminogenic situations; and a unique amenability to rehabilitation.[41] These dimensions of youth, like the amenability to rehabilitation, enunciated in *Roper* after years of brain development research, had motivated the *Gault* Court to take the steps it did.

Still, *Gault* fell short of recognising children as full constitutional rights-bearers, allowing delinquency court to become a watered-down version of the adult-centred criminal system. Despite its announcement that, 'whatever may be their precise impact, neither the Fourteenth Amendment nor the Bill of Rights is for adults alone', *Gault* failed to calibrate procedural interventions, designed to secure those rights, to the unique character and needs of children.[42]

Fifteen-year-old Gerald Gault was arrested and detained for making a lewd telephone call to a neighbour.[43] Neither Gerald nor his parents received a copy of the petition notifying them of the specific allegations; instead, the petition simply alleged that he was in need of care and custody.[44] Gerald's first

---

39 See *In re Gault*, 387 U.S. 1, 14 (1967).

40 *Roper v. Simmons*, 543 U.S. 551, 552 (2005).

41 Ibid., 569–70.

42 *In re Gault*, 387 U.S, 13.

43 Ibid., 4. The caller allegedly asked: 'Are your cherries ripe? Do you have big bombers? Do you give any away?' See B.C. Feld and P.L. Moriearty, 'Race, Rights, and the Representation of Children' (2020) 69 *Am. U. L. Rev.* 743, 766, fn. 140; see D.S. Tanenhaus, *The Constitutional Rights of Children:* In Re Gault *and Juvenile Justice*, University Press of Kansas, 2017, pp. 89.

44 *In re Gault*, 387 U.S., 9.

fact-finding hearing was held in the judge's chambers the day after Gerald had been taken into custody.[45] There was no defence attorney and there were no witnesses – not even the witness to whom Gerald was alleged to have made the telephone call.[46] Instead, the juvenile court judge interrogated Gerald.[47] After a second, similar hearing, Gerald was adjudicated delinquent and committed to the State Industrial School 'for the period of his minority'.[48] Had he been an adult, the most serious penalty he could have received would have been a $50 fine or two months' imprisonment.[49] But because he was a minor, fifteen-year-old Gerald was sentenced to six years' detention away from his family.[50]

Gault revolutionised juvenile court proceedings. The Court acknowledged that children's constitutional rights expanded beyond substantive due process and equal protection entitlements to encompass procedural due process measures as well.[51] By engrafting criminal court procedures on to juvenile court proceedings, *Gault* was meant to limit the state's power and signal a new era of fairness for accused youth. The Court noted that due process should mean that children feel like they are in control of their cases, instead of being subjected to a 'seemingly all-powerful and challengeless exercise of authority by judges and probation officers'.[52] *In re Gault* granted youths in delinquency proceedings the rights to counsel, notice and confrontation, and the privilege against compelled self-incrimination.[53] Further, the importance of the introduction to juvenile delinquency proceedings of defence attorneys, as vehicles for children's agency, cannot be overstated. Having defence attorneys in juvenile court means that children at the mercy of the power of the state have someone in the courtroom to represent their expressed interests instead of just their best interests.[54] The defence attorney is the only adult in a delinquency

45 Ibid., 4–5.

46 Ibid., 5.

47 Ibid., 6.

48 Ibid., 7–8.

49 Ibid., 29.

50 Ibid. Unfortunately, this phenomenon in which children face very serious consequences for violations that adults can only be fined for is not uncommon. See, e.g. *Hedgespeth v. Washington Metropolitan Transit Authority*, 284 F. Supp. 2d 145 (D.D.C. 2003). In *Hedgespeth*, a 12-year-old girl was arrested, searched, handcuffed, booked, fingerprinted and detained for three hours for eating a single French fry inside a Washington Metrorail station in violation of D.C. Code §35-251(b) (2001), which made it unlawful for any person to eat or drink in a Metrorail station. Adults who violated §35-251(b) typically received a citation for a fine of $10 to $50. But because District of Columbia law did not provide for the issuance of citations for non-traffic offences to those under 18 years of age, the girl was taken into custody. The provision has since been revised.

51 387 U.S. 1, 14 (1967).

52 D.S. Tanenhaus, above n. 43, 26, fn. 37.

53 *In re Gault*, 387 U.S., 33, 41, 55–57.

54 Ibid.

hearing who is duty-bound to advocate for the resolution that the child wants instead of the resolution that system actors believe would serve the child's best interests. *In re Gault* enables realisation of the accused child's interests separate from the interests of all the adults in the courtroom, including the child's parents. In this critically important way, *In re Gault* lays a foundation for child-centred Fourteenth Amendment jurisprudence, though a coherent, robust constitutional canon for children remains aspirational. While *In re Gault* starts to chart a truly child-centred jurisprudence, it does so in a context that still allows children's interests to be subordinated to those of adults. Although *Gault* advanced the development of youths' constitutional rights, the fact that this advancement happened in the context of juvenile court proceedings has circumscribed its reach.

3. CONCLUSION

In the Supreme Court's landmark cases addressing children's rights in relation to their parents, the Court consistently rules in ways that affirm the primacy of parents' rights, even as they acknowledge the existence of children's constitutional rights. The Court's watershed decision in *Brown I* that children have a constitutionally protected right to an education unpolluted by racial segregation was eclipsed by a failure to enforce that right, in service to adults' desire to maintain an apartheid regime. And the promise of the Court's decision in *In re Gault* was clipped by the Court's failure to fashion juveniles' procedural protections and protocols to reflect the unique needs and character of children, rather than patterning them after adult criminal protections and proceedings.

Described above are three disparate areas wherein the Court made jurisprudential overtures towards children's constitutional rights but then retreated, leaving children's rights underdeveloped and trapped under an age-tinted glass ceiling. The failure of the Court to curate a comprehensive framework for children's constitutional protections leads to outcomes in cases that are about, and which affect, children, but do not centre or enforce their rights.

Imagine if there were an alienable, unified, coherent theory of children's constitutional rights. The vulnerabilities of youth that the Court recognised and sought to afford Gerald Gault might have been expanded to include additional procedural protections in the juvenile legal context, responsive to his needs and the realities of his childhood experience. Imagine if the Court had given more thought to the constitutional relevance of Victoria's relationship to her natural father. Or if, in *Brown II*, the Court had put its institutional muscle behind its pronouncement striking down the doctrine of separate-but-equal, instead of offering its infamously anaemic directive that states should integrate public schools with 'all deliberate speed', which came at the expense of black children.[55] These decisions provide fodder for a framework that recognises and respects the constitutionality of children's rights, and even though the status of children as rights-bearers remains unrealised, the Court's own rulings confirm that such recognition and respect is possible.

55 *Brown II*, 349 U.S., 301.

UNITED STATES

ABORTION AFTER *DOBBS*

Navigating a Tangle of State Restrictions

Robin Fretwell Wilson*

---

* Mildred Van Voorhis Jones Chair in Law, University of Illinois College of Law. This chapter would not have been possible without the commitment, carefulness and energy of the *Abortion Exceptions and Misconceptions Initiative* at the University of Illinois College of Law: Madelyn Bird, Michael Cerota, Saraf Choudhury, Daniel Donovan, Alexandra Frisch, Joshua Livingston, Anxhela Ndrio, Mai Nguyen, Sara Jane Peal, April Platt, Jafrin Pritha, Shreyas Shastri and Riley Uremovic, as well as my two research assistants, Cameron Samuel Keys and Kimball Yeates. I am also grateful to Professors Phyllis Baker, June Carbone, Brian Gaines, Claire Hill, Kevin Leicht, Jason Mazzone, Nausica Palazzo, Kent Redfield, and Lois Shepherd, and workshop participants at the Antonin Scalia Law School and NOVA School of Law for helpful critiques and comments. This chapter is intended for educational purposes only. It aims to give general information and a general understanding of the law, not specific legal advice. This chapter should not be used as a substitute for competent legal advice from a licensed attorney. Nor is this chapter intended to provide medical advice, and it should not take the place of medical advice or treatment from a physician. Readers should consult their own attorney, doctor or qualified health professional for specific legal or health questions.

Résumé

La législation de chaque État fédéré relative à l'avortement est particulièrement complexe. L'Alabama compte à lui seul plus de 50 textes législatifs distincts réglementant l'accès des personnes à l'avortement (à la différence de la réglementation des établissements pratiquant l'avortement) et le Texas en a 47. De plus, les lois des États fédérés remontent souvent à une centaine d'années, comme l'illustre la récente décision de l'Arizona dans l'affaire *Planned Parenthood Arizona v. Mayes*. La réglementation de l'avortement n'est, par ailleurs, pas inscrite dans un unique texte ou code, mais relève du code pénal, du code civil, des réglementations en matière de santé et d'assurance, des orientations des autorités, des documents budgétaires, etc.

Le présent article part du constat que les débats publics relatifs la réglementation de l'avortement dans les États des États-Unis dits « rouges » (*i.e.* votant traditionnellement pour le parti Républicain) sous-estiment gravement la complexité des lois dont ils sont censés discuter. Les outils de suivi accessibles au public, tels ceux du New York Times, de l'institut Guttmacher ou d'autres encore, tentent de résumer la législation en se plaçant dans une perspective globale visant à dégager des grandes tendances. Mais ces résumés, destinés au grand public, simplifient largement la complexité des textes en indiquant, par exemple, si dans un État fédéré une exception pour viol existe dans la loi, au lieu de donner les caractéristiques de chaque loi et de préciser ce qui détermine l'accès des personnes à l'avortement. En minimisant la complexité et en éliminant les nuances, ces outils de suivi ont alimenté des idées fausses sur l'application de la loi – par exemple lorsqu'il s'agit de savoir si une femme peut être poursuivie pour avoir avorté.

La présente contribution présente une initiative publique en cours. Celle-ci vise à analyser bien plus précisément les législations en vigueur en matière d'avortement dans les 26 États dits « rouges ». Elle effectue des comparaisons entre les États en tenant compte d'un certain nombre d'idées fausses couramment véhiculées sur la réglementation actuelle en matière d'avortement. Sur la base d'une grossesse de 40 semaines, elle rassemble les principales lois régissant l'accès à l'avortement afin que les non-initiés puissent comprendre « quelles sont les options légales en matière d'avortement si une femme est enceinte ? »

1. INTRODUCTION

Forty-nine years after *Roe v. Wade*,[1] *Dobbs v. Jackson Women's Health Organization* returned the regulation of abortion to the states.[2] Instantly, a complex tapestry of state-level abortion regulations, accumulated across decades before and after *Roe*, took on the force of law. Tumult and confusion followed.

Abortion services came to a standstill in states like Oklahoma, where abortion is banned unless necessary to save a pregnant woman's life.[3] Health professionals in Oklahoma had a difficult time trying to 'decipher the law and what they could legally say' to a pregnant woman[4] seeking an abortion,[5] causing

1 *Roe v. Wade*, 410 U.S. 113 (1973) (holding, 7 to 2, that the US Constitution protects a woman's right to choose to have an abortion).

2 *Dobbs v. Jackson Women's Health Organization*, 597 U.S. 215 (2022) (holding, 6 to 3, that the US Constitution does not confer a right to abortion and overruling *Roe* and its later progeny, *Planned Parenthood v. Casey*, 505 U.S. 833 (1992)). The Supreme Court found that '[t]he Constitution makes no reference to abortion, and no such right is implicitly protected by any constitutional provision, including the one on which the defenders of Roe and Casey now chiefly rely – the Due Process Clause of the Fourteenth Amendment.' (*Dobbs*, 597 U.S. at 220).

3 R.E. Kaufman and K. Mayall, 'One Year Later: *Dobbs v. Jackson Women's Health Organization* in Global Context', (July 2023) 48 *Human Rights Magazine*, https://www.americanbar.org/groups/crsj/publications/human_rights_magazine_home/the-end-of-the-rule-of-law/one-year-later-dobbs-in-global-context. Oklahoma's Attorney General issued guidance on that statute in November of 2023. AG Opinion 2023-12, 21 November 2023, https://oklahoma.gov/oag/opinions/ag-opinions/2023/ag-opinion-2023-12.html.

4 This chapter sometimes uses the term 'mother' to denote a pregnant woman, following the Hyde Amendment, a rider to federal appropriations bills since 1976, which prohibits the use of federal funds to pay for abortions except in the case of rape, incest or to save the life of the mother. See, e.g. S. 142 (113th): Hyde Amendment Codification Act, https://perma.cc/W7XN-HH4L.

5 W. Bryen, 'Her pregnancy was non-viable and her life was at risk but Oklahoma law prevented an abortion', *Oklahoma Watch* (19 September 2023), https://perma.cc/4JX2-3QES. In this case, a pregnant woman's foetus was entirely non-viable, missing a skull and most of the brain, with 'not even a 0.1% possibility that the baby would survive' (ibid.). The mother's life was in danger as she had 'one of the largest blood clots her doctor had ever seen and was at risk of going into shock or organ failure if it continued to grow'. (ibid.) Despite this, the hospital refused to terminate the pregnancy.

some women to travel out of state despite Oklahoma law authorising abortions to save a pregnant woman's life 'in a medical emergency'.[6]

Americans' penchant for absolutes was sorely tested as the human costs of state abortion restrictions piled up. A ten-year-old, impregnated by her uncle,[7] ushered in change in Ohio: Ohioans enshrined abortion access in the Ohio Constitution in a 2023 referendum.[8] A woman forced to seek an emergency abortion outside Texas to end a pregnancy that threatened her health and ability to bear children[9] reinforced the Biden administration's effort to press old laws like the Emergency Medical Treatment and Labor Act (EMTALA), the federal anti-patient-dumping law, into service to pry open access.[10] A Kentucky college student who, in the midst of Kentucky's gubernatorial race, narrated what it meant to her to have an abortion at 12 years old after being raped by her stepfather is credited with re-electing Democratic governor Andrew Beshear.[11] Notwithstanding this, Kentucky's law remains one of the most burdensome in the nation, making no exceptions to its ban for non-viable pregnancies or those that result from rape or incest.[12]

For clarity, this chapter uses the term 'foetus' rather than the term 'unborn child' used by some state statutes. Importantly, in public discussions of abortion, there are few terms that are not politically charged. "Pro-choice" and "pro-life" are hotly contested short-hands for substantive positions on abortion, but as noted below, other terms are also seen as loaded. Terms used here are not meant to take sides on the substantive question of access to abortion.

6 Okla. Stat. §1-731.4(B)(1), now enjoined. See also Okla. Stat. §§1-732(A), 1-745.15(A), 1-745.5(B), 1-745.52, and 861.

7 C. Tabachnick, 'Ohio man sentenced to life in prison for rape of 10-year-old girl who traveled to Indiana for abortion', *CBS News*, 10 July 2023, https://perma.cc/J8PD-HF5D.

8 The Right to Reproductive Freedom with Protections for Health and Safety, Ohio Constitution, Art. 1, §22, https://codes.ohio.gov/ohio-constitution/section-1.22.

9 Z. Sottile, A. Killough and E. Lavandera, 'Here's what we know about a Texas woman's battle for an abortion', *CNN*, 12 December 2023, https://perma.cc/T78Z-89Y4. Kate Cox, a 31 year-old mother of two, was forced to leave Texas to receive an emergency abortion after attempting to obtain court permission to end the pregnancy. Cox's foetus had a fatal condition that jeopardised her own health and her ability to have more children. Cox's doctor deemed the abortion 'necessary to protect her health and her chance of future fertility'. Texas' total abortion ban makes an exception for the life of the mother but not for foetal anomalies. Cox received a court order allowing her to terminate the pregnancy, but Texas Attorney General Ken Paxton stepped in. On 11 December 2023, the same day the couple left Texas, the Texas Supreme Court issued a ruling against Cox.

10 Emergency Medical Treatment and Active Labor Act (EMTALA), 42 U.S.C. 1395dd (2024) (EMTALA is a law that requires hospitals to provide emergency medical screening and stabilisation to patients regardless of ability to pay); S. Ranganathan, R. Reingold and E. Schneider, 'Threats to EMTALA: Unpacking the Oral Arguments in *Idaho v. United States*, *O'Neill Institute*, 8 May 2024, https://perma.cc/2MK6-RTEJ. On 27 June 2024, the Supreme Court dismissed an expedited case about whether an Idaho law and EMTALA were incompatible, returning the decision to the lower court. See *Moyle v. United States*, 603 U.S. ___ (2024), https://perma.cc/Q422-FYL6.

11 A. Aquisito, 'On *Dobbs* anniversary, doctors and Gov. Beshear call for repeal of Ky. abortion ban', *Lexington Herald-Leader*, 25 June 2024, https://perma.cc/UDS4-KK8F.

12 Ibid.

In the immediate aftermath of *Dobbs*, Americans grappled with three distinct waves of abortion restrictions. First, *Dobbs* revived every pre-*Roe* law on the books: laws that state legislatures had not repealed in the intervening years.[13] Second, laws took effect that were enacted after *Roe* and before *Dobbs*, either to probe the limits of *Roe* and *Casey* in hopes the laws would take effect if those cases fell, or as a symbolic act of protest, knowing that *Roe* precluded enforcement.[14] Third, state legislatures enacted new restrictions after *Dobbs*, with some states enacting laws in successive waves.[15]

Progressive states also moved into action, ramping up capacity to perform abortions and becoming havens for abortion services, as many predicted in the days after *Dobbs*.[16] They enacted new laws to 'shield' providers in their states; to block prosecution or sanction by other states for providing abortions or pills to out-of-state women.[17]

In the midst of the flux and upheaval after *Dobbs*: what is allowed, when, and under what circumstances in a given state? The degree of complexity Americans have been left to navigate cannot be overstated. Mississippi alone has more than 56 separate statutory provisions regulating access to abortion by persons, as opposed to the regulation of facilities.[18] Texas has 47. Often, state laws

---

13 'Some States Are Ready To Punish Abortion in a Post-*Roe* World', *American Progress*, 24 June 2022, https://perma.cc/KCE7-9GT3. ('Nine states have laws on their books banning abortion that were enacted before *Roe* was decided in 1973. … Alabama's, the oldest, dates back to 1852. Moreover, the statutes have gone unenforced since the decision in *Roe* made them resoundingly unconstitutional.')

14 This included 'trigger laws' in 13 states: Arkansas, Idaho, Kentucky, Louisiana, Mississippi, Missouri, North Dakota, Oklahoma, South Dakota, Tennessee, Texas, Utah and Wyoming. J. Jiménez, 'What is a trigger law? And which states have them?', *New York Times*, 4 May 2022, https://www.nytimes.com/2022/05/04/us/abortion-trigger-laws.html (describing laws passed out of 'frustrat[ion] that they couldn't ban abortion because of Roe v. Wade' that 'would be on the books and operative immediately' if *Roe* fell); E. Nash and I. Guarnieri, '13 States Have Abortion Trigger Bans – Here's What Happens When *Roe* Is Overturned', *Guttmacher Institute*, 6 June 2022, https://www.guttmacher.org/article/2022/06/13-states-have-abortion-trigger-bans-heres-what-happens-when-roe-overturned.

15 K. Crowley, 'Two years ago, SCOTUS overturned the right to an abortion. Here is how each state changed', *USA Today*, 23 June 2024, https://perma.cc/5ZD6-7P7T (listing Arizona, Florida, Georgia, Idaho, Indiana, Iowa, Nebraska, North Carolina, North Dakota, South Carolina, West Virginia, and Wyoming).

16 R. Fretwell Wilson and J. Mazzone, op-ed., 'Illinois should prep for influx of out-of-state abortion seekers', *Chicago Tribune*, 9 May 2022.

17 N. Weixel, 'Red state abortion bans headed for clash with blue state shield laws', *The Hill*, 20 May 2024, https://thehill.com/policy/healthcare/4671299-abortion-bans-clash-shield-laws (discussing laws in '[m]ore than a dozen states', including laws in six states that extend 'protection' for prescribing and sending 'abortion pills to people living in [red] states. … But the laws have only been in existence for about a year and have never been tested in court.').

18 Before *Dobbs*, there was also variation but the same baseline rule, drawn from *Roe* and *Casey*, governed in every state (setting aside circuit splits). The *Abortion Exceptions and*

regulating abortion date back hundreds of years, as Arizona's recent decision in *Planned Parenthood Arizona v. Mayes* illustrates.[19] Moreover, abortion regulations do not exist in a single place in the law but span the criminal code, civil code, health and insurance code and regulations, agency guidance, budget riders, and so forth.[20]

Popular media sources like the *New York Times*, NBC, *USA Today*, Guttmacher and others purport to give contemporaneous summaries of state abortion laws, which this chapter will call 'abortion law trackers'.[21] These abortion law trackers attempt to distill the status of state laws from a 20,000-foot vantage. But these trackers oversimplify matters, to the detriment of the public's understanding of the laws.

Popular trackers do not always agree on whether abortion is available in a given state. Trackers report time-bounded regulations (e.g. a ban on abortions after six weeks of pregnancy) but not reason-based ones (e.g. exceptions for abortions involving pregnancy caused by rape or incest). Trackers fail to show the interplay between time limits and exceptions in broadening access. Trackers often overstate the degree of difference between 'red' and 'blue' states.[22]

Some trackers, for instance, will indicate whether a rape or incest exception exists *anywhere* in a state's law, without connecting the exception to specific provisions. As it turns out, exceptions in some states offer no meaningful access beyond what the state allows in the early weeks of a pregnancy, making the exceptions illusory.[23] Reporting 'fake' exceptions as if they were meaningful ill serves the public. Finally, popular trackers simply do not tell people how bad

Misconceptions Initiative did not code facility regulations, which, for example, might treat an abortion clinic as an ambulatory surgery centre or require abortion providers to hold credentials at the nearest hospital. Using Westlaw's index, the Initiative team gathers all statutes that regulate natural persons.

19 *Planned Parenthood Ariz. v. Mayes*, CV-23-0005-PR (Ariz. Apr 09, 2024).

20 To date, the *Abortion Exceptions and Misconceptions Initiative* has focused on state level statutes and court cases interpreting them. Localities have also begun to regulate abortion access, C. Kitchener, 'Highways are the next antiabortion target. One Texas town is resisting', *The Washington Post*, 1 September 2024, https://www.washingtonpost.com/politics/2023/09/01/texas-abortion-highways/. The *Abortion Exceptions and Misconceptions Initiative* has not attempted to reflect local laws.

21 Media companies and advocacy groups publish trackers that include charts and graphs that purport to summarise the current state of abortion laws in each state. These trackers are not official statements backed up by any government agency, are not necessarily compiled by lawyers, and vary considerably in the sources of the law and definitions they use. See Table 1 below.

22 In many contexts, 'red' and 'blue' denote control by Republicans (red) or Democrats (blue), or by conservative (red) or progressive (blue) lawmakers. This chapter uses 'red' and 'blue' to convey whether or not states are perceived to restrict abortion. A careful review of state laws shows that laws in 'red' and 'blue' states are not always so different. See section 2.2.4. below. Instead, the laws exist on a spectrum. Within a state, there can be a spectrum too, with some laws more difficult to satisfy than others.

23 See section 3.3. below.

it will be if someone violates the law; that is, what sanctions follow an illegal abortion.

In short, existing trackers eliminate nuance and flatten the complexity of laws in red states. By oversimplifying matters, these trackers risk fostering misconceptions about the law's application, for example about whether a woman needs to leave the state to secure an abortion.[24]

State abortion regulations, although extraordinarily complex, can be presented in a way that demystifies the laws people live under. Using examples from the coding of abortion restrictions in 20 red states completed to date by the *Abortion Exceptions and Misconceptions Initiative*[25] at the University of Illinois College of Law, this chapter chronicles how to diagram the contours of state laws that affect whether and how real people access abortion services after *Dobbs*. This initiative fills in the gap between what is being reported and the actual legal availability of abortion in the states.

Section 2 maps what popular media trackers get wrong: how they oversimply complex, often layered, abortion restrictions, flattening the nuance and missing important developments affecting real-world access. Indeed, as section 2 documents, the laws of politically conservative states are not always so different from those of more liberal states but are often presented as starkly so. Section 3 details the reasons the public should be skeptical about trusting popular media trackers, namely that different trackers sometimes code the same state differently, sometimes present conflicting information about a given state, and lack transparency in how they arrive at the top-line summary presented about abortion access. Section 4 shows that it is possible to demystify abortion laws so that people understand the law they live under. Only when misinformation is refuted and the mess of legislation that arose after *Dobbs* is untangled will real people be able to make sense of the law and decide how to proceed.

2. WHAT ABORTION LAW TRACKERS GET WRONG

Americans have been left to navigate a tangled mess of laws in every state that restricts access to abortion. On many subjects, Americans split along 'conservative' and 'progressive' lines, which largely tracks political parties, with

---

24 M. Cook Escobar et al., '171,000 Traveled for Abortions Last Year. See Where They Went', *New York Times*, 13 June 2024, https://www.nytimes.com/interactive/2024/06/13/us/abortion-state-laws-ban-travel.html. ('People in states where the procedure remained legal also traveled for abortions, sometimes because the closest clinic was across state lines or the influx of out-of-state patients made appointments scarce. The data shows that abortions rose in nearly every state where they remained legal.')

25 The *Abortion Exceptions and Misconceptions Initiative* is an effort to analyse and code the abortion laws of all 50 states, and to present those laws in ways that ordinary people can grasp.

Republicans pursuing more 'conservative' policies and Democrats pursuing more 'progressive' policies.[26]

Of course, one of the difficulties with polarisation in America is that it is assumed that parties cannot come together to protect the interests of all persons. The recent federal Respect for Marriage Act and state law unanimously banning gay and trans conversion therapy, passed by an overwhelmingly Republican legislature, suggests that Americans are not so deeply and fatally fractured.[27]

On abortion, it has been useful to separate states into those that heavily regulate access to abortion, shorthanding these as 'red' states, and those that have more permissive access to abortion, shorthanding these as 'blue'. In reality, states exist on a spectrum.

Among the 20 states (out of 34 'red' states) that the *Abortion Exceptions and Misconceptions Initiative* has analysed,[28] the body of law that regulates abortion access includes stacks of laws. At the low end, nine operative statutory provisions in Kansas restrict access by persons to abortion; at the top end, fifty-six provisions, in Mississippi, govern this intimate medical decision.[29] Figure 1 below provides details.

Trackers assign a single 'code' to these complex bodies of state abortion regulation, flattening and obscuring the complexity in important ways.

The whole point of trackers and maps is that the public benefits from the research of others who have more expertise and time to dig through facts. But trackers give top-line estimates of abortion 'access'[30] or 'restrictions',[31] without providing clear guidance about what people can do in their own states, as demonstrated in this section and section 3 below.

---

26 'Democratic Party', *Britannica*, 9 July 2024, https://perma.cc/692R-ZH6W; 'Republican Party', *Britannica*, https://perma.cc/U76S-9L2U, 9 July 2024.

27 The Respect for Marriage Act, HR 8404 (2022); Utah H.B. 228 (2023). For more on the Respect for Marriage Act, see R. Fretwell Wilson, T.C. Berg, C.H. Esbeck and D. Laycock, 'The Respect for Marriage Act: Living Together Despite our Deepest Differences' (2024) *University of Illinois Law Review* 511 (noting that protections for same-sex marriage and protections for people of faith who reject same-sex marriage made possible the most significant federal LGBT protection in the last 15 years).

28 The *Abortion Exceptions and Misconceptions Initiative* will, ultimately, code the laws of all 50 states. Appendix A breaks states into those that all trackers have identified as red (20), states that at least one tracker identifies as red (which, of course, describes the number of states that at least one tracker identifies as blue), and states that all trackers identify as blue (16). As section 2.2. notes, trackers label states as blue and red when some are not so different from one another.

29 In some cases, this will mean much of the law is governed by one statute; in others, there will be a range of statutes governing abortion regulation in the state.

30 'Interactive Map: US Abortion Policies and Access After *Roe*', *Guttmacher Institute* (hereinafter 'Guttmacher Interactive Map'), https://states.guttmacher.org/policies/illinois/abortion-policies. Guttmacher use the term 'access' to describe what their tracker shows.

31 D. Jefferies, J. Carman and N. Chiwaya, 'Abortion law tracker: See where the procedure is currently legal, banned or restricted in the U.S.', *NBC*, 26 June 2024, https://www.nbcnews.com/data-graphics/abortion-state-tracking-trigger-laws-bans-restrictions-rcna36199 (hereinafter 'NBC Tracker'). NBC use the term 'restriction' to describe what their tracker shows.

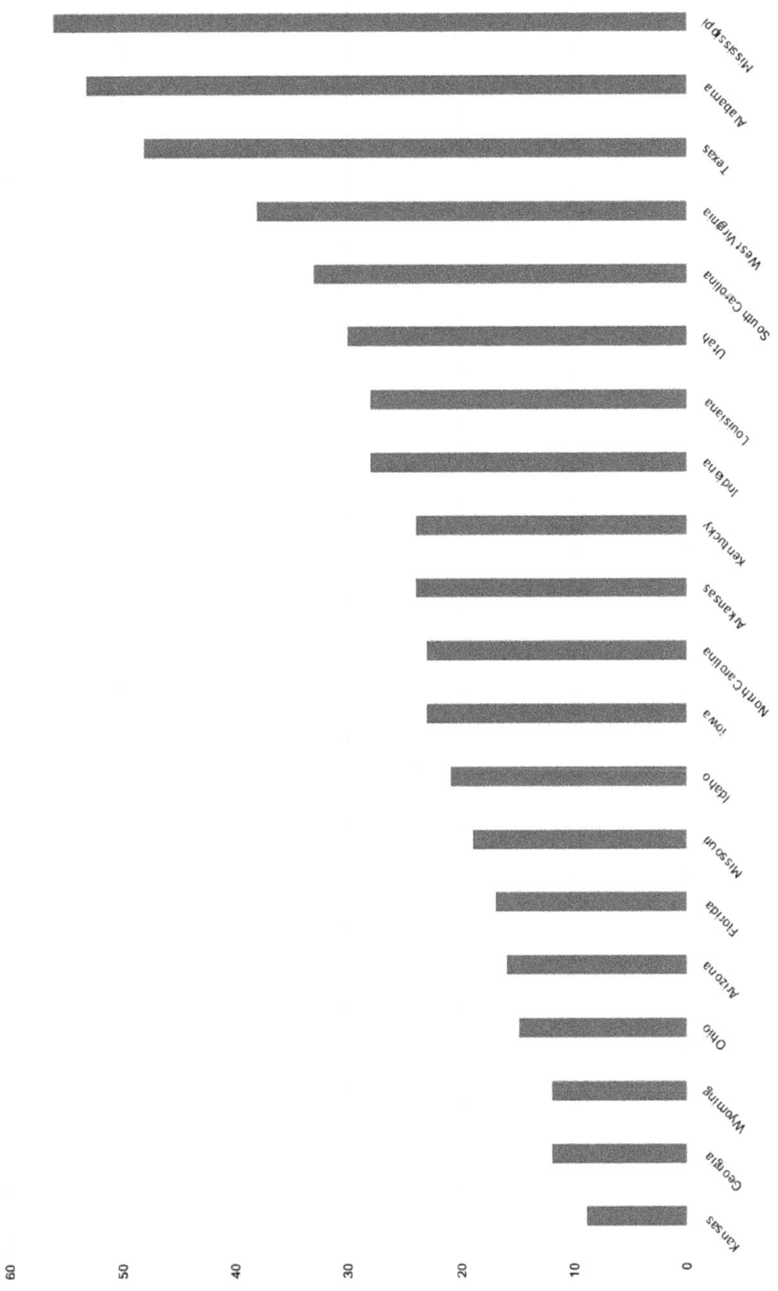

Figure 1. Operative Statutory Sections in Coded States

2.1. EXISTING TRACKERS OVERSIMPLIFY COMPLEX, LAYERED ABORTION RESTRICTIONS

Trackers take multiple – sometimes dozens – of laws in a given state and assign the state a single score. These trackers variously break states into three, four, five or even seven categories to capture the fact of abortion being legal, illegal or somewhere in between. For example, NBC categorise state abortion laws in all 50 states as 'legal and/or protective', 'restricted', or 'banned and/or unavailable'.[32] Guttmacher categorises states into seven categories, ranging from 'restrictive' to 'most protective'.[33]

A typical tracker looks like this:

Figure 2. Typical Abortion Tracker Example[34]

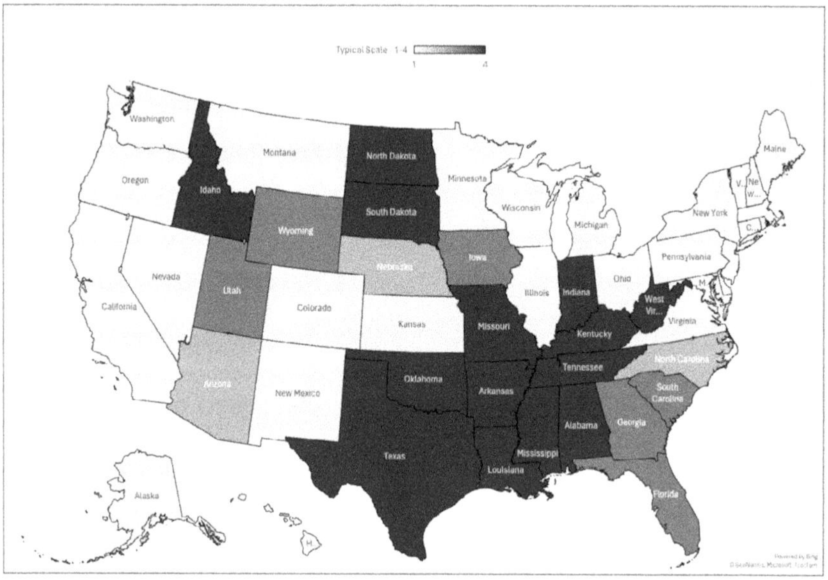

Some trackers, like the *Guardian*'s, give very limited detail about a given state, in a list that appears below the map provided. It describes, for example, abortion in North Carolina as 'banned after 12 weeks' and gives no further detail, such as exceptions available after the time-limited ban.[35]

32 Ibid.

33 Guttmacher Interactive Map, above n. 30, https://states.guttmacher.org/policies/.

34 This stylised tracker combines elements from the *Washington Post* and *Guardian* trackers.

35 C. Sherman and A. Witherspoon, 'Tracking abortion laws across the United States', *The Guardian*, 1 May 2024, https://perma.cc/6WW8-L45X (hereinafter 'Guardian Tracker'). North Carolina's four exceptions, a rape exception, life-of-mother exception, incest exception and foetal abnormality exception, are missing from the Guardian tracker. See NC Code §90–21.81b.

Some trackers are interactive and display additional detail when users hover over a given state, as Figure 3 below illustrates.

The trackers that the *Abortion Exceptions and Misconceptions Initiative* we reviewed present snapshots of state laws in different ways, as Table 1 below shows.

Figure 3. Interactive Tracker Example[36]

Table 1. Details of Popular Abortion Law Trackers

Abortion Law Tracker	Functions	'As of' Date? Reviewed 10 July 2024
The Center for Reproductive Rights https://reproductiverights.org/maps/abortion-laws-by-state/	CRR's abortion law tracker groups each state into one of five categories: expanded access, protected, not protected, hostile, and illegal. Viewers can click on each state for information about post-*Dobbs* abortion access in that state.	No date found.
CNN https://www.cnn.com/us/abortion-access-restrictions-bans-us-dg/index.html	CNN's abortion law tracker provides very little information. Viewers can hover over a state and, if abortion is banned, it will say it is banned 'either with or without exceptions'.	As of 28 June 2024.
The Guardian https://www.theguardian.com/us-news/ng-interactive/2023/nov/10/state-abortion-laws-us	The *Guardian*'s tracker allows viewers to scroll through states to see which states have abortion laws in flux and which have abortion banned or legalised.	As of 1 May 2024.
The Guttmacher Institute https://states.guttmacher.org/policies/minnesota/abortion-statistics	Guttmacher's tracker groups states into seven categories from most restrictive to most protective, based on abortion policies they have in effect. Guttmacher provide details about abortion policies, characteristics of state residents, and key abortion statistics for each state.	As of 3 July 2024.

(continued)

[36] This tracker draws the scale from the Guttmacher tracker and emulates the level of detail from the NBC tracker.

Table 1 *continued*

Abortion Law Tracker	Functions	'As of' Date? Reviewed 10 July 2024
Kaiser Family Foundation https://www.kff.org/womens-health-policy/dashboard/abortion-in-the-u-s-dashboard/	KFF's tracker provides a direct hyperlink to the abortion policy for each state. The site notates with a simple 'X' whether there are exceptions for life, health, rape/incest or a lethal foetal anomaly. The site also lists each state's medical standard regarding abortion.	As of 28 June 2024.
NBC https://www.nbcnews.com/data-graphics/abortion-state-tracking-trigger-laws-bans-restrictions-rcna36199	NBC's tracker tells users what exceptions exist, gestational limitations, whether there is a waiting period for abortions, whether there is mandatory counselling or an ultrasound, and whether minors require parental consent. The site includes a note section on pending legislation.	As of 3 July 2024.
New York Times https://www.nytimes.com/interactive/2024/us/abortion-laws-roe-v-wade.html	*NYT*'s tracker showcases a map distinguishing between states where abortion is legal or illegal. Further down the page, site viewers can access limited information pertaining to state-specific statutes, where the majority of states are labelled as 'abortion is banned in almost all circumstances.'	As of 1 July 2024.
Planned Parenthood https://www.plannedparenthoodaction.org/abortion-access-tool/US	Planned Parenthood's tracker sorts states by whether access to abortion is available, restricted or eliminated. Site viewers can click into a state-by-state guide, which provides limited information about abortions in each state.	No date found.
US News https://www.usnews.com/news/best-states/articles/a-guide-to-abortion-laws-by-state	*US News*' tracker allows viewers to ascertain little information about state-specific laws. For states with abortion restrictions, it merely labels them as 'restricted at viability' with no further detail.	As of 28 June 2024.
The *Washington Post* https://www.washingtonpost.com/politics/2022/06/24/abortion-state-laws-criminalization-roe/	The *Washington Post*'s tracker is unique, tracking bills that have been introduced or have passed one or both chambers, and bills that are in effect. The *Washington Post* does not track the abortion laws in every state. They do not provide any detailed information regarding why they chose which states they present.	As of 28 June 2024.

(continued)

Table 1 *continued*

Abortion Law Tracker	Functions	'As of' Date? Reviewed 10 July 2024
Word in Black https://wordinblack.com/2024/06/two-years-post-roe-abortion-access-patchwork-for-black-women/	This tracker combines data from the *Guardian*, Pew Research and Intersection of our Lives to analyse the impact of abortion regulations on black women and provide information on how women of colour view abortion and abortion rights.	As of 25 June 2024.

Some trackers place great emphasis on state regulations that are essentially nuisance restrictions, like making a woman have an ultrasound even if she does not have to look at it, which is the law in South Carolina.[37] Required ultrasounds are one variety of the 'onerous and irrelevant licensing requirements' known as TRAP (Targeted Regulation of Abortion Provider) laws, designed to 'shut … down clinics'.[38] Without minimising the fact that such requirements can raise the cost of procedures and erect barriers,[39] TRAP restrictions simply do not erect the kind of barrier that an absolute abortion ban does.[40] As section 3.2. below shows, trackers do not transparently explain the importance of TRAP regulations to how they 'code' states.

2.2. TRACKERS ARE WRONG ON (SOME) FACTS

The public place a lot of trust in the organisations that produce these trackers.[41] After all, they are produced by the *New York Times*, CNN, NBC and other

37 S.C. Code Ann. §44-41-330(A)(1)(d) (2023) ('The woman has a right to decline to view and hear the explanation of the live ultrasound images after she is informed of her right and offered an opportunity to view the images and hear the explanation.').

38 R. Benson Gold and E. Nash, 'TRAP Laws Gain Political Traction While Abortion Clinics – and the Women They Serve – Pay the Price' (25 June 2013) 16(2) *Guttmacher Policy Review*, https://perma.cc/NSY6-GPE5.

39 The classic indicia of a TRAP law is that it 'mandate[s] additional requirements not applied to other similarly situated health care practices': 'TRAP Laws – Abortion Facility Licensing Requirements', *LawAtlas*, https://perma.cc/GLP8-66AJ.

40 Put differently, after *Dobbs*, state lawmakers do not need stealth mechanisms to drive abortion providers out or to make abortion burdensome. Missouri and other states have absolute abortion bans. See SB 699, Abolition of Abortion in Missouri Act, https://perma.cc/L5CX-TP7Y.

41 The *Guardian*, *New York Times*, NBC, CNN and *Washington Post* all are among America's 'more trusted' news sources in 2024. See T. Orth and C. Bialik, 'Trust in Media 2024: Which news sources Americans trust – and which they think lean left or right', *YouGov.com*,

household names. But many trackers are flat wrong on the facts – or at least some of the facts. Many overlook key developments in the law impacting access or fail to flag open questions about enforcement of certain restrictions. Many parrot medical jargon from statutes without explaining when key junctures that restrict access are crossed, or fail to explain what key time frames are measured from (e.g. whether the 'number of weeks' in the statute refers to the number of weeks from the pregnant woman's last menstrual period (LMP) or from fertilisation), which can itself mislead the public.

2.2.1. *Trackers Ignore Entire Developments in the Law, Giving Misleading Information*

Trackers overlook key developments that drive whether abortion is allowed and under what circumstances. One need look no further than the NBC's, Center for Reproductive Rights', *New York Times*' and Guttmacher's confusing treatment of abortion access in Wisconsin to see this. Figures 4, 5, 6 and 7 below remake the snapshot of state abortion regulation presented by these trackers as of 8 July 2024.

Figure 4. NBC Abortion Restriction Tracker

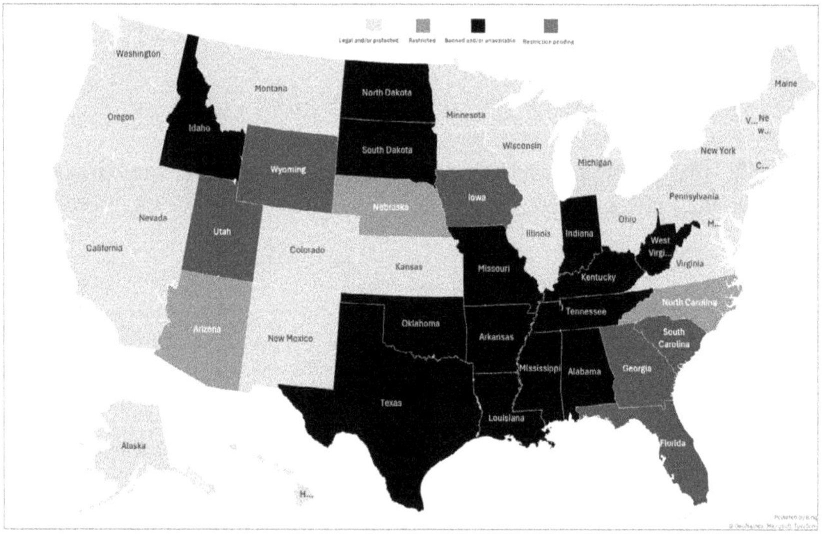

30 May 2024, https://perma.cc/38TH-E9N9. 62% of Americans trust Planned Parenthood: J. Norman, 'Sixty-Two Percent View Planned Parenthood Favorably', *Gallup*, 27 June 2018, https://perma.cc/4EUN-L847.

Figure 5. Center for Reproductive Rights Abortion Restriction Tracker

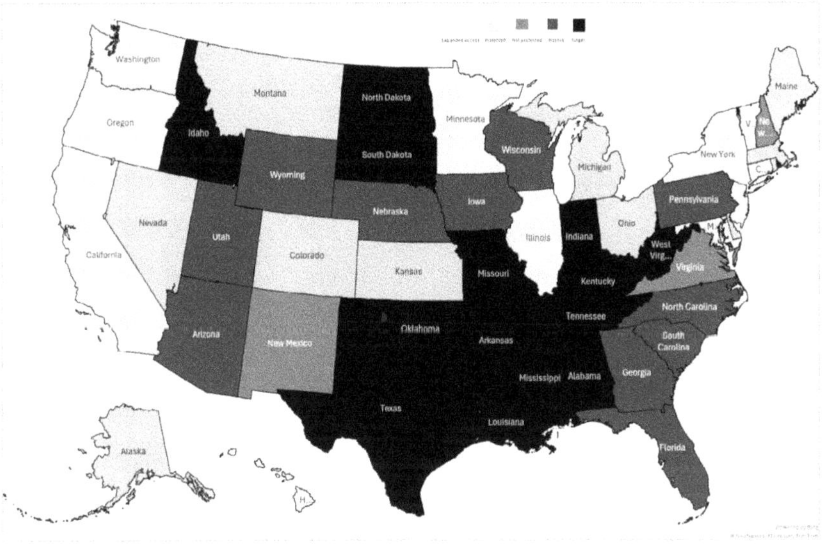

Figure 6. New York Times Abortion Restriction Tracker

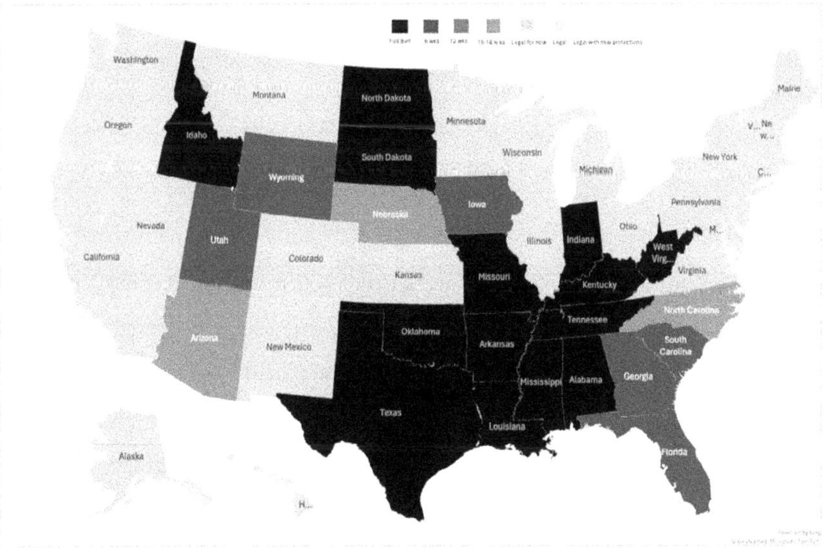

Figure 7. Guttmacher Institute Abortion Restriction Tracker

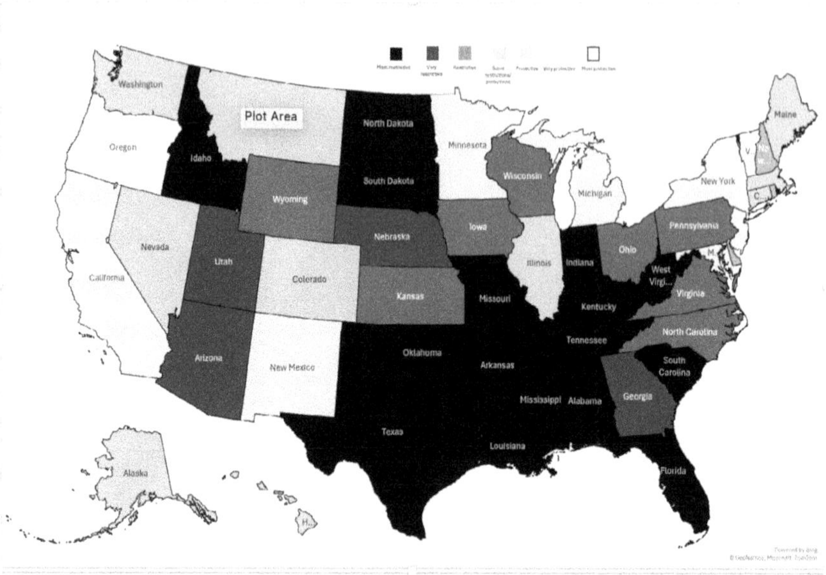

The top-line summary of Wisconsin across these four trackers is wildly different: NBC codes it as 'legal and/or protected', the Center for Reproductive Rights (CRR) labels it as 'hostile', the *New York Times* places it in the 'legal' category, and Guttmacher's tracker writes that abortion regulation in Wisconsin is 'restrictive'.

True, abortion regulation is complex in Wisconsin. The state has three abortion prohibition statutes:[42]

- Section 940.04, a statute that dates from 1849 and is read by some as erecting a complete abortion ban, a challenge to which is pending in Wisconsin state court.[43]
- Section 253.107, a 20-week post-fertilisation ban explained as preventing abortions from harming foetuses that can feel pain.[44]
- Section 940.15, which bans abortion after viability, as determined by a reasonable medical physician.[45]

---

42 M. Kelley, 'Key Abortion Restrictions in Wisconsin', *Wisconsin Legislative Council*, April 2024, https://perma.cc/7DX3-FKQY.

43 Wis. Stat. §940.04 (1849). Section (5) of the statute carves out an exception for 'therapeutic abortions', defined as those abortions 'performed by a physician', 'necessary, or ... advised by 2 other physicians as necessary, to save the life of the mother' and 'performed in a licensed maternity hospital ... [u]nless an emergency prevents'.

44 Wis. Stat. §253.107 (2015).

45 Wis. Stat. §940.15 (1985).

Much of the debate with regard to the 1849 statute is whether it even applies to abortion or instead governs the death of a foetus by means other than abortion. Section 940.04[46] says '[a]ny person, other than the mother, who intentionally destroys the life of an unborn child is guilty of a Class H felony',[47] and that any person, other than the mother, who '[i]ntentionally destroys the life of an unborn quick child' is 'guilty of a Class E felony'.[48] A Class H felony is punishable by up to six years' imprisonment and a fine of up to $10,000.[49] A Class E felony carries a maximum prison term of 15 years and/or a fine of up to $50,000.[50] This statute, which facially appears to encompass abortions done for reasons other than to save the life of the mother, was immediately assumed to be revived by *Dobbs*: Planned Parenthood ceased providing abortions in the state.[51]

On 28 June 2022, Wisconsin Attorney General Josh Kaul and the chair of the Wisconsin Medical Examiners Board, which regulates physicians, filed suit for declaratory relief against the leaders of the Wisconsin Legislature, asking that the trial court find section 940.04 unenforceable.[52] While the procedural history is complicated, with parties intervening on both sides, eventually Joel Urmanski, Dane County District Attorney Ismael R. Ozanne, and Milwaukee County District Attorney John T. Chisholm were substituted as defendants. Defendants argued that section 940.04 must prohibit abortion because two people were prosecuted using the statute in the 1960s. The trial court rejected that argument, instead relying on a 1994 Wisconsin Supreme Court opinion that said section 940.04(2)(a) 'is not an abortion statute' but rather a 'feticide statute only'.[53]

In that case, *State v. Black*, defendant Black was charged under section 940.04(2)(a) 'for destroying the life of his unborn quick child by violently assaulting his wife five days prior to her anticipated delivery date'.[54] The Wisconsin Supreme Court held that 'that the words of the statute could hardly be clearer. The statute plainly proscribes feticide.'[55] Black, however, argued that

---

46 B. Jordan, 'Sheboygan County D.A. says he'll prosecute providers accused of performing abortions in violation of state Law', *WTMJ-TV Milwaukee*, 28 June 2022, https://perma.cc/AF7E-6H3Z.

47 Wis. Stat. §940.04(1) (1849).

48 Wis. Stat. §940.04(2)(a) (1849).

49 Wis. Stat. §939.50 (2024).

50 Ibid.

51 S. Lehr and M. Faust, 'Abortions resume in Wisconsin after 15 months of legal uncertainty', *NPR*, 21 September 2023, https://perma.cc/MCJ4-FEEV.

52 *Kaul v. Urmanski*, No. 22 CV 1594, 2023 WL 11724618, at *10 (Wis. Cir. Ct. July 7, 2023).

53 Ibid. at *6 (citing *State v. Black*, 526 N.W.2d 132, 135 (Wis. 1994)) ('Black's holding that Subsection (2)(a) "is not an abortion statute" and "is a feticide statute only" must apply equally to Subsection (1).'); B. Jordan, above n. 46.

54 *State v. Black*, 526 N.W.2d 132, 133 (Wis. 1994).

55 Ibid.

'the statute was not intended to apply to feticide but to apply only in the context of consensual medical abortions', citing the statute's title, 'abortion', as evidence.[56] The court rejected that argument.[57] Further, the notion that section 940.04(2)(a) 'could be used against a woman or her physician' was 'unfounded'.[58] The court found that using section 940.04(2)(a) 'to charge for a consensual abortive type of procedure … would be inconsistent with the newer Section 940.15', which regulates abortions after viability.[59]

Importantly, the *Black* court observed that attempts to punish physicians for 'performing a consensual abortion prior to viability would be unconstitutional under *Roe v. Wade*'.[60] The fall of *Roe* has, however, thrown the reasoning of *Black* into question.

Wisconsin governor Tony Evers pledged to grant clemency to anyone prosecuted under the law.[61] However, Planned Parenthood did not resume abortions for over a year.[62]

Not everyone agrees, however, on how to read Wisconsin law. In an issue brief from April 2024 listing 'key abortion restrictions', the Wisconsin Legislative Council included section 940.04.[63] In the brief, the Legislative Council notes that section 940.04 is 'commonly referred to as the state's abortion prohibition or abortion ban'.[64]

Both Urmanski and Wisconsin Attorney General Kaul asked the Wisconsin Supreme Court to step in, which would bypass the appellate court.[65] On 2 July 2024, the Supreme Court of Wisconsin granted the bypass.[66] Briefs are due to the court near the end of the summer, with oral arguments to follow.[67]

---

56 Ibid., 134.
57 Ibid.
58 Ibid., 135.
59 Ibid.
60 Ibid.
61 A. Edelman, 'Wisconsin gov. vows to grant clemency to doctors charged under state abortion ban', *NBC News*, 27 June 2022, https://perma.cc/R3R2-4PVA.
62 H. Venhuezin, 'Planned Parenthood resumes offering abortions in Wisconsin after more than a year', *APNews.com*, 18 September 2023, https://perma.cc/9DQN-PH4L.
63 M. Kelley, above n. 42.
64 Ibid.
65 Brief for Petitioner-Appellant to Bypass, *Kaul v. Urmanski*, No. 22 CV 1594, 2023 WL 11724618 (Wis. Cir. Ct. July 7, 2023) (Appeal No: 2023AP002362), https://www.wispolitics.com/wp-content/uploads/2024/02/240220Bypass.pdf; Brief for Plaintiff-Respondent in Response to Petition to Bypass, *Kaul v. Urmanski*, No. 22 CV 1594, 2023 WL 11724618 (Wis. Cir. Ct. July 7, 2023) (Appeal No: 2023AP002362), https://www.doj.state.wi.us/sites/default/files/news-media/2.27.24_Plaintiffs-Respondents_Supplemental_Petition_in_Support_Request_to_Bypass_Court_of_Appeals_0.pdf.
66 Order Granting Defendant-Appellant's Petition to Bypass, *Kaul v. Urmanski*, No. 22 CV 1594, 2023 WL 11724618, (Wis. Cir. Ct. July 7, 2023), https://www.wicourts.gov/sc/order/DisplayDocImage.pdf?docId=822562.
67 *Kaul v. Urmanski*, Appeal Number 2023AP002362, Wis. Ct. Sys., https://perma.cc/GQ9X-V7CA.

Until the Wisconsin Supreme Court authoritatively decides, it is impossible to know whether section 940.04 does or does not reach abortion. Yet the trackers purport to know. The trackers are giving an answer when there is no answer – and in so doing they introduce all kinds of mistakes.

The Center for Reproductive Rights does state that the Wisconsin Attorney General is seeking a 'declaratory judgment that the 1849 pre-Roe criminal abortion ban is unenforceable', but gives no explanation of the potential ramifications if the Wisconsin Supreme Court concludes that the law in fact applies to abortion. If this were to happen, abortion services would likely cease in Wisconsin, as they did in 2022.[68]

As of this writing, on 9 July 2024, none of the trackers in Table 1 note that the Wisconsin Supreme Court has agreed to decide the case in an expedited manner. NBC codes abortion in Wisconsin as legal, as noted above, and makes no reference to the case beyond stating that 'Wisconsin has a near-total ban on abortion that dates back before Roe. The status of the law is unclear, and abortion care in the state was not available from mid-2022 to Sept. 2023.'[69] It would appear that NBC's basis for coding abortion in Wisconsin as legal is that abortions *are being performed.*

As mentioned above, Guttmacher label Wisconsin as restrictive, but they do not do so because of section 940.04. They report that 'abortion is banned at 22 weeks and after' and reference TRAP laws and funding restrictions as the justification.[70] In fact, as of 8 July 2024, Guttmacher make no reference to the case.

While the *New York Times* tracker mentions the case explicitly, it is neither up to date nor particularly informative.[71] The case, it says, 'may come before the State Supreme Court, which has a liberal majority'.[72] Still, it is baffling that the *New York Times* did not, at the very least, label Wisconsin 'legal for now', a category it uses for Montana, Wyoming and Iowa,[73] where appeals are pending, and no dispositive decisions of the state Supreme Courts have been issued.

---

68 S. Lehr and M. Faust, above n. 51.

69 NBC Tracker, above n. 31.

70 Guttmacher Interactive Map, above n. 30: Wisconsin, https://perma.cc/ND6D-QDMY ('Unnecessary regulations are in force and designed to shutter abortion clinics without basis in medical standards.').

71 A. McCann and A. Shoenfeld Walker, 'Tracking Abortion Bans Across the Country', *New York Times*, https://www.nytimes.com/interactive/2024/us/abortion-laws-roe-v-wade.html (hereinafter 'NY Times Tracker'); NBC Tracker, above n. 31. NBC says, '[a]bortion care has resumed in the state. Wisconsin has a near-total ban on abortion that dates back before Roe. The status of the law is unclear, and abortion care in the state was not available from mid-2022 to Sept. 2023', but does not reference the statute itself.

72 NY Times Tracker, above n. 71.

73 Ibid.

Providing wrong information can be worse than a simple omission. Consider the Kaiser Family Foundation (KFF)'s description of abortion access in Wisconsin:

> Current gestational limit is 22 weeks LMP [last menstrual period]. After the SCOTUS decision in Dobbs, the Wisconsin Attorney General challenged the state's pre-Roe ban, arguing it was not enforceable. In July 2023, a judge ruled that the 1849 law was not an abortion ban. The Attorney General had also previously stated that he would offer clemency to anyone prosecuted under the 1849 law. Planned Parenthood has announced it will start providing abortions in the state starting September 18, 2023.[74]

As section 2.2.3. documents, KFF's top-line summary of abortion limited at '22 weeks LMP' is wrong – Wisconsin's ban is keyed to fertilisation.[75] Far more concerning, however, is what KFF say about clemency for performing an illegal abortion. Media accounts report that Governor Evers – not Attorney General Kaul – offered clemency to prosecuted doctors.[76] In Wisconsin, 'pardon authority rests solely with the Governor',[77] so that if Attorney General Kaul in fact offered clemency, it would not matter. Clemency is not absolution. Planned Parenthood themselves appear not to have given great weight to the governor's June 2022 offer of clemency; they did not resume abortions until after trial court's decision, in September 2023.[78] Neither does clemency expunge a conviction from a person's criminal record.[79] State medical review boards can see a crime that has been pardoned[80] and may subject the doctor to professional sanction.[81] True, the Wisconsin medical board might choose not to sanction a physician pardoned by the governor, but any conviction

---

74 'Abortion in the United States Dashboard', *KFF.com*, https://perma.cc/T3ZA-UQYW (hereinafter 'KFF Tracker').

75 Wis. Stat. §253.107 (2015).

76 A. Edelman, above n. 61.

77 K. Bender-Olson, 'Pardons', *Wisconsin Legislative Council*, 6 June 2022, https://perma.cc/EV8Y-V2DF; A pardon is the most relevant form of clemency a doctor convicted under the 1849 statute would seek. Other forms of clemency only delay or reduce punishment, while pardons forgive offenders from legal consequences.

78 J. Harte, 'Planned Parenthood to resume abortions in Wisconsin for first time since 2022', *Reuters*, 14 September 2023, https://www.reuters.com/world/us/planned-parenthood-resume-abortions-wisconsin-first-time-since-2022-2023-09-14/.

79 K. Bender-Olson, above n. 77.

80 M. Koran, 'These Doctors Were Censured. Wisconsin Prisons Hired Them Anyway', *New York Times*, 2 July 2024, https://www.nytimes.com/2024/07/02/us/wisconsin-prison-doctor-health-care.html ('medical boards across the country have access to a federal databank of physicians' disciplinary histories').

81 K. Nelson, 'What Disciplinary Action Can Be Taken Against a Wisconsin Medical License?', *Gimbel, Reilly, Guerin, Brown*, LLP, 19 December 2019, https://perma.cc/MWK3-ZHND.

will follow a physician who relocates to another state[82] and applies for licensure.[83] Because clemency does not expunge the underlying crime, throwing out the notion of clemency without more is itself misleading.

The most generous account of KFF's discussion is that it is out of date. By its very text, the summary appears to have last been updated before 18 September 2023, the date that it gives for Planned Parenthood resuming abortions.[84] As Table 1 above notes, KFF's website elsewhere states that it is current as of 28 June 2024.

The *Guardian* comes closest of any tracker to accurately describing the situation in Wisconsin. They write: "Abortion in Wisconsin is disputed, an abortion ban from 1849 is still on the books, but a judge ruled in July 2023 that it does not apply to what she called 'consensual abortions.' Some abortion providers resumed performing the procedure in September 2023."[85]

While this describes the unclear nature of the current situation in abortion, it does not sufficiently flag that the Wisconsin Supreme Court has accepted review, meaning that an open legal question is pending, the result of which may be to have abortion once more become illegal instantaneously. If the court reaches that result, it means that abortion, other than to save the woman's life, was illegal all along.

True, trackers are inevitably a snapshot unless they are updated regularly. Even recognising that real-time updating is a substantial undertaking, this is a necessary part of providing information to the public.

2.2.2. *Trackers Introduce Errors by not Hewing to Actual Statutes and Medical Knowledge*

Existing trackers do not hew to terminology used in state laws. Instead, many present relevant time frames in weeks from the woman's LMP'.[86] If not done carefully, this can introduce errors.

For instance, when describing Virginia's abortion regulations, no tracker gives enough accurate information to be usable. Virginia law provides that termination of a pregnancy is lawful in the first and second trimesters. However, abortion is only allowed in the third trimester if the procedure is done in a registered

82 L. Bruse, 'How to get licensed in a new state: A physician's guide', *CompHealth Blog*, 4 April 2022, https://perma.cc/ZG3L-Q9P8.

83 Ibid. 'If you are interested in practicing in a new state ... you will most likely need to get licensed in that state.'

84 KFF Tracker, above n. 74.

85 Guardian Tracker, above n. 35.

86 Of the trackers, only those of the CRR and the *Washington Post* explain what LMP means or that most bans are measured from LMP.

hospital and two physicians certify that 'the continuation of the pregnancy is likely to result in the death of the woman or substantially and irremediably impair the mental or physical health of the woman', and, if evidence exists that the foetus is viable, life support must be utilised.[87]

Only the *Guardian*, Guttmacher, and *US News*[88] trackers explicitly state that the ban comes into force at the start of the third trimester. Nonetheless, these trackers never define trimester or explain when the trimester begins.

Worse, the Center for Reproductive Rights tracker incorrectly states that Virginia bans abortion after viability, despite citing the law where Virginia's time limit is set out.[89] NBC's tracker also identifies 'fetal viability' as the gestational limit on abortion but nowhere identifies the specific law or defines viability.[90]

The third trimester and viability are two different things. The American College of Obstetricians and Gynecologists specifies the third trimester as starting at 28 weeks.[91] By contrast, viability is a predictive judgment about when a foetus 'can survive outside the uterus'.[92] A recent *Journal of the American Medical Association* study examining survival rates for premature infants at 19 US university hospitals found a long-term survival rate of 30 per cent for those born at 22 weeks, 55 per cent at 23 weeks, 70 per cent at 24 weeks, 80 per cent at 25 weeks, and so on.[93] The World Health Organization (WHO) states that foetal viability is possible after 20 weeks of gestation (22 weeks past the LMP).[94] The world's most premature baby to survive was born at 21 weeks

---

87 Va. Code Ann. §§18.2-71, 18.2-74.

88 Guardian Tracker, above n. 35; 'Abortion Policies in Virginia', *Guttmacher*, https://states.guttmacher.org/policies/virginia/abortion-policies; Julia Haines, 'Where State Abortion Laws Stand Without *Roe*', *US News*, 28 June 2024, https://www.usnews.com/news/best-states/articles/a-guide-to-abortion-laws-by-state.

89 'After *Roe* Fell: Abortion Laws by State', *Center for Reproductive Rights*, https://perma.cc/9JCM-VT7G (hereinafter 'CRR Tracker').

90 NBC Tracker, above n. 31. As noted below, some states define viability in specific ways, although this nuance is overlooked by abortion law trackers. See 2.2.3.

91 'How Your Fetus Grows During Pregnancy', *ACOG.com*, January 2024, https://perma.cc/Y59A-ZW49.

92 Obstetricians distinguish between foetal viability and pregnancy viability. 'Foetal viability' refers to when the foetus has a detectable heartbeat: C. Pettker, et al., 'The Limits of Viability' (Sep. 2023) 143 *Obstetrics and Gynecology* 725. 'Pregnancy viability' indicates when a foetus can survive outside the uterus (ibid.). Legal restrictions around viability typically concern pregnancy viability: *Colautti v. Franklin*, 439 U.S. 379, 388 (1979).

93 E.F. Bell, et al., 'Mortality, In-Hospital Morbidity, Care Practices, and 2-Year Outcomes for Extremely Preterm Infants in the US, 2013–2018', 327 *JAMA* 1 (18 January 2022), https://perma.cc/9S5J-T2J9.

94 P. Lefèvre, et al., 'Forensic Anthropology and Childhood' in *Encyclopedia of Forensic and Legal Medicine* (2nd ed., 2016). Elsewhere, the WHO labels any child born before 28 weeks as 'extremely pre-term', with prematurity being 'the leading cause of death in children under the age of 5 years': 'Preterm Birth', *World Health Organization*, https://www.who.int/news-room/fact-sheets/detail/preterm-birth.

and 1 day.[95] Thus, Virginia's third trimester ban begins weeks *after* most foetuses are viable.[96]

2.2.3. Trackers Do not Explain when Key Junctures are Crossed

The public may be misled when a tracker accurately describes certain abortion restrictions but does not pinpoint when they occur. The two principal examples are restrictions that kick in either at 'viability' or with a 'foetal heartbeat'.

As noted earlier, viability may occur at different weeks, Laws pegged to viability requires the physician to make a prediction about whether a given foetus would be able survive outside the womb. This predictive judgement varies with the foetus' gestational age and development but also any relevant facts about the mother's pregnancy.[97] Trackers should explain this important context – they need a 'medical corner' or at the very least a link to WebMD.

Existing trackers, at best, make passing reference to viability and move on. CNN, NBC, the *New York Times*, KFF and the CRR nowhere explain that viability determinations may differ by weeks and are sensitive to the specific facts of a given pregnancy.[98] Neither do they explain how viability may be impacted by the degree of deference given to doctors under the legal standard in a given state, as discussed below. When 'viability' serves a gatekeeping function but is not *explained in terms people can grasp*, users cannot possibly know when abortion access is guaranteed and when it is not.[99]

---

95 A. Millward, 'World's most premature baby defies sub-1% survival odds to break record', *Guinness World Records*, 10 November 2021, https://perma.cc/UB7L-N8Q4.

96 The Virginia statute recognises that viability is different in the third trimester – by discussing what must occur if a foetus is 'viable' in the third trimester.

97 'Facts Are Important: Understanding and Navigating Viability', *ACOG.com*, January 2024, https://perma.cc/Z4P4-AAZU. Access to abortion might also depend on which physician is making the prediction, the capacities of the facility to support premature life, and the risk tolerance of the providers.

98 A. Choi and D. Cole, 'See where abortions are banned and legal – and where it's still in limbo', *CNN.com*, 28 June 2024, https://perma.cc/3LHD-3UH6; NBC Tracker, above n. 31; NY Times Tracker, above n. 71; KFF Tracker, above n. 74; 'CRR Tracker', above n. 89.

99 Of course, the predictive nature of viability may have a chilling effect, with providers unwilling to risk sanction for a decision at the leading edge of viability. As technology advances, and the time frame at which a foetus becomes viable increasingly moves forward, access to abortion will become more restricted; put differently, the exact time frame when a foetus becomes viable will depend on the state of medical science when a given woman seeks an abortion. As a result, the week range is susceptible to changes in medical knowledge, technology and techniques. In 1973, *Roe* pegged viability at 28 weeks (*Roe v. Wade*, above n. 1, 160): 'Viability is usually placed at about seven months (28 weeks) but may occur earlier, even at 24 weeks.' By 1992, *Planned Parenthood v. Casey*, above n. 2, described viability as feasibly spanning from 21 to 24 weeks ('The joint opinion agrees with Roe's conclusion that viability occurs at 23 or 24 weeks at the earliest.'). The fact that viability rests on a prediction of the future rather than a present, ascertainable fact may chill provider willingness to perform perfectly legal abortions.

The *Guardian* and Guttmacher do signal that foetuses may be viable at different weeks but suggest that viability occurs within a smaller window: 'around 24 weeks' and 'generally 24–26' weeks, respectively.[100] Contrast the WHO, who place viability as early as 20 weeks post-fertilisation: roughly 22 weeks from the last menstrual cycle, as this section explains below.[101] Women who rely on the trackers' suggesting that viability may occur in a later window may be shocked to learn that they can no longer secure an abortion if their foetus is determined to be viable *before* 24 weeks.

Simply listing viability as a key juncture also misses the considerable variation between states. The CRR's tracker is typical: it notes restrictions tied to viability but does not reference the definition used in a state's statute.

Some states defer to physicians on viability determinations, while others include rules about recording facts in the medical record. For example, in Utah a single physician, in their clinical judgement, determines whether 'there is a realistic possibility of maintaining and nourishing a life outside of the womb, with or without temporary, artificial life-sustaining support' – a determination that may consider 'medical technology and information reasonably available', as well as the particular facts of a woman's pregnancy.[102] In Kentucky, the foetus must 'reasonably be expected to have reached viability'.[103] In Kansas, physicians must 'us[e] and exercise[e] that degree of care, skill and proficiency commonly exercised by the ordinary skillful, careful and prudent physician in the same or similar circumstances' and 'shall enter such findings and determinations of viability in the medical record of the woman'.[104] If the physician determines that the foetus' gestational age 'is 22 or more weeks' but it is not viable, they have to report 'the medical basis and the reasons for such determinations in writing to the medical care facility in which the abortion is performed for inclusion in the report of the medical care facility' to Kansas' secretary of health and environment.[105]

In some states, access is tied to phenomena that may occur across a range of weeks, like foetal heartbeat or cardiac activity. Foetal heartbeat differs from viability in the sense that it does not call on physicians to make a prediction;

100 Guardian Tracker, above n. 35; 'Illinois', Guttmacher Interactive Map, above n. 30, https://states.guttmacher.org/policies/illinois/abortion-policies.

101 P. Lefèvre, et al., above n. 94. As studies like that from *JAMA* emerge, finding that one in three foetuses at 22 weeks are viable, it will become increasingly hard to shrink viability to stretch abortion access.

102 Utah Code Ann. §76-7-310.5. Similarly, Illinois states that '"[f]etal viability" means that, in the professional judgment of the attending health care professional, based on the particular facts of the case, there is a significant likelihood of a fetus' sustained survival outside the uterus without the application of extraordinary medical measures' (775 Ill. Comp. Stat. §55/1-10).

103 Ky. Rev. Stat. §311.780.

104 Kan. Stat. Ann. §§2 (c) 2 and (c) 3, https://perma.cc/QE2X-HHKA.

105 Ibid.

yet it, too, may be found across a set of weeks. In the early weeks of pregnancy, the rhythmic beating of what will develop into a foetus' heart can be picked up on a vaginal ultrasound.[106] Medical authorities report that cardiac activity *can* register around week five, and that a pulse is usually identifiable by the end of the seventh week,[107] but a 'heartbeat' is increasingly likely to be picked up on the ultrasound as the pregnancy approaches week ten, when the actual heart develops.[108]

The trackers do not convey the fact that access depends on a phenomenon that varies from person to person. Consider Idaho's foetal heartbeat statute,[109] which stacks on top of the state's total ban, presently the subject of challenge by the Biden Administration under EMTALA.[110] Only the CRR tracker refers to the heartbeat restriction. However, CRR incorrectly shorthands it as a six-week ban from LMP.[111]

This 'translation' into different terms risks two kinds of mistakes, both of which can have disastrous consequences for women who rely on what they have read. A woman five weeks pregnant with a foetus that has a detectable heartbeat may rely on the incorrect information presented in CRR's tracker and find herself unable to access abortion in her state. Conversely, a woman seven weeks pregnant may believe she cannot secure an abortion in her state, whereas access in fact depends on whether or not a heartbeat can be detected.

Relatedly, trackers do not even explain from when they are measuring in determining the gestational age of the foetus. The standard practice for measuring a pregnancy is to measure from the pregnant woman's LMP.[112] States typically define gestation as 'the development of a human embryo or fetus as calculated from the first day of the pregnant woman's last menstrual period'.[113] This happens of necessity because it is difficult to accurately state when an egg has been fertilised (sperm can survive in the female reproductive tract for up to five days).[114]

---

106 A. Smith Haghighi, 'When does a fetus have a heartbeat?', *Medical News Today*, 29 January 2024, https://www.medicalnewstoday.com/articles/when-does-a-fetus-have-a-heartbeat#timeline.

107 J.D. Jacobson, 'Prenatal care in your first trimester', *MedlinePlus*, 4 April 2022, https://perma.cc/28Z4-YKMJ.

108 A. Smith Haghighi, above n. 106.

109 Idaho Code §18-8804.

110 Ibid. 18-622. Melissa Quinn, 'Supreme Court says emergency abortions can be performed in Idaho'. CBSNews. Jun27, 2024, https://www.cbsnews.com/news/supreme-court-idaho-abortion-ban-emtala/.

111 CRR Tracker, above n. 98.

112 'Committee Opinion No 700: Methods for Estimating the Due Date', 129(5) *Obstetrics and Gynecology* e150 (2017), https://pubmed.ncbi.nlm.nih.gov/28426621/; 'Calculating a Due Date', *Johns Hopkins Medicine* (2024), https://perma.cc/3RPK-8TVF.

113 Fla. Stat. §390.011.

114 P.C. Gargollo, 'How long do sperm live after ejaculation?', *Mayo Clinic*, 5 May 2022, https://perma.cc/V2Y5-UTH6.

People are sometimes baffled to learn that key restrictions are measured from LMP rather than conception. Fertilisation generally takes place in a window between days 11 and 21 of the woman's menstrual cycle.[115] A woman who is researching access to abortion in her state may naturally assume that a regulation that does not specify what it is measuring from is, in fact, measured from conception not LMP. The difference between the two can be several weeks, leading users to believe they have *more* access than allowed under state law.

Trackers often say nothing about these medical facts. For example, Guttmacher simply state that Florida bans abortion 'at 6 weeks and later',[116] without explaining that the six weeks are *not* measured from conception but rather from the first day of the pregnant woman's LMP.[117] Only the CRR and *Washington Post* say that bans are measured from 'LMP', and explain what this means below their maps, although in the case of the CRR this information cannot be found on the state-specific pages.[118]

This lack of clarity matters in states like Wisconsin, where some restrictions are measured *from fertilisation*, not the LMP. One Wisconsin statute bans abortions if the 'probable postfertilization age of the unborn child is 20 or more weeks'.[119] 'Probable postfertilization age' is defined as the 'number of weeks that have elapsed from the probable time of fertilization of a woman's ovum'.[120] As noted above, a statute commonly referred to as Wisconsin's absolute abortion ban will soon be interpreted by the Wisconsin Supreme Court.[121] Assuming that the court decides that the absolute abortion ban is not operative, it becomes even more critical to accurately describe Wisconsin's 20-week post-fertilisation ban. That later postfertilsation ban would then be the law Wisconsinites live under.

Measuring from *probable fertilisation* has proven difficult for the trackers to explain. Guttmacher simply add two weeks to the 20-week fertilisation requirement and state that Wisconsin bans abortion at '22 weeks and later'.[122] The *Washington Post*, *New York Times* and *US News* also do not state what

[115] J. Leonard, 'What days can you get pregnant, and are most fertile?', *Medical News Today*, 21 June 2024, https://perma.cc/HL8H-QKM7.

[116] 'Florida', Guttmacher Interactive Map, above n. 30, https://states.guttmacher.org/policies/florida/abortion-policies.

[117] Fla. Stat. §390.011 (7).

[118] CRR Tracker, above n. 98; C. Kitchener, et al., 'States where abortion is legal, banned or under threat', *Washington Post*, 28 June 2024, https://perma.cc/G7M6-DNL8 (hereinafter 'Washington Post Tracker').

[119] Wis. Stat. §253.107.

[120] Ibid.

[121] J. Kelly, 'Wisconsin Supreme Court seems poised to decide if abortion is protected by the state constitution', *19th News Organization*, 26 June 2024, https://perma.cc/EDR3-DB98.

[122] Wisconsin, Guttmacher Interactive Map, above n. 30, https://states.guttmacher.org/policies/wisconsin/abortion-policies.

they are measuring from when they describe abortions as being banned after 22 weeks.[123] The KFF incorrectly state that Wisconsin's restriction runs from the LMP.[124] The statute does not set out how the physician should determine the foetus' probable post-fertilisation age, but adding two weeks onto the woman's LMP ignores the myriad other ways of estimating foetal age.[125] Perhaps most stunningly, the NBC tracker does not just flatten the nuance of the statute; it gets the statute wrong. NBC codes Wisconsin as allowing abortion up to '22 weeks post-fertilization', despite the statute preventing abortions after 20 weeks post-fertilization.[126] Only the CRR correctly state that 'Wisconsin law generally prohibits abortion at twenty weeks post-fertilization', albeit only on their state-specific page.[127] On the interactive map, the CRR describe the ban as a 22-week LMP gestational ban.[128]

2.2.4. *Blue is not so Different from Red but is Presented as Sharply Distinct*

More puzzlingly, trackers treat states with similar regulations as materially different in terms of access to abortion. Yet red and blue state regulations bleed together far more than these trackers would lead users to believe.

---

123 Washington Post Tracker, above n. 118; NY Times Tracker, above n. 71; J. Haines, above n. 88, https://www.usnews.com/news/best-states/articles/a-guide-to-abortion-laws-by-state.

124 KFF Tracker, above n. 74.

125 K. Naidu and K.L. Fredlund, 'Gestational Age Assessment', *StatPearls*, 24 July 2023, https://perma.cc/22E4-YBV5.

126 Wis. Stat. §253.107 (c) ('"Probable postfertilization age of the unborn child" means the number of weeks that have elapsed from the probable time of fertilization of a woman's ovum.').

127 'Wisconsin', *CRR Tracker*, above n. 98, https://perma.cc/W9US-Y7LK.

128 'Wisconsin', *CRR Tracker* map, above n. 98, https://perma.cc/2L4P-BUJA. States sometimes use medical terms in ways that depart from medically accepted understandings. This idiosyncratic use must be translated into whatever time frames state lawmakers have established so that the public can understand. A concrete example illustrates the risk of misinforming the public. In Florida, special rules apply to abortions in the 'third trimester', specifically that physicians 'must exercise the same degree of professional skill, care, and diligence to preserve the life and health of the fetus which the physician would be required to exercise in order to preserve the life and health of a fetus intended to be born and not aborted' (Fla. Stat. §390.0111 (4) (2024), https://perma.cc/79UG-VPVR. The section goes on to explain that, in a conflict between the life of the foetus and the life of the mother, 'the physician must consider preserving the woman's life and health the overriding and superior concern'. Florida's law defines this stage of pregnancy in an idiosyncratic manner, as beginning with the 24th week. By contrast, ACOG place the third trimester at 28 weeks and 0 days to 40 weeks and 6 days (see 'How Your Fetus Grows During Pregnancy', above n. 91). While definitions that depart from accepted medical definitions do not *inherently* create legal uncertainty, they can mislead the public about when access to abortion is available, when it is not, and what rules will apply. By not clarifying how Florida defines 'trimester', the trackers risk leading users to believe that key restrictions apply at the 24th week, not the 28th.

Illinois and Virginia illustrate this point. Guttmacher label Virginia's abortion policies as '3: restrictive' on their seven-category scale (1: most restrictive, 7: most protective), citing Virginia's prohibition on using Medicaid funding and its parental consent and parental notice rules. But the top-line feature of Virginia law noted by Guttmacher is that '[a]bortion is banned starting at the third trimester'.[129] Medical authorities agree that the third trimester begins in week 28.[130]

In Illinois, abortion is restricted at viability unless necessary to protect the life or health of the patient.[131] As noted earlier, viability involves a predictive judgement about foetal survival.[132] This Some fetuses might be viable at 22 weeks, others at 23, 24 or 25 weeks, or even later.[133] However viability is benchmarked, Illinois' post-viability abortion ban falls weeks earlier than Virginia's third trimester, 28-week ban. Nonetheless, Illinois garners a protective rating (5) from Guttmacher.

This slant is not confined to a single tracker. Indeed, every tracker shows abortion in Illinois as legal.[134] Contrast Virginia, where the trackers come to wildly different judgements on access to abortion, ranging from 'legal' to 'hostile' or 'restrictive'.[135]

3. CAN THE PUBLIC TRUST THE TRACKERS?

The public rely on abortion law trackers to give accurate information about the laws in their state. As this section shows, the trackers often do not agree on a single set of facts, causing confusion. They present conflicting information as to the same state, do not explain how they arrive at their top-line summaries of abortion access or lack thereof, and present information in terms that suggest bias; some trackers present so much information that a user cannot know what the law is.

---

129 Guttmacher's state summary notes that Virginia allows '[q]ualified health care professionals, not solely physicians, [to] provide abortions', expanding access: 'Virginia', Guttmacher Interactive Map, above n. 30, https://perma.cc/U7NY-C4NS.

130 'Week-by-week guide to pregnancy', *NHS* (2024), https://perma.cc/XD9A-BCKE.

131 755 Ill. Comp. Stat. 55/1-25(a) (2023) ('If the health care professional determines that there is fetal viability, the health care professional may provide abortion care only if, in the professional judgment of the health care professional, the abortion is necessary to protect the life or health of the patient.').

132 C. Pettker, et al., above n. 92.

133 E.F. Bell, et al., above n. 93.

134 See Appendix A.

135 A. Choi and D. Cole, above n. 98; 'Virginia', CRR Tracker, above n. 98, https://perma.cc/25J8-9KRX; 'Virginia', Guttmacher Interactive Map, above n. 129.

3.1. TRACKERS PRESENT CONFLICTING INFORMATION, SEEDING CONFUSION

Trackers spark confusion in two ways: they conflict with each other and do not always present internally consistent information. First, trackers do not agree on the 'coding' of states, seeding confusion. Of course, each tracker-maker is free to emphasise what they consider important. But trackers giving different appraisals of abortion access in the same state impede the public's understanding of the law they live under. For example, mismatching appraisals occur with Kansas and its abortion ban at 22 weeks.[136] NBC place Kansas in the 'legal and/or protected' category, while Guttmacher place it among the 'restrictive' states.[137] A comparison of the 'coding' across the eight trackers contained in Appendix A shows different appraisals of access in 14 states: Arizona, Iowa, Kansas, Ohio, Wisconsin, New Mexico, Virginia, Wyoming, Pennsylvania, Rhode Island, Montana, Nevada, New Hampshire and Delaware. Some trackers label abortion in these states as restricted while others label it as legal/protected or in flux.

Some trackers, confusingly, present conflicting information about laws in a single state. For example, Figure 8 below shows how the *Washington Post* reports on South Carolina's laws:

Figure 8. Washington Post Tracker's Report of South Carolina Laws

South Carolina	'Ban on all or most abortions.'	'The all-male South Carolina Supreme Court upheld a ban on abortion after about six weeks of pregnancy Prohibited after: 22 weeks Except for: Life endangerment, Medical emergencies, Lethal fetal anomaly.'

The *Washington Post* tracker accurately notes that a six-week ban is operative, but in bold it says abortion is '[p]rohibited after 22 weeks … Except for: Life endangerment, medical emergencies, Lethal fetal anomaly.' Readers can

136 Kan. Stat. Ann. §65-6723 (f).

137 A 15-week ban is more liberal than what many European countries allow. See, e.g. Germany: 12 weeks (with counselling) ('*Self-management of medical abortion via telemedicine in Germany*', *WHO*, 6 March 2023, https://perma.cc/QDJ9-4J4Y); Spain: 12 weeks (up to 22 in cases of severe foetal abnormalities) ('Abortion rights in Spain over the past decades', *Reuters*, 9 February 2023, https://www.reuters.com/world/europe/abortion-rights-spain-over-past-decades-2023-02-09/); and Italy: 12.8 weeks (90 days), longer if there are severe foetal abnormalities (K. Fox and V. Di Donato, 'Abortion is a right in Italy. For many women, getting one is nearly impossible', *CNN* (2019), https://perma.cc/VF5B-8QPZ). Nonetheless, Europe is generally perceived as more accommodating of abortion than red states are: P. Smith, 'Not just Texas: Europe grapples with abortion laws and limits', *NBC News*, 16 September 2021, https://www.nbcnews.com/news/world/not-just-texas-europe-grapples-abortion-laws-limits-n1279324.

'read more' but hit a paywall at that point. Because the *Washington Post* gives conflicting time limits on the readable page, it would be shocking if the *Washington Post*'s presentation did not mislead some people.

These conflicts extend to exceptions to abortion bans. Consider Ohio's protection for children afflicted with Down syndrome. Section 2919.101 of the Ohio Revised Code requires a physician to certify that they are not performing an abortion because the foetus has or is believed to have Down syndrome. A perfectly legal abortion on a foetus before 20 weeks post-fertilisation[138] becomes illegal if done because the foetus may have Down syndrome. Nearly all trackers omit this important reason-based limitation on abortion.[139]

Planned Parenthood, NBC, the *New York Times*, KFF, CNN, *US News*, the *Guardian* and the *Washington Post* all make no mention of this reason-based ban. Only CRR explicitly says that 'Ohio prohibits abortions sought because of Down syndrome'.[140]

3.2. TRACKERS LACK TRANSPARENCY IN HOW THEY CODE STATES

Abortion law trackers make a second error that compounds inaccuracy about the general availability of abortion. They give accurate information about restrictions on abortion like a minor's need to notify a parent or secure parental consent. But it is impossible to judge *how* the trackers weighed the various considerations in generating a composite label as restrictive or protective.

To see this lack of transparency, consider the treatment by trackers of parental consent laws.

Virginia prevents abortion after the third trimester, 28 weeks,[141] while Illinois prevents abortion after viability,[142] as early as week 21 and up to week 24.[143] These states differ on parental consent: Virginia requires parental consent for a minor's abortion; Illinois does not.[144] The two states differ on funding: in Virginia

---

138 Ohio Rev. Code Ann. §2919.201. Ohio also has a six-week ban on the books, Ohio Rev. Code Ann. §2919.195(A), but this is currently blocked by a preliminary injunction: 'Ohio Lower Court Blocks Six-Week Abortion Ban, Restoring Reproductive Rights Across State', *ACLU*, 18 September 2022, https://perma.cc/9WZV-CMJD.

139 M. Spindelman, 'On the Constitutionality of Ohio's "Down Syndrome Abortion Ban"' (2018) 79 *Ohio State Law Journal Furthermore* 19, https://ssrn.com/abstract=4486239.

140 'Ohio', CRR Tracker, above n. 98, https://reproductiverights.org/maps/state/ohio/.

141 Va. Code Ann. §§18.2-72 (2024).

142 775 Ill. Comp. Stat. 55/1-25, https://ilga.gov/legislation/ilcs/fulltext.asp?DocName=077500550K1-25.

143 P. Lefèvre, et al., above n. 94.

144 'Parental Involvement in Minors' Abortions', *Guttmacher Institute*, 1 September 2023, https://perma.cc/QU4H-X9RF.

public funding is generally not available for abortions; in Illinois it is. But in both states, Guttmacher note, abortion can be done by someone other than a doctor.[145] Even though Virginia allows abortion for what may be a month longer than Illinois, Guttmacher label Illinois as protective and Virginia as restrictive.

Parental consent laws do not follow a red/blue political map. South Dakota and West Virginia, both led by Republican-dominated legislatures[146] and Republican governors,[147] do not require parental consent. This fact might surprise many people.[148] Thoroughly blue Massachusetts and Rhode Island, led by Democrat governors[149] and overwhelmingly Democrat legislatures,[150] do require parental consent for a minor's abortion.[151]

Massachusetts receives the designation 'protective' and Rhode Island 'some restrictions/protections' from Guttmacher, even though both states require parental consent.[152] Presumably these states receive these access designations because they allow free access to abortion up to 24 weeks and 24 to 26 weeks, respectively.[153] But Virginia does, too. The difference in minors' access to abortion in Massachusetts and Rhode Island, while reported by Guttmacher, does not seem to drive Guttmacher's coding.[154] But one plausible explanatory difference in the treatment of Massachusetts, Rhode Island and Virginia is which political party occupies the governor's mansion or controls the legislature.[155]

---

145 Qualified health care professionals, and not solely physicians, can provide abortions. See, e.g. A.M. Ollstein and M. Messerly, 'Blue states expand who can provide abortions as they brace for a flood of patients', *Politico*, 17 May 2022, https://www.politico.com/news/2022/05/17/states-expand-abortions-flood-of-patients-00032815.

146 South Dakota Legislature, https://perma.cc/AAH3-JHEG; West Virginia Legislature, https://perma.cc/6WCK-25WV.

147 South Dakota Governor, https://governor.sd.gov/governor/about.aspx; West Virginia Governor, https://perma.cc/2VFR-G6AQ

148 West Virginia does require notice to be given to the parent or guardian (W. Va. Code §16-2F-3), as does South Dakota (S.D. Codified Laws §34-23A-7).

149 Massachusetts Governor, https://www.mass.gov/person/maura-healey-governor; Rhode Island Governor, https://perma.cc/7BXL-2XLA.

150 Gov't of Mass., 'Composition of the Commonwealth of Massachusetts State House of Representatives', https://www.mass.gov/doc/composition-of-the-commonwealth-of-massachusetts-state-house-of-representatives/download; 'Rhode Island General Assembly', *Ballotpedia*, July 2024, https://ballotpedia.org/Rhode_Island_General_Assembly.

151 Mass. Gen. Laws, ch. 112 §12R (2022); R.I. Gen. Laws §23-4.7-6.

152 Massachusetts, Guttmacher Interactive Map, above n. 30, https://states.guttmacher.org/policies/massachusetts/abortion-policies.

153 Mass. Gen. Laws ch. 112, §12M; R.I. Gen. Laws §23-4.13-2(d).

154 True, Rhode Island and Massachusetts have 'shield laws' that give some security to providers when performing abortions for out-of-state women. It is plausible that parental consent requirements are simply reported but not weighted or are weighted less heavily than general time limits. On Guttmacher's seven-category scale, Vermont and Oregon alone are treated as 'most protective'.

155 Massachusetts Governor Maura Healey is a Democrat: 'Governor Maura Healy and Lt. Governor Kim Driscoll', https://www.mass.gov/orgs/governor-maura-healey-and-lt-governor-kim-driscoll#:~:text=Governor Kim Driscoll,-Maura Healeyandtext=Since taking office%2C Governor Healey,family%2C worker%2C and business. The governor of Rhode Island, Dan

The trackers may implicitly be making predictions about enforcement of laws about abortion that are on the books. In other words, their implicit judgement may be that a doctor in Virginia might find themselves facing prosecution whereas one in Rhode Island or Massachusetts would not. As the example of Wisconsin shows, it only takes a single prosecutor to upend this assumption.

3.3. TRACKERS GIVE USERS REASON TO DISTRUST THEM

Some trackers seem biased. One tracker – that of the CRR – describes restrictions in certain states as 'hostile', a term that does not strike one as objective.

Trackers sometimes disclose that they are guided less by the contours of actual laws than by appraisals of a state's political climate. Guttmacher's methodology explanation says: 'We recognize that any type of restriction may be the one that prevents an individual from accessing an abortion; our map aims to take into account a state's entire policy environment.'[156]

Trackers editorialise. For example, the *Washington Post* gratuitously observes that '[t]he all-male South Carolina Supreme Court upheld a ban on abortion after about six weeks of pregnancy', but notes that the case deciding the ambit of Wisconsin's 1849 ban 'may come before the State Supreme Court, which has a liberal majority'.[157] Of course, statutory interpretation cases are guided by doctrines for reading statutes. And cases granting rights have sometimes been penned by 'conservative' justices, as the Title VII decision *Bostock v. Clayton County* (interpreting sex discrimination to encompass sexual orientation and gender identity discrimination), authored by Justice Neil Gorsuch, shows.[158]

Examples abound. The CRR uses the word 'hostile' to describe abortion laws that erect roadblocks short of an outright ban, like TRAP laws. They describe one TRAP law as requiring '[b]iased counseling', and describe changes to abortion care made during the COVID-19 pandemic as the lawmakers '"exploiting" the pandemic'.[159] Spending words on these observations suggest that the tracker's purpose is not solely to provide information to the public.

McKee, is a Democrat: 'Governor Dan McKee', https://perma.cc/7D2P-DTA9. The governor of Virginia, Glenn Youngkin, is a Republican: 'Governor of Virginia: Glenn Youngkin', https://www.governor.virginia.gov/about/. Massachusetts' state legislature is majority Democrat. Rhode Island's state legislature is majority Democrat. Virginia's state legislature is majority Democrat.

156 'Methodology and Sources', Guttmacher Interactive Map, above n. 30, https://states.guttmacher.org/policies/methodology.html.

157 Washington Post Tracker, above n. 118.

158 *Bostock v. Clayton County*, 590 U.S. 644 (2020), interpreting Title VII of the Civil Rights Act of 1964.

159 Some states required disclosures to women seeking abortions about depression, suicide and even breast cancer risks that have been linked to abortion. See A.L. Schlafly, 'Legal Implications of a Link Between Abortion and Breast Cancer' (2005) 10 *Journal of American*

3.4. SOME TRACKERS PRESENT TOO MUCH INFORMATION

Trackers err in the other direction, too, giving so much information that an ordinary reader cannot possibly glean what is important, and what is not, to the question of access.

Consider the CRR's tracker. It lists every conceivable kind of abortion restriction, including 'pre-*Roe* ban', 'COVID abortion ban', 'mandatory ultrasound requirement', 'biased counseling requirement', and numerous others.[160] For each state, the tracker presents every category with a simple tick or cross next to the category to indicate its relevance to a state.

By throwing an amalgamation of rules at users, trackers deprive users of the ability to understand how elements of the law actually work together in a given state. This granularity simply overwhelms the public, who need a clear, straightforward presentation of facts. As this section shows, the presentation of state abortion laws by popular trackers, and how often these trackers are wrong or slanted, mean that the public lack an objective presentation of data that might guide decisions by actual people. Trackers should help people seeking to understand the law. This is an eminently doable project, as the next section shows.

4. DEMYSTIFYING LAWS

To be sure, the project of making state abortion restrictions comprehensible to ordinary people is a hard one. Three aspects, noted throughout this chapter, make it especially thorny. First, a stack of laws govern access in any particular state. Second, the laws rely heavily on opaque medical terms. And third, laws sometimes use medical terminology in idiosyncratic ways. Unless unpacked, all of this materially impacts on people's understanding of the actual access abortion in a given state.

Yet it is possible to demystify the laws people live under by breaking down each statute and showing how each stacks and interacts with the others. The *Abortion Exceptions and Misconceptions Initiative* deconstructs the complexity of these laws without omitting important features. This initiative is most

Physicians and Surgeons 11, https://www.jpands.org/vol10no1/aschlafly.pdf. The bases for these kinds of disclosures are very much disputed. See, e.g. 'Abortion and Breast Cancer Risk', *American Cancer Society*, 7 June 2024, https://perma.cc/ZNG6-FU9K.

160 Pre-*Roe* ban; telemedicine ban; trigger ban; gestational ban: 6-week LMP, 22-week LMP, viability, total ban; COVID abortion ban; method ban; Texas SB 8 copycat ban; mandatory ultrasound requirement; biased counseling requirement; waiting period requirement; TRAP requirements: facilities, facility requirements; TRAP requirements: providers, reporting requirement, admitting privilege requirement; parental involvement; parental notification and consent requirement.

distinctive in explaining the impact for real people of inadvertent or deliberate violations of abortion laws.

4.1. UNTANGLING A TANGLED MESS

An obvious organising device for the many laws affecting abortion access in a given state is to array restrictions on a single 40-week timeline, which mimics a full-term pregnancy.[161] Figure 9 below presents a stylised timeline that can be used to organise state laws, allowing visual comparisons between states of the density of their laws, their application to particular parts of the pregnancy, whether laws are presently being challenged, and so forth.

Figure 9. Stylised Timeline to Organize State Laws

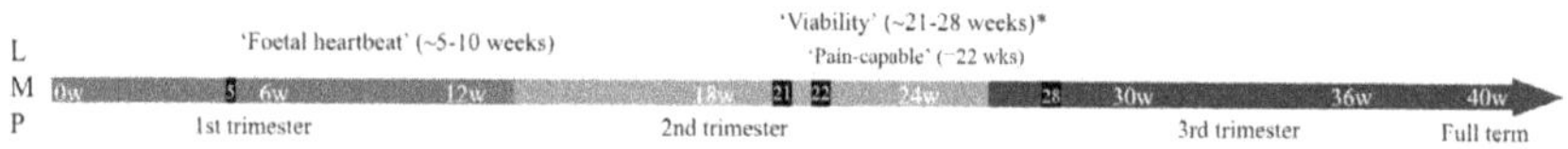

This effort not only drills down on what the actual abortion regulations in the states are, but diagrams the complexity to help people grasp the laws they live under.

Medical jargon scattered across statutes need not be confusing. Demystifying this requires nothing more than sound science connecting specific junctures – viability, presence of foetal heartbeat – to specific weeks in the 40-week timeline. As noted earlier, a foetus may be found to be viable between 21 and 28 weeks. The foetal heartbeat can be detected as early as five weeks.

Thus, Figure 9 includes the key junctures at which states limit access but places these in a medical context. Terms are placed in the context of a typical pregnancy and medical understandings about these phenomena, such as viability (21–28 weeks); foetal heartbeat (around 5–10 weeks); first, second and third

---

[161] Measured from conception to birth, a pregnancy lasts about 40 weeks. See, e.g. 'You and your baby at 40 weeks pregnant', *NHS* (13 October 2021), https://perma.cc/M5RW-HJEZ (reporting that full-term pregnancies can range from 37 to 42 weeks). As noted above, medical authorities measure gestation from a pregnant woman's last menstrual period (LMP): G. Kumar and B. Kumar, 'Embryogenesis and physiology 1' in *Early Pregnancy Issues for the MRCOG and Beyond* (CUP, 2014) ('The average duration of pregnancy is 266 days (38 weeks) after ovulation or 280 days (40 weeks) after the first day of the last menstrual period (LMP). This equates to a period of just over 9 calendar months. Traditionally, the age of a pregnancy has been calculated from the first day of the LMP, but it is easy to appreciate that this cannot be the same as the age of the embryo or the fetus, as conception does not occur until after ovulation has taken place: about 14 days after the LMP.').

trimesters; and LMP.[162] Other key points that figure prominently in statutes, such as 'pain capable', are presented at the time frame prescribed in the statute: 22 weeks.

The *raison d'etre* of the *Abortion Exceptions and Misconceptions Initiative* is to present simple facts, not to push laws in one direction or another. This is not to say that policy implications do not jump out. On the contrary, placing the abortion laws of the 50 states on the same visual depiction allows users to see the key differences.

4.2. UNPACK STACKED LAWS TO EXPLAIN ACCESS

Access to abortion is the sum of overlapping laws, which sometimes establish multiple time limits *and* exceptions. Florida's still-changing abortion law illustrates this point. As Figure 10 below shows, Florida's six-week abortion ban is presently operative, although Floridians will consider a constitutional amendment to expand access in November 2024.[163]

---

162 States also key limitations to contested medical phenomena, limiting the time frame when an abortion may be legally obtained. This is true of abortion restrictions that reference 'pain-capable unborn children'. See Kan. Stat. Ann. §65-6723. Kansas's legislature defined foetal pain as occurring at 22 weeks LMP. The concept of 'foetal pain' is contested: some authorities deny it exists. See S.W.G. Derbyshire, 'Can fetuses feel pain?' (2006) 332 *BMJ* 912, https://doi.org/10.1136/bmj.332.7546.909 ('Avoiding a discussion of fetal pain with women requesting abortions is not misguided paternalism but a sound policy based on good evidence that fetuses cannot experience pain.'). Others say that, while foetal pain is not necessarily pain as we experience it, it is morally significant: S.W.G. Derbyshire and J.C. Bockmann, 'Reconsidering fetal pain' (2020) 46 *Journal of Medial Ethics* 3, https://jme.bmj.com/content/46/1/3#ref-42 ('The precise nature of fetal pain experience remains unknown and will, perhaps, remain forever unknowable.'). Some see foetal pain as a political term or tool: A. Vania Apkarian, 'Nociception, Pain, Consciousness, and Society: A Plea for Constrained Use of Pain-related Terminologies' (2018) 19 *Journal of Pain* 1253, 1255 ('The larger issue regards our community's responsibilities in clarifying such concepts. By carelessly mixing neural nociceptive mechanisms underlying pain with pain itself, we are actively propagating misnomers that can be abused for political interests, like the senselessly titled Pain-Capable Unborn Child Protection Act (the unconscious fetus is neither pain-capable nor a child).'). Unlike viability, states define exactly when this phenomenon is supposed to occur: 22 weeks: W. Va. Code §16-2M-2 (7) (2015) ('"Pain capable gestational age" means twenty-two weeks since the first day of the woman's last menstrual period.'); Ky. Rev. Stat. §65-6723 ('"Pain-capable unborn child" means an unborn child having reached the gestational age of 22 weeks or more.'). An effort at the federal level to regulate abortions of 'the pain capable unborn child' would have regulated abortions at 20 weeks. It has never secured enough votes to get cloture in the Senate: E. O'Keefe, 'Abortion ban bill fails to advance in the Senate', *Washington Post*, 29 January 2018, https://perma.cc/9KNT-C8MA. The trackers do not even reference 'foetal pain'. Instead, they describe these regulations as 22-week LMP bans. See, e.g. 'West Virginia', CRR Tracker, https://perma.cc/RUN9-YQPB and 'Kentucky', CRR Tracker, above n. 98, https://perma.cc/G9QZ-YKJS.

163 *Planned Parenthood of Southwest and Central Florida v. Florida*, SC2022-1050 (Fla. 4/01/24), https://perma.cc/3J7P-WJVA.

Figure 10. Abortion Laws in Florida

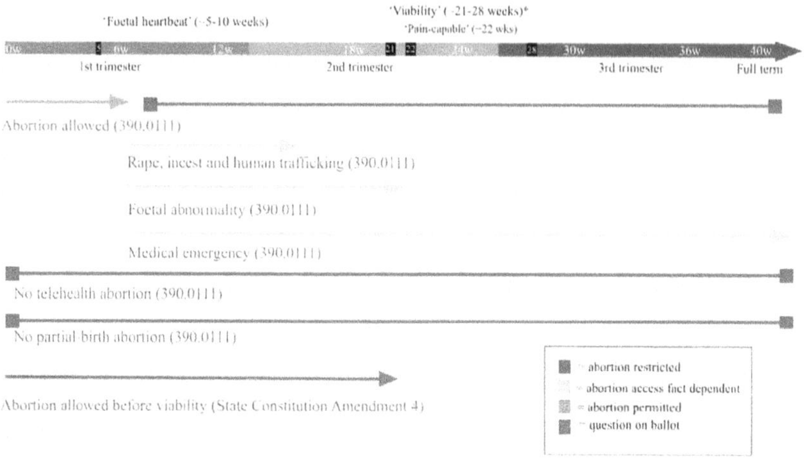

Abortion options in Florida are very constrained under Florida Statutes, section 390.0111.[164] Abortion is freely available until six weeks of 'gestational age',[165] defined as six weeks past a woman's LMP.[166] Exceptions extend this time frame to 15 weeks in cases of rape, incest or human trafficking.[167] In instances of foetal abnormality, abortions are available until viability, which is not specified at a specific week.[168] Abortions are permitted across the pregnancy for medical emergencies where abortion is necessary to save the life of the mother or to 'avert a serious risk of imminent substantial and irreversible physical impairment of a major bodily function'.[169]

Telehealth abortions and partial-birth abortions are not allowed at any time during the pregnancy.[170] The Florida Supreme Court recently upheld section 390.0111 against constitutional challenge.[171]

---

164 Fla. Stat. Ann. §390.0111 (2023).

165 Ibid.

166 Fla. Stat. Ann. §390.011(12)(c) (2023); Fla. Stat. Ann. §390.0111 (2023).

167 Fla. Stat. Ann. §390.0111 (2023).

168 Fla. Stat. Ann. §390.0111(1)(c) (2023) (applying to a pregnancy that 'has not progressed to the third trimester and [where] two physicians certify in writing that, in reasonable medical judgment, the fetus has a fatal fetal abnormality').

169 Fla. Stat. Ann. §390.0111(1)(b) (2023).

170 Fla. Stat. Ann. §390.0111 (2023).

171 *Planned Parenthood v. Fla.*, 384 So.3d 67 (Fla. 2024).

Importantly, if the people of Florida approve State Constitution Amendment 4, abortion will be permitted before viability.[172]

4.3. UNDERSTANDING THE LAW REQUIRES A HANDLE ON TIME LIMITS, EXCEPTIONS AND OTHER REGULATIONS

Abortion laws not only vary significantly between states but can also vary significantly within a single state, meaning that some abortion laws are cabined by exceptions while others are not.

Exceptions sometimes enlarge access but may not necessarily do so, as shown here. Other regulations, like TRAP rules, can add to the regulatory burden, even if they do not block access per se, as discussed in section 4.5. below.

A review of abortion statutes in Utah and South Carolina underscores how differently exceptions can operate. Both states have stacking abortion restrictions, shown in Figures 11 and 12 below. In South Carolina, the operative statutes are:

1. §44-41-630, which establishes the requirement for performing an ultrasound and detecting a foetal heartbeat before an abortion, with a general prohibition if a heartbeat is detected.
2. §44-41-640, which allows an abortion in medical emergencies or to prevent death or serious bodily harm to the pregnant woman.
3. §44-41-650, which allows abortions up to 12 weeks' gestation in cases of rape or incest.
4. §44-41-660, which permits abortions in cases of fatal foetal anomalies.

Arraying these and their respective time limits on a single diagram, Figure 11, illustrates that South Carolina's exceptions meaningfully enlarge access. They take the possible time for an in-state abortion from 6 weeks to 12 in cases of incest and rape, and to the entirety of the pregnancy in cases of foetal anomaly, medical emergency, when continuing the pregnancy threatens the mother's life or risks serious bodily injury to her, and even when conditions occur that are presumed to carry significant risk. These statutes are not enjoined.

172 *Advisory Opinion to the Attorney General re: Limiting Government Interference with Abortion*, 384 So.3d 122 (Fla. 2024).

Figure 11. Abortion Laws in South Carolina

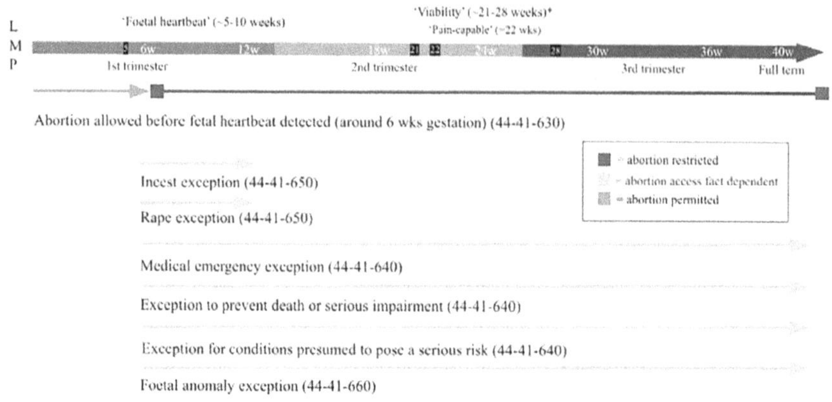

In Utah, a pair of statutes regulate abortion, with one enjoined, shown on the left of Figure 12, and one operative, shown on the right. On the left, section 76-7a-201, presently enjoined,[173] prohibits all abortions, without concessions for early abortion. It makes exceptions for medical emergencies, foetal anomalies incompatible with life, and pregnancies resulting from rape or incest, which, if met, extend access to abortion until 18 weeks. Its belt-and-suspenders companion,[174] section 76-7-302, shown on the right, makes abortion freely accessible until 18 weeks' gestation, with exceptions that operate for 18 weeks, for medical emergencies, foetal anomalies incompatible with life, and pregnancies resulting from rape or incest.

Instantly, one sees from Figure 12 that Utah's exceptions to its operative ban – at 18 weeks – do not extend access to abortion beyond what is already given.

4.4. PRESENT THE DETAILS OF EXCEPTIONS BECAUSE THEY MATTER

Not all exceptions are equally onerous, although trackers only record the fact of exceptions. Utah, South Carolina and Mississippi laws illustrate nicely that not

---

173 This statute is presently enjoined, and the challenge to it is awaiting a decision by the Utah Supreme Court, which held oral arguments in August 2023: *Planned Parenthood Ass'n of Utah v. State*, No. 220903886, 2022 WL 2314556 (Utah Dist. Ct. June 27, 2022), https://perma.cc/CMK5-W4PT.

174 See E.J. Leib and J.J. Brudney, 'The Belt-and-Suspenders Canon' (2020) 105 *Iowa Law Review* 735, https://perma.cc/C9DX-F5P7 (presenting reasons why risk-adverse lawmakers might choose to draft without perfect parsimony, doubling up protections).

Figure 12. Abortion Laws in Utah

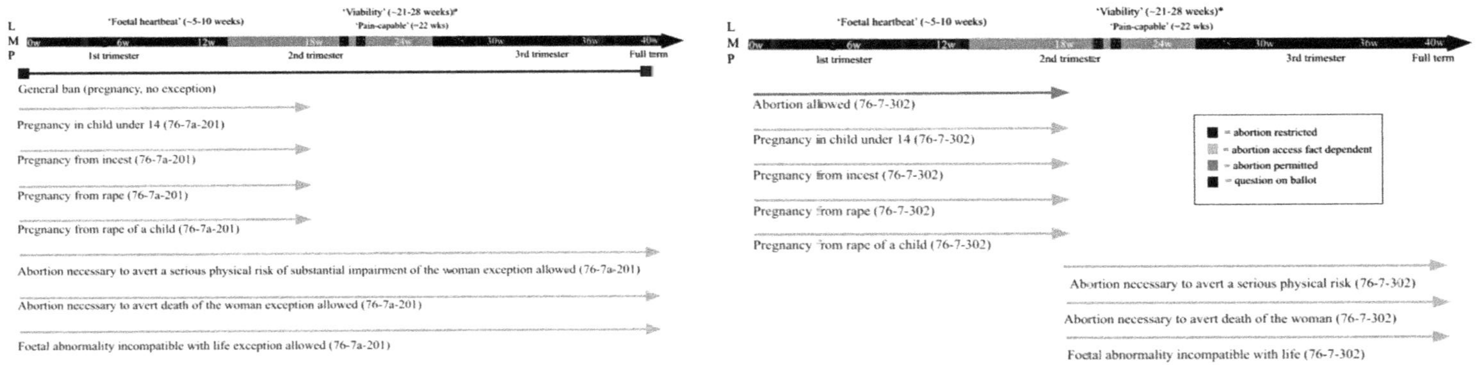

all exceptions are equally demanding to make out – meaning that some states erect bigger roadblocks to access than others.

The rape and incest exceptions in South Carolina are both more restrictive and more generous than Utah's. In Utah, rape and incest can provide access under the presently enjoined statute, up to the eighteenth week.[175] For a woman to receive an abortion under the rape or incest exception, the physician who performs that abortion must verify that the 'incident described has been reported to law enforcement'.[176] South Carolina extends access in such instances up to 12 weeks' gestation, making such access more restricted, but requires only that the woman report the fact of a rape to the provider, who must then report it to the local sheriff within 24 hours, with the woman's contact information.[177] In South Carolina, falsely filing a police report is an offence,[178] but reporting a rape to an abortion provider is not subjected to this 'check' on veracity.

At the other end of spectrum, Mississippi requires a 'formal charge of rape [to have] been filed with an appropriate law enforcement official' in order for the exception to apply.[179] But Mississippi also removes the criminal sanction for illegal abortion – which can be punished by imprisonment 'for not less than one (1) year nor more than ten (10) years' – 'where the pregnancy was caused by rape'.[180] Other state statutes contain the ability to prosecute women obtaining an illegal abortion, as the next subsection shows.

It is clear that the rape exception in Utah differs significantly from that in Mississippi, which in turn differs from South Carolina, yet the trackers do

175 Utah Code Ann. §76-7a-201(1)(c) (West 2024) ('the unborn child has not reached 18 weeks gestational age and: (i)(A) the woman is pregnant as a result of: (I) rape, as described in Section 76-5-402; (II) rape of a child, as described in Section 76-5-402.1; or (III) incest, as described in Subsection 76-5-406(2)(j) or Section 76-7-102').

176 Utah Code Ann. §76-7a-201(1)(c)(ii)(A) (West 2024) ('before the abortion is performed, the physician who performs the abortion: (A) for an abortion authorized under Subsection (1)(c)(i)(A), verifies that the incident described in Subsection (1)(c)(i)(A) has been reported to law enforcement').

177 S.C. Code Ann. §44-41-650(B) (2023), https://perma.cc/6K9J-JZ2K ('A physician who performs or induces an abortion on a pregnant woman based on an exception contained in this section must report the allegation of rape or incest to the sheriff in the county in which the abortion was performed. The report must be made no later than twenty-four hours after performing or inducing the abortion, may be made orally or otherwise, and shall include the name and contact information of the pregnant woman making the allegation.').

178 S.C. Code Ann. §16-17-722 (2023). Individuals who falsely report a felony are guilty of a felony, and those who falsely report a misdemeanour are guilty of a misdemeanour.

179 Miss. Rev. Stat. §41-41-45 (2, 3) ('(2) No abortion shall be performed or induced in the State of Mississippi, except in the case where necessary for the preservation of the mother's life or where the pregnancy was caused by rape. (3) For the purposes of this section, rape shall be an exception to the prohibition for an abortion only if a formal charge of rape has been filed with an appropriate law enforcement official.").

180 Miss. Rev. Stat. §41-41-45 (4).

not acknowledge this. For South Carolina, the CRR, CNN, *New York Times*, KFF and *US News* do not reference any exceptions. Planned Parenthood, the *Guardian* and the *Washington Post* state that exceptions exist but give very little detail. Only NBC states that there are exceptions 'up to 12 weeks for rape and incest', yet even this does not provide the important detail that the exception can be accessed simply by informing the provider, without having to file a police report.

Differences similarly exist among states that allow abortion for foetal abnormality, too. In South Carolina, fatal foetal abnormalities must be determined to be fatal 'according to standard medical practice'.[181] In Utah, abortion is permitted when the foetus has an 'abnormality incompatible with life' if 'two physicians who practice maternal fetal medicine concur'.[182]

The 'medical emergencies' exception is identical in both states.[183]

4.5. DIFFICULTY-OF-ACCESS SCALES

As noted earlier, access is the sum total of time-limited bans, exceptions and other regulations that can burden women and providers. The *Abortion Conceptions and Misconceptions Initiative* has developed scales that show that not all burdens are equally onerous. These scales, applied to the law in a given state, also show that the whole picture of access varies dramatically between states.

States differ in the harshness of their abortion regulation along eight different dimensions:

- Hard time limits to access abortion without qualifying for an exception.
- The severity of punishment.

181 S.C. Code Ann. §44-41-610(5) (2023) ('"Fatal fetal anomaly" means that, in reasonable medical judgment, the unborn child has a profound and irremediable congenital or chromosomal anomaly that, with or without the provision of life-preserving treatment, would be incompatible with sustaining life after birth.'); S.C. Code Ann. §44-41-660(A) (2023) ('It is not a violation of Section 44-41-630 if an abortion is performed or induced on a pregnant woman due to the existence of a fatal fetal anomaly. Section 44-41-630 does not apply to a physician who performs or induces an abortion if the physician or person determines according to standard medical practice that there exists a fatal fetal anomaly.").

182 Utah Code Ann. §76-7a-201(1)(b) (2024) ('two physicians who practice maternal fetal medicine concur, in writing, in the patient's medical record that the fetus has a fetal abnormality that in the physicians' reasonable medical judgment is incompatible with life').

183 In Utah, it is met when 'the abortion is necessary to avert: the death of the woman on whom the abortion is performed; or a serious physical risk of substantial impairment of a major bodily function of the woman on whom the abortion is performed'(Utah Code Ann. §76-7a-201(1)(a) (West 2024)); South Carolina also allows abortion 'if an abortion is performed or induced on a pregnant woman due to a medical emergency or is performed to

- Burdens associated with obtaining abortions.
- What is required to satisfy the exceptions for:
  - rape;
  - incest;
  - foetal anomaly;
  - mental health of the mother; and
  - life and (sometimes) health of the mother.

Like the trackers do, it is important to begin with the hard time limits. The hard time-limits scale places states on a continuum from no time-based limit on abortion[184] to a total ban.[185] This scale, shown in Figure 13 below, allows individuals to visualise at a glance how restrictive state laws are when no exception to the time limit is available. The intervals for each scale have been created with reference to the states coded so far and may change as additional detail from states emerges.

The severity-of-punishment scale shown in Figure 14 below presents what no other tracker does: the penalty incurred if a specific state restriction is breached. The penalties on the scale run the gamut from civil sanctions, like an award of attorney's fees in a private lawsuit, through to criminal sanctions for the death of 'mother or child'. Often neglected, this aspect is vitally important to fully understand the law people live under, as the next subsection explains in detail.

As is shown in Figure 15 below, the third scale, 'burdens to access', includes some restrictions found in existing trackers but also others that are not. At the low end, this scale considers nuisance TRAP restrictions, for example requirements to take ultrasounds or requiring follow-up visits; and things like bans on advertising, preventing advertising of 'advice direction, information, or knowledge … for the purpose of causing or procuring the miscarriage of any woman pregnant with child', as in Florida.[186] Higher on the scale are reason-based limits to abortion (e.g. if it is discovered the foetus has Down syndrome),[187] since these materially impact on access (although nearly every tracker makes no mention of these). Appearing at the top end of the scale are prohibitions on certain types of procedures, like partial-birth abortion and, of course, a total ban on all abortion.[188]

prevent the death of the pregnant woman or to prevent the serious risk of a substantial and irreversible impairment of a major bodily function, not including psychological or emotional conditions, of the pregnant woman' (S.C. Code Ann. §44-41-640(A) (2023)).

184 18 Vt. Stat. Ann. §9497 (2023).

185 Ala. Code §26-23H-4 (2024).

186 Fla. Stat. §797.02 (2023).

187 Ohio Rev. Code Ann. §2919.10 (2024).

188 Mo. Rev. Stat. Chapter 188 – Regulation of Abortions, https://perma.cc/4SJG-KN4J.

Figure 13. Hard Time Limits Severity Scale

Hard Time Limits

1	No Limit	
2	Third trimester (measured by medical authorities as 28 Weeks)	
3	24 Weeks	
4	22 weeks (This is labelled as pain capable)	
5	Viability * *This can be as early as 20 weeks but is a medical judgment	
6	20 weeks	
7	18 weeks	
8	15 weeks	
9	13 weeks	
10	12 weeks	
11	6 weeks after last menstrual period	
12	Foetal heartbeat/ cardiac activity	
13	Moment of conception/ absolute ban	

Figure 14. Criminal Action Severity Scale

Criminal Action

1	Low-level criminal liability (misdemeanour or less)	
2	Crime where penalty isn't specified	
3	Threat to livelihood (medical licence)	
4	High-level criminal liability (felony)	
5	The statute makes you guilty of the death of the mother or the child	

Figure 15. Civil Action Severity Scale

Civil Action

1	Low-level civil liability/sanctions (ex. civil contempt)	
2	Attorney's fees awarded in civil actions	
3	Injunction	
4	Civil suits by private citizens (caps at $10k+ attorney fees)	
5	Civil malpractice	
6	Civil suits for wrongful death	
7	Civil money penalties	
8	Punitive damages	
9	High-level civil liability/sanctions	

Figure 16. Burdens to Access Severity Scale

Burdens to Access

1	Very low burden (ex. taking ultrasounds or sonograms, can't advertise/coerce abortions, limits where abortions can be performed and who can perform them, women's welfare needs to be considered, medical disclosures, follow-up visits/counseling, notifying woman about information located on a website *see Arkansas*)	
2	Consent, waiting periods	
3	Physician action is required (ex. certifying informed consent, medical record retention is longer than usual, disclosing info to health dept. or AG)	
4	Reporting the abortion to the medical board or state	
5	Prohibited reasons for abortion (down-syndrome, sex-based, race-based)	
6	Limits/prohibits insurance/public funding for abortions or requires doctor to have a certain amount covered by their insurance to perform an abortion	
7	Parental permission or leave of court needed for minors to access abortion	
8	Ban on taking minors out of state	
9	Medical hurdles (ex. ban on a particular procedure, life of child preserved at all cost, ban beyond stated fetal age)	
10	No rape exception, no incest exception	
11	No health of the mother exception	
12	General/total ban	

The *Abortion Exceptions and Misconceptions Initiative* uncovers the deep variability between states in the *exceptions* to their hard time-limited bans. When trackers state that a rape exception exists and give no more information, they tell only part of the story. The purpose of the exception scales is to reveal that apparently identical exceptions are, in fact, not alike.

First, consider rape, shown in Figure 17 below. The scale below runs from a requirement to state that the pregnancy was caused by rape; to the more onerous requirement that the rape has to be reported to the Department of Health; to duties on the doctor to notify police; to the pregnant woman having to present documents, including a police report, to be preserved in her medical records, in order to receive an abortion; to confirmation by two doctors of a rape; to hard time limits on the exception, such as unavailability after 18 weeks or 15 weeks; and, finally, unavailability after the first trimester.

Figure 17. Rape Exception Severity Scale

Difficulty of Qualifying for
Rape Exception

1	Pregnancy is caused by rape	
2	Reporting to Department of Health number of abortions performed for rape	
3	Doctor needs to notify police	
4	Copy of police reports and other documents that show proof of rape preserving the documents in the medical records	
5	Need confirmation from two doctors	
6	Cannot be obtained after 18 weeks	
7	Cannot be obtained after 15 weeks	
8	Cannot be obtained after the First Trimester	
9	No exception available	

Similarly, exceptions for risk to the life of the mother vary significantly. The range within each category of exception makes clear the need for greater explanation than is given by any of the current public trackers. Importantly, some states have no rape or incest exceptions at all.[189]

Like rape, exceptions for incest, the mother's mental health, life of the mother and foetal anomaly can all be harder or easier to show, depending on the state and the specific statutory provision. Figures 17, 18, 19, 20 and 21 contain details that materially impact on the ability to claim an exception to a state's ban.

Figure 18. Incest Exception Severity Scale

Difficulty in Qualifying for the Incest Exception

1	Pregnancy is the result of incest
2	Reporting to Department of Health number of abortions performed under the exception
3	Copy of police reports and other documents that show proof of incest and/or preserving the documents in the medical records
4	Doctors need to notify police
5	Cannot be obtained after 20 weeks
6	Cannot be obtained after 15 weeks
7	Only available if the woman's father caused the pregnancy and the women's mother gives permission
8	No exception available

189 Alabama.

Figure 19. Life of the Mother Exception Severity Scale

Difficulty of Qualifying for Life of the Mother Exception

1	Low difficulty: danger to health of the mother & danger resulting from any physical ailment	
2	Must be performed at medical facility w/ specified resources, doctor needs to certify the procedure in writing	
3	Need the medical judgment of a second unrelated doctor.	
4	Danger must result from the pregnancy	
5	Must ensure survival of the child when possible	
6	Must be a medical emergency/danger to life of mother	
7	Does not allow a certain kind of abortion to be used (like partial birth)	

Figure 20. **Foetal Anomaly Exception Severity Scale**

Difficulty in Qualifying for the Foetal Anomaly Exception

1	Foetus wouldn't be able to survive outside the womb (ectopic pregnancy, dead fetus removal, etc)	
2	Need confirmation from two doctors	
3	Cannot be performed after third trimester	

Figure 21. **Mental Health Severity Scale**

Mental Health Severity Scale

1	Any pregnancy that causes distress upon the mother (including mental health) can be aborted	
2	If the pregnancy is causing a mental health condition, there can be an abortion	
3	If the mental health condition must be certified by two or more doctors	
4	The woman must be at risk of committing self-harm to abort	
5	Two doctors must certify self-harm risk	
6	The woman must have caused harm to herself to get an abortion	
7	No exception available - Even if a woman is at risk of causing harm to herself, she cannot get an abortion	

4.6. EXPLAIN HOW BAD IT WILL BE TO VIOLATE STATE LAW

Many people are rightly concerned about sanctions for advertent or inadvertent violations of the law. Sanctions generally divide into civil and criminal categories. Some trackers note whether persons who 'aid and abet' an abortion that is not permitted under state law open themselves up to civil liability, like that created by Texas's controversial Senate Bill 8, which awards attorneys' fees and a $10,000 'bounty' in lawsuits filed against persons who aid and abet an illegal abortion.[190] Elsewhere, Alabama prohibits all abortion unless necessary to prevent serious health risk to the pregnant woman.[191] Those who perform an abortion in violation of Alabama statutes can be found guilty of a Class A felony, for which penalties range from 10 to 99 years in prison, or a Class C felony, which can incur a penalty of up to 10 years in prison. Yet criminal sanctions and fines are much more serious than 'bounty hunting' laws like SB 8, in terms of the loss of liberty and the possible damages at stake.

None of the trackers show severity of criminal punishment in any detail. At best, they state that an action may constitute a crime.[192]

Explaining sanctions is crucial. Many people labour under the misconception that women cannot be prosecuted – or the misconception that they can.[193] *Both* fears are wrong, depending on where a person lives.

Some states exempt the pregnant woman from criminal sanctions. Mississippi, for instance, punishes by prison, 'for not less than one (1) year nor more than ten (10) years', '[a]ny person, *except the pregnant woman*, who purposefully, knowingly or recklessly performs or attempts to perform or induce an abortion in the State of Mississippi.'[194]

Other state statutes include the ability to prosecute women obtaining an illegal abortion. In Texas, anyone who violates section 170A.002's absolute abortion ban is guilty of a felony of the second degree.[195] The felony is upgraded to the first degree if an unborn child dies.[196] The penalty for a second-degree felony

---

190 R. Fretwell Wilson, op-ed, 'Perspective: On deputizing private citizens as snitches, where do we draw the line?', *Deseret News*, 7 February 2022, https://perma.cc/7Z73-R7L4.

191 Alabama Code §26-23H-4.

192 The CRR describes Texas law as 'prohibit[ing] abortion and include[ing] civil and criminal penalties', https://reproductiverights.org/maps/state/texas/.

193 Change Research, 'NATIONAL SURVEY: Intense Concern Over Consequences of Abortion Bans; Sustained Outrage, Half of All Women "Motivated" to Take Action in Support of Abortion Access' (2023), https://changeresearch.com/wp-content/uploads/2023/01/PPFA-_-Poll-Results-January-2023-1.pdf (reporting that, in a 2023 national survey of 1,443 adults conducted on behalf of Planned Parenthood Federation of America, 75% believed that women who got an abortion could be charged with a felony or sent to prison).

194 Miss. Rev. Statutes §41-41-45 (4) (making exceptions for abortions needed to preserve the mother's life or 'where the pregnancy was caused by rape')(emphasis added).

195 Tex. Code Ann. §170A.004.

196 Ibid.

is 2 to 20 years' imprisonment, 'in addition to' a fine not exceeding $10,000.[197] The penalty for a first-degree felony is far worse: 5 to 99 years' imprisonment and a fine not exceeding $10,000.[198] In Texas, the minimum sentence just for attempting an abortion is two years' imprisonment.[199]

Criminal penalties differ significantly from state to state. North Carolina bans abortion after 12 weeks, absent an exception.[200] Two separate statutes prescribe the penalty for administering an illegal abortion.[201] Section 14-44 of the North Carolina General Statutes makes it a Class H felony to willfully administer 'to any woman, either pregnant or quick with child, or prescribe for any such woman, or advise or procure any such woman to take any medicine, drug or other substance whatever, or ... use or employ any instrument or other means with intent thereby to destroy such child'.[202] Class H felonies are punishable by 4 to 25 months' imprisonment.[203] Section 14-45 makes it a Class I felony to procure the miscarriage of a pregnant woman.[204] Class I felonies are punishable by 3 to 12 months' imprisonment.[205]

Amping up the complexity of state abortion laws, different statutory sections may impose distinct penalties, meaning that one provision in a state carries one penalty, while another provision in the same state imposes a different one. For example, Alabama allows a woman who has a 'dismemberment' abortion[206] to

---

197 Tex. Code Ann. §12.33.

198 Ibid., §12.32.

199 Ibid., §170A.004.

200 N.C. Gen. Stat. Ann. §90-21.81B(2) (2023) ('Notwithstanding any of the provisions of G.S. 14-44 and G.S. 14-45, and subject to the provisions of this Article, it shall not be unlawful to procure or cause a miscarriage or an abortion in the State of North Carolina in the following circumstances: ... (2) During the first 12 weeks of a woman's pregnancy, when the procedure is performed by a qualified physician licensed to practice medicine in this State in a hospital, ambulatory surgical center, or clinic certified by the Department of Health and Human Services to be a suitable facility for the performance of abortions, in accordance with G.S. 90-21.82A or during the first 12 weeks of a woman's pregnancy when a medical abortion is procured.').

201 N.C. Gen. Stat. Ann. §§14-44, 14-45 (1979).

202 N.C. Gen. Stat. Ann. §14-44 (1979) ('If any person shall willfully administer to any woman, either pregnant or quick with child, or prescribe for any such woman, or advise or procure any such woman to take any medicine, drug or other substance whatever, or shall use or employ any instrument or other means with intent thereby to destroy such child, he shall be punished as a Class H felon.').

203 N.C. Gen. Stat. Ann. §15A-1340.17(d) (2013).

204 N.C. Gen. Stat. Ann. §14-45 (1979) ('If any person shall administer to any pregnant woman, or prescribe for any such woman, or advise and procure such woman to take any medicine, drug or anything whatsoever, with intent thereby to procure the miscarriage of such woman, or to injure or destroy such woman, or shall use any instrument or application for any of the above purposes, he shall be punished as a Class I felon.').

205 N.C. Gen. Stat. Ann. §15A-1340.17(d) (2013).

206 Alabama describes a 'dilation and evacuation' abortion as a 'dismemberment abortion'. See Ala. Code §26-23G-2 (3) (defining 'dismemberment abortion'). The American College of Obstetricians and Gynecologists caution that the term is inflammatory.

sue the physician and directs the court to award reasonable attorney fees to her if she prevails.[207]

As the severity scale in Figure 14 shows, private parties can seek injunctions,[208] sue for damages for wrongful death of the 'unborn child',[209] and file suit for civil malpractice for performing an abortion after viability, with an award of punitive damages possible.[210] In addition, the government may levy '... civil fines of either less than or greater than $10,000'.[211]

At the other end of the scale are criminal penalties, which can range from mere misdemeanours – a charge that physicians in Ohio may face if they perform an abortion on a minor without parental consent or judicial bypass[212] – to the threat of an extreme loss of liberty for homicide, like that described above.

5. CONCLUSION

People need a clear, straightforward presentation of facts and statutes that inform and shape the reality surrounding abortion in their state. The public must be able to trust a tracker's top-line summary.

This chapter has shown that one relies on public trackers at one's own peril. In many instances, it appears that one cannot rely on the trackers for an overall understanding of whether, when and under what circumstances abortion is permitted in a given state.

The gap between what is being reported in the abortion law trackers and the laws people are living under is massive. Popular media trackers emphasise hard time limits and gloss over exceptions and other differences between state laws, even though exceptions are meaningful points of access for those seeking abortions. Trackers treat states that are alike in their abortion laws as starkly different and treat those that are different as alike. They overlook or neglect important medical facts and legal developments.

---

207 Alabama Code §26-23G-6. Alabama also awards reasonable attorney's fees to a defendant if the suit was 'frivolous and brought in bad faith'.

208 Under Indiana law, a parent can ask the court to enjoin a physician who attempted to do an abortion on their minor child without complying with state law. See Burns Ind. Code Ann. §16-34-2-9. See also Kentucky Revised Statutes §311.800.

209 See Ohio Revised Code Ann. §2919.13.

210 See Ohio Code ORC Ann. §2919.17.

211 Under Arizona law, a health professional can be subject to a fine up to $10,000 for not reporting violations of the prohibition on providing abortion-inducing drugs via courier/mail service. See Arizona Code §36-2160. Under West Virginia law, in addition to possible imprisonment of up to two years, any person who knowingly performs a partial-birth abortion and kills the human foetus may also be fined not less than $10,000 and not more than $50,000. See W. Va. Code §33-42-8.

212 See ORC §2919.12.

The errors and conflicts between trackers create confusion and can lead to access being more difficult to achieve for Americans. Women scattering to different states for abortions may be doing so unnecessarily, based upon imperfect and partial information from trackers they believe are good sources of information.

Some misinformation about abortion access is inevitable given how quickly laws are changing, either by enactment or court challenge. However, it is important to prevent 'unnecessary misinformation'.

It is possible to present this complex and rapidly changing body of law in clear, cogent terms that people can process. Only then will actual people be able to make sense of the law and how to proceed.